PELICAN BOOKS
African Affairs
General Editor: Ronald Segal

LONRHO

Michael Lonsdale

Suzanne Cronjé was born in Vienna in 1925. She went to South
Africa in 1946, taught science in Ghana and Nigeria, and came
to London in 1963 with her husband and children. She is now a
freelance journalist and writer, specializing in African affairs, and
has written for many publications, including the *Financial Times*
and the *New Statesman*. She was editor of *African Horizon*
(published by the Northern Nigerian Government) for a year,
and is the author of *Biafra, Britain's Shame* (with Auberon
Waugh; 1969) and *The World and Nigeria: the diplomatic history
of the Biafran war, 1967-70* (1972).

Margaret Ling was born in England in 1948. She graduated in
1970 from Newnham College, Cambridge, with an honours
degree in social anthropology, and holds a diploma in social and
administrative studies from Linacre College, Oxford. She is now
working in the Research Department of the International Defence
and Aid Fund for Southern Africa, with particular responsibility
for Zimbabwe and Namibia.

Gillian Cronjé was born in South Africa in 1951 and came to
England in 1963 to finish her secondary education. She graduated
from the London School of Economics in 1974 with a first-class
honours degree in economics. At present she is a research student
in the Economic History Department of the London School of
Economics researching into tuberculosis in nineteenth-century
Britain. She has also written *The Middle Class and the 1889 Dock
Strike: a critique of Outcast London*.

Suzanne Cronjé,
Margaret Ling and
Gillian Cronjé

LONRHO

Portrait of a Multinational

Penguin Books

in association with
Julian Friedmann Books

Penguin Books Ltd,
Harmondsworth, Middlesex, England
Penguin Books,
625 Madison Avenue, New York, New York 10022, U.S.A.
Penguin Books Australia Ltd,
Ringwood, Victoria, Australia
Penguin Books Canada Ltd,
41 Steelcase Road West, Markham, Ontario, Canada
Penguin Books (N.Z.) Ltd,
182–190 Wairau Road, Auckland 10, New Zealand

Published simultaneously by Julian Friedmann Books Ltd
and Penguin Books 1976

Copyright © Suzanne Cronjé, Margaret Ling
and Gillian Cronjé, 1976

ISBN 0 904014 13 4

Made and printed in Great Britain by
Richard Clay (Chaucer Press) Ltd, Bungay, Suffolk
Set in Monotype Times by
The Lancashire Typesetting Co Ltd, Bolton, Lancashire

Contents

Introduction

People will say 'Tiny Rowland has gone mad', but this year Lonrho will make £23 million profit and have a turnover of £250 million. With a turnover of nearly a million a day you no longer have money problems – what is needed is ideas, creativity . . . the future lies with international companies, with consortia set up by different nations getting together and tackling today's needs all over the world. (*Rowland, June 1973*[1])

Lonrho has found it difficult to escape hitting the headlines. Crisis has followed crisis, interspersed with news of brave new ventures. In 1973 the company's internal dissensions produced a boardroom row which was followed by hearings in the High Court. It was one of the rare occasions on which business quarrels festooned the front pages, not only of the financial papers, but also of the popular press. As one Lonrho director said later: 'I deeply, bitterly regret that anyone should have thought it necessary to drag all these matters out into public daylight.'[2]

Lonrho is a multinational company whose main sphere of operations is in Africa, both the white-ruled south and the independent African states. It has over five hundred subsidiaries and associated companies, and its interests are extraordinarily diverse: they include gold and copper mines, sugar-cane plantations, shipping lines and property, breweries and newspapers. In this it is like other large companies operating in Africa. In other respects it is quite different.

Behind an unpretentious façade of shoe-shops and boutiques, Lonrho's office shared until recently Cheapside House in the City with Post Office Telecommunications and the Mining Development Corporation of Zambia. Those who have followed Lonrho's exploits in the press, and who might be taken aback by the modesty of its premises, may care to remember that in 1971 Lonrho entered unsuccessful negotiations to rent Centre Point, Harry Hyams's notorious skyscraper in London's Tottenham

Court Road. But Lonrho is, of course, a company which has grown accustomed to thinking big. The advent of Mr Rowland to Lonrho's board in 1961 galvanized the Rhodesian mining and cattle-ranching business into action.

Roland W. Rowland, or 'Tiny' as he signs himself in his letters to shareholders, is probably the first name that people think of when Lonrho is mentioned. As chief executive of the company he has masterminded the group's spectacular expansion, and he has been tireless in his efforts to translate his dreams into practice. At the end of 1973 Rowland submitted an application for the appointment of Lonrho as oil consultants to the Organization of African Unity. Had it come off, such an influential role would have opened great vistas of opportunity for the company on the African continent. Earlier that year, Rowland had talked about buying Rolls Royce Ltd: 'By using the Rolls Royce name and prestige, we would have been welcome all over the world putting up factories with the revolutionary engine [i.e. the Wankel] in Russia, China and so on . . .', he explained.[3] But his ambitious schemes often came to nothing. From the late 1960s financial circles became cautious of such ventures, despite Lonrho's spectacular growth.

Rowland is a loner. For about twenty weeks of every year he is away from his colleagues, travelling, and he has excellent connections among the African and Arab élites. Lonrho's contacts with influential figures have certainly led to a number of profitable contracts.

If Rowland is the first name that springs to mind when the company is mentioned, the Cayman Islands also have a place in public memory. These small and remote islands in the Caribbean are now a well-known tax haven, firmly associated with Lonrho's 1973 boardroom crisis, in the course of which it emerged that Duncan Sandys, the Conservative politician, had not only been paid a very large sum by Lonrho for his services, but that this had been paid in the international tax haven of the Cayman Islands. The disclosures arising from the row led Britain's Conservative Prime Minister, Edward Heath, to coin his celebrated phrase, 'the unpleasant and unacceptable face of capitalism'. The phrase has since become so much a part of British thinking that an allusion to it – the 'acceptable face of capitalism' – is even used to advertise a well-known brand of lager.

Lonrho has acquired a persistent reputation for unconventional behaviour. Indeed, at the height of the boardroom crisis came the announcement that it was to be the subject of a Department of Trade and Industry inquiry. Much of the research for this book was carried out by the authors while the thirty or so assistants of the Department of Trade were unravelling Lonrho's affairs at the behest of the government-appointed inspectors. At the time of writing, their report had not been published.

For the first eighteen months of the inquiry, Lonrho kept a low profile in London, but towards the end of 1974, the company's activities again made news. In August 1974 Lonrho's shares had reached a low point of 47p on the London stock market, but even before the general rise in the *Financial Times* ordinary share index in the first months of 1975, Lonrho's share price began to climb. By the end of February it had topped 150p. This phenomenal rise was largely due to the world commodity boom and to the new interest shown in Lonrho by Kuwaiti investors. Gold, copper and sugar, three products in which Lonrho was strong, all did extremely well during the 1974 financial year, and contributed to a fifty-eight per cent rise in the group's pre-tax profits.

In February 1974, Rowland said in his Review of the group's operations that 'our connections with the Arab world are likely to provide opportunities for Lonrho to join in projects in partnership with African and Arab interests. We hope that this will become the most important aspect of our business.'[4] A year later, a twenty-two per cent stake in Lonrho's issued share capital had passed into Arab hands, challenging Rowland as the pre-eminent shareholder in the company. Apart from an agreement made in 1972 to construct a major sugar scheme in Sudan, however, the promised ventures in joint partnership had not made their appearance.[5] Press comment suggested that the service which Lonrho was to provide for the Kuwaitis was that of middleman in helping them place their money in British-based stock market investments.[6] Lonrho later denied this. With rising Arab oil profits, Kuwait, like other rich Middle Eastern states, was looking for lucrative but safe investment opportunities, and it seemed to have decided that Lonrho would provide a suitable channel.

Some of Lonrho's existing interests could, however, inhibit the further development of such relations. In a climate of Arab–Israeli hostility, the *Financial Times* pointed out that an Israeli company, Savkel, had been licensed to build the Wankel rotary engine, in which Lonrho owns forty per cent of the patent rights.[7] This licence had been negotiated by Audi NSU and Wankel in 1969.

Whether Lonrho's hopes for long-term cooperation with Middle Eastern interests will be realized remains to be seen. The fact of the matter is that the vast bulk of Lonrho's profits are still earned in Africa, and it is here that the most deep-rooted contradiction within the company lies. Rowland's emphasis on the development of independent Africa – with or without Arab support – must be weighed against the group's substantial involvement in white-ruled southern Africa. Lonrho's operations in Rhodesia and South Africa have been very profitable, but the company's contacts here are an embarrassment in its dealings with independent African governments, and neither country was mentioned by name in Rowland's Review of Operations for 1974. This Review invited shareholders to 'write to us if you want to know more' about the operations of the group's subsidiaries.[8]

The authors in writing this book approached members of the board of Lonrho with requests for information, but it proved impossible to arrange a meeting on terms acceptable to Lonrho, although recently Lonrho have provided us with some information, when they read and commented upon a draft of this book. Our investigations did, however, take us from the lower vaults of the Bank of England to the equally dim but rather more dusty recesses of Companies House. Officials in the Foreign Office and the Department of Trade were helpful, as were a number of Embassies and High Commissions. Many individuals gave us their views and provided us with information. Our thanks go to all concerned.

March 1975

One

The Colossus of Cheapside House

One of the witnesses to give evidence on 'Tiny' Rowland's behalf
in 1973, when Lonrho's feuding directors fought out their boardroom battle before the High Court, was the German pilot of the
company's Mystère executive jet, Captain William Wilming.

'I have frequently seen Mr Rowland after an extensive flight
leave the Mystère to rush immediately to a conference with
Lonrho managers, African heads of state, Ministers and other
businessmen,' Captain Wilming said. 'It doesn't appear to matter
that he may have been ill or tired, he always endeavours to make
the meetings on time, even though he often has to snatch the only
sleep he can aboard the Mystère. He also has to eat aboard the
plane where necessary . . . I believe it to be virtually impossible for
most people to work the hours and to the extent that Mr Rowland
does but he appears to thrive on it.'[1]

This catalogue of personal virtues led to the crucial point which
all of Rowland's supporters stressed:

It is astonishing and admirable how quickly people take to and trust
Mr Rowland in the countries of Africa and the Middle East where I so
frequently see Europeans finding much difficulty in being accepted and
gaining confidence. I have been told, and I believe, that their confidence
in him is because of his frankness and human qualities, with which I
have become so familiar.[2]

The most sympathetic profile of Rowland to appear in the
British press at that time described him as 'a real sun-worshipper'.
There was the inevitable reference to the tireless jet-borne tycoon:
'When he is flying round Africa in Lonrho's own Mystère jet he
takes a collapsible chair so that he can set it out on the airfields
and sunbathe during stops . . . In an hour or so of sunbathing
(or merely keeping still) he can recharge himself amazingly.'[3]
This energy has gone into nurturing Lonrho's African links:

Certainly he does have a great affinity with Africans, and in many black countries he is regarded as an ambassador extraordinary, with access to the head of state whenever he wants it. Should he be sacked, his friends say, Lonrho would inevitably lose the greatest part of its African business.[4]

Sir Roy Welensky, the last Prime Minister of the one-time Central African Federation, is reported to have said of Rowland that he was 'the best thing to hit Africa since Cecil Rhodes'.[5] And, certainly, Rowland has something in common with the empire-builder whose grand schemes for Africa were the product of contemplation under the sun of the South African *veld*. It has been said of Rhodes that: 'The colossal was something that everyone recognized about him at first impact. His plans were always on an immense scale: to monopolize the diamond industry, to paint the map of Africa red . . . '[6]

The Hon. Angus Ogilvy, Princess Alexandra's husband, also spoke of Rowland as 'a Cecil Rhodes', 'a genius . . . but with defects'.[7] The qualifying note was understandable, in view of the revelations then emerging about the way that Lonrho was being run. Ogilvy had resigned as a Lonrho director as soon as the company dispute became public in April 1973. Until then he had been one of Rowland's closest associates on the board. Indeed, he had been instrumental in recruiting Rowland for Lonrho on behalf of Harley Drayton, the head of the London-based 117 Old Broad Street Group of investment trusts, and an influential shareholder of the London and Rhodesia Mining and Land Company Ltd, as it was then.[8] Ogilvy himself had joined the board of Lonrho in 1958, as alternate to Major-General John Dee Shapland, to represent the 117 Group.

Ogilvy recalled in 1973:

Twelve years ago Lonrho was a bit of an embarrassment to Drayton. We had bought the shares for about fourteen shillings and they had slipped to 2s. 6d. Then it was just a ranching company with a couple of tin-pot mines. My feeling then was that we should either sell out or find a good man to run it. I went to Southern Africa and heard about Tiny Rowland in Rhodesia. They said he was a smart farmer. I brought him in, hoping that he might be able to raise the Lonrho profits to about £300,000 a year. No-one can say he was not successful. Shareholders have seen profits of £19 million and their five bob shares valued at £3. Even today's 70p is not too bad. Plainly Tiny Rowland was more than an ordinary farmer.[9]

This picture of Rowland the man, and how his 'genius' turned a sleepy company into a vast business empire is what might be described as the 'authorized version' of Lonrho's history – the myth. The truth is more interesting – though the whole truth is hard to establish, particularly since Rowland's early life remains shrouded in speculation.

He was born on 27 November 1917 in India, a British subject. His father, reportedly a pharmacist by trade, was called Furhop – Rowland changed his name after he came to England, in October 1939. It has been suggested that Rowland speaks a number of Indian dialects and fluent German.[10] In 1939 he described himself as a shipping agent,[11] and at the end of that year he joined the British Army. He served as a non-combatant in the Royal Army Medical Corps during the Norway campaign, and attained the rank of Corporal. On 19 January 1942 Rowland was discharged and, when peace came, is said to have been working as a porter at Paddington Station. The Rowland legend usually includes this particular interlude, although the details vary; according to one account he started on the road to prosperity 'by persuading a signalman down the line at Slough to telephone exactly where the First Class carriages were in each incoming express'.[12]

Soon after the war he is reported to have acted as an unofficial buying agent in Holland for a number of local authorities, followed by a period in London as owner of a refrigeration company.[13] Rowland's activities must have shown some profit, for in the late 1940s he was able to emigrate to Rhodesia and buy himself a farm at Gatooma. Farming was only one of his preoccupations in Rhodesia, however, for he soon set up Shepton Estates as a private holding company for other business ventures. One of these was Norton Motors, which held the franchise in Rhodesia for Mercedes-Benz. Besides cars, he accumulated interests in gold and copper mining, and dabbled in early plans for an oil pipeline. One of the components of Shepton Estates was Kanyemba Gold Mines (Pvt) Ltd, a profitable venture, and one with which Angus Ogilvy, according to the Mining Editor of the Johannesburg *Financial Mail*, was associated in the late 1950s.[14]

Rowland apparently gained a foothold in the mining industry during the 1950s as a contact man and go-between for a number of established companies. One of his most important deals was to arrange for the purchase by the Rio Tinto Company Ltd of the Sandawana emerald mine in Rhodesia.[15] Rowland's connection with Rio Tinto is closer than is generally known. In 1973 the *Investors' Chronicle* pointed out that 'when Rowland claims that his entire life since joining Lonrho has been devoted to the company, shareholders should know that between 1961 and 1969 he was very well paid as a consultant to the main board of Rio Tinto-Zinc'.[16] Rio Tinto itself was at pains to deny that the connection had been close; in 1971 the deputy chairman of Rio Tinto-Zinc, Sir Mark Turner, was quoted as saying that Rowland 'produced businesses for us, but he was not in our employ'.[17]

In the late 1950s the Rio Tinto Company began a large-scale exploration programme for new mineral deposits in various parts of the world. (It was a few years later that it amalgamated with Consolidated Zinc to form the well-known Rio Tinto-Zinc Corporation.) The company had plans to expand their base in Rhodesia, and set about acquiring a number of established mines, one of which involved them in negotiations with Lonrho itself – at that time a staid member of the Rhodesian business establishment. Towards the end of 1959, Rio Tinto made a bid for the Cam and Motor Goldmining Company (1919) Ltd, a public company in which Lonrho had a shareholding, and whose two gold mines Lonrho managed. Rio Tinto's bid, in the absence of any competing offers, was successful early the following year, and Rowland negotiated the purchase. It is said that, as compensation for loss of office, he arranged for a total of £33,000 to be divided between three of the Cam directors who had resigned on the change of ownership – Joseph Ball, his son Alan Ball, and Brigadier Stephen Thorburn. All three were on the board of Lonrho at the time.[18]

Rowland himself was appointed to the board of Cam and Motor immediately after the transfer, and he may at this stage have contemplated the possibility of making his career with the Rio Tinto group. Rio Tinto was certainly at the time a thrusting concern, and in 1960 it attracted two senior members of Lonrho's staff to its Rhodesian operations, one of whom, Mr R. S. Walker, was in 1976 chairman of Rio Tinto (Rhodesia) Ltd, and served as commercial director for the group's southern African interests.[19] Rio Tinto's intention was to link up Cam and Motor with its other Rhodesian interests, and to operate all the mines it had acquired as a single group. In July 1960 the name of the Cam and Motor Company was changed to Rio Tinto Rhodesian Mining Ltd, and through a special Act passed in the British Parliament, permission was granted to move the company's domicile to Salisbury. Here it took over responsibility for Rio Tinto's Rhodesian head office, and besides managing the gold mines, undertook exploration work for further deposits.

If Rowland had indeed had ambitions to stake his business career with Rio Tinto they were short-lived, for in 1961 he joined the board of Lonrho Ltd. The story of how he came to do so dates back a few years. In the Rhodesia of the late 1950s, Lonrho and its then associate, Willoughby's Consolidated, were landowners on a considerable scale. Around 1955 Glazer Brothers of Johannesburg made a bid for the share capital of Willoughby's, followed two years later by one for Lonrho itself. But this came to nothing. Together with Harley Drayton, the London financier who joined them in this venture, the British South Africa Company and the Anglo American Corporation of South Africa Ltd bought up enough shares in the two companies to discourage Glazer Brothers. A related effect, however, was to push up the price of shares in Lonrho and Willoughby's, so involving the buyers in an outlay of some magnitude and landing them with sizeable stakes in two companies whose records were far from exciting. The prospect of a lively managing director who could push the Lonrho share price up to a level at which Anglo American, BSA and Drayton could dispose of their holdings at a profit, or make such holdings worth their price, must have seemed an attractive one.

The fact is that Rowland, far from waiting in peaceful obscurity on his Gatooma farm to be 'discovered' by Ogilvy, was by the end of the 1950s a visible feature of the Rhodesian business scene. He was well known to Rio Tinto as a reliable 'broker' and had probably known Ogilvy since around 1957. He was, however, a man who kept his personal life and background entirely to himself. It may have been on Rio Tinto's recommendation that Rowland was recruited for Lonrho, and in August 1961 an important deal was struck between him and the company. Through the agreement signed between Lonrho and Shepton Estates (Rowland's private holding company) on 16 August 1961, Rowland gained nearly a third of Lonrho's issued share capital and effective control of the company through a joint managing-directorship with Alan Ball, at a salary of £2,000 a year. In return for one and a half million fully paid-up shares in Lonrho Ltd, Rowland handed over the bulk of Shepton's subsidiary interests,[20] his personal estate. He did, however, retain his holding in the

15

Nyaschere copper mine, which was to become very profitable. It was still held by Shepton which, under the conditions of the deal, was to remain effectively owned and controlled by Rowland. Shepton was, furthermore, given the option of buying two million Lonrho shares on Rowland's behalf at a fixed price of 7s. (35p) each, in addition to the one and a half million already issued. By the time that the option was taken up in 1967, the market value of the shares was a good deal higher than this.

Through their deal with Rowland, Lonrho had branched out into new spheres of business. The motor companies in particular were a somewhat surprising departure from convention. 'It will be interesting to see how the company fares by the incursion into commerce and also what difference an energetic person like Mr Rowland will make on it as a whole,' commented *Property and Finance* in Salisbury. 'This development may be the start of a period of acquisitions and mergers which, given the low prices current for Rhodesian shares and assets, could be very profitable.' It was estimated that the assets that Lonrho had acquired from Rowland himself would more than double the company's usual income over the first full year.[21]

Rowland joined Lonrho at a time of increasing uncertainty about the future of the Central African Federation, with Zambia (then Northern Rhodesia) and Malawi (then Nyasaland) stepping up the pressure for its dissolution.[22] In Rhodesia, destined to remain white-dominated, African nationalism, manifested to the European population in a wave of strikes and riots, proved an unnerving influence. As one African country after another gained its independence from colonial rule, the feeling grew among shareholders in Britain that this was the time to pull out of Africa, before the value of their investments dwindled further. It is possible that Rowland's confidence in his own schemes had a special appeal in an atmosphere of business gloom and uncertainty.

On the other hand, without Rowland Lonrho might still have prospered, if not perhaps boomed. The fall in the company's net profits over the financial year 1960, from £82,372 to £65,139, was in large measure due to the loss of the administration of the Cam and Motor Company whose gold mines had brought in considerable revenue from fees, buying and insurance commissions. Between 1958 and 1959 Lonrho's net profits, after tax and minority interests, had doubled from £41,532 to £82,372 and there is no means of knowing precisely what would have happened if the company had continued to receive its usual income from the two mines that had been handed over to Rio Tinto. Their sale was probably responsible for the drop in the London price of Lonrho shares to which Ogilvy referred in his interview in 1973.[23] Rowland's redoubtable coup in acquiring a 27.3 per cent slice of Lonrho's share capital as part of the terms on which he joined the board was a reflection of this low price.

It has sometimes been suggested that in 1961 Lonrho was not merely a rather pedestrian kind of company but virtually moribund. It had been incorporated in 1909 as the London and Rhodesia Mining and Land Company Ltd for a number of functions, including to 'purchase, take on lease, or otherwise acquire, any mines, mining rights and metalliferous land in Rhodesia, South Africa, or elsewhere in Africa, and any interest therein, and to explore, work, exercise, develop and turn to account the same'.[24] It might also farm, acquire property, construct roadways and factories, and engage in wholesale and retail trading. In the early 1960s Lonrho operated or managed a handful of gold mines and owned nearly 700,000 acres of land, on which it raised some of the largest herds of cattle in Rhodesia. It had been prepared to be venturesome in its investment portfolio, and in 1959, for example, had been involved in the setting up of Rhodesian Television (Pvt) Ltd, which had just gained the contract to introduce television to the Federation. Also in 1959, Lonrho had finished building its new headquarters in Salisbury at a cost of £275,000, on a large and valuable site that the company had owned for some time in the centre of the city. The block was designed to house a range of departments of the Federal Ministry of Posts as well as Lonrho's own offices, a tribute perhaps to the company's standing in the eyes of Federal officialdom. Lonrho's property interests in 1961, in contrast to its cattle ranches and mines, are rarely mentioned, but the company did own a number of valuable office blocks in Salisbury and a central transport depot for the industrial sector.

In 1961 motor trading was a new and talked-about departure for Lonrho. The Shepton gold interests, on the other hand, slotted easily into the company's existing operations and must have appeared to many as the sensible element in a colourful bargain. In the months following the deal with Rowland, however, it became clear that the transaction had been anything but well judged. From the figures which Rowland had presented to the board, his gold mines, Kanyemba and Empress, seemed a sound enough investment, with a productive future ahead of them. In January 1962, however, Lonrho's newly-published Annual Report revealed that Kanyemba's proven ore reserves were now only a third of the figure calculated at the end of 1960, and that 'probable reserves', which in 1960 had been put at 600,000 tons, were now apparently down to nil.[25] The figures meant that the life of the mine, previously estimated at twenty years, was reduced to a mere eighteen months. In the first few weeks of 1962, the Kanyemba share price plummeted from the eight or nine shillings paid in the late 1950s to less than three shillings.

It would appear, however, that the mines had been a profitable investment for Rowland before he joined the Lonrho board. Up to 1958 Kanyemba had been a private company owned and controlled by Rowland through Shepton Estates. In that year he received £350,000 in shares on its flotation as a public company on the South African and Rhodesian stock exchanges, with a further £150,000 for the sale of the adjacent Hepworth mine to the new company. Share prices went as high as 9s. 6d. (over 45p) and production boomed. The massive drop in ore reserves suggested a somewhat hasty, if highly profitable, emphasis on exploitation rather than development.

Soon after Kanyemba Gold Mines' Annual General Meeting in Johannesburg early in 1962, angry shareholders, who felt that they should be compensated on at least the same terms as Rowland had been when he sold his own interest in Kanyemba to Lonrho, were reported to be planning a protest meeting and demanding a public inquiry into the drop in the share price.[26] Hurried attempts were made to calm frayed tempers. Lonrho, obviously embarrassed, announced that it was switching from a policy of high production to one of development; shareholders agreed to give Kanyemba the benefit of the doubt for the time being and it seemed as if the storm might blow over. But in 1963 shareholders were informed that the Kanyemba mine had no future and that Coronation Syndicate, a company in which Lonrho had a majority holding, was to take over what remained of Kanyemba Gold Mines Ltd. Disgruntled investors, offered a choice between Coronation shares and cash (3s. a share – 15p), pocketed the money and disappeared from the scene.[27]

About six months after he joined the board, Rowland made his first takeover bid, for Willoughby's Consolidated Company Ltd.

This old British concern had similar interests in Rhodesia to Lonrho and the two had become closely associated in the 1950s, when Willoughby's took over the management of Lonrho's ranches. The fact that Lonrho had been a shareholder in Willoughby's and had two of its own directors on the board may have contributed to the success of the offer.[28] The deal illustrated the ease with which companies already closely linked to Lonrho could be absorbed into the group, and the pattern was soon repeated in the takeover, in September 1962, of the Chicago-Gaika Development Company Ltd, an associate of one of Willoughby's wholly-owned subsidiaries. A feature of both these transactions was that Lonrho's offers were in cash, rather than by the exchange of shares as would so often be the case later. The mopping-up operation increased the size and financial security of the group as a prelude to more glamorous ventures.

Subsequent developments on the Lonrho front convinced many people inside Rhodesia, in particular the increasingly influential Rhodesian Front, that Rowland was a man to be watched. Not much was known about him, but more disturbing than this were his contacts, by 1963, with black African leaders.[29] Rhodesia, where the whites were in a much more powerful position than in the rest of the Federation, also had its suspicions of the Federal government – though for opposite reasons to those which motivated the black nationalists in Zambia and Malawi. The whites in Rhodesia feared a Federal sell-out to black nationalism; and although Federal leaders were in fact paying little more than lip-service to non-racialism when they spoke of the equality awaiting all citizens who had attained 'civilized standards', even this was almost too much to bear. As Lonrho began to secure important contracts, the conviction grew among certain sectors of the Rhodesian business community that the company was seeking to establish itself in key economic sectors of the Central African Federation. Alarm mounted to such a peak that there was even a call in the Rhodesian parliament for a government inquiry into Rowland's dealings. Mr W. Harper, a former Rhodesian Leader of the Opposition and an MP for Gatooma, raised his fears during the Rhodesian budget debate on 19 July 1962. He said:

There is rather an extraordinary thing going on in this country at the moment, and I am disturbed about it. ... We seem to be having a general-post arrangement between some of the major mining and finance houses, at the head of one of which is a certain individual, a Mr Rowland.

By the time that Rowland teamed up with Lonrho, he had built up for himself an enviable private empire of mining and motor companies. One of the most important factors behind his alliances with companies such as Rio Tinto and Lonrho may have been an urge to secure the capital and backing needed to bring his more ambitious schemes to fruition. One of the most far-sighted projects of Rowland's career, considering his comparatively unknown status at the time, was a plan born in the late 1950s to build an oil pipeline from Beira, on the east coast of Africa, to Umtali, just inside the Rhodesian border. Rhodesia is a landlocked country and was at this time dependent for a significant proportion of its energy resources upon oil supplies transported across the Mozambique hinterland from Lourenço Marques. Rowland's oil pipeline was a brilliant scheme to bypass the laborious and expensive rail transport that was then available. On the other hand, it was a project which in due course was costed at £3½ million and it was clear that a private businessman had little hope of bringing it into operation unaided. In 1957 Rowland had set up Associated Overseas Pipelines, a private company in Salisbury with a nominal capital of £4,000, to negotiate the concessions for a pipeline with the Portuguese, Federal and Rhodesian governments. His partners in the venture were three Salisbury businessmen, J. H. Carvill, V. W. Coats and A. B. Maxwell. Maxwell became secretary of the company, and Rowland, Coats and Carvill formed the board. Maxwell and Coats both died within five years of AOP's formation and after three Lonrho directors, Alan Ball, Forbes Davies and Colin Braun, had come on to the board in 1961, Carvill bowed out. Rowland was now, as managing director of Lonrho, in a position to forge ahead with negotiations in the knowledge that he had influential sponsors behind him. However, the agreements on the pipeline which were in due course signed by the various bodies concerned were a major source of the antagonism towards Rowland that developed among certain sectors of the Rhodesian community. In November 1962, after the Federal government had finally committed itself to the scheme, *Property and Finance*, representing the right wing of Rhodesian business, summed up the affair in sarcastic terms:

The signing of the agreement has been described as a triumph for the Minister. In fact, it is a triumph for Mr R. W. Rowland who, having emerged from obscurity to assume preponderant executive control of Lonrho a year ago, is a man who combines ability, astuteness and persuasiveness to a quite remarkable degree with a single-minded dedication to his business interests. For his determination and resource, and for his starting to build what has been described in Parliament as a new financial 'empire' in the Federation, he may earn admiration in the business world; but only time will show whether a major business achievement is necessarily in the national interest when applied to the sole right to transport a commodity utterly essential to a landlocked country.[30]

A year later, after fuller details of the pipeline deal had been made available, the magazine commented:

It will come as a shock to the Rhodesian public (as it did to *Property and Finance*) that another monopoly for the Portuguese has been negotiated; and that the negotiators were a Federal Ministry (Mr Owen's) and Mr R. W. Rowland (chief executive of Lonrho and the actual pipeline promoter).[31]

There were two main components to the scheme: first, the pipeline itself; and second, an oil refinery, to be built at Feruka near Umtali, fourteen miles inside the Rhodesian border. The pipeline was eventually constructed by Lonrho, and the refinery by a consortium of international oil companies who undertook to pay a fixed amount to the owners of the pipeline for every ton of crude oil delivered through it. The key figure in the whole series of negotiations was Mr F. S. Owen, a Federal MP. Up to 1962 he had been the Minister of Commerce and Industry in the Federal government and, as such, mainly responsible for the two-and-a-half-year negotiations for the refinery. In 1962 he moved to the Ministry of Transport, where he presided over the signing of the main pipeline agreements between October and December of that year. As the negotiations over the pipeline approached completion, it seemed clear that Rowland had friends and supporters within the Federal government who were prepared to use their influence to advance this particular project.[32] Accusations were made that an alternative scheme had been pigeonholed by the Federal authorities without being adequately discussed.[33] Other Federal MPs, Saul Udwin and Peter Staub, also seem to have been on close terms with Rowland; Udwin and Vrettos, in which Saul Udwin was a partner, was appointed by Lonrho as its consulting engineers during the pipeline negotiations, while

Staub was associated with Lonrho in a scheme, never realized, to set up an Agricultural Development Corporation to promote African small-holding. The distaste which the right-wing Rhodesian Front felt for Federal 'liberalism' – as they saw it – was later a liability to Lonrho when the Front gained political ascendancy in Rhodesia and the Federation was dissolved.

As negotiations for the pipeline scheme neared completion, its opponents in Rhodesia became increasingly agitated by the secrecy in which the project was wrapped. Despite requests for more information, the details of the pipeline agreements were not made public until several weeks after the final signing. Throughout the months of negotiation, debate continued about the scheme in both the Federal Assembly and the Rhodesian parliament. Questions were asked about Lonrho's credentials, and fears voiced about the implications of the scheme. Not everybody was convinced that the pipeline would in fact lower the cost of oil and petrol for the Rhodesian consumer, in comparison with rail transport. The final cost would depend upon the terms of the agreement with the Portuguese, through whose territory the pipeline would pass. One factor in what was bound to be a very complicated deal was the compensation which would have to be paid to the Mozambique State Railways for loss of revenue arising from the switch from rail freight to the pipeline.[34]

Potentially even more serious than the economic cost to Rhodesia was the scope that the agreements might give to the Portuguese to subvert Rhodesia's political integrity. Such fears were intensified by the uncertainty surrounding the future of white supremacy in southern Africa at this time. The only elected European Independent in the Federal Assembly, Mr R. Williamson, expressed this sense of insecurity when he spoke in the Federal budget debate on 23 July 1962:

When erected, the pipeline, of course, will form a very important artery in the Federation, and it will be essential that the government maintains some control over the financing and the running of it. Through being operated by private enterprise, it could possibly fall into the wrong hands and would affect the Federation considerably from an economic point of view, and even from a defence point of view.[35]

Williamson was not the only Federal MP to call for government involvement in the project. Questions were also asked about government measures to insure the pipeline against sabotage, especially in the event of Mozambique falling into enemy hands. Owen gave his assurance that these matters would be fully covered in the agreements.[36] As Minister of Transport, he signed the Federal agreement on the pipeline in November 1962, a month before the Portuguese ratified their own side of the bargain. Clearly, the construction of the refinery could not get under way until the agreements over the pipeline had been finalized. Rowland's urge to get this first prestige project off the ground as soon as possible was probably one of the factors underlying his desire to become a member of the Lonrho board, whose members, used to a more leisurely pace, must now have been taken aback by the speed of the events that had overtaken them and the publicity to which they were now exposed.

The concessions made by the Federal government to the Portuguese were writ large in the articles of association of the Companhia do Pipeline Moçambique-Rhodesia SARL, an indirect subsidiary of Lonrho set up to control the pipeline, and the agreement between Lonrho and the Mozambique government.[37] Although Lonrho has in its Annual Reports since 1963 consistently referred to the project as 'our oil pipeline', one of the terms most galling to the Rhodesians was that the Mozambique stretch of the pipeline was to be handed over to the Mozambique government free of charge after a maximum of seventy-five years, during which Lonrho would hold the concession. While Lonrho was to have a sixty-two per cent holding in the share capital of the Companhia do Pipeline, its head office was to be in Beira and five out of the nine directors, including the chairman, were to be Portuguese. Furthermore, a maximum of only fifteen non-Portuguese were to be employed in the construction of the pipeline, and there was limited scope for the participation of Rhodesian industry. Finally, if at any time the pipeline ceased operations without the Mozambique government's consent, the latter could immediately take possession and have the project publicly administered. The legal implications of this must have worried Lonrho considerably when the imposition of sanctions against Rhodesia closed the pipeline down at the end of 1965.[38] The Portuguese had clearly driven a hard bargain and made a number of important gains; control of the pipeline seemed, for many of its opponents, to have been effectively withheld from Rhodesians.[39]

There was one further hitch before Rowland was home and dry. In December 1962 elections were held which put the Rhodesian

Front, Rowland's most influential critic, into power as the Rhodesian government. Although it was now the eleventh hour, the Rhodesian Front was left with one last bargaining counter. The pipeline had been given right of way over the fourteen-mile stretch of Rhodesian territory from the Mozambique border to the Feruka refinery by an Act voted through the Rhodesian parliament in 1962, but this could always be repealed by a government hostile to the scheme. As the press took up the debate, a working party of Federal and Rhodesian civil servants was set up to investigate the affair. Ignoring the fuss, Lonrho announced that it had appointed contractors and intended to start the construction work on 1 April 1963. On 2 April, the Rhodesian Front capitulated and recognized the validity of the pipeline agreements.

There seem to have been severe weaknesses in the civil servants' working party. It was expected to report with alacrity, despite the complexity of the issues and the fact that some of its members had little expertise. Secondly, hanging over the government's head were its legal obligations, for an agreement had after all been signed with Lonrho. On 27 March Rowland had stepped into the limelight to threaten the Rhodesian government with legal action to the tune of £5 million. Whatever the reason, the government did give way, and on 3 April the announcement that a bottle of champagne had been broken over a bulldozer blade heralded the start of construction work. Shortly after, the two key figures in the whole affair took a well-earned break: Owen, on holiday to Europe; and Rowland, to attend Angus Ogilvy's wedding to Princess Alexandra in London. That summer, Denis O'Donovan, recently retired as Federal Government Solicitor and a member of the working party, was appointed as legal adviser to Lonrho. There were no more setbacks and by the end of January 1965 crude oil was being pumped through the pipeline on a commercial basis to the newly-built refinery.

The pipeline scheme was dramatic proof that Rowland appeared to have a 'Grand Design'[40] for the strategic sectors of the economy. As the pipeline negotiations drew to a close he embarked upon a new round of discussions, this time for the handling of one of the Federation's most valuable exports – maize. At that time it was transported to the port of Beira by the same rail link that carried the oil, and here it had to be laboriously transferred from individual sacks into the holds of the ships. Bulk handling was the obvious way to cut costs and streamline the operation in a highly competitive world market. Rowland now stepped in with a neat project, although one that must have added insult to injury for the opponents of the pipeline. The plan was to convert the railway tanker trucks, previously used for carrying oil but shortly to be made redundant by his own pipeline, into bulk carriers for maize. To begin with, the scheme, which would have been a great improvement on the existing arrangements, was greeted with considerable interest. But as its authorship became widely known, support for it faded. In the end, Rowland quietly withdrew the scheme, remarking pointedly that he 'wouldn't like to be the target for a monopoly charge . . . I don't want a monopoly on anything'.[41] He added that 'it was the negative attitude of people that he did not understand. A lot of positive action was necessary for development here, but there was not much evidence of potential interest in the country. When someone came up with a development scheme, therefore, it seemed reasonable that he should be encouraged.'[42] Barely eighteen months later, Rowland was negotiating with Portuguese interests for purchasing all the output of all the major sawmills in Mozambique,[43] to the considerable dismay of the Rhodesian timber processing industry which relied heavily on supplies of Mozambique hardwood. By this time, too, he was deeply involved in Malawi, Rhodesia's black-governed and therefore potentially hostile neighbour.[44]

Although Malawi was part of the Federation and still in a sense 'home ground' for Lonrho, it was a country where African aspirations, personified by Dr Banda, were in the ascendancy. In retrospect, Malawi was perhaps the easiest of Rowland's black African successes[45] in view of Dr Banda's readiness, particularly after his country had achieved independence, to cooperate with his white neighbours in Portugal and South Africa. While Banda's loathing for Welensky and for all things Federal might otherwise have made matters difficult for Lonrho, with its Federal government associations from the pipeline deal, the importance of private investment as a symbol of Malawi's economic and political self-sufficiency seems to have enabled Rowland to establish excellent relations with Malawi's leader. This was illustrated a few months before Malawi's independence, when negotiations between Lonrho and Banda for what was to become the country's most impressive agricultural investment project, a large-scale sugar scheme, drew to a successful close. In November 1963 Ball and Rowland were entertained at a dinner in their honour at the Shire

Highlands Hotel in Blantyre, attended by government and consular representatives and many of Malawi's top businessmen. He had never given a party for businessmen before, Banda explained, and the reason he was doing so now was because Rowland had told him: 'We believe your country has an important future.' It was this kind of confidence, from those who possessed the capital, the technical know-how and the ideas, that would enable Malawi to achieve real standing in the world community. Lonrho and any other company that showed itself willing to throw in its fortunes with Malawi's were welcome so long as they minded their own business and avoided meddling in affairs that did not concern them:

You can make all the money you want and take as much as you like to London, but after I have taxed you, of course, after I have done that, I won't restrict you at all. But here if you try to make this country a Banana Republic or a Sugar Republic, then you will hear from me and my people.[46]

Banda went on: 'These men have said to me: "We are businessmen and not politicians." That is good . . . I shall judge Lonrho by its achievements.'[47] Here, indeed, was a veiled warning. But Lonrho seemed sufficiently eager to keep on good terms with Banda for *Property and Finance* to comment, somewhat maliciously,

The new Lonrho–Banda entente, of course, has a pointed similarity to the closeness of relations between Mr Rowland and certain personalities in the Federal Administration – when the Federal Government still seemed reasonably secure.[48]

Rowland's close connections with Roy Welensky and other Federal MPs such as Peter Staub may have persuaded him to maintain a low profile in Malawi. It was Ball, Banda had learnt, who was the 'real boss' of the company,[49] and it was Ball's photograph that adorned the front pages of the *Times* of Blantyre as Lonrho's empire expanded. In 1963 Gerald Percy, a recruit from the Northern Rhodesia Liberal Party and a follower of Sir John Moffat, a prominent opponent of the Federation, was put in charge of the company's Malawian operations.

The dinner party came almost exactly a year after the company had secured one of their most important contracts in that country – the appointment as Local Secretaries and Consulting

Engineers to Malawi Railways Ltd[50] and its wholly-owned subsidiary, the Central African Railway Company.[51] Until 1970, when Banda formally opened a second rail link with the northern border of his country to the port of Nacala in Mozambique, these British-based companies operated the only rail outlet to the sea, at Beira. Malawi had always been the poor man of the Central African Federation. Apart from deposits of coal and bauxite, the country has no substantial mineral resources, and it failed to attract the spin-off of infrastructural development that went with the opening-up of mining claims in Zambia. The northern portion of Malawi in particular remained economically backward and difficult of access. After independence in 1964, Malawi's fortune was its agricultural potential and the foreign exchange to be earned from exports of tobacco, tea, ground-nuts and other crops. Being a land-locked country, the availability of cheap and efficient transportation was crucially important, and in 1962 it was this that made Lonrho's takeover of the railway such a coup. Lonrho itself seems to have remained rather quiet about the whole affair. But Owen, the Federal Minister of Transport, went on the radio to explain to the Rhodesian public at large that administrative changes were about to be made in the running of the railway, whose headquarters were to be moved from London to Salisbury.

At that time the Federal government had by far the largest stake in the Malawi Railways Company, having earlier that year bought additional shares which increased the size of their holding to seventy-six per cent of the issued capital. With their holding in debentures and loans, their interest amounted to some £4 million worth of the total assets, valued at between £5½ and £6 million; and they held the right to nominate two government representatives to the board. In the long run, therefore, it was the Federal government who would probably have the final say in matters concerning the railway. The shares were, however, of two kinds, 'A' Ordinary, and Ordinary; the latter carried the right to appoint the remaining five of the maximum of seven directors, and hence conferred effective control over the day-to-day running of the company. Lonrho now owned the bulk of the Ordinary shares. Nonetheless, 'There is no change in the government's position on the Railways,' Owen stated. 'The government's shareholding is unaltered and it retains the right to appoint two government directors, with reserved powers, to the board.'[52] The report of the announcement in the *Nyasaland Times* added that, following

Lonrho's acquisition of a 'substantial interest' in the ordinary capital of the railway company, four of the directors had resigned, to be replaced by Rowland, Ball, Ogilvy and Colin Braun, Lonrho's local Rhodesian manager.[53] For the *Financial Mail* of Johannesburg, Lonrho had simply bought the railway and that was what mattered.[54]

Who was effectively in charge of the railway, Lonrho or the Federal government, now appeared a matter of opinion; and to the critics the deal was further evidence of Rowland's adroitness in handling relations with the Federal government. 'In point of fact,' *Property and Finance* commented, 'Mr Rowland, having doubtless earned much Government goodwill . . . for his success with the pipeline, is now, to all intents and purposes, the Government's agent in the running of Nyasaland Railways.'[55] A few months later, indeed, Lonrho's control over the railways was significantly strengthened when it was granted the sole buying agency for stores and equipment by the board, and Rowland was given a general power of attorney to assist him in his task as managing director of the railway company.

Although Malawi Railways appear to have been a paying proposition over the years immediately preceding Lonrho's takeover, they were in 1962 short of capital and heavily indebted to the governments of both Malawi and the Federation for loans that had been received. No dividend was paid by the company in either 1961 or 1962, and five new diesel-electric engines imported from Britain in the summer of 1962, to cope with an increasingly heavy volume of traffic, had to be ordered on deferred payment terms. Apart from sharing a director, Jacques Kiek, with Rhodesian Railways, Lonrho had no experience of running a railway. However, while the suggestion made later, that Rowland bought up Malawi Railways so that he could finance his other schemes from the ready cash raised by the sale of passenger tickets,[56] may be discounted, if on no other grounds than that this was preeminently a line for the carriage of heavy goods, in the long run the company became a valuable asset for Lonrho. The first year of Lonrho management, 1963, was definitely not a success. The two railway companies, Malawi Railways and the Central African Railway Company, together made an operating profit of only £156,956 compared with £405,989 the year before, and registered overall a net loss of £47,000, partly attributable to the expenses incurred as a result of Lonrho's reorganization, but also to a fall in the tonnage carried in the face of increasing competition from road transport. By 1966, when Zambian exports sent via Malawi to avoid breaking the UN sanctions barrier against Rhodesia were added to the increasing volume of Malawi's own agricultural exports, profits had shot up to £806,864.

It was at this point that Banda seems to have decided that things had gone far enough. Lonrho's association with the railways lasted for barely four years. During the break-up of the Federation, the responsibility for railways in Malawi, plus the Federal government's seventy-six per cent holding in the Malawi Railways Company, were transferred to the Malawi government with effect from 1 October 1963. In 1964 Malawi became independent, and the following year its government indicated that they did not intend to renew the management agreement with Lonrho after the expiry of its three-year term in December 1966. At the beginning of 1966 they announced that they were now planning to buy the outstanding shares in Malawi Railways; and on 8 August the directors of Lonrho accepted an offer from Banda of £1 for each Ordinary share in their possession. A total outlay of around £420,000 bought the Malawi government the whole of the outstanding share capital from both Lonrho and such minority shareholders as still existed. Funds were provided for the purchase by the Farmers' Marketing Board, and in November Mr V. H. Gale, its chairman, was appointed to the boards of both Malawi Railways and the new Malawi Railways Holding Company set up by the government. The purchase of the controlling interest in the railways by Banda was not achieved without something of a struggle, however, and Lonrho was paid the par value, in sterling, of the shares – which then stood at only 7s. 6d. on the London stock exchange.

In a speech to the Malawi parliament in Limbe on 23 August, Banda revealed that for more than twelve months he had been personally involved in the negotiations to buy the railway. He had been hearing complaints from businessmen, he said, at the high charges made for the carriage of goods on the Beira route and this had convinced him that the railways could continue no longer as the private preserve of a foreign company: 'otherwise industrial development in this country would be almost impossible'.[57] In June 1965, when Banda had been in London for the Commonwealth Prime Ministers' Conference, he had warned the directors of Lonrho that he was intending to purchase their block of shares in Malawi Railways for the government. The reaction had apparently been one of some intransigence:

Needless to say they refused – and with vigour. But I did not give up or give in . . . I made it quite clear that while I did not want to resort to expropriation or confiscation of anyone's property in this country, in the interest of development in this country I was ready to use other means than buying that block of shares, if free negotiations were impossible, or if the directors were unreasonable.[58]

Lonrho had, perhaps, become too successful for Banda to tolerate its continuing control over such a strategic part of the economy as the main export route to the sea. At the end of August 1966 the five Lonrho directors on the board of Malawi Railways submitted their resignations.

Lonrho remained, nevertheless, one of the largest foreign investors in Malawi, and in this respect the railways had fulfilled a useful function. In 1973 Rowland commented that, from Salisbury, he had 'moved north and across. I started with Malawi where I bought the railway. Everyone said that I was mad because railways never make money, but it enabled me to obtain other interests.'[59] This Lonrho certainly did. From 1963 the company expanded inside Malawi into tea and sisal, sugar and textiles, garages and motor-car distribution. In setting up the first locally registered building society in partnership with the government, it helped to promote the development of state participation schemes. In October 1963 it set up a joint venture with the French oil giant, Total, to distribute petrol and oil throughout Malawi. It was an important move in view of Total's interests in Mozambique, where Lonrho was then building the Beira–Umtali pipeline. Total had a substantial interest in Sonarep, the Portuguese company operating the refinery at Lourenço Marques from which, after UDI when the pipeline was closed, Rhodesia received the bulk of its oil supplies.[60]

During 1963 Lonrho figured frequently in the Malawi press. At the Central African Trade Fair in Bulawayo that year – a Federal event – it was Lonrho, rather than the Malawi government, which arranged an exhibition on Malawi. A few months later Banda announced in a special broadcast that a cane sugar project was under way. With an estimated investment of £4 million, it was to be the biggest scheme in the country's history. For Lonrho, which a few days later was revealed as the sponsor, it was the first important venture into sugar production. In the 1970s sugar was to become Lonrho's leading agricultural profit-earner.

For Banda, growing sugar was a landmark in the struggle for Malawian economic independence. For years the country had depended for its sugar upon imports from Rhodesia, which used up precious foreign exchange to the tune of nearly £1 million a year. In 1962 a Federal Sugar Commission had recommended the development of a sugar industry in the Great Elephant Marsh in the valley of the Shire River, Lake Malawi's only outlet to the sea. Now came the news that Lonrho was to establish a sugar cane estate and mill, with an eventual capacity of 60,000 tons of refined sugar a year, at Nchalo on the west side of the marsh. The scheme was to provide employment for between two and three thousand people and by 1966 or 1967 would be producing enough sugar not only to satisfy Malawi's domestic needs but to leave an export surplus as well. 'This boost to the country's secondary industries shows that people will invest here, whatever Welensky thinks,' remarked Dr Banda.[61] It was rumoured that he himself had suggested the scheme to Lonrho.[62] Less than a week after his broadcast announcement came the famous dinner party.

In 1965 an agreement was signed between Lonrho and Banda's government, under which Lonrho was to supply Malawi with its entire requirements of sugar, present and future. Barely two years after the first stretch of bush had been cleared, the first sugar produced by Lonrho's wholly-owned subsidiary, the Sugar Corporation of Malawi, was being marketed under its trade name, SUCOMA. It was perhaps some consolation to the Rhodesians, who had lost an export market, that the bulk of the work for constructing the scheme and installing the equipment went to building firms in Salisbury and Bulawayo. The South Africans were also involved: a Durban firm, Partick Murray (Pty) Ltd, were the main contractors. They secured a guarantee from the South African Industrial Development Corporation – a state body – for this purpose. It was South Africa's first official aid to Malawi, and the first practical sign of the alliance which was developing between Banda and the *apartheid* regime, with Lonrho in an active role.[63]

Lonrho had supported Banda in his bid to break away from the hated Federation by demonstrating that Malawi could attract foreign investment in its own right. In the process, new links were being forged between Malawi and its powerful white neighbours.

Two

Black African Allies

Over the five years following the break-up of the Central African Federation, Lonrho expanded its sphere of operations northwards into newly independent Africa, and by the end of 1967 had offices in fourteen countries. The enormous range of ex-colonial and rather humdrum companies that were acquired, particularly in Zambia and Kenya, set the seal on the group's transformation from a Rhodesian land and mining company to a multinational. Its interests were now extremely diverse, covering breweries, motors and transport, newspapers and publishing, sisal, tea, cotton and sugar, warehousing and packaging. This pell-mell growth bewildered commentators who attempted to discern some underlying pattern. Growth in Zambia was described as

... such a hotchpotch of companies that nobody could imagine what lay behind the policy. A nail factory, a match factory, a transport company, a garage or two, breweries, newspapers – anything that had a willing seller found a willing buyer. Naturally the price was right, and Lonrho got cheap assets and the odd asset which could be quickly realized for the cash which the company had always needed.[1]

These acquisitions, although individually not outstanding profit-earners, were collectively a secure financial base for the break which came in 1968, when Lonrho moved for the first time into West Africa.

One Lonrho asset which caught public imagination at the time of the boardroom row was the white Mystère jet that Rowland then used for his excursions into black Africa. In the autumn of 1963 the company had acquired a white Beechcraft Queen Air 80. Remarking on this acquisition, Gerald Percy, managing director of Lonrho (Malawi), said: 'Our interests in Africa now extend as far north as Nairobi, and we have projects under consideration in practically every country in East, Central and Southern Africa. This aircraft is invaluable to the group.' One of the first uses to which the plane was put was to carry Dr Kaunda for talks with President Nyerere.[2] No doubt it was hoped that, as in Malawi, friendships with African leaders would reinforce the company's established strategy of expanding into areas where contact with the élite had already been made. One of the early acquisitions in Tanzania was Central Line Sisal Estates Ltd, later a subsidiary of the Central Africa Company which Lonrho took over completely in 1968. In November 1964 a controlling interest was bought by the company in Riddoch Motors Ltd which held the Ford franchise in Tanzania. Although operations here were in due course expanded to include two cotton ginneries, a newspaper and a brewery, from the late sixties onwards the Tanzanian government's nationalization plans put paid to any more ambitious schemes. In Zambia, on the other hand, Lonrho built up a more secure footing within the economy.

Lonrho had, in fact, acquired a small interest in Zambia as early as 1961. Consolidated Motors, a company dealing in motor spares, which was one of those included in the package deal with Rowland, had an office in Lusaka. Early in 1964 two more motor companies were taken over, Puzey and Diss (which held the BMC franchise in Zambia) and Milne's Motor Supplies Ltd.

In 1963 a feasibility study for a 500-mile rail link between Zambia and Tanzania – later to become the famous Tanzam railway – was undertaken by the company. Lonrho's proposals were submitted to the Zambian government, but no further mention was made of the scheme in Lonrho's annual reports, although further efforts were subsequently made to get in on the project. Its failure to gain the contract may have been connected with its request for a monopoly over the copper traffic to the coast.[3] There are also suggestions that the Zambian government was upset by reports that Lonrho directors were talking as if the contract was in the bag. Probably the established mining houses in Zambia contributed to Lonrho's disappointment by opposing the award of a contract to a newcomer, muscling in on what had for so long been their exclusive preserve.[4] The feasibility of the railway itself had also been questioned by a series of adverse reports from international bodies.

Other acquisitions which followed shortly after included interests in amethyst mining, newspapers and brewing. The profitable Chibuku breweries were among the assets of Heinrich's Syndicate Ltd, a company set up in 1955 by a German-born businessman, which Lonrho bought in 1964. With Heinrich's Syndicate came one of Lonrho's first senior African executives, Tom Mtine, an employee of the company, who was Mayor of Ndola, a prosperous town on Zambia's copperbelt, and who had access to important Zambian leaders. Mtine soon joined the board of Lonrho's Zambian subsidiary and eventually became chairman; he was then on the boards of a number of other companies including Rothmans, a South African controlled company in the Anton Rupert group.[5] Mtine was to play an important part in Lonrho's 1973 boardroom row.[6]

Heinrich's Syndicate owned two newspapers in Zambia, the *Zambia News* and the *Zambia Times*; and at the time it was taken over by Lonrho its newspapers in particular were going through a bad financial patch. Shortly afterwards Lonrho took over Northern News Ltd, a subsidiary of the Rhodesian Printing and Publishing Company Ltd, which published the daily *Northern News*. All three papers circulated in the northern part of Zambia, in the copperbelt: the *Northern News* from Ndola, and the two Heinrich papers from Kitwe. Lonrho now carried out a reorganization: the *Zambia Times*, a weekly, was discontinued; the *Zambia News*, which had been a daily, became a weekly; and the *Northern News* became a daily paper, the *Times of Zambia*.

It was perhaps the general expectation that Lonrho was eager to push forward with its takeover strategy that prompted Kaunda to announce early in 1965 that he intended to have his own government newspaper. The Lonrho paper, *Zambia News*, reported that 'vital talks' had been held between the Zambian Information Minister, Rowland, and representatives of Lonrho's main competitor in this field, the *Central African Mail*, owned by the Astor group in London.[7] Mr Changufu, the Information Minister, said that the government paper would be a daily and printed in English. It seemed that a choice was to be made between Lonrho's *Times of Zambia* and the *Central African Mail* as the future vehicle for government pronouncements. From Lonrho's point of view a joint participation scheme with the government might well have been a mutually satisfactory solution, but only if combined with the demise of the *Central African Mail*. It was later rumoured that Mr Astor had been offered £100,000 by Rowland for its purchase.[8] The government, however, opted in the end for the *Central African Mail*, which was renamed the *Zambia Mail*, to appear as a bi-weekly. Rowland was obliged to content himself with the acquisition in October 1966 of another, less important Astor paper, the *Financial Mail of Zambia*, a monthly business journal published in Lusaka.

A second opportunity for Lonrho to become involved in a joint newspaper scheme with the Zambian government occurred in 1968. The *Zambia Mail* was still a bi-weekly, although with plans to become a daily, when the Zambian government announced its intention of bringing about a merger between its own Zambia Publishing Company and Lonrho's Zambia Newspapers Ltd (the former Northern News Ltd). The *Times of Zambia* was at that time the only daily and Lonrho was also publishing the Sunday paper, *Zambia News*. The plan was to give each side a fifty per cent shareholding, with one per cent, for voting purposes, floating between Lonrho and the government, depending on whether a financial or an editorial aspect was under discussion. In any event, Kaunda was to have the right to nominate the senior editorial staff. The *Times of Zambia* was to remain the country's only daily, and the *Zambia Mail* would have been turned into a Sunday paper. The other publication involved, Lonrho's *Zambia News*, was to be killed off. The plan came to nothing, partly because it was discovered that the assets of the government's *Zambia Mail* were worth £1.25 million while the Lonrho publications had assets worth only £100,000 (their printing press and other machinery were heavily mortgaged, and the buildings were owned by outside interests).[9] It was too unequal a deal from a financial point of view; but there may have been political considerations as well. Admittedly, this was to be a joint participation scheme, but Lonrho remained a company with Rhodesian antecedents, a state of affairs which perhaps prompted second thoughts. The scheme would also have continued to leave Zambia with only one daily paper for the whole country. Nevertheless, there was one legacy from this plan; Kaunda's First Secretary, Dunstan Kamana, had taken over as editor of the Lonrho daily in expectation that the scheme would go ahead, and he remained in the post. The Zambian President also appointed Mr Kamana's editorial successors. In June 1975 it was announced that the Lonrho papers in Zambia were to be nationalized.[10]

Lonrho's African papers have from time to time reflected the company's interests. It has often been said that Lonrho never interferes with the editorial policy of its African press. As early as 1965 the newly-acquired *Northern News* carried a five-column banner headline, 'Rail-Link Dream Could Be Reality Within Four Years of Kaunda Giving the Go-Ahead' – the second time the railway scheme through Tanzania had been mooted.[11] The leading article brushed aside a series of adverse reports and called for a quick decision. The right-wing Rhodesian press commented, 'Clearly Lonrho's astute Mr Rowland fully appreciates the value of a press mouthpiece . . .'.[12] Other notable editorial decisions by *Times of Zambia* editors included a hostile attitude towards Kaunda's nationalization of the copper mines, and hints that Lonrho might reconsider its policy in Zambia if the company's negotiations with the government over the valuation of their Smith and Youngson assets failed.[13] Dunstan Kamana went too far for the Zambian national assembly in March 1970 when he described the Zambian parliament as 'a rubber stamp', and was compelled to publish an apology.[14] This earned him the reputation of sturdy independence in British circles. He was replaced at the beginning of 1972 by Vernon Mwaanga, who subsequently became Foreign Minister. During the 1973 boardroom row, the *Times of Zambia* congratulated Rowland on remaining at the helm of the company: 'It is quite amazing how the personality of one man can triumph over opponents who use every dirty trick in the book.'[15] Mwaanga's former editorship of the newspaper became a disadvantage during his candidature for the post of Secretary-General of the Organization of African Unity in 1974;[16] and shortly afterwards Zambia's state-owned broadcasting corporation, which had regularly quoted the *Times of Zambia*'s opinions in its radio bulletins to the exclusion, almost, of those of other newspapers, switched abruptly to the government *Zambia Daily Mail*.

In December 1974 the *Times of Zambia* was castigated by President Kaunda for releasing details of recent diplomatic moves for a Rhodesian settlement, contrary to his own instructions. The President said that negotiations were at a delicate stage and that 'I personally requested editors of our newspapers to cooperate with the Government and I further made a special appeal that nothing should be published on the Rhodesian issue'.[17]

In Tanzania Lonrho owned the daily *Standard* and the *Sunday News*. Both were nationalized in February 1970, and new editorial staff appointed. This still left Lonrho with the Kenyan *East African Standard*, a newspaper which provoked sharp criticism in 1973. It was said that while 'particular persons who may be in the good books of that particular group of Lonrho and the *East African Standard* appear on the front page of such papers', Vice-Presidents and Ministers were sometimes relegated to the back pages.[18]

Lonrho's major acquisitions in Kenya and Uganda were made in 1967, when it gained control of Consolidated Holdings Ltd and Tancot Ltd, with interests in primary produce, packaging, engineering and printing, office supplies and newspaper publication. The Express Transport Company Ltd, a subsidiary of Consolidated Holdings, was responsible for the warehousing, sorting and despatching of Kenya's entire coffee crop and a large part of Uganda's as well.

Not all of Lonrho's East African ventures came off. In 1966 it lost the contract for a £16 million oil pipeline between Tanzania and Zambia. The Italians won it and, according to one observer, Lonrho's 'fund of unrequited pipeline know-how' remained unrequited, because the company wanted to own as well as run it. The Italians, while offering to lend the money, allowed Zambia and Tanzania majority control of the scheme. 'Lonrho's offer was cheaper, the Italians' irresistible.'[19] Three years later Lonrho was reported to be behind another East African pipeline plan, this time from Mombasa in Kenya to Kampala in Uganda, via Nairobi. The success of this plan was said to depend on the response of British oil companies: the Italians had already started a survey for it, but London reportedly 'has not been amused at the way the Italians sweep all before them in East Africa'.[20] In view of Lonrho's apparently secure foothold in the Kenyan economy, its failure in this instance must have been particularly disappointing.

In 1967 Lonrho East Africa was formed in Kenya to provide services for the group in Kenya, Uganda and Tanzania. The Kenyan government's policy of encouraging private enterprise provided Lonrho with ample scope for expansion and by the end of 1972 the group had around fifty subsidiaries there. Not everyone in Kenya was happy with this state of affairs, however, and in April 1973 Lonrho's burgeoning economic power provoked Mr J. M. Kariuki, the Assistant Minister for Tourism and Wildlife, to declare in Parliament:

> I found that they have taken over very many businesses in this country. I understand that even when we are discussing this matter here today, they are negotiating to buy some African liquor businesses. Very soon, Sir, if you are not going to be careful, you will go back home

only to find that even the utensils which your wives are using have been bought by the Lonrho group companies.[21]

This criticism was made in the course of a long parliamentary debate in which the company's extensive Kenyan interests and political influence were discussed. Towards the end, one member, Mrs Gecaga, intervened to point out that her son was managing director of Lonrho in Kenya, and that there were 'very many big companies in Kenya, much bigger than Lonrho, that do not have African managing directors or even directors'. She then asked, 'Why has Lonrho been discussed in this House for the last ten days? Is it because there might be a friend or friends of someone in this House who wanted this managing directorship in Lonrho but failed to get it?'[22] Her inquiry was not answered, and it is quite possible that what she suggested was true. It illustrates the way in which Lonrho had come to operate in independent Africa.

Udi Gecaga was a well-connected young Kenyan who later became the first African to be appointed to Lonrho's main board in London. His uncle, the Foreign Minister Dr Mungai, was a nephew of President Kenyatta. Gecaga received an excellent education and ended up with three degrees from prestigious universities – Princetown, Cambridge and the Sorbonne. He then became an executive with the Bank of America and the National Bank of Kenya, until he was recruited for Lonrho by one of the company's most important African connections – Gil Olympio. Shortly after joining Lonrho, Gecaga married a daughter of President Kenyatta, thus strengthening his and Lonrho's ties with Kenya's ruling family – a fact to which he proudly points: 'Before I was related to my wife by marriage, I was related to her by blood.'[23] One of Gecaga's uncles, Ngethe Njoroge, was High Commissioner in London in 1973, when Lonrho's dissident directors and Rowland's supporters brought their quarrel before a High Court.

Kariuki feared that Lonrho's well-placed connections might influence government policy, and he complained that the company was borrowing locally and was not injecting sufficient capital into the country. Lonrho was taking over as many firms as possible, including tea companies and farms, Kariuki said, and then it asked the government for a letter of approved enterprise which would allow it to repatriate the money to its own country.[24]

During the mid sixties Lonrho undoubtedly enjoyed a period of rapid growth, although primarily through the takeover of existing companies rather than by internally generated expansion. From 1963 to 1967 the group's total net assets increased from around £3.5 million to nearly £15 million. However, by the end of the 1967 financial year its current liabilities stood at over £19 million.

A number of the group's early acquisitions, such as Willoughby's and Chicago-Gaika, had been paid for in cash, and it was noted at the time that Lonrho was selling off several tracts of ranching land and mining rights in Rhodesia. *Property and Finance* commented that while it had been hoped that Lonrho's 'valuable assets in Southern Rhodesia might be put to work for the good of the company and the country as a whole', there was little evidence that this hoped-for policy had been carried out. 'Little has been done to develop existing assets, and expansion has been substantially in the turbid waters of the Pan-African seas.'[25] The takeover of Halls Holdings in Malawi was an early instance of the issue of new shares to finance a deal, and, from 1967 especially, the growth of Lonrho's share capital accelerated as further takeovers were secured.

Political contingencies had obliged many multinationals to accept majority government participation and a new role for themselves. At their Annual General Meeting in April 1965, Lonrho passed a special resolution to insert an additional clause into its Memorandum of Association, empowering the company to act 'generally as representatives, agents and consultants in all spheres and as members of local or advisory committees of other companies, corporations or concerns of any kind whatsoever . . .'.[26] It was in the capacity of consultants and management contractors that Lonrho then launched into some of its most prestigious schemes.

Despite Lonrho's statements that it welcomed African partnerships, at the beginning of 1973 there were only two companies where African directors were in the majority: Chibuku Breweries in Zambia, owned 51 per cent by the state and 49 per cent by Lonrho; and Ashanti Goldfields in Ghana. *African Development* reported at that time that 'this arrangement has presented the company with many problems in the day-to-day running of the company, even with the best will in the world, when important decisions have to be referred back through a plethora of government departments'.[27]

Chibuku was a subsidiary of Heinrich's Syndicate in Zambia, and Kaunda pointed out that it had a monopoly in its own field. He also said that Chibuku and another brewery, which was specializing in bottled lager, were making excessive profits and could make even more if they curbed their expenditure on advertising. Following the state takeover the large profits would be made partly for the nation, 'which will put them to proper use'.[28] Chibuku was taken over by Indeco (Industrial Development Corporation, a state holding company) in 1968 by the acquisition of 51 per cent of the shares without payment. Lonrho was compensated by continuing its royalty for ten years on every gallon of beer sold. The other brewery affected received cash for its 51 per cent of shares.

Another takeover by the Zambian government was of Smith and Youngson. This transport company was originally acquired by Lonrho in March 1966 from two brothers-in-law, who were apprehensive about independence, and who accepted Rowland's cash offer and a place on the local board, in which capacity they continued to manage the business. They were engaged in operating regular road freight services between Lusaka and Fort Jameson on the Malawi border, and they had special contracts for carrying maize, livestock, petroleum and building materials. Since independence they had expanded their operations. They were carrying copper and tobacco to the Malawi railhead at Salima and bringing back bulk fuel in association with the government of Zambia which, according to Lonrho's Annual Report, was importing a large number of new freight and tanker vehicles and trailers, for hiring out to road transport operators. This expansion was one consequence of UDI in Rhodesia, and the increase in the volume of Zambian exports through Malawi contributed to the sharp upturn in the profits of Malawi Railways during the final year of Lonrho's railway management.[29] Rowland got the agency for Canadian Kenworth trucks: big expensive vehicles, which he expected the managers of Smith and Youngson to incorporate into the fleet. The vehicles were used to bring in oil over the emergency 'hell run' from Dar-es-Salaam; by 1968, when the Zambian pipeline to the coast which Lonrho had hoped to build came on stream, they were in a poor condition.

Kaunda's 1968 Mulungushi nationalization plan – named after the place where it was announced – included the transport sector. It was later said that

The then Lonrho management in Zambia made the bad mistake of holding out for a substantial price for 51 per cent of Smith and Youngson. Indeco, which to begin with might have been prepared to pay about K750,000 [£437,250], came to realize that the state of the truck fleet was such that the company was effectively worth less than nothing. It allowed Smith and Youngson to pile up heavy losses during the eighteen months after the pipeline opened.[30]

In the end Lonrho had to guarantee Indeco an overdraft of 2 million Kwacha (£1,166,000) before Andrew Sardanis, the brilliant Cypriot-born director of Indeco, would agree to take the firm off Lonrho's hands.[31] Possibly the company's acceptance of this hard bargain was influenced by the critical attitude shown to it by Vice-President Simon Kapwepwe. Lonrho had tried for the government contract to establish a second transport operation on the Great Northern Road, parallel to that already worked by Zam Tan Road Services Ltd which had set up an operation after Rhodesia's UDI to turn the road into a serious import–export route. According to Anthony Martin,

Kapwepwe not only vetoed that proposal but laid it down that Lonrho should not be allowed to expand in any direction until it had been determined that the company was not already too closely involved in Zambia for the country's good.[32]

Lonrho's concern that its Rhodesian image might prove an obstacle in the path of further deals with African governments had led to earlier attempts to change the company's name. 'It is the intention to adopt, as soon as feasible, a more appropriate new name,' announced the Annual Report for 1966. But two years later, 'despite many suggestions', none had been found that 'is acceptable in all the countries in which we operate'. Lonrho's southern African links were to prove an embarrassment in many of the countries into which Lonrho expanded and which were less accustomed than Zambia or Malawi to dealing with Rhodesian or South African interests.[33]

A Zairean venture was spearheaded by the acquisition of a share in the Belgian company, Cominière, in 1968. Like Lonrho, Cominière's interests covered a wide range of activities and most of these were in Zaire. They included the supply of water and the distribution of electricity, timber plantations and a minor railway, engineering, motor distribution and insurance. Cominière was the third largest company trading in Zaire.

Zaire had nationalized its copper interests, owned by the Belgian giant, Union Minière, in 1966. But this company continued to hold the management contract for the mines and to control the shipment of the metal to refineries in Belgium, where its stockpile of copper constituted a powerful counter in bargaining with the Zairean government. Compensation terms for the nationalization were still under discussion, together with the renewal of Union Minière's management contract. As long as these issues remained unsettled, none of the major mining houses was willing to step into Union Minière's shoes; nor would the World Bank advance loans for major economic developments in the country. This was Lonrho's opportunity to move in. It was generally assumed that the company's ultimate aim was to win the management contract from Union Minière.[34] As a first step, Lonrho, on the advice of Cominière's president, Martin Theves, and in association with a Japanese firm, Nissho-Iwai, offered to carry out a free survey for a railway from the Katanga copperbelt to the Atlantic Ocean. This link was important to Zaire's President Mobutu for political, economic and strategic reasons; it would offer an alternative route to the Benguela railway through Angola for Zaire's copper.[35]

The negotiations were carried out by Theves, who was said to be on close terms with the then Foreign Minister, Justin Bomboko. Amongst other reasons, Lonrho's shares rose in early 1969 in anticipation of an announcement about the management contract. Although no official statement by the company about this contract was made, press reports predicted an announcement after the monthly board meeting of Lonrho on 16 July. As a correspondent subsequently described it, 'the Lonrho deal was all but sealed. In fact, everybody was wondering whether the announcement would be made on Great Britain day' at the Zaire International Trade Fair in July 1969:

Martin Theves was there, demonstrating his perfect relations with Bomboko at the innumerable cocktail parties and in front of a score of foreign journalists, flown to the Congo [Zaire] at the expense of the Congo government. 'Tiny' Rowland, in Lagos at that time, was expected in Kinshasa any day (a room was reserved for him in the overcrowded Regina Hotel). But, to everybody's surprise, Rowland went straight to London from Lagos, for the 16 July Lonrho board meeting. No announcement was made.[36]

It became clear from then on that Lonrho's bid for the management contract had failed. As it happened, Union Minière's tenure was renewed as part of the general compensation terms, and an announcement to this effect was made in September of that year. Lonrho's Zairean copper ambitions had not been taken very seriously by the established mining houses which dominated the Zairean industry, and it is not unlikely that President Mobutu had used Lonrho as a lever in his negotiations with the Belgian interests. However, it is also possible that Lonrho, through Theves, had backed the wrong political horse; in August 1969 Bomboko was dismissed by Mobutu, and the company lost its most important contact in Kinshasa.

It was reported that Lonrho had bought the Watergate Steam Shipping Company with the Zairean venture in mind and that the cargo vessels had been intended to carry Katanga's ore to refineries in Europe and Japan.[37] The profitability of the railway project largely depended on the Katanga copper freight, but it had its own mineral possibilities: along with the contract for the construction of the line was to have gone a concession for the exploitation of territory along the route 'said to be rich in hidden wealth'.[38] Early in 1970 the feasibility study was presented to the Zaire authorities. From the start, of course, Lonrho must have hoped to get the contract for building the railway as a reward for the 'free' survey, and in June 1970 the company was certain that the deal was in the bag. Alan Ball was reported by Reuter's on 22 June and by the *Financial Times* on 23 June as saying that a protocol would be signed shortly between the Zaire government and a syndicate consisting of Lonrho, its Belgian subsidiary and Nissho-Iwai. This display of over-confidence gave Mobutu the opportunity to disown Lonrho. In a sharply-worded statement on 22 July the Zairean government, while it reaffirmed that the line was 'indispensable to its overall transport system and policy', denied that the contract had been awarded to any group, 'and in particular to Lonrho'.[39] The statement also alleged that Lonrho had tried to subvert the 1969 discussions between Kinshasa and Union Minière on the management contract for the mines, and it referred to Lonrho's Rhodesian connections. Mobutu was also alarmed at the potential economic strength of the Lonrho–Cominière combination in Zaire. A further factor was the publication in the Lonrho-owned *Times of Zambia* of comment unfavourable to Zaire at a time when President Mobutu was visiting Lusaka. The Zairean statement ended: 'The Congolese government therefore, true to its policies of economic independence, wish publicly to announce their refusal to have any further dealings with Lonrho.'[40]

A few weeks later, Zaire decided to place Cominière under government supervision – it was denied that this move amounted to nationalization – so as to safeguard the country's interests during a bitter legal wrangle between Lonrho and Cominière. This had resulted from differences between Theves and the Lonrho directors over the control of Cominière. After the British company's fall from favour, Theves was under pressure in Kinshasa to reassert Cominière's independence from Lonrho, and the complicated manoeuvres in Brussels were not resolved before his death in November 1970. In July 1971 Lonrho purchased enough shares to give it undisputed control of Cominière.[41]

Eighteen of the companies – excluding Cometrik, the electricity supply undertaking – were eventually returned to Lonrho in February 1973. Duncan Sandys may have played a part in this complex story. As founder of the European Movement, Sandys must have had good connections in Brussels. But Lonrho's relationship with Mobutu in December 1970 may not have been as bad as the hostile tone of the July 1970 statement implied: in December Rowland and Ball were due to visit Kinshasha, where they apparently expected a 'cordial' reception.[42] In 1974 Lonrho was again reported to be conducting feasibility studies of the projected railway. At the end of that year there was press speculation that the company's domicile would be moved out of Britain and that 'the most likely base could be Belgium with Rowland's eyes still fixed on the Union Minière'.[43]

That Lonrho had rebuilt its contacts in Kinshasa with some success was indicated by the appointment in 1973 of Mboti Litho, a cousin of President Mobutu's father, to the board of the company's Zairean subsidiary. Litho was one of the richest men in Zaire, after Mobutu himself. After a political career during which he served as Minister of Finance and Minister of Agriculture, he bought a chain store and founded the Société Générale d'Alimentation which, according to *African Development*, was responsible for 'the distribution of most foodstuffs ... He also gets supplies from Rhodesia and southern Africa.' He owned what was said to be the biggest supermarket anywhere in Europe or Africa, 'an edifice so large that it would hold six full-sized football pitches while 480 American cars could be garaged in the cold store'.[44]

Lonrho reportedly helped him to stock his supermarket; his portrait hung in the company's London boardroom.

In 1968, the year of Lonrho's expansion into Ghana and Zaire, it acquired David Whitehead and Sons (Holdings) Ltd, a British textile firm with mills in Malawi, Rhodesia, South Africa and Nigeria. The Nigerian factory, Kaduna Textiles, was then the biggest in West Africa. This introduced Lonrho into the continent's most populous state. What is more, Nigeria was potentially black Africa's richest country, with vast oil reserves which produced a comparatively small return at that time because Nigeria was in the middle of a civil war. The Federal government was hard put to it to finance the military operation, and was running into a big balance of payments deficit, with foreign investors difficult to find because of the great political uncertainties. The war had already affected old-established firms, particularly John Holt, which had established itself in the Niger Delta during the last century. John Holt had acquired what might be described as a respectable colonial image of solidarity, dealing in produce and general merchandise. Among its subsidiaries were the West African Drug Company, one of West Africa's largest pharmaceutical outlets; tanneries; various secondary industries; an agricultural engineering company; and J. Allen, a large motor distributor. The Holt Maritime Enterprises and Holt's Transport operated an important river fleet which had been virtually immobilized because it was situated in Eastern Nigeria, where the civil war was being fought. Many other John Holt enterprises had been affected, although the company's port in Warri was already recovering and doing good business. John Holt also had branches and associated companies in Ghana, and wine-trading firms in Britain and France.

In October 1968 John Holt rejected a takeover bid by an unnamed group: the board decided that no commercial or financial advantage could be derived from accepting. In February the following year, the company's chairman reported a marked recovery in the group's fortunes. Trading profits for the year ending 31 August 1968 amounted to £853,000, compared with a loss of £355,000 in the previous year. Nevertheless, there was a drop in turnover of £4 million, reflecting the fact that the company had 'throughout the whole year been cut off from our trading ventures, motor agencies and other activities in the east of Nigeria'.[45] An

45

increased dividend was paid. But the group was not in good shape and had sold properties surplus to its needs, realizing capital profits amounting to about £500,000. At the end of August 1968, John Holt's net tangible assets were put at £4.7 million – almost £2 million less than in the previous year.

The group could not withstand the Lonrho offer when it was made in March 1969, and the deal went ahead soon after Jessel Securities of London, which held twenty per cent of the John Holt capital, announced its willingness to accept the bid. Lonrho acquired the company for about £8 million – though not for cash: for each ordinary John Holt share of 5s. (25p), John Holt shareholders received two ordinary Lonrho shares of the same par value. Lonrho shares were then at their peak price of over £3; three years later they had fallen to less than a third of this. An interesting aspect of the takeover offer was that it stated Lonrho's intention 'that John Holt will be continued under its existing identity'.[46] So strictly was this intention adhered to that most Nigerians were completely unaware that the company had changed hands, and there was no need for reassuring statements that Lonrho was practically divorced from its southern African background, such as had to be issued in Ghana and elsewhere. In any case, Nigeria was in the middle of a bloody conflict and too preoccupied to take much notice of the transaction.

Rowland visited Lagos in July 1969, and soon after his return to London there were reports that Lonrho was negotiating with 'certain Nigerian interests' about forming a tanker fleet which would transport Nigeria's rapidly increasing oil output. The British press suggested that this development 'could open the way to Lonrho moving into the oil exploration and prospecting business itself'.[47] There were no suggestions about the sources of the finance for the five super-tankers which, it was said, would be required, but Shell, the Russians and Kuwaiti-based interests were mentioned, and there was talk of a partnership with the Federal government.[48]

Rowland had meanwhile established an acquaintance with Joseph Tarka, at the time Federal Commissioner for Transport. The Kuwaiti interests were probably represented by the Gulf Fishing Company, a subsidiary of Gulf International – the empire of Khalil Osman, the Sudanese tycoon, who was to play such an important part in Lonrho's future expansion.[49] Lonrho's hopes of entering the international oil business through Nigeria came to nothing, for a large number of possible reasons, although in May 1973 Rowland still expressed hopes of exporting Nigeria's natural gas to the United States in partnership with an American firm.

He and Tarka may first have met over the negotiations which followed the Nigerian announcement, immediately after Lonrho's takeover of John Holt, that the Federal government intended to nationalize all foreign-owned ports – including that at Warri, one of the John Holt Group's most valuable assets. By 1969 Warri had turned into an oil city, catering for a vast commercial and industrial complex based on the operations of the British and American oil companies. But even before this boom the port had been an important trade terminal, handling, under John Holt's control, imports of capital goods, heavy machinery, building materials and consumer items. The mooring facilities had just been expanded to take four more ocean-going vessels by the end of 1969, and although the Lonrho Annual Report for that year mentions official Nigerian assurances that the government would pay fair compensation for the port 'together with its equipment, workshops and shipping facilities', the accounts in subsequent years did not note the receipt of such compensation. John Holt's own reports also failed to record the outcome of the Warri negotiations with the Nigerian authorities. But their 1972 accounts cite a credit of £277,300 for 'nationalized assets'. In the year before the port was nationalized, according to John Holt's chairman, Warri port contributed approximately £200,000 to Holt's profits.[50]

John Holt did employ senior African management, and Lonrho extended directorships to Nigerian employees. During the 1973 boardroom row, one of them commented privately that he was now aware that he was working for Lonrho; though until the scandal broke, the connection had seemed unimportant and remote. The only Nigerian to identify himself publicly with Lonrho was Mr S. K. W. Ogungbade. In May 1973, when appearing in the Woolwich County Court to apply for an order to evict the tenants of his London house, he stated that he had come to London in order to organize support for Mr Rowland in the boardroom row.[51]

A few days before the Woolwich court hearings, Rowland had been photographed with Ogungbade on his right and Tom Mtine on his left outside the High Court during the Lonrho boardroom hearings.[52] *West Africa*, which published the full group photograph, described Ogungbade as a director of Lonrho (Nigeria).[53] A fortnight later *West Africa* carried an editorial correction stating that 'in fact, Mr Ogungbade has no connection with the Lonrho group, and there is no such entity as Lonrho (Nigeria), although the company has a variety of interests in Nigeria. A number of well-known Nigerians are directors of the separate Lonrho companies there.'[54]

While Ogungbade's precise connection with Lonrho remained unclear, he seems to have known, according to his evidence at the Woolwich County Court, about the directors' feud at least a fortnight before it became public, indicating some link with the company. Certainly he was concerned enough to pay, in the following year, for a full-page advertisement in Nigeria's most important newspaper, the *Daily Times*, in which he defended Lonrho's OAU consultancy deal, stressing Rowland's lack of racial prejudice. The company's chief executive, he said, was 'a true lover of Africans and pan-Africanism' who regarded Rhodesia's declaration of UDI as 'unforgivable and therefore insufferable. He left Rhodesia. Since then he has not been to Rhodesia.'[55] Ogungbade's reference in his advertisement to Lonrho's purchase of John Holt made it more difficult for Nigerians interested in the OAU affair to claim that they had no means of knowing of the company's interests in their own country.

Lonrho's relative anonymity explains at least in part why the Lagos press could put in banner headlines, 'Nigeria Will Not Deal With Lonrho – Says Arikpo', when the news of Lonrho's appointment as consultants to the OAU broke.[56] Nigeria's ambassador to the United Nations, Edwin Ogbu, referred to this matter at a press conference in New York: 'My country and a number of other countries are opposed to the agreement,' he said, and accused Lonrho of 'aiding and abetting South Africa because of its investments down there'. The extent of Lonrho's involvement in southern Africa had not been understood before, but now that it was, attitudes would change.[57] They did change at the OAU headquarters in Addis Ababa. But Nigerians, who must by then have had plenty of opportunity to find out about the company's Nigerian interests, considering the amount of publicity that the consultancy had received, continued apparently oblivious to what Mr Ogbu and others had said. In June 1974 the Governor of Nigeria's Western State, Brigadier Oluwole Rotimi, in making a speech when the Ibadan branch of Phoenix Motors (Nigeria) Ltd was opened, stressed that John Holt had offered the best conditions for partnership with the state government in this new company, in which the Western State owned forty per cent of the equity, while John Holt had a controlling share.

Nigeria's oil, size and economic potential make it the most promising area in black Africa for entrepreneurs. But the leadership of such a rich country has had no need to cultivate individual businessmen and multinational investment in the way that small countries with few resources, such as Malawi or Swaziland, have done. Furthermore, military leaders are often outside the established and interrelated élites of East and West African countries, in which important families tend to produce a high proportion of the politicians, technocrats, businessmen and intellectuals. In Nigeria this nexus of top people was dislodged from the most important posts in public life when the military came to power, and the officers who took over did not as a rule come from influential families. Nevertheless, Lonrho established a presence in Nigeria, both through the acquisition of long-established companies such as John Holt and Costain, and through new ventures. In addition, Rowland overcame the obstacles to establishing personal contact with influential political circles, and even became personally acquainted with the head of state, General Gowon.

Rowland also got to know Joseph Tarka, who was a federal commissioner – the equivalent of a minister in rank, though not in political power. Tarka was also tipped as a likely Prime Minister when Nigeria changed back to civilian rule, and Rowland and Tarka kept up their business contacts even after the oil tanker scheme had been quietly dropped. In 1973 there were moves to form a joint Lonrho–Nigerian construction company to take advantage of Nigeria's building boom. A meeting took place in Bath House, London – the headquarters of Lonrho Exports – on 13 September 1973. Among those invited to attend were Tarka and Mr G. W. Whitelaw, the General Manager of Lonrho Exports. The proposal was that Lonrho and Bovis, the British construction firm, would own thirty per cent each of the shares, while private Nigerian interests would hold the remaining forty per cent. Bovis dropped out of this venture, which did not receive publicity either in Britain or in Nigeria, where Tarka's association with Lonrho might have caused some embarrassment in view of his official position. Unfortunately Lonrho lost this valuable contact in 1974, when Tarka became the first federal commissioner to resign, following press accusations of corruption, which he strongly denied.

But in 1975 Lonrho acquired indirect building interests in Nigeria through its acquisition of a holding in the construction company, Richard Costain.

Another West African country to which Lonrho turned its attention in the late sixties was Ivory Coast, which had been receptive to the idea of a 'dialogue' with South Africa. By 1969 Lonrho's southern African sugar empire was well on the way to becoming a major contributor to group profits. In Ivory Coast, Lonrho's initial idea was a sugar scheme, from the first stage of growing the cane to the ultimate refining. Probably the resistance which Lonrho met from the established French businesses was one of the main reasons for its failure to secure the wide-ranging contract it had anticipated.

The first Ivory Coast venture, in 1969, was one in which Lonrho and the government had respectively 40 per cent and 60 per cent interests. This was the Société Ivoirienne d'Exportation S.A. (SOCIVEX), which was set up as a commodity marketing enterprise. By 1972 it was exporting about 5 per cent of the country's cocoa and 4 per cent of its coffee. In November 1970 a protocol agreement was signed for a £14 million plantation-to-market sugar complex to be built at Ferkessedougou in the extreme north of the country. It was envisaged that by the end of 1973 the project would be producing refined sugar at the rate of 50,000 tons a year. Negotiations were also in progress for the formation of a new bank in which Lonrho, the Ivorian government and the Standard Bank would have 50 per cent, 40 per cent and 10 per cent interests respectively, as an alternative to the traditional sources of French finance for promoting exports of agricultural commodities. There were yet more plans to establish an insurance company in which Lonrho would again have an important stake.

In February 1971 it was announced that Lonrho had won the sugar contract and that the basis of a partnership with the government was now being established in the form of a state sugar corporation, SODESUCRE.[58] The scheme was to include an irrigation system covering 12,000 acres of cane, and possibly a dam as well. It was on a scale to make Ivory Coast entirely independent of imported sugar and was undoubtedly the most important deal ever concluded by a British firm in this erstwhile French colony. A spokesman for Lonrho in London, however, remarked that the contract had been secured only as a result of 'a major effort made in the face of strong, and natural, opposition'.[59] The drawbacks from Lonrho's point of view became clear a few weeks later when the final details of the contract were released. It emerged that Lonrho had failed to secure unrivalled control of the sugar scheme. The agreement even fell short of a fully-fledged management contract, because the government's approval would be required before each consecutive stage of the scheme could go ahead. Lonrho would also act as consultant in giving technical advice and assistance. The £14 million required was put up in equal parts by the First National City Bank and the Export-Import Bank of America. The American loans were tied to American suppliers of engineering equipment, so that it was Lang Engineering of Florida, rather than Lonrho, which in due course installed the Ferkessedougou refinery.

That Lonrho achieved the success it did in Ivory Coast, albeit less sweeping than originally intended, was in no small measure due to the part played in the negotiations by Gil Olympio, newly recruited from the International Monetary Fund to become Lonrho's West African manager. Olympio had impeccable connections: he was the second son of the late President of Togo, Sylvanus Olympio, and had a younger brother who was married to the daughter of the Ivorian President, Houphouet-Boigny. Being a French-speaking African who had received a training in economics at Oxford University, he was admirably suited to blaze a trail for a British firm in what had to date been the exclusive province of French big business. It was not long after the Ferkessedougou contract was signed that the strategic value of going right to the top was given further recognition in the appointment of Dia Houphouet-Boigny, the President's nephew, to the chairmanship of La Securité Ivoirienne, an insurance company in which Lonrho and the Guardian Royal Exchange between them had a forty per cent holding. The thirty-three Ivorians who held the balance of the shares included a number of government corporations and four ministers.

At the end of 1974 it was announced that the first Ferkessedougou sugar would shortly be on the market.[60] Ivory Coast remained Lonrho's principal interest in the former French African colonies. In Dahomey an agreement was signed for the development and management of a sugar complex which was to be the largest single investment in Dahomey since independence. It was due to start production in 1976 with an eventual capacity of 40,000 tons of sugar a year.

Towards the end of 1973 – a year after the Dahomey agreement had been signed – Lonrho was reported to be establishing trade links in Cameroun, home country of the OAU Secretary General, Nzo Ekangaki. Rowland's bid to become consultant to the OAU was not yet known – except, perhaps, by those who were in his confidence. The fact that Rowland had met Cameroun's President Ahidjo probably helped in December that year, when the consultancy was discussed in Addis Ababa.[61] The company's initial fact-finding mission in Cameroun was only vaguely defined: it was to discover the government's priority projects 'which could be carried out on the basis of participation with Lonrho'.[62] The company's representative, Francis Shoniwa, a black Rhodesian, also inquired about the possibility of Lonrho being appointed as buying agents for the government. He offered facilities to importers, reinforced by financial credits, and the patronage of the Chamber of Commerce. The vice-chairman of the Cameroun Chamber of Commerce – who was also chairman of the Cameroun Development Corporation, a state-owned concern – was Victor Mukete, a minister in Nigeria's Federal government before independence.[63] Ekangaki, who came from the same area as Mukete, was then studying in Nigeria, and if the two men did not meet then they are certain to have done so after Ekangaki entered politics and became a minister in the Camerounian government. During Lonrho's 1973 visit, Mukete chaired meetings between the company and leading Camerounian businessmen; later he headed a committee of experts to draft a memorandum and articles of association for presentation to the Camerounian government.

After a second visit Mr Whitelaw, who headed the Lonrho delegation, said that his discussions with the authorities had been very fruitful; Lonrho would 'soon' start operating in Cameroun. He was reported to have 'stated categorically' that the company intended to act as buying agents for the Camerounian government. Plans were in progress to create the Cameroun National Industrial and Commercial Company, to be jointly owned by Lonrho and Camerounian businessmen. 'He added that ninety per cent of Lonrho's investments are in Africa, where it now operates in Zaire, Ivory Coast, Nigeria, Kenya, Tanzania and Zambia.'[64] Rhodesia and South Africa were not mentioned.

The most important contact that Rowland made in Lonrho's years of growth was Khalil Osman, a Sudanese millionaire, who was making efforts to expand his business in black Africa.[65] He had started his career as a veterinary surgeon, and is said to have been given his first big chance when he cured a cow belonging to the ruler of Kuwait.[66] Within a few year he controlled a large collection of Sudanese enterprises, including textile mills, glass factories, insurance companies and fishing fleets. He was reputed to be the richest man in Sudan. Precisely how Rowland and Osman met is not clear, but it is likely to have been in West Africa where Osman was almost as much of an outsider as Rowland. The meeting was to have important consequences for Lonrho: the 'Kuwaiti interests' often mentioned by Rowland and those around him as backers of various plans are Osman's patrons in the ruling family of Kuwait.

Rowland was a man after Osman's own heart. Osman has called himself 'a black Tiny Rowland',[67] and he invested in Lonrho by buying a large number of shares. At the 1974 Annual General Meeting, Osman was introduced by Duncan Sandys as chairman of Gulf International, 'one of the largest privately owned industrial groups in the Middle East, employing over 25,000 people . . . I propose to invite him to say a few words'. This he did at great length, concluding with a panegyric on Lonrho and Rowland:

Lonrho is aggressive. Lonrho is great. This Mr Rowland. I have been many times with him, meeting him in Kuwait when the temperature was 43° C and one Bedouin, seeing him – he [Rowland] had a fever and put on an overcoat over his head – said 'What's wrong with this Englishman? He's having a coat at 43° C? What has he got, an air-conditioning in his head?' I said, 'No, the man is sick. He is sick but he works, and works very hard. He is a very rich man. He doesn't need to work. He can enjoy the Riviera, but he works as if he doesn't have money for his breakfast tomorrow. I like that kind of man. You should like him, your children should like him.' I am not here to advertise him . . . I expect from Lonrho a great future.[68]

Three

Gold and Diamonds

Lonrho's acquisition of Ashanti Goldfields at the end of 1968 was perhaps the most important single takeover in the company's history. It was rightly hailed as a commercial coup and a fine example of Rowland's entrepreneurial ability. The benefit that the mine was to bring to the group was foreshadowed in Ashanti's 1967 figures, with pre-tax profits of £2.2 million compared with the Lonrho group's total for the same period of £3.6 million. Indeed, Ashanti was one of the richest gold mines in the world though by no means the biggest. A senior manager of the mine, pointing to a lump of quartz streaked with gold, once said, 'in South Africa there are men who have been mining for a lifetime and have never glimpsed anything as rich as this'.[1]

When Lonrho arrived in Ghana there were six producing gold mines, five of which – Tarkwa, Prestea, Konongo, Bibiani and the Bremang gold dredges – had been nationalized by Nkrumah and were owned by the State Gold Mining Corporation. The Ghana government quickly welcomed Lonrho's takeover of Ashanti Goldfields and authorized the company to say that it had also invited Lonrho to carry out a feasibility study of the state mines (eventually produced in 1971) and to take a direct interest in their operations.[2] There was talk of Lonrho investing in breweries, in the sugar industry and even in developing Ghana's diamond areas – which, according to Rowland, would be 'a priority item' for the company.[3]

Ashanti Goldfields was acquired according to the increasingly common pattern: no money actually changed hands and Ashanti holders were given Lonrho shares in exchange for their own.[4] Lonrho promised to preserve the separate identity of Ashanti Goldfields and that management staff would not be deprived of any of the advantages and conditions of service which they had previously enjoyed. Sir Edward Spears, who was chairman of the Ashanti Goldfields Corporation, was invited to join the Lonrho board, and he resigned from Ashanti in August 1971. It may be important that Harley Drayton, who had been involved in getting Rowland to join the Lonrho board in the early sixties, was a director of Ashanti Goldfields and remained so until his death in 1966, when he was succeeded by Martin Ellison Rich, who was then a director of Consolidated Goldfields and of companies in Drayton's 117 Group. Duncan Sandys, who had joined Ashanti's board after the war but had resigned when he became a minister, also rejoined the board in 1966. He resigned a second time when he became chairman of Lonrho in 1972. Rowland became managing director of Ashanti at the end of 1968.

Not everybody in Ghana welcomed Lonrho's arrival. There were suggestions that the takeover infringed Ghana's decree applying UN sanctions against Rhodesia. Ghana press attacks on Lonrho's Rhodesian connections sent Rowland and Ball on a flying visit to Ghana in their private jet. Soon afterwards the Ghana government issued a statement in terms which were to become a familiar theme in the repertoire of Lonrho's African friends: Lonrho's holding in Rhodesia, it claimed, was only an historical accident. It continued, 'None of the company's present directors was either born in, or lives in Rhodesia, and out of 20,000 Lonrho shareholders there is not a single Portuguese national.' This would appear to have been something of a *non sequitur*, indicating perhaps that Lonrho's equally unacceptable Portuguese connections were very much in the spokesman's mind.[5] In addition, the statement pointed out that Lonrho had not remitted any funds to Rhodesia since sanctions were enforced, nor had it invested money there. It had resisted pressure from the Smith regime to operate the Beira–Umtali pipeline.[6] Rowland himself assured the Ghanaians that only five per cent of Lonrho's assets were in Rhodesia, and in a message to the Ministry of Lands and Mineral Resources the company stated that 'so far as Rhodesia is concerned, Lonrho never made any secret of its antipathy towards the policy of the present regime'.[7]

But there were other difficulties. The Adansi chiefs on whose land the Obuasi concession of Ashanti Goldfields was situated disputed the transaction. They cited an 1897 agreement which, they claimed, prevented transfer of the concession without written government consent. The case was settled out of court. Soon afterwards, Mr R. S. Amegashi, Commissioner for Lands and Mineral Resources, stated that his government was not happy about Ashanti Goldfields' annual payment of only 132 new cedis (about £54) to the Adansi traditional council for the land, and the government would enter into negotiations with the company to improve this figure. In December 1968 Amegashi, accompanied by the Adansihene – the Adansi chief – and two senior government officials left for London to discuss with Lonrho 'the terms of a new lease which it is proposed to grant' Ashanti Goldfields.[8] Eventually it was agreed that the Adansi traditional council would receive over £100,000 annually. The Adansihene became a member of the board of Ashanti Goldfields. He resigned in 1970. It was said that he was dissatisfied with the terms of the new lease.[9] This was at a time when the company came under criticism from the government for having failed to improve amenities for its employees.[10]

The Adansi episode was more than simply a matter of compensating the chiefs for a long-standing grievance. The issue was used as an opportunity to renegotiate the entire relationship between Ashanti Goldfields and the Ghana government. President Nkrumah's government had already come up against stubborn resistance from Ashanti Goldfields, particularly from the board's chairman, Spears, when it was suggested that the state should participate in the ownership of its main gold mines. General Ankrah's government which overthrew Nkrumah in 1966 was much more friendly towards foreign investors. Nevertheless, the new government was also eager to derive more direct benefits from the mine's prosperity, possibly in exchange for an extension of Ashanti's lease. There was a feeling in Ghana that Ashanti may have been developing the mine too slowly to meet the country's currency needs. To this Spears had replied that while there was 'a lot of gold' in the mine, it had to be 'treated properly', and that there had never been any government pressure for hasty development in the past.[11] He also said that more than seventy-six per cent of profits in 1968 had gone in taxation. Spears's resistance to increased Ghanaian control continued even after Lonrho's takeover. While he still held the post of chairman early in 1970 he sought a meeting with Ghana's newly-elected Prime Minister, Dr Busia, who had said that his government was 'going to look into' the question of taking a fifty-one per cent share in the holdings of mining companies.[12] Afterwards Spears said that Busia had assured him there would be no nationalization. This reinforced the Ghanaian impression that Spears, as an old colonial, was determined to resist any progressive move.

In January 1969 Lonrho and the Ghana government agreed on a state participation of twenty per cent in Ashanti Goldfields, with an option on a further twenty per cent at £1 a share. In return, the lease of the Obuasi concession, which was to have run out in 1986, was extended for a period of fifty years, starting on 1 January 1969. Lonrho also promised to extend the milling capacity of the mine from 45,000 tons of ore a month to 80,000 tons, and to compensate the government if its dividend from the twenty per cent shareholding fell short of royalties under the old lease.

If everybody in the Ghanaian establishment and the Lonrho boardroom was pleased with these arrangements, there were lesser people who were not. To start with, the farmers in the Adansi traditional area claimed one million new cedis (about £410,000) for damage done to cocoa and food crops by pollution from the mine. Amegashi had already noted that unscrupulous people had taken advantage of the mine takeover to create trouble and political dissension, and he had promised that the government would take into consideration all grievances during the negotiations with the company.[13] But the only benefit arising from the deal appeared to have gone to the chiefs. The most dissatisfied group were the 6,000 miners working for Ashanti Goldfields. They demanded three months' 'severance pay', claiming that the takeover would deprive them of benefits under a collective agreement. Amegashi said that their demands were 'unjustifiable', since workers' appointments had not been terminated.[14] Although the term 'severance pay' seemed misleading, there was, in fact, a precedent in the Nkrumah period, when the Konongo mine was taken over by the state on the recommendations of a commission of which Amegashi had himself been a member. Severance pay had been paid on that occasion, and while the Lonrho takeover was not an exact parallel, the miners were not without a case.

This seemed to be conceded when the company offered a fifteen days' *ex gratia* payment; but this was, unfortunately, referred to as 'dash' in the letter making the compromise. The word 'dash' means a tip or a small bribe. This compromise was rejected by the workers, who decided at a meeting in the Obuasi mosque on 2 March 1969 to go on strike, although strikes were at that time illegal in Ghana. Their own union and the Ghana Trades Union Congress were not involved in the decision; in fact, both were so unrepresentative of mine-workers' opinion that considerable anger against officials had gathered, and the house of at least one union leader was stoned in the days leading up to the strike. At the mosque meeting, sticks and stones were hurled at union representatives who called for 'moderation'.

The strike began the following day. There was a serious clash with the police in which two miners were shot dead, and another later died of his wounds. Twenty-eight people were wounded: rioters and policemen, except for three railwaymen, reportedly hit by stray bullets. The government's first statement held that the miners had attacked the police station and that the police had fired in self-defence. This contradicted local reports which described fifty policemen, 'mostly armed with rifles and truncheons', as having rushed to the scene of the demonstration and fired warning shots.[15] Ghana's state-owned radio broadcast the government statement, but added to it a report of the mine-workers' claim that the bodies of the dead miners had been found near the mine and not at the police barracks. A commission of inquiry later found that the police station had not been attacked, and that the police officers may have lost their nerve when they heard of the disorders – news 'which in such situations tends to dim one's powers of observation'.[16]

The government's stand during the March unrest was remarkable. It promised full support for the company and ordered the miners back to work, claiming that many 'loyal' employees wanted to return and promising them police and military protection. Miners 'should take advantage of the generous offer of fifteen days' pay made earlier by the management and accepted by the Ghana Mine Workers' Union'.[17] The secretary of the Ghana TUC, Mr Bentum, also appealed to the workers to end their strike, promising that the TUC would continue to help the miners in all their legitimate demands. At a meeting on 6 March the miners decided not to resume work and criticized the government for condemning their action. The following day only about five hundred employees out of six thousand complied with the government order to return, and the mine stayed closed.

Six strike leaders were arrested. On 10 March the miners returned but announced that the strike would be resumed if their demands were not met by 1 April. Before that date Major-General John Anderson, Lonrho's deputy chairman in Zambia, arrived on the scene and announced that he and the other directors were 'very much upset' at unjustified Ghana press criticism of the company. Lonrho might reconsider its investment in Ghana as a result.

It would be stupid to link Lonrho with Rhodesia, he said, and give the impression that Ashanti Goldfields had been taken over by a racist company. He himself had been dismissed as General Officer Commanding the Rhodesian armed forces by the Smith regime because he was opposed to UDI.[18] But Rowland himself smoothed things over and announced that Lonrho would go 'full speed ahead' with its Ghana investment plans.[19] A Lonrho delegation then held talks with the mine management at Obuasi, and shortly afterwards Ashanti Goldfields agreed to give the miners three months' basic pay as a goodwill award.

'There hasn't been anything like it in the seventy-three years the mine has been going,' Spears's secretary, Miss Nancy Maurice (who subsequently became the second Lady Spears), said about the strike.[20] There had been strikes, but never any serious violence. During the official inquiry into the incident, the counsel for Ashanti Goldfields told the press that the company had not agreed with the police decision to shoot. This reflected the widespread Ghanaian suspicion that the mine management had been responsible for the tough official action. The change in ownership seems to have crystallized longstanding grievances, such as those over accommodation and transport. During the inquiry, the general manager admitted that the last set of houses built for employees dated back to 1937 and provided accommodation for less than one thousand. The apprehension among workers about the changeover from the paternalistic but familiar rule of Spears to new owners – unknown entities without local links – helped to create the emotional atmosphere in which the disturbances took place.

Visitors to Obuasi sometimes remarked on the manorial air of the mining town. The company provided the whole of Obuasi with water, and it had built a modern maternity hospital. The mine was self-sufficient in timber, and its carpenters made furniture for all the houses. The senior and junior staff clubs were said to be well equipped. Besides, there was no other employer in the area; even farmers often worked for the mine in some capacity. It was reported that at the memorial service for the first Lady Spears in the Anglican church near the mine, the Ghanaian clergyman referred to 'our father General Spears'.[21] Although Spears arrived in Obuasi soon after the takeover to assure the union executive that he was still chairman, miners continued to be uncertain about the real position.

The mine's labour force had increased rapidly, rising by one thousand in the year preceding the strike, and many of the new employees had come from state mines, where there had been industrial trouble in 1968. The management suspected that this influx had encouraged militant activity; others blamed outside agitators. But the demands of the miners may well have been the result of the benefit which the deal with Lonrho had brought to the chiefs and to the government, and the argument was that the most deserving people were those who actually produced the gold.

Feelings ran high and in June 1970 another strike closed the mine, in protest at failure to publish the report of the commission of inquiry into the March 1969 incidents. This second strike went on for a week before union officials appealed to the workers to return, and then the majority still refused to do so. The government arrested 108 of the strikers, but released them in the hope of ending the dispute. Most workers returned in the first week of July, but production did not really pick up again until September.[22] The Ghana government lost an estimated £300,000 in revenue through the action, but neither Lonrho nor Ghana officialdom was ready to concede anything on this occasion to the workers. In fact, Ashanti Goldfields subsequently dismissed six men, believed to be the leaders of the strike, who had also been expelled from the Ghana Mine Workers' Union because of their unofficial action. A company spokesman said, 'we had to dismiss them as the company has an agreement not to employ non-union members.'[23]

The last (1969) Annual Report of Lonrho which contained any reference to the March 1969 strike added that labour relations 'are now excellent'[24]; the next Annual Report was silent on this subject, despite the much longer 1970 strike. In the autumn of 1971, some 7,500 workers at Ashanti Goldfields decided to leave the Ghana Mine Workers' Union and form their own national union, reportedly in reaction to the argument by the Ashanti Goldfields management that it could not raise wages, however much it might have liked to do so, because it had to pay in accordance with the levels at the much less profitable state-owned mines. Lonrho in Ghana supported the authoritarian regime and was supported by it in turn. The paternalist Spears, who had disdained the new breed of African rulers, may not have been willing to collaborate so closely with the authorities. In 1971 when the British press suggested that Lonrho was becoming unpopular in Ghana, the Ghana High Commission in London went so far as to issue a statement 'categorically denying this'.[25]

Meanwhile, several other projects which Rowland had planned for Ghana failed to materialize. At the beginning of 1970 the company closed the *New Ashanti Times*, Ghana's oldest mine journal, which had been published by Ashanti Goldfields, on the grounds that its losses could no longer be sustained. The staff described the decision as 'pathetic'.[26] The only project which got off the ground was that for brewing *pito* (indigenous beer). There was some difference of opinion within the Ghana government on the wisdom of proceeding with this enterprise. At least one minister, Professor Twum-Barima, Commissioner for Agriculture, described the project as 'ill-conceived'.[27] A year later, in October 1970, the Tamale factory in the north was closed, although the management said that it would eventually reopen it to produce a different type of beer. The initial venture had, it seems, been badly planned. To some extent, the brewery had been established for political rather than economic reasons, not only to prove to the Ghana government that Lonrho would fulfil its promises of investment in other industrial fields, but also because there had been pressure to site the project in the north, where economic development had lagged behind. The Tamale factory had an initial production target of 1,000 gallons a day – a figure at which it could have just broken even – but could sell only 300 gallons a day. The manager blamed inadequate publicity, local competition, high taxation and the weather for the failure. But the brewery ran into serious difficulties when it started to buy up all available supplies of maize and guinea corn, with the result that local prices of basic foodstuffs started to soar. The other brewery operated by Lonrho at Obuasi was still making a loss in 1971.

Lonrho did eventually produce, in mid-1971, its promised feasibility study on the five state-owned gold mines. In 1970 a report by Bibiani gold mines had mentioned the discovery of large deposits said to be of even higher quality than other Ghana ore. This had been denied by the government. The state gold mining company had provided about £200,000 for mopping-up operations at the Bibiani North mine, due to close down, and the government now said that it had no plans to reopen the main Bibiani mine, which had already been flooded. At the end of 1969, some 700 workers at Bibiani affected by the closure had been told that they would be transferred to other enterprises. Now the Ghanaian press, and in particular the *Ashanti Pioneer*, said that Bibiani could be more profitable than any other mine if the mill were re-started. This would have required at least £1.5 million. By May 1971 work at Bibiani was at a standstill and the remaining work force of five hundred was being assigned to other duties, including stone quarrying. Local politicians and mining experts still insisted that there were important gold deposits, but Bibiani was due to be closed finally. The Lonrho study pointed out that equipment at the mine had so deteriorated that heavy expenditure would be required to put it in order, and recommended that the mine should be closed immediately. Mr I. L. Mensah, member of parliament for the area and a member of the ruling party, threatened to resign if the government did not make more exhaustive studies of the reported ore discovery, and he was supported by geologists who pleaded that the mine should at least be put on a care and maintenance basis while an exploration programme was undertaken. These pleas appeared to fall on deaf ears until the end of the following year, when another government change had taken place, and the resident mine superintendent announced that Bibiani North would soon be reopened.[28]

The Lonrho experts also reported on the Tarkwa mine which, they said, would require five years' heavy expenditure on shaft-sinking and exploration to make it economic. If expectations of ore deposits in the vicinity were to be fulfilled, 'the effect on the economy of Ghana would be far-reaching'.[29] The problem at Tarkwa was not one of mining technology, however, but of sound management: the Lonrho report alleged that on any day a quarter of the labour force was absent on full pay. Nonetheless, early in 1969 Lonrho had already been in negotiation for the takeover of the Tarkwa gold plant. Construction of a plant near Tarkwa had been a Russian project which was stopped soon after the first military coup, when the Ghana government abrogated the agreement with the Soviet Union on the grounds of financial difficulty. Better management was also called for by the Lonrho experts in the case of another state mine.

Before the Ghana government could act on this report and ask Lonrho to undertake the heavy investment in the state mines which seemed to be needed, as well as to supply its managerial skills, Busia's civilian government was overthrown by another military coup. Lonrho was now faced with a much less sympathetic administration. Ghana's first military rulers had reacted against Nkrumahism and the socialist concepts which Nkrumah's government had popularized. After 1966 capitalism and foreign investment became not only respectable concepts but part of a system which was to be entrenched to keep out everything considered 'subversive'. Busia, Nkrumah's old political opponent, came to power after elections in 1969 in which left-wing parties were eliminated from the start, and his administration carried the conservatism of his military predecessors even further. The Busia regime was particularly repressive towards trade unions. The population, on the other hand, had a nostalgic longing for the Nkrumah days, when Ghana had set the pace in Africa and had been respected as a progressive Third World force. In 1971 a political rally in Ashanti had sold more than 2,000 portraits of Nkrumah, and soon afterwards Busia made it a political offence to display or distribute pictures of the former leader. The opposition attacked the new law as unnecessary, suggesting that the popular longing for Nkrumah arose from the failures of the Busia government. Soon afterwards the government introduced an act which, in essence, abolished the TUC of Ghana and caused much resentment. Colonel Acheampong's coup in 1972 was therefore widely popular, particularly among those who still thought of Nkrumah as Ghana's greatest leader. There was talk of restoring him and, although such intentions were strongly denied by the military, it was only his death in the same year which ended speculation about his eventual return.

In such circumstances the new government was impelled in a Nkrumahist direction, at least superficially. In July 1972 it announced that it wanted 'participation' in foreign-owned mining companies and other extractive industries. Rowland paid a visit to Accra and returned to London declaring that Lonrho had already allowed the Ghana government to participate, and that no change was envisaged. Lonrho was 'extremely happy', he stressed, with its agreement, which gave Ghana an option to buy a further 20 per cent in Ashanti Goldfields.[30] This gave rise to some optimism in London, where it was hoped that the Ghana government's participation demands would fall short of the 51 per cent controlling share which had originally been expected. Nevertheless, local rumours insisted that the terms sought by the government were a 25 per cent shareholding for which no compensation would be paid, with a further 30 per cent payable from dividends: or 55 per cent altogether. Acheampong underlined this possibility when he told a gathering in Accra that 'our cocoa, our gold, our diamonds, our manganese, our timber, and the energies of our people have for too long been utilized for the benefit of foreigners'. While his government's policies would not be unjust to such interests, 'those who seek to resist us will only provoke their own destruction'.[31]

The following month Rowland returned to Accra for further talks with the government, but no agreement was reached. In December 1972 the Ghana government announced the failure of the negotiations and, on its own terms, took over fifty-five per cent of the company's assets. The Ashanti Goldfield miners cheered the Acheampong regime, particularly when the Commissioner for Labour, Major Kwame Asante, urged them to be 'watchdogs' against foreign sabotage.[32] The miners at Tarkwa had already resolved not to go on strike or engage in any labour unrest while the existing administration was in power, to show their support for Acheampong's change of economic and industrial policy. They were particularly pleased at the new government's decision to embark on a five-year 'exploration and exploitation programme' of Tarkwa goldfields at the cost of some £3 million.[33] Soon afterwards it was reported that another gold mine, Prestea, had discovered further large gold deposits. The Ghanaian press was jubilant, and the state-owned *Ghanaian Times* spoke of objections by the mining companies to tax assessments, adding: 'if the mining companies have nothing to hide, why were they insisting on having their companies still incorporated in London instead of Accra?'[34]

Compensation terms were substantially agreed a few months later with the other mining company in which Ghana took a fifty-five per cent share, Consolidated African Selection Trust, which mined diamonds. But the Lonrho negotiations were still proceeding in 1974. Rowland's company apparently found it more difficult to come to terms with the Ghana government than one of the old-established 'imperialist' concerns had done.

Before 1972 Lonrho owned 80 per cent of Ashanti Goldfields, and the fall to only a 45 per cent share, from October 1972, would clearly reduce its future profits. The question of how large this loss would be gave rise to widely different estimates. *African Development*, for instance, often close to Lonrho sources, reported that 'Lonrho maintains that its loss in profits due to government participation would be some £170,000 but of this some sixty per cent is due to be paid in tax, so the net loss to Lonrho shareholders would only be some £65,000.'[35] This figure was disputed by a leading London stockbroker, who put the loss to shareholders at an after-tax £1 million or £2 million.[36] In 1973 Lonrho's 45 per cent share of Ashanti's £5.1 million profit was about £2.2 million. Had they still owned 80 per cent of the corporation, it would have been £4.1 million. Even so, Ghana's gold contributed about a fifth of the group's net profit of £11.2 million that year. Alan Ball was right in describing Ashanti Goldfields as 'Lonrho's largest single asset' when he addressed the Annual General Meeting in March 1971.[37]

Ashanti contributed 31 per cent of the group's net profit in 1969; 20 per cent in 1970; 29 per cent in 1971; and in 1972, in consequence of the high gold prices on the world market, 45 per cent.[38] On the whole, Lonrho did well out of the mine and expanded it through capital investment, as its previous owners would probably also have done, given the rise in gold prices. Some of the extensions had already been planned under Spears. At the end of 1970, Rowland expressed the hope that 'production is in the process of being doubled'.[39] By the end of 1973, throughput at the mine's treatment plant amounted to 74,500 tons of ore a month, which came close to the 80,000 tons per month aimed at after Lonrho bought the mine in 1969.

Rowland seldom mentioned in his annual review of operations the people most closely connected with Ashanti – the miners and the inhabitants of the surrounding area. Yet when Lonrho's claim of contributing to Africa's development is tested, as for example in this case, on-the-spot inquiries present a different picture. The expansion in production at Ashanti has worried many Ghanaians, concerned that the company has been exhausting ore reserves too rapidly. (However, Spears had been accused of not expanding fast enough.) In 1973 Cameron Duodu, one of Ghana's best-known reporters, wrote about Ashanti Goldfields: 'The mine from which over £10 million worth of gold is being dug this year has reduced the people to such abject poverty as to make the stories of Lonrho's squabbles seem like an obscene irrelevance.'[40] Complaints about the inadequate housing and transport facilities seemed the same four years after Lonrho's takeover as they had been under General Spears. Junior workers paid rent for small rooms in which they were supposed to live with their wives and children, while senior officials, particularly whites, were allocated spacious rent-free bungalows. Workers had to rely on buses purchased by their union, but senior officials were helped to buy their own cars and given transport allowances. The hundred-square-mile mining concession surrounding the mine was partly used for the growing of timber for underground shoring, with the result that food needed by villagers close by had to be brought in at greater cost. Duodu met a woman carrying plantains and asked her where she had bought the fruit: 'It's from Dakyiwaa, fifteen miles from here,' she said; she had to go so far 'because we are not allowed to farm here. All this place is mine land. You can see the trees they've planted. No one is allowed to cut down any of them in order to make a farm. If you do that, the mine's security officers will uproot your crops and then they will look for you and arrest you and take you to court.'[41]

In 1969 Lonrho was still engaged in establishing itself in West Africa, and one of the most alluring prospects was Sierra Leone's diamonds. Echoes of Lonrho's exploits in Sierra Leone were heard three years later in the London High Court, when Gerald Percy spoke of a quarrel between directors in 1969/1970:

Mr Rowland insisted on pursuing proposals whereby a certain African government should nationalize the assets of two other British companies in the country concerned, and then transfer them to a new corporation which would be jointly owned and/or managed by such government and Lonrho.[42]

Percy was referring to Sierra Leone, and the two other British companies were CAST, which mined and marketed diamonds, and William Baird, which mined iron ore under the name of Delco. In fact, Rowland's plans were more grandiose than this. Sierra Leone was to have been only a part, although a crucial one, of a scheme to challenge the virtual monopoly position then enjoyed by De Beers, a South African company. This was at a time when the balance of power among the diamond producers was shifting, and the Central Selling Organization (CSO) – De Beer's diamond marketing instrument – which had dominated the entire field could no longer be sure of its continued power to control international diamond transactions. The CSO still marketed 80 per cent of world output, but independent African states were mining about a quarter of the West's production, while the Russians were selling about a fifth of the world total. This meant that De Beers directly controlled only 42 per cent or so, by value, of the total mining output (as opposed to world sales), and the mining of diamonds in new areas outside De Beers' control was expanding. Rowland's ambition to challenge the established South African mining houses[43] was bound to be boosted by such a prospect, and in 1969 it was proposed that Lonrho could take on at least a part of the Soviet Union's diamond sales – undertaken indirectly by De Beers. The Russians are said to have shown some interest initially. There were also reports that Lonrho wanted to combine the Sierra Leonean diamond interests which it hoped to acquire with Ghanaian and other African concessions. For instance, a prospecting and mining agreement was signed with the Lesotho government. And Zaire, another diamond producer, was mentioned as a potential field of action, although the company had already lost out to Union Minière in its bid for the Zairean copper mine management contract.[44]

The possibility that Sierra Leone might demand a 51 per cent controlling interest in its mines was first suggested in August 1969, when Prime Minister Siaka Stevens announced that his government would review existing agreements with CAST. CAST mined about two-thirds of the country's diamonds, exporting some £15 million worth a year. Stevens had recently visited Zambia, where government acquisition of 51 per cent holdings in mining companies had already become official policy. It was therefore suggested that Sierra Leone was contemplating a similar move. These rumours were confirmed in December, when Stevens announced that his government would take a 51 per cent controlling share in all mining companies operating in Sierra Leone, with the transfer to be completed before the end of March 1970.

The main British firms affected were CAST's local subsidiary, the Sierra Leone Selection Trust (SLST), and Delco, which mined iron ore.[45] Negotiations with SLST opened in February; the Sierra Leonean team, which was led by the Minister of Mines, Mr Kamara-Taylor, was advised by Theodore Sorenson, a former counsellor of President Kennedy.[46] The main issue at stake was not so much the question of state ownership and compensation as managerial control. Sierra Leone wanted a look at the books. Stevens explained that even he did not know exactly how the foreign concerns operated, and his government was often embarrassed by requests from its domestic supporters or foreign investors for details about Sierra Leone's mineral wealth. This complaint was also echoed in the local press, which had to rely on the reports of the London parent companies for news about subsidiaries operating in Sierra Leone. The case of Delco, whose profit figures were released through the accounts of William Baird in Britain, led to editorial demands that 'the Government must now legislate to ensure that at least information can be made available to Sierra Leone and Sierra Leoneans, by enacting that reports of all companies must be published in Sierra Leone'.[47]

It is possible that Lonrho brought these grievances out into the open. Rowland's conviction that rule from head office was obsolete, and that Africans were entitled to seats on the boards of British companies operating in their countries, may have seemed to offer an alternative to established practice. Before the SLST talks got off the ground, Rowland and Ball arrived in Freetown, accompanied by 'a leading Ghanaian'.[48] Their prime interest was said to be the development of iron ore deposits in Tonkolili, in northern Sierra Leone. This was surprising because the iron ore had been examined both by Delco, which had spent £1.5 million on the study, and a Soviet team. In each case, the conclusion had been the same: the deposits were of low grade and uneconomic because they were so far inland. Lonrho, however, without any indication that it had made new tests, suggested the possibility of processing the ore so that it could be 'piped' to the port of Freetown, possibly in order to avoid having to build an extension to the nearest railway, which belonged to Delco and which used the Delco port of Pepel. The Tonkolili deposits were in Delco's concession area.

It was generally supposed that Rowland's principal objective in Sierra Leone concerned the diamond business, and Tonkolili was used as a bait to catch the favourable attention of the government. The area round Tonkolili was one of the most underdeveloped in the country, and badly in need of industry; it also happened to be the area from which the government derived its chief support. There had been complaints that the Prime Minister relied too much on the southerners or on the influential creoles of Freetown. It was clearly important for Stevens to encourage the project, which would have meant an economic upsurge for the Tonkolili district.

Significantly, in the light of later events, Tonkolili was also the district in which the constituencies of Mr M. O. Bash-Taqi, Development Minister, and Dr M. S. Forna, Finance Minister, were situated; the development of the area must have been of particular interest to these two politicians, as well as to a former Minister of Mining, Dr Karefa-Smart, who was a Tonkolili man. But the iron ore scheme was left in abeyance while the SLST talks dragged on. When the 31 March deadline had passed, it was admitted that the negotiations had run into difficulties. Nevertheless, agreement in principle was reached in May, and an agreement was expected to be signed within two weeks. The details of the settlement were not revealed but some members of the government were reported opposed to its terms: there was talk that parts of it would have to be renegotiated before it was signed and ratified.[49] Then Lonrho came into the limelight.

In a statement released in Freetown on 12 June, the formation of a new company, the Commercial and Industrial Corporation of Sierra Leone (Comincor), was announced. The new company was to be a partnership in which the Sierra Leone government held 55 per cent and Lonrho 45 per cent of the shares. According to the official statement, it was the 'considered view of the Sierra Leone government that the London-based company of Lonrho Ltd, with its wealth of experience of industry, mining and commerce in Africa, is well qualified to be of valuable assistance to Sierra Leone in its present crucial state of development'. The company would serve the general economic development of industry, mining and commerce, and in particular the establishment of new agricultural and commercial projects on a profitable basis. The vital phrase announced that 'through this partnership government will promote the development of all known viable mineral resources in the country. It will take a special interest in Tonkolili Iron Ore.'[50]

The Tonkolili project was the only one specifically mentioned, but when the news broke in London interest was concentrated on the meaning of 'all known viable mineral resources'. In reply to inquiries, Lonrho was rather vague about the effect that this would have on SLST but gave the distinct impression that the deal would allow it to take over the country's diamond marketing and, perhaps, the management of the mines as well. *The Times* reported that 'it is believed by some sources that Lonrho would like to relieve De Beers of the business of selling Sierra Leone's diamonds, which are high quality gems'.[51] De Beers, through its subsidiary the Diamond Marketing Corporation, had a management contract for running the Government Diamond Office in Sierra Leone. This contract was due to expire at the end of the year. Perhaps it was Lonrho's record in Zaire which suggested a parallel in Sierra Leone: the stepping-in by Lonrho when a management contract was about to run out and negotiations were in progress.

There were those who suggested that Lonrho had a 'more acceptable image' in African eyes than CAST.[52] Certainly Lonrho did not stress its southern African links to the Sierra Leonean press. One leading newspaper in Freetown, in an unsigned article entitled 'Who Is Lonrho and What Does It Do?', described it as 'a modern progressive company, active in more than twenty-seven countries', without mentioning South Africa or Rhodesia. It stated that Lonrho's insurance and produce brokerage interests were world-wide,

but the greater part of its commercial and industrial activities is on the African continent ... The company has large interests in textiles in Africa. It is the largest single manufacturer, producing no less than 120,000,000 yards of cloth per annum ... Already it has two experts in Sierra Leone studying the possibility of establishing a textile industry.

The writer stressed Ogilvy's royal connections and concluded by saying that 'there is already strong support for his appointment to the board of directors of Comincor'.[53]

Nonetheless, there was some local criticism. This came, for instance, from Dr D. M. Yillah, an opposition M P. He considered it surprising that the government was associating itself with a company which had heavy investment and interests in South Africa and Rhodesia. Yillah also seemed to assume that Lonrho was to replace SLST; he criticized the government for not handing diamond-bearing land over to the people rather than bringing in 'another set of capitalists'.[54] The Minister of Finance, Forna, denied that the partnership with Lonrho was intended to squeeze SLST out of the country. In fact, revised settlement proposals submitted by the government to SLST were under consideration. But in Freetown, as in London, the conviction that Comincor would step in continued to grow.

The negotiations with SLST continued, and Forna was reported to have led the cabinet opposition to certain clauses in the May draft agreement. As Finance Minister, Forna was in a key position: that he was a Tonkolili man with a concern for the development of his neglected home area must have been a common interest between him and the Lonrho executives who visited Freetown frequently during this period. In August *African Development* reported that Forna – 'the young Sierra Leonean Minister of

Finance who masterminded the formation of the Commercial and Industrial Corporation' – had had contact with the Soviet government, 'and it is quite on the cards that common problems in the marketing of diamonds were discussed'.[55] Lonrho was at that time believed to have plans for an African diamond-marketing organization independent of De Beers.

Meanwhile, political tensions developed in Sierra Leone. Stevens subsequently connected these with the return that summer of Karefa-Smart, who had served in a previous government and who had spent some years in Geneva as an official of the World Health Organization. There were rumours of a cabinet split, with Forna and Bash-Taqi, the two Tonkolili men, opposing the Prime Minister on a number of issues. In any event, at the beginning of September the agreement with SLST was concluded, giving the government 51 per cent of the company and setting up a new firm, Diminco, to run the new partnership.

One of Diminco's directors was Andrew Sardanis, who had recently left his position in Zambia where he had masterminded the 51 per cent takeover of the copper mines and other business concerns, including Smith and Youngson.[56] In February 1971 Lonrho proudly announced that 'we have been fortunate in securing, with the agreement of His Excellency, President Dr K. Kaunda of Zambia, the services of Mr A. S. Sardanis'.[57]

The deal which had been concluded between the Sierra Leone government and SLST had been negotiated by the Minister of Lands, Mines and Labour, Kamara-Taylor. News of it broke on 10 September 1970, and that day the Acting Prime Minister, Mr S. B. Kawusu-Konteh – Stevens was attending the Non-Aligned Summit Conference in Lusaka – declared that he was not aware of rumoured threats by the Ministers of Finance and Development to resign, though he was also not in a position to say that these rumours were unfounded. Forna and Bash-Taqi resigned on 12 September, and the following day Stevens rushed back to Sierra Leone. He had stopped over in London after the Zambia meeting but had hastened his return when he heard of the political upheavals. He immediately declared a state of emergency.

Forna and Bash-Taqi explained their resignations as a protest against Stevens's plans for a republic, with himself as executive president; they also accused him of economic mismanagement. Stevens said that the government's proposal to acquire a fifty-one per cent interest in the mining company was at the root of the crisis, and that 'some people in the country were receiving support from foreigners who had vested interests'.[58] Whom exactly he had in mind is not clear. What cannot be denied is that the political revolt against Stevens, which was also joined by Karefa-Smart, was led by northern politicians from Tonkolili, and that the crisis occurred just after the SLST agreement was concluded. Lonrho once again seems to have miscalculated; Forna, the man on whom the Sierra Leone government's goodwill so largely depended, was out of office and the company achieved none of its Sierra Leonean plans.[59]

'Comincor so far seems to be little beyond a press release,' said one observer at the end of the year.[60] None of the ambitious schemes mooted when the company first arrived had been realized. It had not confined its avowed interests to iron ore and diamond marketing; textiles, timber, insurance and banking had been among the subjects discussed in connection with Lonrho's future in Sierra Leone. As had been the case elsewhere, lack of preparation seems to have jeopardized these plans and to have harmed Lonrho's standing in the country. For instance, its project for a textile industry, submitted to the government, proposed that the plant be eventually supplied with locally-grown cotton. This aroused considerable suspicion among local experts and officials, who knew that three independent studies on cotton growing in Sierra Leone had recommended against it because of the country's high rainfall.

The last reported visit to Sierra Leone by Rowland and Ball took place in December 1970. They arrived the day before parliament ratified the SLST agreement, and left a couple of days later. Were they engaged in a last-ditch attempt to prevent the partnership between SLST and the Stevens government? Perhaps it was merely Rowland's way of operating; 'creative capitalism', he had once told a correspondent, meant keeping touch with the top political leaders, and on that occasion his itinerary took him from Sierra Leone to Ivory Coast and on to Zaire and Zambia. 'Mr Rowland believes passionately in this kind of personal approach to his group's interests in Africa . . .'[61] A few weeks later, Kamara-Taylor said in parliament, in reply to a question by Yillah, that the agreement between his government and Lonrho setting up Comincor had never been signed.

Four

The White 'Homelands'

Around the time that Lonrho entered Ghana, another mining venture took shape in completely different circumstances and surroundings. This was to become the Western Platinum mine on the famous South African Merensky reef, near the biggest platinum producer in the world, Rustenburg Platinum Mines in the Transvaal. In May 1969 Lonrho shares were first quoted on the lists of the Johannesburg Stock Exchange. It was said that the listing was a condition of a deal signed a few weeks before, when Lonrho had taken over Glendale Sugar Millers (Pty) Ltd, an Indian-owned cane sugar enterprise in Natal, but later Lonrho explained that it was in connection with the takeover of the Swaziland Sugar Milling Company. 'Lonrho sidles in,' announced the Johannesburg *Financial Mail*; '. . . seldom can a major share have come on to the Johannesburg Stock Exchange Lists in such a blaze of obscurity'.[1]

At the end of 1968, Lonrho had made a bid for the outstanding share capital of three South African subsidiaries – Witbank Consolidated Coalmines, Tweefontein United Collieries and Coronation Syndicate – as well as its Swazi subsidiary, the Swaziland Sugar Milling Company Ltd. The bids involved offers of Lonrho shares as well as cash, and until they went through there would only be a small number of Lonrho shares available on the South African market. The listing offended Stock Exchange convention by putting a share onto the market which was not merely in short supply, but little known to South African investors besides. The *Financial Mail* 'deplored' the situation in which a share – 'even one of the undoubted calibre of Lonrho – should be granted a listing, although the average investor . . . is in no position to obtain even the most elementary information on the company'.[2]

In the event, the bid for the outstanding share capital of the three South African companies fell through, and except for those stemming from the Swazi sugar deal, the Lonrho shares which should have been issued failed to come onto the market. It reduced Lonrho to a less marketable commodity than had been hoped, and trading in such shares as were available in South Africa remained relatively quiet throughout that year. Western Platinum, however, forged ahead.

South Africa's platinum deposits are probably the most extensive and valuable in the world. Those in the Rustenburg area supplied about two-thirds of the West's demand for platinum in 1969. At the end of 1972 the South African government estimated the value of the Republic's platinum reserves at R20,000 million.[3] This was 'sixty per cent above the value of the Republic's gold reserves at ruling prices'.[4] Taking a more optimistic view of future platinum prices, in relation to the same reserves, Mr S. C. Newman, chairman and managing director of Lonrho South Africa Ltd, gave the figure of R84,000 million as the potential value of platinum from the central Transvaal.[5]

These fabulous forecasts reflected to some extent the new uses that had been found for platinum: mainly by the petroleum industry, to produce lead-free petrol, and as the most likely catalyst in car exhaust converters. The international concern about the deterioration of the environment, and in particular the pollution-consciousness of Western industrialized states, was a major factor in the platinum boom of the early seventies. In the summer of 1972, the United States decided to enforce clean exhaust standards from 1975 onwards, and General Motors sent a mission to South Africa to assess the Republic's reserves as a source of supply. The South Africans gleefully calculated that 'the number of cars manufactured in America in 1975' would be 'around eleven million, each requiring about one tenth of an ounce of p.g.m. [platinum group metals] in the mandatory exhaust converters'. And since Canada had experienced a sharp fall-off in production, while 'Russia is rather a dark horse', it was concluded that 'South Africa will thus be the main supplier'.[6] Financial circles grew lyrical: 'Roses for Rustenburg' enthused the *Financial Times* of London over a report on improved prospects at the Rustenburg mine.[7]

This was in sharp contrast with the gloom which had prevailed in 1971, when large-scale sales by Russia had depressed the market. Rustenburg Platinum Mines, for instance, had been forced to cut production by half and lay off more than fifty per cent of its labour force, though even then it had had to stockpile large quantities. The dramatic change in the fortunes of platinum illustrated the uncertain prospects of a metal as valuable as this, but lacking the monetary attractions which gold enjoys.

The first reports of Lonrho's South African platinum wealth appeared in 1968, when the company announced that its farms at Wonderkop and Turffontein in the Transvaal contained 100 million tons of the ore, with an estimated £600 million worth of the metal. Early the following year the first borehole results were published, to reveal extremely promising yields. South African mining houses, by convention, never publish platinum values; when Lonrho did so it was received as a break with tradition – and a surprising one at that for a company with a reputation for reticence about its operations. Its confidence 'must have upset those circles . . . who regard disclosure of any quantitative facts on platinum as a breach of the Official Secrets Act'. But perhaps Lonrho was destined to start a trend. 'Now that Lonrho has bravely made the breach, perhaps some of the other tight-lipped platinum tycoons will be a little more revealing,' remarked the South African press.[8] Lonrho shares in London rose to an all-time high of over £3 at the good news and, not long afterwards, a South African merchant bank valued Lonrho's twenty square miles of platinum-bearing farmland at between £75 million and £100 million.[9]

The borehole results came from the Wonderkop farm and from a depth of more than 2,000 feet – deeper than any other major platinum mines in the area were expected to reach for many years. Plans were announced for a mining venture to produce 250,000 oz. a year by 1973 from two mines, but there was a snag. Wonderkop and Turffontein were separated by a railway and another farm, Middelkraal, which belonged to Union Corporation, owners of the Impala platinum mine in the same district. It was reported that Lonrho would have had to mine through Middelkraal to get at its platinum,[10] and a deal was arranged whereby Lonrho swapped land with Union Corporation on terms which neither side was prepared to disclose. But Union Corporation was said to have driven a hard bargain, retaining a third of Middelkraal – enough to be developed independently. A South African expert subsequently pointed out that while the initial results came from Wonderkop, Lonrho's platinum mining development started at Middelkraal, where the deposits were shallower but of a much lower grade: when Union Corporation had drilled on this farm, the metal content for the Middelkraal ores had been found to be only half that of the nearby Impala and Rustenburg mines.[11]

Soon after the land swap, Lonrho announced that it had gone into partnership with Falconbridge Nickel Mines, a Canadian company, and its associate, Superior Oil of the United States, with Lonrho retaining a fifty-one per cent share in the mine. An investigation subsequently confirmed that, as part of the Lonrho–Falconbridge agreement for the development of Western Platinum, Falconbridge

undertook to use its best endeavours to obtain permanent finance for this development from outside sources. This finance was not forthcoming, and consequently substantial sums have been advanced by Lonrho, Falconbridge and Superior in proportion to their interests.[12]

The Western Platinum venture became the main cause of Lonrho's 1971 liquidity problem.

Through Western Platinum Lonrho expanded significantly in the South African mining world. And clearly, for the powerful establishment of mining houses – a tight circle of related interests – this brash new competitor, which seemed to ignore the unwritten rules, was less than welcome. The announcement of the Falconbridge partnership coincided with new, increased figures for the mine's projected output. Instead of 250,000 oz. of p.g.m. per year, 430,000 oz. would be produced.[13] The initial production target, scheduled for 1971, of 50,000 oz. was increased to 60,000 oz.,[14] but in May of that year Newman spoke of a shortfall of about ten months' production.[15] Then, in July, the London office stated that the project 'is on schedule'.[16] The uncertainties which these conflicting reports generated in the City also contributed to the liquidity crisis. By February 1972 the company had advanced £4.8 million towards the development costs of Western Platinum, on top of its original investment of £3 million in the mine. With the improvement of platinum prices in 1972, it looked as if the investment would realize its early promise; and despite the 1973 Middle East war and the world energy crisis, which diverted international attention from problems of pollution, platinum prices were sustained by the general commodities boom. Western Platinum became self-financing at the end of September 1972.

Lonrho's calculation that there would be a long-term demand for platinum seemed eminently justified.[17] The weakness of the scheme was that the company, in its haste to get it under way, lacked adequate finance. It may also have lacked the expertise:

Rowland himself explained the choice of Falconbridge as partners 'because they are expert refiners [and] they have an established marketing organization'.[18] He added that Falconbridge 'like us . . . have interests in independent Africa' and were free of control from South Africa.

This was presumably meant to reach an African public. Lonrho had already acquired its major West African interests, and was about to expand into Sudan. In South Africa, however, the company made no apparent attempts to break away from the customary apartheid rules of South Africa's racialist system. Western Platinum itself was embarrassingly associated with the institution of Bantustans. These form the basis of South Africa's racial economic policy, which has two crucial aspects. The first is that Africans in the Republic are regarded as no more than temporary workers in the white areas, where they are permitted to remain only while their labour is required. The second is that they have no claim to South African citizenship, and are expected to confine their economic and political aspirations to the Bantustans, the so-called 'homelands' or native reserves which constitute only thirteen per cent of South Africa's land surface, though Africans comprise seventy per cent of the Republic's population.

In all, eight Bantustans were visualized but, with the exception of the Transkei, these areas consist of scattered fragments of land, which do not form cohesive administrative units. Zululand, for instance, is composed of more than two hundred unconsolidated areas in Natal. Moreover, it has been admitted even by South Africa's rulers that these 'homelands' are not economically viable, being incapable of growing sufficient food to support the populations they are theoretically intended to accommodate and having little if any industry. The South African government has, to be sure, pointed out that 'today most chrome and platinum producing mines are situated in the homelands and new discoveries of these minerals cannot be ruled out'.[19] But all precedent suggests that nearly all the benefit of such mines will accrue elsewhere.

Bophuthatswana – the 'homeland' where Western Platinum ore is situated – consists of eight large and eleven small pieces of land, scattered across a 300-mile arc in the Western Transvaal, Northern Cape and Orange Free State. In 1973 the South African Deputy Minister of Bantu Development, Mr A. J. Raubenheimer, announced proposals for the consolidation of Bophuthatswana. The realization of these pious plans would lead to the formation of between three and six pieces of land. Despite the fact that a number of platinum mines were what Raubenheimer called 'intrusions' into the surrounding white territory, the mines would be allowed to remain part of Bophuthatswana. They were considered valuable Bophuthatswana assets, despite the fact that their inclusion did not make for 'good rounding-off of the homelands'.[20]

According to South African law, mines situated in the Bantustans must pay to the Bantustan administration royalties equal to about ten per cent of profits. This amount can be written off as costs before the South African government tax is assessed, while companies which can show an assessed loss make no such payments. As Newman pointed out: 'This leads to the situation in South Africa in which new mines are able to pay dividends long before the tax-paying stage is reached.'[21] In 1971 an official South African government publication reported that the people of Bophuthatswana 'have already earned more than R500,000 in mining royalties alone' from the Rustenburg and Impala platinum mines.[22] But this must be placed against the fact that in 1970 Rustenburg alone recorded *net* profits of R34 million and, while the following year's figures were seriously affected by the platinum slump, the company still recorded a respectable R19.4 million net profit.

The expressed hope of the South African government has been that the platinum mines would 'assist future economic developments in this homeland, which also has asbestos, manganese, chrome, vanadium, limestone and diamonds. Future mining development through the Bantu Mining Corporation will be on a White agency basis, and royalties will be paid to the Tswanas [who inhabit this 'homeland']. Hereby the Tswanas will benefit from White capital and skills.'[23] One of the functions of the Bantu Mining Corporation, established by Act of Parliament in 1969, was supposed to be the creation of increased employment opportunities. It has been calculated that in Bophuthatswana 11,300 new jobs would have to be created each year until 1980, simply to absorb the natural increase of men in this 'homeland'. (Apart from those within the Bantustan, about a third of the Tswanas live and work in white areas.)[24]

Companies investing in South Africa, however, have continued to follow an established pattern in making heavy use of migrant labour, and the intention to provide employment locally for the inhabitants of the Bantustans remains no more than that.

Lonrho's South African mines, for example, have derived eighty per cent of their labour force from outside South Africa, while the majority of the remaining twenty per cent were 'also migrants to the Transvaal mines from other parts of the Republic'.[25] In 1970 both Rustenburg and Impala were employing less than two per cent of the local Tswanas in their African labour forces, since it did not pay them to recruit in the 'homelands' where their mines were situated. As a UN publication pointed out, South Africa's 'white Mineworkers' union has delivered an ultimatum to the government against the training of Africans in skilled mining operations. The government has recently made a major concession to the Union by limiting the advancement of Africans to skilled jobs to only those Africans of the specific ethnic group in whose homeland the mine is situated.'[26] In other words, Africans recruited outside South Africa or in other areas of the Republic could not be trained, and could be paid as unskilled labour, whereas local recruits could demand training and higher wages.

From all the evidence, therefore, Western Platinum, with its labour force of more than 4,000 African workers, has done little to ease the severe unemployment problem in Bophuthatswana, from which it derives its huge profit-earning potential. Indeed, even by South African government criteria the mine has contributed little if anything to the improvement of African living standards. It might even have been a negative factor, because it took out profits and depleted the 'homeland's' mineral resources, giving little in return. The project's failure to impart technical skills to the Bantustans is also underlined by the fact that the platinum refinery is situated at Brakpan, a 'white' town, many miles away from Bophuthatswana. In all this, Lonrho is by no means exceptional, but merely one of many companies which continue to invest under the system.

Western Platinum was not, in fact, the first time that Lonrho had moved into a non-white area. At the end of March 1969, it was announced that agreement had been reached on a deal between Lonrho and the Paruk family, owners of the Glendale sugar mill and estates in Natal. Lonrho's purchase of the land and assets of Glendale Sugar Millers for a total of R2.5 million in cash and shares removed the only Indian-owned sugar scheme in South Africa from the hands of the Asian community, which meant an end to plans to build up around it the first Indian industrial complex in the Republic. The Natal Indian Cane Growers' Association and Illovo – the South African arm of Tate and Lyle – were unable to meet the Paruk family's terms and this gave Lonrho the chance to enlarge their expanding empire of sugar plantations.

In 1973 Newman estimated that Western Platinum, the largest of the company's investments in the Republic, would earn a total profit for the year of R2,700,000 after interest. The first figures for working profit were not published until early in 1974, but for the first six months of the 1974 financial year, they in fact topped the three million rand mark. Profits on this scale are in sharp contrast with Lonrho's repeated assertions that its South African interests are insubstantial, historical and inherited. Early in 1974, Rowland maintained that 'it is only in three principal South African companies that Lonrho has interests through its subsidiaries, and even then they are not in themselves majority interests'.[27] In its memorandum to a British Parliamentary Select Committee a year earlier, the company had stated:

Lonrho South Africa Ltd is owned as to 96.89 per cent by Lonrho Ltd. The effective ownership by Lonrho Ltd of the other three subsidiaries is as follows:

Tweefontein United Collieries Ltd   55.49 per cent
Witbank Consolidated Coal Mines Ltd   62.89 per cent
Western Platinum Holdings Ltd   48.87 per cent.[28]

In addition, Lonrho had other South African interests, such as Glendale Sugar. Tweefontein United Collieries also owned a majority share of Coronation Syndicate, a controversial undertaking which operated Lonrho's Rhodesian mines, and whose affairs were connected with the arrest in South Africa at the end of 1971 of several directors of Lonrho's subsidiaries.

At the time of the memorandum Lonrho was also assisting the South African government with a strategic problem in that they agreed to make disused coal mines belonging to its South African subsidiaries available for oil storage purposes. In January 1974, at the very moment when the appointment of Lonrho as consultants to the OAU was being defended by the OAU Secretary General, it was reported in South Africa that

Lonrho's Witbank Cons is to open a new coal mine, the cost of which will be met from compensation paid by the Government arising from its acquisition of the old mining area for strategic storage facilities.[29]

Over the years, the company has been involved in numerous South African schemes. In its review for 1969 it reported the taking-up of options on uranium-bearing ground near Klerksdorp, and nickel in the Western Transvaal. In 1971 there was a reference in the review to a 'sizeable kaolin deposit in the Cape Peninsula', with indications that 'a good saleable grade can be produced'. But from 1968 on, references to the group's interests in South Africa became less and less frequent, a fact which was observed in the South African press. For instance, commenting on the Annual Report for 1973, the *Rand Daily Mail* declared:

It is almost amusing to note that in Mr Rowland's review of the group's operations specific projects under way in East, Central and West African countries are specifically noted and full progress is reported. However, under the subheading coal, for instance, the group's two collieries remain anonymous, and both the platinum and copper production figures are not attributed to any country.[30]

By 1968 Rowland had started belittling the importance of the company's southern African links,[31] and at the beginning of 1972 he told the British press that Lonrho was considering relinquishing its interests in white-ruled Africa and concentrating on black African countries.[32] But by 1974, when Western Platinum was beginning to pay off and Lonrho's Rhodesian mines had been expanded and were showing handsome profits, Rowland had apparently changed his tune again. Although the company would have preferred to dispose of its historical South African interests, he said, 'we were advised not to sell by several African leaders who thought that to do so would be increasing the strength of the enemies of Independent Africa. They considered that it made more sense to have a foothold in the enemy's territory.' He added, 'Of course, there is also the question of the interests of the shareholders . . .'. What was more, 'I, the Chief Executive of Lonrho, am not on the board of any South African company, and I am not even allowed to enter the country.'[33] Rowland's reference to visiting South Africa was mysterious, although there was good reason why he and his fellow directors should have avoided travelling to South Africa between 1971 and 1973. This arose out of the arrest of Mr. F. Butcher, Lonrho's finance director, on an allegation of fraud, which was subsequently withdrawn.[34] Rowland himself referred to the incident in a television programme in 1973, when he said that he was 'not absolutely sure how many warrants there were for the arrests, or for how many directors . . . Not one of us thought it safe to go to South Africa, or even to Rhodesia. Therefore we avoided southern Africa and Mozambique.'[35]

Lonrho's troubleshooter in South Africa was the Hon. Duncan Sandys, MP, a former Conservative Colonial and Commonwealth Secretary who had been engaged as consultant to the London board in September 1971, shortly after the arrest of the directors.[36] He was already a director of Ashanti Goldfields, with which he had been associated since 1947, except for the period he spent as a member of the government. In 1972 he became chairman of Lonrho. On the face of it, the choice of Sandys seemed surprising for a company which was busily constructing a non-imperialist image. As Colonial and Commonwealth Secretary, he had scarcely shown himself in harmony with the political aspirations of African nationalists. One objective in his ministerial post had been to keep South Africa in the Commonwealth; another, to preserve the Federation of Rhodesia and Nyasaland. Together with Sir Edgar Whitehead, the Rhodesian Prime Minister, he drafted Rhodesia's 1961 constitution, subsequently rejected by the African nationalist leadership. He authorized the retroactive validation of elections in Gambia which had been declared null and void by the local courts. In 1963 he sanctioned a constitutional framework for Zanzibar which made the island almost the only British dependency to gain freedom without having first been granted universal adult franchise. Zanzibar's unpopular government survived independence by only five weeks. Towards the end of his career as the Commonwealth Secretary, Swaziland was evolving its constitution, and this meant securing power for a coalition of traditional chiefs and conservative whites, along with retrospective legislation absolving royalist candidates from the electoral offences they had committed to gain office.[37] In opposition Sandys opposed the imposition of sanctions against Rhodesia and was associated with meetings in favour of Rhodesia's whites. He advocated the repatriation from Britain of coloured immigrants.[38]

A spokesman for Keyser Ullmann, the company's merchant bankers, commented on Sandys's appointment as chairman of Lonrho by saying that he was 'very familiar with the African scene and is a strong man. This is just what is needed.'[39] Several newspapers remained unconvinced, and speculation about the appointment continued. The Financial Times, for instance, described him as 'perhaps the last of the paternalist–imperialist Secretaries, and one who found the "wind of change" hard to interpret', and suggested that his importance to Lonrho was his commitment to Europe.[40] He had founded the European Movement in 1947.

At Lonrho's Annual General Meeting in March 1974, in the sumptuous ballroom of the Hilton Hotel in London, Sandys declared that it was impossible to apply British standards to 'a country which has got an entirely different flavour and laws' – meaning South Africa. This observation was in reply to questions about the wages paid to black Africans in Lonrho's South African mines, a subject topical at the time since the report of the British Parliamentary Select Committee on Wages and Conditions of African Workers employed by British firms in South Africa had just been published.[41] Lonrho was listed as one of those firms paying the great majority of its black African workers below the poverty datum line (PDL). The PDL has been defined as the 'lowest possible amount on which a family can live under humanely decent conditions in the short run'.[42] The Select Committee commented that the PDL 'excludes many items on which expenditure is actually made by African households ...': for example, medical care and education.[43] The PDL level in money terms varied according to geographical location, but was around R70 a month at the time of the survey. Lonrho, according to the information it supplied to the committee, showed an average African wage of R5.11 a week at its Tweefontein mine, R5.47 at Witbank, and R6.76 at Western Platinum. The lowest wages were considerably below this level, but the company added R30 per month to the cash earnings when estimating total remuneration. This was the Lonrho valuation of 'benefits' received by African workers in the form of board and lodging, medical attention, and transport to and from their home areas at the beginning and end of contract.

Like most South African mining companies, Lonrho relied on migratory labour recruited mainly outside South Africa, where the families of these workers subsisted on food grown on their own land. 'This, and the fact that they received free food and accommodation while on the mines, provide a cushion against the increase in the price of food and other essentials,' explained the Lonrho memorandum. Since R30 a month was effectively deducted from the workers' wages to pay for board and lodging and other benefits, food and accommodation could scarcely be called free. It might be argued that the fact that miners' families supported themselves by farming during the main wage-earners' absence cushioned the employer and represented a subsidy to the mining companies and their shareholders from the African peasants. The Select Committee report stated that

It was clear that companies had the power to raise the wages of their employees; in no case were wage increases expressly prevented by statute, Government policy or employers' agreement, and in the case of mining the maximum wages, formerly laid down by the Chamber of Mines, had been abandoned early in 1973 . . .[44]

At the Annual General Meeting Sandys stated:

I have made it quite clear that we fully accept, endorse and approve the principles and objectives [of the Select Committee Report]. We are, I believe, endeavouring to realize those principles and we shall continue to do so. I am looking further to say that if the laws in South Africa were different, I think we would be prepared to go further still in some respects than is indicated in the Report.[45]

Persistent questioning at the Annual General Meeting by a group of Anti-Apartheid Movement supporters irritated the bulk of the shareholders, one of whom complained about the 'very loaded questions' on South Africa. Finally Ball, the deputy chairman, intervened by announcing that 'very considerable detail' was available for any shareholder wishing to acquaint himself with the complicated South African wage structure – after the meeting. When that time came, a small group rushed to the podium, and Newman handed out a few copies of what turned out to be a South African Chamber of Mines document entitled 'General Conditions of Recruitment and Service of African Employees on South African Mines', dated 25 March 1974.[46] This said nothing specific on Lonrho or any other company; it was impossible to check on statements of fact, since no mines were cited to which the conditions described specifically applied. Paragraph 14, for instance, stated that 'the ration scale for married workers is increased for their families. Indunas [a South African word for chiefs], for example, receive 21 lbs of meat'. But Paragraph 7 pointed out that 'government regulation restricts to three per cent the proportion of Africans who may live on the mines with their families. The balance is thus migrant labour.'[47] This illuminated the first item of information given by Lonrho to the Select

Committee, on 'fringe benefits' for their African workers at Witbank Consolidated Coal Mines. 'Married workers are housed free of rent in cottages consisting of two bedrooms, one living room and one kitchen with communal toilets. Electricity, coal and water are supplied free of charge.'[48] Lonrho did not point out that this system applied to three per cent of the workers at most, and that the so-called fringe benefits described for single workers were enjoyed by the great majority of their black mine employees: 'twenty workers are housed per room, which is equipped with beds and a stove. Communal toilet facilities are conveniently situated.'

Still at Witbank, Lonrho listed 'fish and chips, chicken, meat, bread, mealie meal [maize flour], vegetables and citrus in season' as the food supplied to African workers. In Tweefontein the list was given in 'grams/feeding shift' and chicken did not feature on the menu, but there was a lot of offal, beef and fish, with the bulk made up by mealie meal. In Western Platinum the diet was not itemized, but a modern kitchen 'remains open for 22 hours daily where the issue of basic food, i.e. maze [sic] meal porridge is not restricted'. Benefits included cinema, tribal dancing and sports. Despite such facilities the miners do not appear to have been sufficiently distracted to prevent what was described as a 'Sunday evening tribal brawl' in September 1974, when South African police killed two of the black Western Platinum miners and injured four others. Lonrho had called in the force after five hours of 'rioting' by four hundred men. The two dead miners came from Malawi.[49]

The Lonrho memorandum pointed out to the Committee that the three mining companies, as members of the South African Chamber of Mines, were bound by the wage policy of the Chamber. Lonrho Ltd, meaning the British-based board, owned 96.89 per cent of Lonrho South Africa Ltd, and was therefore in some position to determine management policy at the three companies for which employment details were submitted. However, while the company admitted to being in command of 'major issues of financial policy', control of all matters mentioned in the memorandum on employment 'is vested in Lonrho South Africa Ltd, and not in Lonrho Ltd ... No one director of Lonrho Ltd is responsible for the South African operations.' The memorandum also stressed that control of Western Platinum was shared equally between Lonrho and Falconbridge Nickel Company of Canada and Superior Oil of the United States. Of the main Lonrho board in London, one director was on the board of Lonrho South Africa Ltd; two on the board of Western Platinum Ltd; one on the board of Tweefontein United Collieries Ltd; and two on the board of Witbank Consolidated Coal Mines Ltd.

For a company which so often stressed its concern for African welfare, it seemed inconsistent to conform so easily with the Chamber of Mines rules, in particular since the question of South African wages must have been of interest to Lonrho's black African friends and business associates. However, Rowland denied that Lonrho had such a bad record when the matter was put to him in an interview early in 1974:

INTERVIEWER: It has been suggested that your company is among British companies that pay the lowest wages to their black employees in South Africa and in independent Africa. What do you say?
ROWLAND: That is not true. We pay above average wages. In some African countries wages are regulated by law, and we operate within the limits set down by the Governments.[50]

South Africa was not the only place where Lonrho paid low wages; in one of the few developing countries outside Africa where the company had interests, Sri Lanka (Ceylon), tea workers on Lonrho's Delmar estate were said in 1974 to be among the lowest paid on the island. The scandal that broke over starvation wages in the Sri Lankan tea industry as a whole made headlines in the British press in March 1974, following the publication of a War on Want pamphlet, 'The State of Tea'. While campaigns directed in the previous year against Brooke Bond Liebig, which handled a large part of the Sri Lanka crop, seemed to have resulted in improved conditions on their estates, those obtaining at Delmar were described as the worst on the island, with severe cases of malnutrition the rule rather than the exception among the workers and their families. When the report appeared, Lonrho's personnel manager admitted that conditions were a matter for 'concern', but said that the company was making hardly any profit in Sri Lanka.[51] The author of the War on Want report, Edith Bond, found this claim difficult to understand in view of a profit bonus of two and a half months' gross salary paid to the local management.[52]

Apart from South Africa itself, Lonrho had extensive investments in neighbouring countries which fell within the Republic's sphere of influence, and from the end of the sixties changes were made in the group's management structure which accentuated the southern African identity of these interests. Lonrho's Annual Report for 1969 recorded that, because of the wide geographical diversification experienced by the group, 'it has become necessary to establish local services on a regional basis. Besides those already formed in east and central Africa, new companies are now in operation in Swaziland and west Africa, and an administrative reorganization of the group's interests in southern Africa is in train.' This reorganization was particularly comprehensive in the case of Lonrho's sugar interests in South Africa, Swaziland, Malawi and Mauritius, all of which were brought under control from Johannesburg. Although the Swaziland Sugar Milling Company, the holding company, was incorporated in Swaziland, its registered office, along with those of a number of other Lonrho group companies, was at the time in the Trust Bank Centre, Eloff Street, Johannesburg, and Lonrho South Africa then acted as Secretary for it.

In March 1968 it was announced that talks were in progress between Lonrho and the directors of the Swaziland Sugar Milling Company Ltd, an enterprise owning substantial cane plantations at Big Bend, in the east of Swaziland, through its subsidiary Ubombo Ranches Ltd. Later that year, an agreement was reached which not only gave Lonrho fifty-two per cent of the shares of the Swazi company, but brought the group's other sugar schemes – three mills in Mauritius, one in Malawi and one in South Africa – under the latter's control. As part of the deal, Lonrho's sugar interests in Mauritius – Britannia and Highland Estates – were sold to the Swaziland Sugar Milling Company. Glendale Sugar Millers and the Malawi Sugar Corporation were ultimately owned by Swazi Sugar.[53] In acquiring a stake in Swazi sugar, Lonrho had moved into a promising sector of the country's economy. Sugar was Swaziland's most important foreign exchange earner; ninety per cent of the crop was exported. In 1974 the sugar industry employed about one in five of all Swaziland's wage earners, and profits rose to high levels as world prices soared. Sugar became far and away the most important component in Lonrho's agricultural operations, which in 1973 contributed £4.98 million to the group's pre-tax profits. The Swaziland venture was a valuable addition to the company's portfolio, and in 1969 Lonrho set the final seal upon its success by acquiring virtually all of the outstanding share capital of the Swaziland Sugar Milling Company.

In September 1968 Swaziland achieved independence after more than five years of protracted and sometimes stormy negotiations with the British government. Six weeks later Lonrho's was the first mining prospecting contract to be issued by King Sobhuza as an independent monarch. He granted the company prospecting rights over several square miles of land near the country's single asbestos mine at Havelock. The Havelock mine was operated by a subsidiary of the British firm Turner and Newall, but it was now expected that another would be opened by Lonrho. The venture had still not taken off by the end of 1973, but the contract, signed by the king himself, illustrated the influence which Lonrho had managed to gain. Angus Ogilvy was no doubt an asset; in September 1969 he accompanied Princess Alexandra on a royal visit to Swaziland, to mark the first anniversary of independence and the opening of the new parliament buildings. 'The visit of Princess Alexandra has been a wonderful tonic for Anglo-Swazi relations – and they needed improvement . . .' commented the *Times of Swaziland*,[54] and Lonrho must have felt its future in Swaziland to be secure indeed. Nevertheless, in 1973 even the docile Swazis, feeling perhaps that they too should benefit from the high world prices, imposed an export levy of fifty per cent on the excess proceeds from the sale of sugar over a ceiling of R90 per ton. This levy hit Lonrho; the taxed profit of the Swaziland Sugar Milling Company fell by about R1 million to R2,520,000 for the year ending March 1974.

'The climate of racial goodwill and peacefulness; Swaziland's potential as an exporter to the independent African states; consideration for new industries, and guarantees that there will be no interference with private enterprise'[55] may all have been factors attracting Lonrho to the country. The possibility, eventually realized, of acquiring full voting control of the Swaziland Sugar Milling Company made it a sound base from which to administer the group's sugar interests in Malawi and Mauritius. Although Malawi's profits were included under 'East and Central Africa', and Mauritius's under 'Europe and other', in the regional breakdowns given in Lonrho's Annual Reports, they were effectively treated as part of a southern African regional sugar enterprise. The 'administrative reorganization' which took place in 1969 was in tune with certain political and economic alignments emerging in these two countries.

After Malawi achieved independence in 1964, Banda encouraged the development of diplomatic and economic links with the white-ruled south. From Banda's point of view, his 'alliance with the devil' – his own phrase – had very positive results. Development projects backed by South African capital included the £4.7 million first stage of the new capital city, turned down by British aid-dispensers as a low-priority project, and the £6.4 million rail link with Nacala on the coast of Mozambique.[56] South African businessmen, in contrast to the South African government, were more hesitant in staking their capital on Malawi's future; but Lonrho, whose sugar scheme at Nchalo was in 1963 the largest single investment that Malawi had ever attracted, brought in a South African contracting firm, Patrick Murray (Pty) Ltd of Durban, to manage the building of the SUCOMA factory. In 1966 the South African Industrial Development Corporation, a government body, advanced a loan of R6 million to Patrick Murray, on condition that sixty per cent of the construction materials were supplied from South Africa. The SUCOMA scheme was hailed as a breakthrough at the time for the record speed with which it had been brought into production, and the care that had been taken to involve experts of the highest calibre from the planning stage onwards. Dr McMartin, former director of the South African Sugar Association's experimental station at Mount Edgecombe in Natal, was engaged by Lonrho as consultant.

The plant went into production in the late summer of 1966, and by 1968 it had achieved its first-stage target of 30,000 tons of refined sugar a year. The factory had always been planned with expansion in mind, and the opportunity came in 1971, when an export quota of 15,000 tons of sugar was approved for Malawi by the United States Congress to take effect from the beginning of 1972. It was estimated at the time that the expansion of production to meet the quota would increase Malawi's export earnings by 3.7 per cent and plans were made virtually to double the capacity of the SUCOMA estate and refinery. Once again South African companies were involved: the Elgin Engineering Company (Pty) Ltd of Durban won a R1.25 million export contract, the biggest it had ever negotiated, while Roberts Construction built irrigation channels and provided engineering know-how. When the SUCOMA scheme first entered production, a number of Mauritian operators and supervisors were recruited to man the factory. Mauritius, an island whose economy was almost totally dependent on sugar, was well suited to supply Malawi with the technical expertise for a project like this. The executive director of the Malawi Sugar Corporation, Mr J. R. Leclezio, was also a Mauritian, and one who had connections with the largest sugar producers on the island, Flacq United Estates.

This link was no doubt a valuable introduction for Lonrho to the sugar-growing aristocracy of Mauritius when it took over Anglo-Ceylon and General Estates, with their Mauritian sugar plantations, in November 1967. Anglo-Ceylon was not particularly prosperous at the time because of declining world prices for tea and sugar, and its directors apparently considered Lonrho's offer the best that was likely in the circumstances. They were also concerned at the prospect of Mauritian independence, scheduled for March 1968, and the uncertainties of the political climate that might ensue. Despite its position far out in the Indian Ocean, the island had close links with Africa and was to become a member of the Organization of African Unity. In 1974 sugar accounted for over ninety per cent of the island's export earnings. Its population, the result of several centuries of colonial occupation, was mixed. The Hindus and Creoles were numerically dominant and with independence wielded the majority in the parliamentary system. The aristocratic Franco-Mauritians, on the other hand, although relatively few in number, controlled the balance of power in the island's economy, as the owners of virtually all the largest sugar plantations. These families of European descent had close links with South Africa. Many had friends and relatives in the Republic, and business connections were close. Not surprisingly, the Mauritian clique had extremely conservative political attitudes, and warded off attempts after independence by the ruling Labour party to bring the sugar plantations under state control. In contrast with those for a number of other sugar-producing countries in the Third World, quota and price-fixing negotiations for Mauritius were dominated by private interests. Although after independence South African businessmen and holidaymakers continued to be welcomed on the island, these close South African links were an embarrassment to the government's policy of solidarity with black Africa.

In 1969 Lonrho took over Rogers and Company, a shipping and general services enterprise that was a member of the Rogers group, whose interests touched virtually every aspect of the island's economy. This had a large stake in the Mauritian tourist industry, owned shipping lines and construction companies and, not surprisingly, had interests in sugar. The managing directors were two brothers from one of the old colonial families on the island, René and Amédée Maingard de la Ville-es-Offrans. They were married to two sisters, Jacqueline and Françoise Raffray, whose family, also well established, had connections with Flacq United Estates, the major sugar producer on the island.

Through Rogers, Lonrho added more luxury hotels to its numerous interests, and in January 1970 was reported to be investing £2 million in hotel construction. A new company was being formed with two local and two Lonrho directors and, as chairman, Amédée Maingard. The appointment of Maingard, a leading member of the Franco-Mauritian 'plantocracy', indicated the interest groups to which Lonrho gravitated.

Meanwhile the political climate was growing turbulent as the influence of the left-wing Mouvement Militant Mauricien grew under the leadership of Paul Berenger. In September 1969 the unrest on the island was considered sufficiently serious to warrant the cancellation of a royal visit by Princess Alexandra, part of the same visit which took her to Swaziland. Paul Berenger, who was imprisoned for alleged security reasons at the time, said: 'We planned to demonstrate peacefully against Princess Alexandra's visit. The government threw eighteen of us in jail. Why Alexandra? Well, Alex's husband is Ogilvy, Ogilvy is Lonrho, and Lonrho is extremely powerful here – hotels, sugar factories, import-export.'[57]

Lonrho's centralization, in the Swaziland Sugar Milling Company, of its Malawian and Mauritian sugar interests was coincidental with South Africa's often-declared aim to set up some kind of southern African 'Common Market', including countries that had shown themselves sympathetic to the idea of 'dialogue' with Pretoria and, of course, Rhodesia. If any more formal grouping of these countries had been established, it would have almost inevitably worked to the advantage of South Africa – the richest, the most highly industrialized and the most powerful country on the African continent.

After the end of the sixties, Lonrho expanded its sugar interests into countries geographically far removed from South Africa. By 1974 the company was actively involved in schemes in the Ivory Coast, Dahomey and Sudan. Nevertheless, its sugar interests in southern Africa, far from being diminished, were to be significantly expanded. In March 1974 the *Rand Daily Mail* remarked of Lonrho's annual report that 'no mention is made of the group's recently announced feasibility study to set up a 600,000-ton-a-year sugar mill in Natal'.[58] This new sugar project had previously been reported in American and British as well as South African publications, and was being initiated at the request of the South African Department of Trade and Industry.[59] According to one report, the sugar mill was to be 'located in the impoverished Kwazulu Bantustan (the partly autonomous Zulu 'homeland')'. If the project went through, the $7 million mill would eventually have an annual crushing capacity of one million tons of cane. 'The mill would be one of the first major industries for the Bantustan.'[60] During Lonrho's Annual General Meeting in March 1974, Ball declared in general terms that it had not been Lonrho's policy to expand in southern Africa; 'for that and other reasons, we have concentrated on investing north of the Zambesi and, more latterly, in the Middle East'.[61] However, after the meeting Newman, perhaps more familiar with the company's South African operations than the British board, confirmed that the Bantustan feasibility study was going ahead. He stressed that only the growing of sugar would take place in Kwazulu and the mill itself would be situated in the white 'homeland' of Natal. The reason for this, he said, was that the whites had more expertise.[62] Technical expertise for the study, and in due course for the mill, was to be provided by the Swaziland Sugar Milling Company, and the feasibility study was to be completed in July 1974.[63]

In January 1975, Lonrho increased its interests in South Africa even further by buying a 29·5 per cent stake in London Australian and General Exploration (LAGS), a satellite of the troubled Jessel Securities group.[64] LAGS possessed substantial engineering interests in the United Kingdom, including companies manufacturing mining equipment, which could be fed into Lonrho's own ventures. It was also strong in South Africa where, among other companies, it controlled Duiker Exploration, a mining venture formerly known as Free State Gold Areas.[65] At the time of the deal with Jessel, a heavily qualified auditor's report on LAGS had just been published which estimated the company's maximum liability at £3.4 million.[66] Lonrho, as they were acquiring a controlling interest, paid substantially more than the market price for Jessel's shares in LAGS. One of the attractions may have been the fact that, since the previous June, LAGS had made a paper profit of over £2.5 million in Unisel, a new South African gold mine in which Duiker had a sizeable stake.[67] It seemed possible that Lonrho was considering moving further into the highly profitable South African gold industry.

Five

City Trouble

In 1969, when Lonrho's expansion was in full swing, mining circles spoke of four major long-term projects for the group: the Zaire scheme, asbestos mining in Swaziland, diamonds in independent Africa, and South African platinum. Substantial finance would obviously be needed; platinum, for instance, 'must perforce require a very great sum of money'.[1] Only the platinum scheme, however, went ahead. The others, like the diamond plan, died after some publicity. The asbestos project was put into cold storage. In the 1969 Annual Report, Lonrho's directors announced that plans were in hand to expand the operations of the newly-formed Ivory Coast company into Senegal, Togo, Dahomey, Cameroun, Gabon, Upper Volta and Burundi. Such a growth of activities would presumably have required sustained and substantial expenditure, without any short-term gain. But little more was heard of these ventures, apart from Dahomey, where Lonrho eventually participated in a sugar scheme, and Cameroun.[2]

Following the announcement of the glittering platinum development, share prices rose to an all-time high of over £3.50. This came at an opportune moment for Lonrho because of its numerous acquisitions at that time: Ashanti Goldfields, interests in East and Central Africa bought from Slater Walker Securities, John Holt in West Africa, Anglo Ceylon, and David Whitehead, the textile firm with interests in Rhodesia, South Africa, Nigeria, Malawi and England. While this impressive list of bargains was expected to bring in revenue – Ashanti, in particular, was hailed as a 'master stroke'[3] – Lonrho nevertheless had to finance the deals. While share prices remained high, this was possible through the exchange of relatively valuable Lonrho shares for the low-priced shares of the companies it was buying. For example, when John Holt was acquired, 2,400,000 Lonrho shares were issued in exchange for all Holt's ordinary shares; in the case of Ashanti, the transaction also included convertible unsecured loan stock;[4] the Slater Walker deal involved the issue of 1,200,000 fully-paid Lonrho shares.

Not all of the companies purchased were financed only by the issue of shares and loan stock, however. In April 1968 an agreement was concluded with the Belgian company, Cominière, under which Cominière's President, Martin Theves, received 200,000 Lonrho shares and 120 million Belgian francs (£1,004,600) in return for Lonrho's acquisition of a share in the company. A year later Lonrho bought Glendale sugar mills in South Africa for 125,000 of its own shares and R875,000 (about £400,000). In September 1969 the entire share capital of the Watergate Steam Shipping Company Ltd was acquired for 960,671 fully-paid Lonrho shares and, 'in addition, a small number of £1 preference shares were purchased for cash at par'.[5]

The Slater Walker deal was particularly significant because it involved Rhodesian interests. The assets acquired by Lonrho were Motor Mart Holdings Ltd and the East African Tanning Extract Company (EATEC), both of which operated in Kenya, together with Crittall-Hope of Rhodesia and the Rhodesian Wattle Company Ltd. The transaction was conditional on a contract being concluded between Lonrho and EATEC, on the one hand, and the Forestal Land Timber and Railways Company Ltd, which was to be EATEC's sole distributor throughout most of the world, on the other. An important condition was that Lonrho undertook to ensure that the Rhodesian Wattle Company would enter into a similar distribution contract with Forestal.

The practice of acquiring businesses by share exchanges is a common one. Nevertheless, a shortage of cash has been at times one of Lonrho's most pressing problems. Speculation about how the company was financing its expansion accompanied the beginning of its rapid growth in the sixties. Although there was no substance to the story that Lonrho was so short of ready cash that the prospect of earning some by ticket sales was one of the attractive aspects of Malawi Railways, it was indicative of the company's reputation that such rumours should have been given any currency. The unease which Lonrho's financing operations aroused was expressed in a Zambian paper early in 1965: 'Somehow, rumour seems to object that Lonrho should create shares rather than pay cash for some of its takeovers. This is, of course, a normal commercial practice, but what rumour really dislikes is the practice by Lonrho of taking over political discounted businesses.' The paper, quoting a statement by Ball that it was the aim of the group to acquire 'on favourable terms sound businesses capable of profitable integration with those of our existing subsidiary companies', commented: 'Provided their creditors do not start acting up, that is all there is to it . . .'. The article ended by expressing the sentiment often found later in City comment: 'The structure of Lonrho is that of an iceberg. To gauge whether the acquisition of politically volatile companies will be profitable is not something which can be done by studying a balance sheet.'[6] Six and a half years later, creditors did start 'acting up'. Those who had become Lonrho shareholders through share exchanges also had a very good case for feeling aggrieved: by 1971 they had seen their shares, valued in 1968 at more than £3, fall to less than a third of this. By 1974, in a generally depressed market, they fluctuated around the 50p mark.[7]

Lonrho's high share price in the late sixties was an important aspect of its ability to grow by acquisition, and the company did all it could to keep the share price high. In the second half of 1969, however, the price halved and Lonrho came in for some adverse comment in the financial press.[8] This collapse was not due to any failure to meet profit targets; the two main causes were the disappointing outcome of the Zairean plans and the secrecy surrounding, in particular, the mining operations.[9] The point was made that while Lonrho had not in the past been regarded as an orthodox mining company, now that it was describing itself as 'primarily . . . a mining finance house', it should conform with general practice, and make regular and detailed reports of its activities.[10]

Lonrho's justification for its reticence, in particular over Western Platinum at this time, was that to reveal details of its southern African activities would prejudice its operations in black Africa. 'In fact it claims that, like mushrooms, it grows best in the dark,' commented the City press, pointing out that the company did not even list in full its subsidiaries and the size of its stake in them.[11] It was suggested that Lonrho had obtained exemption from the 1967 Companies Act, which requires companies to list their subsidiaries, together with certain details concerning them, in their annual reports, on the grounds that to do so would prejudice its interests in black Africa.[12] When inquiries were made about this in 1974, Lonrho answered them by reference to Section 3(4) of the 1967 Companies Act[13] and refused to confirm or deny the press report. According to *African Development*, Lonrho explained its reticence about the geographical spread of its operations by reference to 'the Companies Act, assorted Board of Trade regulations, and internal requirements of countries like Burundi'.[14] In Rhodesia Lonrho's reticence was attributed to the Official Secrets Act of the Smith government, which precluded detailed reports of progress at the Inyati and Nyaschere copper mines. The Johannesburg *Financial Mail*, however, remarked that other mining houses, such as the South African-based Messina group, apparently found it unnecessary to interpret the official rulings with such diligence and rigour.[15] The obscurity surrounding the company's activities began to be a liability in the City. When Lonrho acquired a publicity officer in 1969, the hope was expressed that this appointment would help the share prices, provided 'he has the knowledge and the authority to dispel the mystery that is Lonrho's self-imposed cross'.[16]

Lonrho's image as a whizz-kid of Central Africa did not discourage stock market speculators, but it did lead to City worries over the group's ability to operate profitably in what were seen as politically unstable areas. For instance, the decision by Zambia in the late sixties to take a fifty-one per cent government stake in the country's copper mines promoted doubts about the ease with which Lonrho could continue to sidestep the hazards of economic nationalism in Africa. Some of these anxieties seemed confirmed by Tanzania's takeover of Lonrho's sisal plantations and newspapers. But this was nothing compared with the backwash from the failure of the Zaire plans.[17]

Neither this nor the collapse of hopes in Sierra Leone[18] did anything to improve share prices. From their peak of over £3 until the liquidity crisis, the decline was steady, so that by October 1971 they reached their lowest point at 56p. Overseas troubles apart, the fall in gold and platinum prices on world markets was undoubtedly a depressing factor. The group's profit record was good, but the City no longer believed in Lonrho's ability to work apparent miracles where other companies had failed. Share prices would not recover until Lonrho had been seen to carry out one of its much publicized schemes, and it was in this context that Western Platinum was so important to the company's fortunes. The 1971 fall in platinum prices was therefore extremely serious for Lonrho. The stock market in general was depressed at this time, but financial analysts pointed out that the Lonrho share price was not simply part of this decline; Mr R. Rolfe, a southern African mining expert and commentator, for instance, stressed that 'since there are so few other developing enterprises in Lonrho, any failure at Western Platinum would be bearish. To an extent, the failure of Western Platinum is now being discounted. This is not a "balloon of despair" but a market judgement.'[19]

Lonrho was unable to continue on its course of expansion by acquisition; the consistently weak share prices of 1970 and 1971 did not allow for the sort of deals in which Lonrho had used its shares as currency. Growth would now have to be internally generated and liquidity or the ability to obtain substantial credit became even more important. Total borrowings grew from £14.8 million in 1968 to £43.7 million in 1969, and £58.7 million in 1971.[20] In 1968 roughly a third of the total capital employed was borrowed and by 1971 this ratio had risen to much nearer half. Commitments were heavy: they included three new 34,000-ton ships at a cost of £11 million; development at Ashanti Goldfields at £1 million; and the acquisition of Wankel, which came at the precise moment when Lonrho could least easily lay its hands on ready cash.

Added to the spiral of worry and doubt that low share prices caused was the problem of unremittable profits – profits which could not be sent to the United Kingdom because of exchange control restrictions in the countries where they were earned. In the sixties many African countries in which Lonrho operated had increasingly applied such restraints. The most important instance for Lonrho was Rhodesia, where, as a result of UDI, no profits could be remitted directly to the United Kingdom.[21] This, together with the weak share prices, was a fundamental reason for the 1971 liquidity crisis.

The news of the arrest in South Africa of Lonrho directors in September 1971 came as a last straw. Shortly afterwards, two Lonrho directors, Andrew Hunter and Philip Caldecott, resigned over fundamental policy differences: reportedly over whether expansion should take place in North Africa, but probably also over the too rapid rate of growth, the Wankel acquisition and, finally, perhaps because they felt that non-executive directors were not kept adequately informed about company policy.[22] S. G. Warburg, Lonrho's merchant bankers, severed its links with the company at the same time, reportedly because of uneasiness over the Wankel deal. The bank also seems to have become increasingly concerned about the lack of contact between Rowland and its own executives.[23]

At this juncture, the board had to act decisively if investor confidence was not to drain away. On 14 October the directors decided to call in the leading firm of accountants, Peat Marwick Mitchell and Company – referred to in the City as 'Peats' – to investigate and report to the board on Lonrho's financial position and in particular the liquidity situation, the management structure and future prospects. For Rowland, however, the investigation did not constitute an obstacle to further grand designs. 1972 started with a bang when someone close to the company leaked the news that Lonrho was involved in a £200 million petrochemical project with the Libyan government. Lonrho was to provide expertise and participate in the marketing of the products, but would reportedly only make a small financial contribution to the scheme. A preliminary agreement was said to have been reached already, and the company, while refusing to reveal details, declared that talks were incomplete but amicable. The company hoped that 'the Egyptians would also be involved in the construction'.[24] But the scheme gave rise to some comment about Lonrho's lack of expertise in the petrochemical field, and nothing more was heard of it in Britain.

In the absence of further exciting developments, the publication of the Peats report held out the best hope for Lonrho's shares. The company encouraged suggestions that this would be published at the end of January. It was eventually released on 1 March 1972. It confirmed the existence of a liquidity crisis; and share prices, which had risen in the expectation that Peats would give the company a clean bill of health, plummeted from a peak of 109p to 70p. The leaks did not go unnoticed: the financial editor of *The Times* observed, 'Since the autumn the market in Lonrho shares has been conducted on a series of fantasies and still is.' He went on to say:

The Stock Exchange has heard consistent and persistent rumours about Wankel, about the chairmanship, about merchant banks, about the content of the Peat Marwick report, even about vast petrochemical investments with the Libyan government. The favourable rumours carried one message – Lonrho was financially in the clear – and that message doubled the share price in four months of official boardroom silence. In fact, of course, Lonrho is not yet in the clear and the Peat Marwick report was an unpleasant shock.[25]

But this was not a unanimous verdict: the *Economist*, for example, hailed the report as showing that 'the patient is healthy but weak'.[26]

The Peats report was not published in full; shareholders got only a summary of the salient points. Peats defined the greatest problem as being the 'excessively high level of short-term indebtedness in the United Kingdom'.[27] The main cause of Lonrho's liquidity problem was given as the failure to raise long-term loans to finance the development of Western Platinum. The report also revealed that the Wankel group, another major cause of the liquidity problem, had good potential but would not be in a position to contribute to Lonrho's cash flow until 1976, by which time the money paid for the acquisition of the group should have been recovered. The Peats report gave details of the cost to Lonrho of the project.[28] It recommended that Lonrho should develop more projects in the United Kingdom and try to reverse the negative cash flow.

The point that made most headlines was that Lonrho had to raise £10 million by 30 September that year. The Peats report said:

Since 30 September 1971 the London bank overdraft has increased from £2.2 million to £6.1 million. The cash flow projection for the year ended 30 September 1972 indicates that the London bank overdraft will increase to £11 million by that date. Lonrho's principal bankers in the UK have indicated that they expect the London overdraft to be reduced to £2 million by 30 September 1972.

Shortly after the Peats report was published, Rowland announced that he had agreed to lend the company £1 million. His concern for the company needs no explanation, in view of the fact that he was both its largest shareholder and the leading member of its board. But the conditions which accompanied the loan were interesting: no change was to be made in the composition of the board without Rowland's consent as long as the debt remained; and he was to be a board member when any call on the loan was made. In part these conditions show an understandable caution on the part of someone lending a large sum of money – although they do not display undue confidence by Rowland in his colleagues' business judgement. But they also suggest that even at this stage he felt that his position on the board was less secure than it might be.

In the period between the liquidity crisis and the publication of the Peats report Lonrho had taken some preliminary steps towards raising cash by selling a few of its less remunerative undertakings: Chibuku Holdings Ltd, Consolidated Motors Ltd, and Freight Lines Ltd, all in Rhodesia; Rogers and Company Ltd, a Mauritian company; Anglo-Mauritius Assurance; and Lesotho Diamonds.[29] It was suggested that the £10 million would be raised by selling a major subsidiary. But in the event Lonrho had little difficulty in raising the necessary cash by a rights issue in May 1972, which was over-subscribed. This feat would have been at the very least much more difficult seven weeks earlier.

Meanwhile, however, Lonrho had augmented the image of its board by the advent of the Hon. Duncan Sandys, MP,[30] the Hon. Edward du Cann, MP and Sir Basil Smallpeice, lately at Cunard and BOAC. Du Cann was chairman of Keyser Ullmann, which now became Lonrho's merchant bankers. Keyser Ullmann described the appointment as a 'most interesting and stimulating challenge' which would not have been undertaken unless it was thought that the company had a very good future.[31] At the same time, Peats became Lonrho's joint auditors. The appointments to the board were part of the face-lift recommended by Peats and accepted by the Lonrho board. The report had pointed out that 'the group is currently managed in effectively the same manner as it was in the early 1960s'.[32] Not surprisingly, a large multinational required a somewhat more sophisticated management structure than a ranching and mining concern based in provincial Rhodesia. Until March 1972, Rowland and Ball had been joint managing directors, with Ball occupying the additional office of chairman. Ball, Rowland and Ogilvy had been the board's triumvirate.[33] Peats' recommendations for strengthening the management led to the search for an independent chairman. Ball gracefully stepped down to become executive deputy chairman.

The chairmanship was offered to several prominent City figures who turned it down, and when it became clear that Lonrho was having difficulty in finding a suitable candidate, Sandys accepted the post in a part-time capacity.[34] It was not generally known at the time that Sandys' association with Lonrho was closer than his membership of the board of Ashanti Goldfields indicated. For the six months preceding his appointment, he had held the post of consultant to Lonrho South Africa. His qualifications to be an 'independent' chairman may have needed closer scrutiny than they received. Smallpeice was put in as an Establishment figure;[35] he was also administrative adviser to the Queen's Household. Peats recommended that three senior Lonrho executives – R. F. Dunlop, T. R. Prentice and W. H. N. Wilkinson – should join the board and that Rowland should become chief executive.

Peats also urged changes in the accountancy practices. Expenditure on various projects in the course of investigation or development, which had hitherto been entered under Current Assets, were no longer to be capitalized, except where there was a reasonable prospect that the scheme would materialize. Further, Lonrho had been in the habit of recording the value of nationalized assets, before compensation had been agreed, at their book value; Peats recommended that the value should be assessed at the compensation likely to be realized[36] – generally a somewhat lower figure. Another innovation was the geographical breakdown of profits and turnover. The report itself provided figures for net assets under this classification, but this was not repeated in any annual account. This breakdown was widely hailed as penetrating the secrecy with which Lonrho surrounded the origin of its earnings.

Shareholders had in the past received no information about the proportion of profits which were actually remittable to Britain; many African countries had imposed exchange control regulations and in Rhodesia, for example, where it was estimated that somewhere between a quarter and a third of profits were earned, post-UDI regulations made it extremely difficult to transfer funds to the United Kingdom. Following the Peats report, the ratio of remittable to unremittable profits was given for the first time in the 1972 Annual Report, although 'remittable' meant profits 'which have already been, or may be expected to be capable of being remitted to the United Kingdom' within the generous allowance of thirty months after the end of the financial year.[37]

The day after the report was published, an accountant, Roger Moss, joined Lonrho to implement Peats' accountancy recommendations.[38] Moss found a somewhat eccentric accountancy system, which was substantially the same as it had been when Rowland joined Lonrho in 1961: the dynamic force of the company, Rowland, took little interest in accountancy and had tended to leave this field alone. According to Moss, 'When I arrived on the scene, I inherited a book-keeping staff looking after inherited London books.'[39] Accountancy was done for the head office rather than the group: Lonrho had in the past merely added up the results of its subsidiaries and associated companies. Moss set about modernizing this system, paying particular attention to the treatment of remittable profits.

The Peats recommendations and the changes which followed marked the end of the liquidity crisis, but the report was central to the boardroom dispute that broke out a year later. Not only had such changes created the conditions for the row that was to follow, but the argument about whether Rowland had tried to implement certain major recommendations was also an important issue. The liquidity situation and level of share prices continued to be a matter of concern to Lonrho. During the boardroom row, Percy and Smallpeice said that another liquidity crisis was pending, because the chief executive was not taking the appropriate measures to correct the developing situation.[40] In fact a fresh cash crisis did not erupt, and in 1974 liquidity improved. This was in large measure due to the high – and rising – commodity prices.

At the end of 1974, in generally depressed market conditions, Lonrho, according to the *Financial Times*, emerged as one of the top ten big groups (which had market capitalization of over £10 million on 1 January 1974) for share price performance over the year.[41] In contrast with a number of other British companies at this time, Lonrho appeared to have access to cash for development projects. In December 1974 Sandys, commenting on the group's recent sale of eight million shares to Kuwaiti interests,[42] said that although Lonrho was not short of cash, the extra money 'won't do us any harm'.[43] At the beginning of 1975, as the FT ordinary share index rose, Lonrho seemed to be re-embarking on a programme of acquisitions. The purchase of a large stake in London Australian and General Exploration[44] took place amidst rumours that other acquisitions were being explored.[45] At the beginning of February, Lonrho announced that negotiations were well advanced for the purchase of Balfour Williamson and Company, a subsidiary of Lloyds Bank International.[46] Some connection with Lonrho did already exist insofar as Sir George Bolton, former chairman and director of the Bank of London and South America (BOLSA), a member of the Lloyds Bank International group, had been appointed to Lonrho's board in 1974. Other companies mentioned in press speculation about Lonrho's acquisition plans were Messina, a South African mining company, and Richard Costain, the construction firm.[47]

Six

The Public Daylight

The boardroom crisis became public in mid-April 1973, when Rowland obtained a temporary injunction to prevent eight of his fellow directors from dismissing him from his post as chief executive. There was no great surprise in the City at the news: it had been clear for some time that there would be an explosion resulting from tensions in the changed board. But the sensational publicity demonstrated that more was at stake than a clash of personalities. The board was split almost evenly between those who felt that for Rowland to remain at the helm would on balance damage Lonrho's prospects, and those who considered it vital that Rowland should stay. The anti-Rowland faction was led by Sir Basil Smallpeice, a non-executive deputy chairman, and Gerald Percy, the deputy managing director who had been with Lonrho for over a decade.

Smallpeice was in many ways the antithesis of Rowland. A trained accountant, he was the personification of City orthodoxy. He had had a distinguished if not outstandingly brilliant business career: an adviser to the Royal Household since the early 1960s, he had become managing director of BOAC at a time when it was making heavy losses, and resigned when its management structure was reorganized in 1963. He later joined Cunard as chairman, also at a time when this prestigious shipping line was in financial difficulties. The company was taken over by Trafalgar House in 1969 and shortly afterwards Smallpeice resigned. His concern for precise details did not mix with Rowland's flair for seeing the overall potential of schemes, and the resulting clash was seen in Rowland's complaint during the row that Smallpeice was 'terribly interested in petty cash vouchers'[1] and that, instead of visiting Lonrho's subsidiaries, he had sat in Cheapside House going through the accounts.[2] Smallpeice replied that considerably larger sums than this were in question. He had made determined efforts to bring about a change in Rowland's style of management, which he regarded as extremely irresponsible, and to institute formal decision-making machinery. He had succeeded only in infuriating Rowland and had contemplated resignation, but had decided that this would be a dereliction of duty. He spelled out his objections concerning Rowland during the May court case which Rowland brought to extend the temporary injunction already granted. Smallpeice said that Rowland had refused to submit to the discipline of the board and in some cases actually deceived it. In certain instances, according to Smallpeice, Rowland 'appeared to have acted without any regard to the true interests of the company . . .'.[3]

Percy's opposition to Rowland occasioned some expressions of surprise in the press; why had it taken him so long to make this stand? Percy had met Rowland in southern Africa in the early 1960s, when he was trying to raise funds for the Northern Rhodesia Liberal Party. Rowland had not made a contribution but had offered Percy a job, which was later accepted. In the 1960s, Percy did much to build up the company's interests in Malawi. He joined the London board only in 1969. Initially his relations with Rowland seem to have been good: at one time Rowland is said to have expressed the wish that he had six men like Percy.[4] Like Rowland and Ball, he had been given a company house for his personal use, and all three had accordingly been criticized in the Peats report. The appearance of bad feeling in the period before the row became public was indicated by Sandys, who said, 'Mutual antipathy which had grown up between Mr Rowland and Mr Percy . . . reached the point where they were unable to work together.'[5] During the May court case, Elliott, another director, said that he had heard Rowland describe Percy in highly disparaging terms when speaking on the telephone to a manager in Africa.[6]

According to the testimony of Ian Marcus Hossey, a South African executive, during the court hearings, Rowland was willing to delegate considerable authority in many matters to local management. This had presumably applied to Percy while in Africa. But matters were different at head office: a major complaint of the eight dissident directors against Rowland was that he took important decisions on his own initiative, without consulting the board. During the May court hearings, Percy joined Smallpeice in accusing Rowland of bad management, as did many other directors; Rowland's 'preoccupation with the long-term future, and his highly egocentric approach to business and management problems, coupled with his lack of interest in, or concern for, day-to-day management' was creating a situation detrimental to Lonrho's future well-being.[7] Tensions may also have arisen from Percy's ambitions, or Rowland's suspicion of them, which he expressed during the row: '. . . he wants my job. Why not? It's a very nice job.'[8] Percy dismissed this as an obvious jibe, but he was named by the anti-Rowland directors as their candidate for the top Lonrho job once Rowland had been ousted.

Another anti-Rowland director, William Wilkinson, previously with a merchant bank, had been promoted to the board from a senior management position on the recommendation of the Peats report. Rowland subsequently described him as a 'paper merchant' because of the large number of documents he had produced in planning company strategy. There was, too, a long history of personal animosity between Rowland and General Spears, summed up when Rowland said, 'He cannot die happily until he sees me kicked out of Lonrho. That is his ambition in life.'[9] During the court hearings, Spears made indignant comments about Rowland's dictatorial style of management. Stanley Dalgliesh, who had joined Lonrho when it took over Watergate Steam Shipping, was the largest individual Lonrho shareholder after Rowland. He opposed the latter's retention of office.

Of the remaining three anti-Rowland directors, John Nicholas Rede Elliott must in some ways have been one of Rowland's greatest disappointments. Reputed to be a former member of MI6 who had played a key part in the uncovering of Philby, he had been recruited to Lonrho because 'we thought he would be useful in making contacts with ambassadors and those sort of people'.[10] These did not materialize, and Rowland said he was sure that Elliott had 'masterminded the conspiracy against me'.[11] Elliott denied this, declaring that, as administrative director, he had a duty to safeguard the interests of the company which Rowland, despite the great good he had done Lonrho in the past, was putting in jeopardy. Rowland was puzzled about the opposition to him of Major Colin Mackenzie, 'the salt of the earth' with whom he had always got on 'terribly well'.[12] The last director, Alfred Gerber, was in many ways the odd-man-out; Rowland said he should not have been on the board at all. A Swiss who had joined Lonrho on the Wankel acquisition, he was a qualified engineer who had advised the government of Pakistan on industrialization.

Besides expressing 'utter astonishment at the way in which Mr Rowland runs Lonrho', Gerber criticized his negotiations with Arab governments and businessmen as lacking 'sincerity, technical knowledge and methodical approach'.[13] Rowland had offered him no assistance in the day-to-day management or the policy background for the Wankel company.

During the May court hearings, the eight directors made major complaints, which are essential to an understanding of the more specific issues. Rowland, they claimed, was utterly intolerant of criticism or suggestions about policy; his bad temper had led a number of directors to question his self-control. He insisted, Wilkinson alleged, on treating Lonrho as if it were his personal property.[14] Rowland, in a letter to shareholders after the court hearings, conceded that he was sometimes short-tempered or even rude, but he pointed out that he worked extremely hard for the company. Lonrho's chairman, Sandys, who emerged as one of Rowland's most devoted supporters, also said, 'It is perfectly true that Mr Rowland has been reluctant to pay sufficient attention to the opinions of his executive co-directors and at times has behaved in a high-handed manner to which his colleagues have understandably taken exception.' Rowland's frequent absences abroad made it difficult for him to 'conduct the day-to-day business of management'.[15]

Nevertheless, Rowland retained the full allegiance of nearly half the board. Robert Dunlop and Thomas Prentice, promoted from senior management positions at the same time as Wilkinson, supported him. So did Frederick Butcher, the company's finance director.[16] Butcher's support strengthened Rowland's case against the argument of the dissident directors that his irresponsible policies might give rise to another liquidity crisis. Even more important from this point of view was the support of Edward du Cann, another director brought in as part of the face-lift following the Peats report. A prominent Conservative politician and Member of Parliament, he was chairman of the Conservative 1922 Committee, and had been chairman of the Conservative Party in 1965–7. He was also chairman of the company's merchant bankers, Keyser Ullmann, which stood firmly behind Rowland. During the May court hearings, Mr R. Franklin of Keyser Ullmann testified to the financial soundness of Lonrho under Rowland's management.[17] Du Cann declared that he would resign from the Lonrho board if the attempt to dismiss Rowland was successful.

Of the other two members of the triumvirate, Ball, not unexpectedly, supported Rowland. Ogilvy had been absent at the crucial board meetings in March when the directors had attempted to vote Rowland out of his position as chief executive, and shortly after the row became public he resigned. It is possible that his absence in March explains the timing of the row: it was generally agreed that he was a Rowland man, and in his absence the eight were in a clear majority. In view of Ogilvy's description in May of Rowland as a genius with defects and a Cecil Rhodes, Rowland's claim that he would have had Ogilvy's support is not improbable.

For much of the public slanging match which followed the May court hearings, Lonrho's chairman, Sandys, maintained the position of neutrality he had adopted when the row became public. Shortly before the Extraordinary General Meeting (EGM) of shareholders on 31 May, which Rowland, by virtue of his twenty per cent holding in Lonrho, was entitled to call, Sandys made a statement which, most were agreed, came down firmly on the side of Rowland. Sandys himself, however, insisted that he continued to be neutral. Reactions from the dissident directors which followed made it clear that there had been at least implicit tension between Sandys and some members of the board, particularly in the weeks before the public row. Sandys suggested that Smallpeice, at least up to mid-September 1972, had been satisfied with the state of affairs at Lonrho; that he had on 12 March 1973 refused to explain to Sandys his specific complaints so that they could be examined by the board; and that the criticisms of Rowland were 'mostly of a very vague nature'. Rowland had been willing to accept the suggestion of a compromise solution, while Smallpeice had not. Sir Basil had wanted to move to the vote to dismiss Rowland without discussion.

Smallpeice retorted that he had made repeated efforts to try to get Rowland to change his ways, and had warned Sandys about an approaching liquidity crisis on several occasions. He said that there had been two hours of discussion at the crucial board meeting in April, and even then Sandys had insisted on awaiting the outcome of Rowland's application for a temporary injunction. The proposal for Rowland's dismissal, 'and therefore the grounds on which it was demanded, was excluded from the boardroom discussions at Mr Sandys' own request in order, as he himself put it, to keep the temperature low and to give him time to find an alternative solution . . .'. Finally, Smallpeice said, 'Mr Sandys also knows that it was the revelation of his own consultancy compensation arrangement that finally brought the eight individual directors together, in insisting that Mr Rowland must go, whether Mr Sandys wished it or not.'[18]

The issue that sparked off the public row, and which made the greatest sensation when it became public during the May court hearings, was Duncan Sandys' appointment as a consultant, and the compensation paid to him when he gave up his job to become chairman at £38,000 a year. Sandys had been appointed as a £50,000-a-year consultant in November 1971,[19] with effect from 1 September. In February 1972, Sandys' appointment was extended to up to six years and his pay upped to £51,000 of which £49,000 was to be paid in the tax-free Cayman Islands. The full board, however, was not told of this until 22 March 1972, when they were asked to approve the agreement, two weeks after they had agreed to invite Sandys to join Lonrho as an independent chairman. Nor were they informed that on 19 March 1972 Butcher had terminated the consultancy agreement by letter, agreeing to pay Sandys £130,000 for loss of office.[20] Discovering that the full board had not been informed, Sandys paid back the money he had already received in compensation.

Rowland said in court that he considered the size of the payments justified in view of Sandys' experience and contacts.[21] Sandys had agreed to become chairman only when it had proved difficult to find an alternative candidate. Rowland admitted that 'I may well have made an error of judgement',[22] but he pointed out that Smallpeice was on the committee of inquiry which subsequently approved the payment. Later, in a television interview, he said that the concealment from the board was deliberate: Sandys was a national figure and 'I felt it perhaps wrong for twelve or fourteen people to know that a sizeable amount was being paid to him. What appeared to me a reasonable and fair amount would not necessarily have meant a fair and reasonable amount to all my colleagues.'[23]

What the dissident directors objected to, of course, was that they had not been informed either of the original consultancy appointment or of the compensation decision when Sandys became chairman. But the interesting point for the public was that he was receiving a large part of these payments in the international tax haven of the Cayman Islands, whose extremely generous tax laws had recently made them very popular with those wanting to avoid tax. (After June 1972, when they were excluded from the Sterling Area, their attractions for those resident in Britain and fortunate enough to be able to avoid the normal obligations of wage and salary earners, faded slightly.) British residents can pay income into a tax haven in the Sterling Area if such earnings arise 'wholly and exclusively' from overseas work. Any money paid outside the Sterling Area has to be cleared with the Bank of England.

As was stressed in court, Sandys did nothing illegal in having these large amounts paid in the Cayman Islands. The majority of the board learned of the payments and, with them, fuller details of the consultancy deal, eleven months after they were approved. Then, in the course of audit, Peats received details of a £75,000 loan from Lonrho's subsidiary, Anglo-Ceylon, to Consultancy and Development Services Ltd, a Cayman Islands subsidiary. It was revealed that Sandys had been paid £23,000 in fees in the Cayman Islands, as well as the first £44,000 of the compensation payments.

Stories of tax-free payments began to filter through to the public at the end of April. A spokesman for Rowland immediately stated that:

The payments were known to and considered by the full board, a committee of which ratified the position. The accounts have been approved by the auditors without qualification on this point. Mr Rowland wishes to make it clear that there is no question of any such payment having been made to him.[24]

The publicized High Court revelations must have been embarrassing to the whole board, particularly as it was discovered that Sandys had not been the only one to enjoy the benefits of tax havens. Smallpeice had also received £2,500 of his £12,000 salary in the Cayman Islands. Charles Ball, a director of Kleinwort Benson, the anti-Rowland faction's financial advisers, said that some Lonrho directors received up to three-quarters of their salaries through tax havens.[25] Smallpeice pointed out that 'this is quite a common practice in companies which trade internationally. My fees were arranged by Mr Edward du Cann . . .'.[26] But, as Charles Ball said, the practice 'does not look good'.[27] This matter elicited hasty statements from some directors. Wilkinson said that the habit of paying salaries into foreign tax havens did exist in certain cases. He himself received fees from a Belgian Lonrho subsidiary, 'but this is taxed in Belgium and taxed again when I bring it back to England'.[28] Smallpeice said that he would be 'happy to give up' the part of his salary paid in the Cayman Islands, adding that, if the anti-Rowland faction were successful, they would re-examine the company's system of foreign payments.[29] Percy hastened to stress that 'as far as I am concerned, I have never received a penny of my money in any tax haven'.[30] Rowland said that at the time of the compensation payment, he had not even heard of the Cayman Islands: 'This was negotiated by perhaps Mr Butcher and Mr Sandys. I'm not sure. I know nothing about that.'[31] The tax-free payments, almost an accidental revelation, caused extremely strong and widespread indignation.

For the board, the consultancy deal seems to have been the last straw, and the decision was reached that Rowland must resign. Signatures were collected for a motion presented on Monday 19 March, asking for his resignation and stating that if he did not resign a resolution would be introduced for his removal at the next board meeting on 22 March. Rowland said that the decision to dismiss him was taken without consulting him; the plan was leaked to him one Sunday morning and came as 'a bolt from the blue', because he regarded his fellow directors as his friends.[32] At the 22 March meeting, however, the dissident directors agreed not to implement their decision until attempts had been made to find an alternative solution. Percy subsequently described this as a 'tactical defeat':

The resolution to remove Tiny was being put before the board but we agreed to stall it for fourteen days while he sold his shares in the firm. It was understood then that he was going to leave the company. That was where we fell down, because the selling negotiations fell down and it gave Tiny time to mount a personal campaign against us.[33]

After this they had lost the initiative. There followed weeks of manoeuvring and at first it seemed that Rowland was willing to sell out to the financier Oliver Jessel – at a price, it was said in court, of 100p a share. There was later some dispute about whether Rowland would, in fact, have been willing to sell out: the anti-Rowland faction thought he was, but Rowland later said in an interview that he had had no wish to accept the proposed bid.[34] Jessel was still interested in the offer in late March, but the deal fell through. The intervening period may have given Rowland time to prepare the case he so energetically mounted later. It was suggested in the press that the dissident directors had then unsuccessfully tried to find other takers.

Another suggested solution revealed later by the eight was their offer to buy Rowland out by handing over to him operations in the Arab world, North Africa, East Africa, Zambia and French West Africa – apart from the Ivory Coast sugar project, but including that in Sudan – with an agreement to avoid competition for five years, in exchange for the twenty per cent of Lonrho shares that he held. The offer included the Mystère jet, but the future of Rhodesia was left vague. The pro-Rowland faction initially said that the offer was totally illegal: 'You simply cannot sell assets to one shareholder. We took legal advice and were immediately told this.'[35] Although it was subsequently established that under certain conditions the offer would have been legal, Rowland's supporters continued to discount it as impractical. Dunlop, for instance, said:

They wanted to get rid of Zambia because they know they can't handle it without Tiny. They have never met the people in these countries. In fact they were so anxious to get rid of these possessions that they discounted the whole deal by £3 million and offered to throw in the company's Mystère jet for good measure. The only thing they wanted to keep in East Africa was a ranch.[36]

At the beginning of May, Rowland turned the tables, offering to buy the Lonrho shares of the dissident directors at forty per cent above the market price, provided that they themselves would resign. This the directors felt they could not accept. Rowland then proposed to arrange an injection of £8 million into Lonrho; although Keyser Ullmann, informing the board of the offer – which it strongly recommended – in a letter dated 13 April, stressed that over the past year Lonrho's liquidity position had greatly improved. The sum was to come from two sources: the Sudanese, Khalil Osman, and a Zambian company, Muzaona. This last had been formed on 4 April with an authorized capital of 100,000 kwacha (£62,000), but the issued capital was the minimum two kwacha required. The two directors of the company, Tom Mtine and Vic Brown, chairman and secretary respectively of Lonrho (Zambia), each held one of the issued shares. Rumours that Muzaona was to be a vehicle for the £8 million injection, or for Zambian government involvement, were denied by the two directors, who said that the company had nothing to do with either Lonrho or the government.[37] The injection of cash was to be made by issuing new shares at 115p each. There were conditions attached to the offer: the Zambians and Osman wanted the right to nominate Lonrho board members, and Rowland was to remain chief executive. Not surprisingly, the eight rejected it. Later, Rowland said in a letter to shareholders that if he was successful in retaining his post, he would do his best to get the offer renewed. But nothing more was heard of the Muzaona scheme, although Osman, along with other Arab interests, bought shares in Lonrho.

This ended all attempts to reach a private solution. The crucial vote to dismiss Rowland was to be taken on 18 April. On that day, Rowland obtained his temporary injunction preventing the action contemplated by his fellow directors. According to Smallpeice, when the motion to dismiss Rowland was put to the meeting, 'Mr Sandys refused to put it to the board because of his insistence on waiting for the court injunction applied for that afternoon by Mr Rowland . . .'.[38] Rowland obtained his injunction, and the fight became public when the eight opposing him contested its renewal during the May court hearings. But the matter was resolved only at the 31 May EGM of shareholders which Rowland had called.

The court hearings had in some ways a curious air of unreality. Called by some a 'war of affidavits', it was an event outwardly dominated by lawyers, in particular Charles Wheeler, representing Rowland, and Samuel Stamler, who represented the anti-Rowland group. The participants confined themselves to affidavits, read out by lawyers, in which accusations and counter-accusations were made. The hearings, which lasted from 8 May to 14 May, made headlines not only in the quality press, where they were reported in the detail usually reserved for matters of national importance, but also in a number of more popular papers. Substantial personality differences emerged clearly, as did the fact that there had been policy clashes, but it was the former that the pro-Rowland faction tended to emphasize. In his final summing-up, Wheeler suggested, as did Rowland himself, that the row was predominantly a matter of personality. But apart from the tensions created by Rowland's highly individual management style, there were possibly more important policy issues. Such difficulties exist in other companies, but what perhaps made Lonrho a special case was Rowland's reaction to any criticism of his decisions. Convinced that he knew what was best for Lonrho, Rowland would have got his own way even at the risk of provoking the kind of situation that did in fact arise.

One of the clashes that resulted between Rowland and some of the other directors over the move into Sierra Leone was cited by Percy during the hearings.[39] The South African executive, Hossey, otherwise loyal to Rowland, had also opposed this decision.[40] Another disagreement had arisen from Cominière's Zairean interests which, Wilkinson said, had been placed under government surveillance because of Rowland's 'ill-judged political behaviour'.[41] But when it was suggested that the situation would be resolved if Rowland resigned from certain Belgian company boards, he 'flew into a rage'.[42] Obviously the management team was not altogether happy with some of Rowland's excursions into African politics and Spears thought that Rowland's claims of preferential treatment gained for the company in Africa had been exaggerated.[43]

The Peats recommendation that more United Kingdom projects should be found to combat the problem of unremittable profits was also the subject of dispute. Wilkinson, backed by other directors, said that Rowland had consistently and vigorously refused to consider proposals to make British acquisitions by issuing Lonrho shares, partly because he did not want to dilute his personal shareholding in Lonrho. Rowland denied this, pointing out that his holding had in fact been diluted considerably, but it was an accusation that Smallpeice subsequently repeated. Rowland did stress that Lonrho's future had to be determined in accordance with African conditions,[44] but he was concerned to develop the group in Europe and elsewhere; indeed, Lonrho had only missed the opportunity to buy Rolls Royce because of the boardroom row. (Rowland later explained that he had had plans to build Rolls Royce factories in Russia, China and elsewhere.)[45]

Rowland's emphasis on his own importance in the retention of Lonrho's black African interests led the eight to deny that his removal would alter the company's policy. They stressed their intention of remaining in Africa but when during a press conference they said that the company should examine its investments in areas where remittability of profits was low, it seemed that this had indeed been a subject of dispute. The attitudes adopted by African governments to the dispute later became a critical factor.

The dissident directors felt that Rowland was not implementing the Peats recommendations. One instance of this was Rowland's house, Hedsor Wharf. The eight said that the Peats report had criticized the fact that three of the directors – Percy, Ball and Rowland – were all living in free company houses. They had agreed to purchase the properties before 30 September 1972, but by the end of April 1973 only Percy had done so. Rowland conceded this but stressed that he used the house mainly for weekend entertaining on Lonrho's behalf, for which he did not claim expenses. Moreover, he had personally spent £200,000 to £300,000 on the house and its contents, maintained it at his own expense, and personally met the cost of the staff of ten. Hedsor Wharf would, he said, be transferred to one of his overseas personal interests before 30 June.[46] As both Wheeler and Rowland pointed out, Rowland was debited with the interest on the capital cost of the house to the company, and Rowland said that this came from substantial credit balances that he had with Lonrho. Part of these may have been his £1 million loan to the company the previous year. It was also suggested that the credit arose from Rowland's 5.3 million Lonrho shares held by Shepton which, as a Rhodesian company operating under that country's exchange controls, could not transmit dividends. Consequently, Shepton and Lonrho had agreed that the accumulating sum should remain with Lonrho and earn a commercial rate of interest.[47]

The argument about the Wankel acquisition was a rather more technical matter. But it provided a clear example of the way that members of the board felt they had been left in the dark by Rowland about his activities, until Lonrho had been firmly committed to the course of action on which he had decided. The nub of their complaints was that when it was proposed to the board that Lonrho acquire the two Wankel companies which together owned forty per cent of the licensing rights, they authorized Rowland to purchase 100 per cent of the companies for DM64 million (£7.8 million), and to vary the terms 'in his absolute discretion'.[48] They learned in October 1971 that Lonrho was to pay the higher sum of £12.14 million for only eighty per cent of Wankel International, the company formed to hold the acquisitions. Finance was to be raised by loans from a Swiss bank and, according to a former director of a Lonrho subsidiary, Arab banks offered to guarantee the loan and were paid a commitment fee. Wilkinson said that when he found out about the extra sum to be paid, he raised the matter with Rowland who told him that the sum was his personal responsibility, but it later became clear to Wilkinson that this was not so. Rowland, in his evidence, denied that he had ever made the statement.[49]

Rowland explained the discrepancies in court by the fact that the negotiations were lengthy and complicated. The extra DM36 million was licence fees payable by General Motors to the Wankel companies over a period of time. Lonrho had paid this, intending to recoup the cost from General Motors. It emerged that twenty per cent of Wankel International had been promised at no extra charge to the British Israel Bank and a freelance entrepreneur, Max Bunford, who had had a prior option on the companies. Another contact, Captain Klein, who had assisted with the negotiations, also took a slice of the new company as his fee. Rowland said that the directors could at any time have ascertained the true state of affairs by consulting the records, but these were apparently in German which few of the directors understood. He pointed out that the Peats inquiry had had the full details and that shareholders had been informed of the true arrangements, but he did not satisfactorily answer the claim by the dissident directors that, between 9 August and 10 October, he had failed to inform the board fully about the terms of the deal. Dunlop, who was closely involved in the Wankel negotiations, said that the extra sum was specifically mentioned in the agreement, and that it was quite obvious at various meetings attended by Wilkinson that Lonrho would only get eighty per cent of the rights. In his summing up, Wheeler only said that *at the end of the day* there had been absolutely full disclosure. Rowland dismissed the matter to shareholders by pointing out that Wilkinson himself had said the Wankel investment was a major growth point for the future.

But perhaps the gravest allegation against Rowland concerned the Nyaschere copper mine in Rhodesia, rather than Wankel. The major point of dispute in this affair was the ultimate ownership of the mine and the finance that Lonrho had provided for its development. Rowland's interest in Nyaschere dated from August 1958, when he had formed a private company, Nyaschere Copper, in partnership with the owner of the copper prospects, Mr J. C. Reynolds. Reynolds had discovered the deposits himself but had had insufficient capital to develop them. Rowland had paid him £1,000 for a half share and the negotiating rights,[50] but despite approaches from, among others, Rand Mines of South Africa, the prospect remained unworked for a number of years.

Nyaschere Copper was not one of the Shepton companies ceded to Lonrho in late 1961 as part of the package that brought Rowland to the board. He is reputed to have offered them his own half on joining, but Lonrho, having sent an engineer to inspect the mine, refused.[51]

The development of Nyaschere did not begin until after UDI. By this time Reynolds' business had become insolvent and Rowland offered a derisory £250 for Reynolds' half share in the mining prospect – which eventually earned profits of about £600,000 a year and was valued by Reynolds at the time at £250,000 at least.[52] Although Rowland had been awarded an option over all outstanding shares and held the management rights besides, making the mine of limited interest to an outsider, he was persuaded to raise his offer to £18,500. But in the event he did not buy, negotiating the purchase on Lonrho's behalf instead. A condition of the sale of Reynolds' half of the mine to Lonrho was that Rowland would not be called upon to put up the capital to develop the mine, or have any management responsibilities. Nevertheless, Rowland remained on the board of Nyaschere Copper until 1969.

The ownership of Reynolds' half of Nyaschere had now passed into Lonrho's hands and, early in 1970, a Johannesburg-registered company, HCC Investments (Pty) Ltd, was set up especially to hold all the Nyaschere shares. In 1973, therefore, 50 per cent of HCC was owned by Lonrho Ltd. The other half was owned by a Swiss company formed in 1970, Borma,[53] which was itself a subsidiary of a company incorporated in the Bahamas called Yeoman Investments. Yeoman had been formed in 1966 for the purpose, among others, of taking up Rowland's option in Lonrho shares which he had held since he joined the company in 1961. In 1967, Rowland gave the Ball trust a 20 per cent interest in Yeoman, and later the Ogilvy trust a 10 per cent interest, so that he remained with 70 per cent. As a result of these complex manoeuvres, by the time of the boardroom crisis 50 per cent of Nyaschere was owned by Lonrho, 35 per cent by a company nominated by Rowland, 10 per cent by the Ball family trust and 5 per cent by the Ogilvy family trust.[54]

During the court hearings the news broke in the British press of another issue in the Lonrho row: the accounts showed that by the end of the previous financial year the group had made substantial loans to Nyaschere. The company hastened to stress that the loan had been on commercial terms[55] and from funds frozen in Rhodesia.[56] The anti-Rowland group nevertheless saw serious implications for Rowland's position, both as a Lonrho director and as a private individual whose property was benefiting from Lonrho finance. Percy said during the High Court hearings that 'the development of Nyaschere has been financed by the group and as at 30 September 1972 the total indebtedness of Nyaschere to the group was in excess of £3 million, whereas the equity capital of the company is equivalent to approximately £5,000'.[57] Nyaschere Copper had apparently caused considerable controversy on the board.

It was another instance where it seemed that Peats' recommendations were being ignored. Both Peats and Keyser Ullmann had indicated that Rowland's position was open to criticism: in 1972 it does not seem to have been known that the Ball and Ogilvy family trusts both had holdings in Nyaschere.[58] In September 1972, Percy said, Rowland had asked him to discuss with the board his offer to sell Lonrho his private holdings in Nyaschere for £600,000. This offer was not taken up, but he later renewed it, changing the price to £750,000, when Peats said that the situation ought to be dealt with in the 1972 directors' report. According to Percy, the board rejected this second offer too, partly because, as with the first, Rowland made it a condition that he should be paid in sterling or Swiss francs. Percy also said that Rowland had announced that he had already contracted to dispose of his interest in Nyaschere – three months before his first offer. Percy commented: 'I found Mr Rowland's behaviour in relation to this matter inexplicable and extraordinary, and the fact remains that Mr Rowland's original very small investment in Nyaschere has increased in value by his own claim to £700,000 – largely as a result of the use of Lonrho resources.'[59]

The 1972 Annual Report stated: 'Mr R. W. Rowland has advised the Board that during the course of the year, he contracted to dispose of his indirect interest.' An addendum, reported to have been inserted at the insistence of the dissident directors, declared: 'The contract entered into by Mr R. W. Rowland was with a relative by marriage who has for some twenty-five years past been a business associate of his.' This was his father-in-law, Lionel Taylor, who said, 'He knows he can have them [the shares] back whenever he wants them.' And Taylor added, 'No written contract has been entered into and no money has changed hands.' He had not asked for the shares or made an offer.[60] Rowland's main response was to point out that Nyaschere was very profitable for Lonrho, and that he had not taken up the offer of the other half of Nyaschere for himself, lucrative as this would have been. Stressing one of Rowland's most important themes, his lawyer said that it was a great embarrassment to Rowland to own property in Rhodesia: 'African leaders do not exactly like Rhodesia.'[61] Nyaschere was, after all, a mine being successfully worked despite United Nations sanctions against Rhodesia.

For some weeks after the boardroom split became public, the anti-Rowland directors had remained officially silent on their reasons for wanting to dismiss him, although they did make some public statements. Percy said in late April that the issues at stake were 'fundamental'. Charles Ball of Kleinwort Benson voiced one of the main complaints: Rowland was still behaving like a 'one-man band'.[62] Smallpeice said that to make any statement before the court hearings would be *sub judice*, although he felt that there was a 'substantial case' against Rowland.[63] One reason for waiting until the court hearings may have been that the anti-Rowland group considered the court to be the best forum for an orderly, clear and well-publicized presentation of their case.

In the period before the hearings were due to start, there was a final attempt to reach a compromise and to keep Lonrho's affairs out of the headlines. The initiative, coming from the Governor of the Bank of England and the senior partner of Peats, was rejected by Rowland's opponents, although he himself was apparently willing to accept it. The proposals were to abandon the court hearing and the EGM which Rowland had called, and to attempt to reach a compromise by negotiation. If this failed, the directors were free to make fresh proposals to dismiss Rowland. The reasoning behind their rejection is clear: the directors had become convinced that to remove Rowland was essential, and if the compromise solution leaving him in office had been accepted, they would have failed in this central aim.

The judge's decision, given on a Monday morning, was a refusal to renew Rowland's temporary injunction and the dissident directors were free to proceed with the dismissal. Extraordinarily, however, in view of their previous determination to get rid of Rowland, they now decided not to press ahead. This astonishing reversal must have had something to do with what they judged to be their chances of carrying the day at the EGM. By this time it was widely predicted that Rowland would win the support of the majority of shareholders and there was probably little to be gained by dismissing him, only to see him triumphantly reinstated on 31 May. They would only have laid themselves open to the accusation that they had deprived Lonrho of leadership at a crucial time – du Cann had said that he would resign if Rowland was dismissed, as had some senior African executives, and it was assumed that Sandys would follow suit – or that they were after the key jobs at Lonrho, an accusation which Rowland made in any case. Moreover, the judge had said in his summing-up: 'It is a matter for the defendant directors to decide whether it is wise or desirable for them to take any action in advance of the decision of the shareholders on 31 May, now that they are free to do so.'[64] Finally, there was the question of costs, which had not yet been settled, and the prospect of further legal action for the full hearing of Rowland's case.

Rowland himself said that the decision was the result of a Zambian government threat that 'action which would have been taken, probably tonight, would have meant freezing Lonrho's assets, stopping the transfer of funds to London, not paying bills, and even nationalizing Lonrho's assets'. Smallpeice categorically denied that this had been a factor in the decision.[65] The two sides disputed who had made the first move. Whoever it was, the announcement made later on the day of the judge's decision gave the terms of a compromise agreement: the dissident directors promised not to dismiss Rowland before the 31 May EGM and, in return, Rowland was to abide by all reasonable board decisions, keep the board informed of his executive activities and do everything in his power to further the best interests of the company. He was also to pay the bulk of the legal costs. Further court moves were dropped.

The question of Lonrho's future cash position was an integral part of the argument about the company's recent profit performance, remittable profits and Rowland's management style, stressed by the eight in the campaign that followed in preparation for the EGM. The proportion of remittable to unremittable profits was included for the first time in the 1972 Annual Report, issued during the crisis. This break with past habits was said to be at the insistence of the dissident directors, though it may also have had something to do with the improved accounting methods recommended by Peats.[66] Smallpeice said in court that Rowland's conduct was leading to a deteriorating liquidity situation. Percy stressed that 'the liquidity problem had been discussed at at least half the board meetings over the past year and three out of four of the regular general purposes committee meetings'.[67] He pointed to the rapidly rising overdraft, which stood at about £6 million on 30 April 1973.[68] In his affidavit, Butcher said that 'the overdraft position will be tight compared to agreed facilities up to June 1974', but from then on the position should improve.[69] Rowland himself replied to all these allegations in a letter to shareholders.[70] He did not know what effect the boardroom row would have but in its absence the company would have been able to finance its developments until 1974, when there would be a positive cash flow from Western Platinum. He subsequently reiterated this point,[71] again referring to Western Platinum's profits.

Franklin of Keyser Ullmann, acknowledging that there was a negative cash flow, said that he was confident the situation could be contained. The eight dissident directors stressed that while Lonrho cost £6.4 million a year to run from London – of which nearly £1 million a year was 'being spent on supporting Mr Rowland's personal initiatives and uncontrolled development schemes'[72] – the after-tax profits remittable to the United Kingdom were only £4 million.[73] Percy claimed that the money raised by the £10 million rights issue had not been invested, but spent as income. On current trends, he said, the overdraft would exceed £9 million within a year.[74] He later elaborated on this theme, saying that 'the £2.4 million of dividends paid over the last year have been paid out of the proceeds of the rights issue.'[75] Syd Newman, the chairman of Lonrho South Africa, who was one of Rowland's more important supporters, replied that Western Platinum would contribute a substantial profit, not only in 1974 but also in 1973, because of foreign exchange earnings. Finally, at the EGM du Cann said, 'I don't think there is a financial crisis and I don't think there will be a financial crisis.'[76] In the event this proved to be correct.

Rowland was forced onto the defensive about Lonrho's profit record. After the court hearings Smallpeice had attacked it, saying that earnings had only just kept pace with the cost of living while dividends had fallen and share prices had declined by sixty per cent. But the attack that really seemed to upset Rowland came not from the directors, but from the *Sunday Times* of 20 May 1973. There,

Graham Searjeant wrote that in terms of earnings per share since 1967, Lonrho's performance had been worse than several other companies chosen more or less at random, and he questioned whether Rowland's entrepreneurial flair was more successful than traditional management. Rowland replied in a circular to shareholders,[77] saying that if the starting point of 1962 was taken, Lonrho's record was outstandingly better. While this was conspicuously true, the starting base of Lonrho of 1962 had, of course, been small. Percy drove home the attack, saying that 'Lonrho has been ex-growth since mid-1969.'[78]

An important part of the argument was concerned with the remittability of profits. In 1972 unremittable profit formed nearly half of total profit, and consequently of earnings per share.[79] In court, the anti-Rowland directors had complained that Rowland had failed to carry out the Peats recommendation questioning the advisability of earning such a high proportion of profits in areas from which they could not be recouped and advising a review of activities with this in mind. Percy was prepared to admit that about half the unremittable profits were earned in Rhodesia – i.e. nearly twenty-five per cent of the total.[80] The question of remittability raised important issues affecting Lonrho's future policy. While the eight emphasized that it was their intention to remain in independent Africa and 'to continue to work as closely as possible with the Governments and peoples of our host countries in Africa,'[81] they were committed to a policy of concentrating on the fields in which Lonrho was strongest and on areas from which profits could be remitted. This was bound to lead to a change away from the Rowland strategy. Percy, pointing out that the remittability of Zambian profits was very restricted and that the company had not expanded there in the past few years, said, 'We do not say that the policy of Lonrho towards investments in Zambia should be changed at all.'[82] However, while no decision had been taken to run down investments in countries like Zambia and Rhodesia if the eight were victorious, Lonrho's interests there were unlikely to be expanded.

It was this aspect of their approach that allowed Rowland to make some of his most effective points in developing his own theme of the importance of Africa to Lonrho. He replied to a question about unremittable profits that 'in Africa our ability to bring home profits varies from State to State, and time to time – we can remit just about everything from the Ivory Coast, for example, as we can from Europe and the Middle East'.[83] Interestingly, in his subsequent forecast of earnings doubled or trebled in the next few years, the only specific project he mentioned as a major profit-earner for the future was Western Platinum, a South African venture, although he did say that European and Middle Eastern profits would also 'build up strongly'. As well as receiving support from Keyser Ullmann, his case was further strengthened by the fact that one of the company's auditors, Fuller Jenks Beecroft, filed an affidavit during the court proceedings, dealing mainly with accounts and financial controls.

But Rowland's main theme, and one in which there was truth, was that his opponents wished to reverse the policy of dealing with African countries where there were political risks. He stressed Lonrho's pioneering role:

What I sell is Western technology and expertise. As for myself, I have ideas and create competition. Where Lonrho goes, other companies, many of them British, and indeed other countries, follow. This is what we have managed to do for many African countries.

He was in the business of development: 'I would put against the face Mr Heath has discovered, the "smiling face of development" '[84] – a reference to the Prime Minister's celebrated remark immediately after the court hearings.[85] Heads of African governments, said Rowland, knew him, and his African friends were upset at the way the eight were trying to remove him. Their success might lead to the nationalization of Lonrho's African assets.

From the start, Rowland was supported by some of the company's African executives. Tom Mtine, Udi Gecaga and Gil Olympio signed a statement backing him shortly after the row became public. Mtine also gave some support in an interview with a Zambian paper. Here he said that he did not mind who took over the reins so long as he had 'sound policies'. Rowland had proved he was practical and progressive, while the eight had yet to do so.[86] A few days later, Brian G. Chapman, a senior Lonrho executive in French-speaking West Africa, also suggested that Rowland's dismissal might not be acceptable to the company's Ivorian associates. In his application for a temporary injunction, Rowland had said that his removal would be disastrous for the company's African interests. He mentioned in particular the possible consequences for Lonrho's interests in Zambia and Sudan. A Keyser Ullmann spokesman said: 'Mr Rowland exercises immense influence in Black Africa. The company he has developed is virtually unique in being the only UK company in Africa which does not have the usual imperialistic overtones.'[87]

This mention of imperialism was the opening shot for the central theme of Rowland's campaign. In an interview with *African Development* he claimed that the row was the result of his pressure for African directors on the London board.[88] Wheeler said: 'It is a fact that General Spears, in African eyes, unhappily represents the old regime – what Africans regard as the worst of imperialism.'[89] Rowland must have thought that Sandys did not have this image. His claims to be non-imperialist, moreover, must be evaluated in the light of the importance to Lonrho of its southern African earnings. Some Africans also seem to have regarded Rowland's relatively 'liberal' policies as being the issue at stake. A Ghanaian newspaper suggested: 'The move in London to oust Mr Rowland from office stems from some of the London board members' anger at his negotiations with African Governments, including the Ghana Government, which secured fifty-five per cent equity shares in the company's concessions at Obuasi.'[90] Rowland's supporters said that Percy had gained most of his African experience in southern Africa and might be *persona non grata* in many African countries, but Percy firmly countered this.[91]

During the May court hearings, a number of executives from Africa gave evidence for Rowland. Tom Mtine said in his affidavit that he had been 'authorized by the High Commissioner for Zambia in London, speaking on express authority from the Government, that if Mr Rowland is removed from the office of chief executive the company's whole operation in Zambia would not only be in jeopardy, but would cease'. He understood that the government of Zaire would follow any course which Zambia took.[92] Wheeler said that a dignified letter from a Zairean diplomat gave a warning about the consequences of dismissing Rowland.[93] A statement from Khalil Osman emphasized Lonrho's non-imperialism and said that if he were removed it would be difficult for Lonrho to find new projects, while existing ones would be in danger.[94] It was also suggested that Ghana would take action if Rowland were removed.

Stamler dismissed claims of African retaliation as a 'paper tiger':

We are not dealing here with unreasoning masses who, having read in the Nairobi evening papers that Mr Rowland is to be dismissed, would storm the British embassy. We are talking about governments – and they have been very careful to hedge about their words, saying 'We shall have, naturally, to reconsider'.[95]

Wheeler replied that the Ugandan response had been personal and emotional. While Stamler did have a point about governmental reactions, however, both were wrong about the 'Ugandan reaction'; there was none, as General Amin, the country's leader, had already nationalized Lonrho's assets.

One of the most convincing arguments in favour of Rowland's case seemed to be the support that he received from the Zambian government. Most people who followed the events must have been in little doubt that it had made an official threat to nationalize Lonrho's assets should Rowland be dismissed. Because of Zambia's importance in the row, the claim is worth examining. In a moment of high drama on the eve of the court hearings, the Zambian High Commissioner in London, Amock Phiri, came out in apparent official support for Rowland. He said in a statement:

The Zambian government was very strongly of the view that in these circumstances it should take immediate control of the assets of Lonrho in Zambia . . . It was only as a result of urgent representations from Mr Rowland that the Government of Zambia has refrained from taking such a step.[96]

Phiri seems to have been particularly annoyed at the news that an ex-employee of Lonrho, Anthony Mitchley, a lawyer who had recently been in Zambia, was to give evidence on behalf of the dissident directors and to say that there was no climate of opinion in Zambia for a Lonrho takeover in the event of Rowland's dismissal. But at a subsequent press conference Phiri took a modified view, putting more emphasis on future policy than on personalities: the Zambian government had the utmost confidence in Rowland and if his removal meant a drastic change of policy, then Lonrho would cease to be welcome in Zambia as an independent company. Percy hastened to stress that policy would not be changed in Zambia except for the better.

Despite this partial reversal, the impression must have remained that the Zambian government supported Rowland and had authorized Phiri's statements. Soon after, however, there were reports in the British press that Zambian government officials were refusing to confirm any official authorization. No official pronouncement was, in fact, ever made by the Zambian government.

It is believed that one was intended shortly before the EGM, expressing support for anyone who could assist with the development of Zambia, but it was never issued. Phiri's statement aroused considerable controversy and Zambian government circles continued to discuss its implications for months after the crisis. Clearly it caused great embarrassment in Lusaka.

Doubts about whether Phiri had official authorization were reflected in the Zambian press; the Lonrho-owned *Times of Zambia* said: 'Whether the strong views contained in his statement were authorized word for word we shall probably never know ...'. It went on to suggest that 'there can be no question of the Zambian government wanting to become part of the Lonrho boardroom scene'.[97] There were other mysteries in the Zambian 'support' for Rowland. The Zambian official who was reported to have passed on the nationalization threat to Rowland was Bitwell Kuwani, Governor of the Bank of Zambia.[98] Phiri expressed surprise at this supposed intervention, calling it 'misplaced enthusiasm' and saying that Kuwani's presence in London had been coincidental.[99] Rowland claimed that he had had lunch with Kuwani on 14 May, the day he flew in.[100] Kuwani, however, denied that he had conveyed such a threat[101] and later repeated the denial, saying, 'I did not see Mr Rowland at the time he made his statement about me ... I only met him in March. I do not even know the man well.' Asked about Rowland's claim of Zambian nationalization threats, he remarked, 'It is the way the British conduct their boardroom battles.'[102]

Rowland undoubtedly had powerful friends in Zambia; for example, the Minister of Mines, Humphrey Mulemba. But even he was careful to say that he talked 'as a friend of Tiny and not as a cabinet minister'.[103] Rowland's claim that his dismissal would lead to nationalization was tantamount to saying that Lonrho was a firm which received special treatment. Some Lonrho assets in Zambia had already been affected by the government's economic policy.[104] Others were in fields where the Zambians would probably want greater control eventually. But it is difficult to see why Rowland thought the Zambian government would be willing to break established procedure just for Lonrho.

The other African country of which much was made was Ghana. During the boardroom crisis, the Ghana government issued a press statement which stressed that, although directors were free to squabble among themselves, this would in no way deflect the government from its determination to guard Ghanaian sovereignty and to participate in the country's extractive industries. Rowland's counsel quoted this in court, interpreting it as 'an iron fist in a velvet glove', a description which in the context implied that Rowland's dismissal would have serious consequences. To most people, this must have seemed logical; Ghana, after all, said that it followed the stand of Zambia, Kenya and Sudan. But the statement in fact implied no open support for Rowland whatsoever. Zambia seems to have been a case of influential friends rather than government backing. Kenya's position was much more clear-cut. At the time of the boardroom crisis, Lonrho came under prolonged attack in the Kenyan Parliament from a junior minister, J. M. Kariuki.[105] The parliamentary reaction showed that his hostility was by no means the expression of a unanimous sentiment, but it did lead to a statement by Dr Kiano, Minister for Commerce and Industry, that the Kenyan government had no desire to become involved in the boardroom row. 'Boardroom fights for power within Lonrho Company or any other foreign company is no concern to the Kenyan government. Our government is not and shall not be in the pockets of any persons or any company.'[106] The situation was complicated by internal political manoeuvrings, which amounted to an attack on the Kenyan ruling family via Udi Gecaga.[107] But the Kenyan High Commissioner in London, Ngethe Njoroge, repeated shortly before the EGM the Kenyan government's wish to stay out of the affair, and assured foreign investors in Kenya that their investments were secure and regulated by the Foreign Investments Act of 1964.[108]

Ghana's reference to Sudan is rather mysterious; as far as is known, no official stand for or against Rowland was forthcoming from this quarter. The only Sudanese backing came from Khalil Osman who was, of course, a businessman. Some of Rowland's supporters may have been hoping for Ghanaian support. While the slanging match was going on in London, it was reported in the Ghanaian press that General Spears had said that the takeover by the Ghanaian government of fifty-five per cent of Ashanti Goldfields would never have happened had he still been at the helm: 'Ghana's Colonels and Majors could not have looked a British Major-General in the face and proposed the measures.'[109] It was reported that 'Ghana's acquisition of the senior partnership in Ashanti Goldfields last October is known to be one of the causes of the row.'[110] This added ammunition to a popular campaign against all foreign companies exploiting Ghana's resources. At the time of the row, all the places in Obuasi called after General or Lady Spears were being issued with new Ghanaian names.

Thus influential friends did not add up to official, public support for Rowland from Africa. Nevertheless, Rowland, during the EGM of 31 May, claimed that evidence had come from many parts of Africa of the 'appalling consequences' that might follow his dismissal.[111] Rowland's account of what he would do if he did not win the day at the EGM of 31 May varied. In one interview he said that he had been so moved by the African support he had received – 'there is no jungle in the whole of Africa like the jungle of the City of London'[112] – that he would offer his services, free, to the Organization of African Unity; elsewhere he said that he would call another EGM to oust the dissident directors; and again, that 'I and twenty-five senior African executives will get out of Lonrho and start again'. To this he added that, 'in the event, my Lonrho shares will be for sale',[113] an implicit threat of some magnitude, for to put twenty per cent of the shares on the market at once would have been catastrophic for the all-important share price.

In the event, shareholder support for Rowland was even stronger than had been anticipated. In part this must have been due to the fact that he seemed able to deliver the goods in the form of profits and dividends, at least for most of the time. By contrast with Rowland's confident and positive approach his opponents talked of possibilities, probabilities and ways of averting crises. To many it seemed that it was indeed Rowland rather than any of the eight who was best qualified to understand and operate in a black African framework. His opponents' campaign was sound: they had established an alternative to Rowland in Percy, obtained the advice of one of the most respectable City firms and put forward a plan of action. Some of their accusations were serious and not all were adequately refuted by Rowland. But as Sir Douglas Glover, a Lonrho shareholder, put it at the EGM, Rowland's flair for handling his campaign had 'seen off' his opponents 'into the outer darkness'.[114]

One reason for Rowland's overwhelming victory may have been Lonrho's unusual position in having very few institutional investors. Most of the company's shareholders were at the time small; there were just under 50,000 of them, each holding an average of 1,000 shares.[115] Many rallied to Rowland's flag, free from the pressures to which institutional investors are subject, and organized by several energetic and interested people who themselves owned shares in the company.

Several different shareholders' groups were distinguishable. The best known was the Lonrho Shareholders' Action Committee which first made headlines when its founder, Timothy Segrue, sent a telegram to Smallpeice demanding his resignation. At the same time, he took steps to form the Action Committee, which began its activities at the end of April. Segrue probably spoke for many shareholders when he expressed impatience at the 'continual bickering for the best part of three years' in the Lonrho boardroom.[116] He was an unequivocal supporter of Rowland and the essential part of his campaign was to unseat Smallpeice, because 'Lonrho would hardly be Lonrho without its chief executive'. His appeal was blunt: 'Resign now, Sir Basil. Don't castrate Lonrho.'[117] He described the Cayman Islands press rumours as 'an apparent attempt at muckraking . . . secret tax-free payments to a tax haven for a director for overseas service could be interpreted by any businessman who has covered Africa as meaning just that. In Dr Livingstone's day it was baubles and beads.'[118]

At the meeting of shareholders called by Segrue, he asked his fellow investors to offer Rowland 'our whole-hearted support', although he did feel that Rowland should be 'a little more amenable in future'.[119] The meeting approved Segrue's motion: 'That Sir Basil Smallpeice be removed from the Lonrho Board'. Segrue was not on the committee which was formed as a result of this meeting but he continued to make statements about the row. Initially the Action Committee tried to adopt a neutral pose, saying that it wanted to protect the interests of all investors[120] and that its aim was 'to have Mr Rowland's future with the company decided by the shareholders'.[121] But there can be little doubt that, like Segrue himself, it soon took a strongly pro-Rowland stance, and shortly before the Emergency General Meeting sent out a circular which made clear where its votes would be going. Almost immediately after it was formed, three of the Committee's members went to see Rowland who said he was 'very grateful to the Committee for its support'.[122] The Committee also saw Smallpeice, but apparently found his attitude, in contrast with that of du Cann whom it also approached, unsatisfactory. It attacked Smallpeice's refusal to comply with its request not to contest Rowland's application for a renewal of the injunction. Despite allegations to the contrary, the Committee's spokesman, David Fulton, insisted that it was independent.

Another group was the Lonrho sub-committee of Sir Gerald Nabarro's National Shareholders' Protection Committee, whose major action was to nominate Nabarro for election to the Lonrho board. He said that he was sponsored by a large number of private investors in Lonrho as well as by merchant banking interests. His group was 'utterly impartial and is intended to sort out the trouble in the boardroom in the interests of shareholders without pre-empting the position of Mr Rowland'.[123] Nabarro, who was a Lonrho shareholder, seemed quite confident that he would be a match for Rowland but in the event he did not get a chance to confirm this. Segrue suggested that Nabarro was being an opportunist.[124]

Nabarro's group was frequently confused with another, which made an attempt to nominate shareholders to the Lonrho board. The leading figure of this last group was Martyn Marriott, a diamond consultant. Marriott has described his action as 'an experiment in shareholder democracy'; it seemed to him that it was the small shareholders who were the losers in the row, and that the Action Committee was not really doing much to help them.[125] 'The main purpose', Marriott said, 'is to ensure that shareholders can exercise their statutory right to be represented on the board . . . It is important that the shareholders' interests are protected in the future and that the general interest is seen to be protected . . . However, the most important task is to build a united management for our company, to restore its public image and to develop a clear strategy for its development.'[126] His original intention was to persuade well-known figures, or those with some experience of Africa, to stand as directors, and he approached a number of possible candidates, including Sir George Bolton, who later joined the board, and Lord Goodman. All refused, so he himself stood and nominated two fellow shareholders, Major Edwin Marley and Mr Jack Fryer, to act as caretakers 'until the right people are available'.[127] Still, Marriott was clearly more sympathetic to Rowland than to the dissident directors. He felt that what was lacking was an orderly management structure under Rowland to implement decisions and that Rowland himself should continue at the top, making deals and flying around Africa.[128]

The three groups were thus all more or less on Rowland's side. The Lonrho Shareholders' Action Committee did much to help him, mainly by making shareholders more aware of what was going on – after which Rowland's excellently judged campaign could take effect. Once spurred into action, there was in any case not much doubt that Rowland had the support of the small shareholders – with the added advantage that he himself owned twenty per cent of the voting stock. Rowland was, after all, the man who had built up Lonrho and seemed able to keep the profits and dividends flowing. Shareholders did not in the main seem to care about the courtroom revelations; their reaction was largely 'good luck to Rowland', and this was made clear by his overwhelming victory on 31 May.

The Lonrho Shareholders' Action Committee was probably the most successful of the shareholders' groups. Ignoring Marriott's argument that 'it is essential that strong, independent, non-executive directors compatible with the managing director are appointed to the Lonrho board',[129] the shareholders made clear their disapproval of the nominations, particularly Nabarro's, at the EGM. The announcement that the nominations had been withdrawn was greeted with cheers.

The 31 May EGM was in many ways a fitting climax to the Lonrho affair. Company meetings are generally rather sedate, with interruptions to the proceedings usually coming, if ever, from minority groups objecting to company policy on political or humanitarian grounds. On 31 May some Lonrho shareholders seemed determined to show that the Prime Minister's description of certain Lonrho practices as 'the unpleasant and unacceptable face of capitalism' was close to the mark. There were in fact two meetings on 31 May. One was the EGM called by Rowland to confirm him in office and to dismiss the dissident eight. The other was the routine Annual General Meeting, which followed the EGM after a break of five minutes. The venue had been removed from its original site a very few days before, when it became clear that large numbers would wish to attend the meetings. These were now held in the more spacious premises of Westminster Hall. The EGM was bound to be emotional and noisy; the public squabble that had preceded it, together with the strong support for Rowland, guaranteed this. Shareholders must have felt that for once they had the power to make important decisions. The meeting was not improved by the fact that at times Sandys, as chairman, was unable to control the proceedings, which provoked demands from some dissatisfied shareholders that he should be replaced by du Cann. Du Cann refused the offer, although he did at times practically take over from Sandys.

The respect in which Rowland was held by many of the shareholders amounted at times almost to hero-worship. His performance was as well judged as the rest of his campaign had been. In a low-key speech, during which he introduced executives from Africa, he gave a brief background to the row – more in sorrow than in anger – and went on to the subject of the all-important profits: British profits would be increased and the board strengthened. Smallpeice's speech reiterated the main complaints of the directors but at times it was almost inaudible above the shouts of 'rubbish', 'get out', and 'what about Cunard and BOAC?', particularly when he talked about Lonrho's recent unimpressive profit record. The chairman of the Lonrho Shareholders' Action Committee gave a six-minute speech in praise of Rowland, saying, 'You can't shackle a man like Rowland'. Other characters appeared ludicrous in the situation, like a shareholder from Grimsby who gave an impression of Winston Churchill, Sandys' late father-in-law. Another thought that Rowland had constructed a huge organization for the welfare of Africans. Questions concerning Lonrho's relationship with Rhodesia went unanswered.

Inevitably, Rowland won overwhelmingly. The proxy votes went more than three to one in favour of the dismissal of the dissident directors, while the votes for Rowland remaining chief executive were more than six to one in favour. One procedure which might have struck observers as slightly curious was that the results of the proxy votes were announced before the vote at the meeting had been taken. The announcements were greeted with rounds of applause, with that following Smallpeice's dismissal being particularly long and fervent. Adding a final touch to the air of unreality, Rowland shook hands with Smallpeice, saying, 'I hope now this is over we can be friends.' He added, 'I bear you absolutely no animosity.' To which Sir Basil, gentleman that he was, replied, 'All the best. You certainly pulled in the votes this time.'[130] Percy took his defeat perhaps less gracefully; leaving the hall he observed that companies got the governments they deserved, and that shareholders had only themselves to blame.[131]

The Annual General Meeting that followed was something of an anticlimax. Sandys made a statement about his remuneration in the Cayman Islands: 'I was amazed and horrified when I heard from the auditors . . . that the Board as a whole had not been told about it. It shook me to the core.'[132] It was decided that the matter of new directors should be left for the time being. There was, said du Cann, no shortage of 'really valuable candidates'.[133] The meeting drew to a close and the shareholders departed, leaving the chairmanship in Sandy's hands, where it still remained in 1976; and in 1974 he was elevated to the peerage.

Seven

The Unacceptable Face

Suggestions that a Department of Trade and Industry inquiry might be held into Lonrho's affairs were heard when the boardroom split first became public at the end of April 1973.[1] Speculation increased when it became known that lawyers from the DTI had attended the High Court hearings; Sir Gerald Nabarro made demands in parliament that an inquiry should be held.[2] Less than twenty-four hours after his request came the announcement of the inquiry. A DTI inquiry is set up to acquire more information about the affairs of a company than is currently available. The Department, if it so wishes, may publish the report. If it appears from the report that an offence has been committed, the Department can refer the matter to the Director of Public Prosecutions.[3]

The decision to hold the inquiry was welcomed by the press: the *Investors' Chronicle* had already called for such action,[4] and a *Times* editorial gave the move its approval.[5] Following the announcement, the Stock Exchange Commission decided on 21 May not to suspend the quotation of Lonrho's shares. This was interpreted by some as a snub to the DTI. A Stock Exchange spokesman explained that enough financial information was available to the public for investors to estimate a fair share price. The *Guardian* suggested that the decision was a Stock Exchange judgement that 'the Board of Trade investigation is no more than a political sop'.[6] This indeed was what some Members of Parliament feared. There was considerable indignation in parliament among Labour Party MPs at the fact that the inquiry was to be held in private. They suspected that it was a method of sweeping the whole matter under the carpet for political reasons and were afraid that the final report of the inquiry might not be published.[7]

The inspectors were appointed under Section 165B of the 1948 Companies Act, which allowed an investigation when there were circumstances suggesting that those concerned with the company's management had 'been guilty of fraud, misfeasance or other misconduct towards it or towards its members', or that shareholders had not been given the information about company affairs 'which they might reasonably expect'. The DTI press notice naming the two inspectors – Allan Heyman, QC and Dennis Garret[8] – pointed out that 'the terms of the appointment place no restriction on the scope of the investigation. The inspectors have power to investigate anything that appears to them to be relevant.'[9] The general procedure is for the Department to point out to the inspectors in preliminary conversations the areas which it feels need inquiry.

In answer to Labour Party protests about the nature of the inquiry, the government stressed that 'the inquiry will proceed and publication will be decided by exactly the same standards as other governments have applied under the Companies Act. That is as it should be and as it will be.'[10] It was pointed out that publication of the report might prejudice possible legal proceedings and consequently could not be guaranteed. Labour unease remained, however, and was voiced by Anthony Wedgwood Benn: 'A long private inquiry with no certainty of publication at the end would totally fail to erase the anxiety that has been aroused by the Lonrho case and which extends into many other companies.'[11]

Information on the extent of the inquiry was requested in parliament: William Hamilton, the well-known anti-monarchist MP, asked whether the affairs of the Drayton Corporation (formerly the 117 Old Broad Street Group), the Yeoman Company in the Bahamas, and its Swiss subsidiary, Borma, were being investigated.[12] Jo Grimond, the former leader of the Liberal Party, wanted to know whether the inspectors would be able to investigate fully the activities of Lonrho subsidiaries outside Britain. The most detailed and penetrating questions, however, were put by Michael Meacher, MP, a member of the Fabian Society, in December 1973.[13] He asked about the extent of the investigation into the allegations of sanctions breaking, and into Lonrho's complex company structure in South Africa and Rhodesia. Members of the government pointed out that inquiries could be made into the affairs of overseas subsidiaries but that the inspectors could not require any non-British subjects to give them information, or command the production of books and papers from such subsidiaries.[14] The Lonrho investigation proved to be a complicated one, with over thirty people working on it full time.

In view of its complexity, it is not surprising that the investigation dragged on.

Both sides of the boardroom dispute welcomed the inquiry. Rowland issued the optimistic statement that 'the inference . . . is that the purpose of the inquiry is to investigate generally remuneration paid overseas rather than to investigate Lonrho itself'.[15] He pointed out to shareholders[16] that he himself had suggested to his colleagues that if doubts remained about the company's affairs, the DTI should be invited to hold an inquiry. In fact, there were several issues apart from remuneration which caused public concern and prompted the DTI investigations. The High Court revelations gave good grounds for thinking that information had been withheld from the full board. As serious, if not as publicized, was the Lonrho loan to Nyaschere. A Department of Trade official has since indicated that the Department considered this to be a more serious matter than the consultancy payments.[17] There were some activities of which shareholders had not been informed – such as the scheme to divide Lonrho's assets between Rowland and the rest of the company.

The decision to hold a DTI inquiry indicated the importance to officialdom of the issues which the public row had raised. As a senior official at the Department of Trade declared, the Lonrho affair touched matters about which most people feel very strongly, and above all raised the question of the relationship between the company and the community, with which existing company law did not deal. Public reaction and concern certainly played a large part in initiating the inquiry, for the courtroom proceedings had aroused a remarkable degree of public interest. Nor did this disappear when the judge had reached his decision. The sensation continued with the description which the Prime Minister, Edward Heath, gave to the revelations – 'the unpleasant and unacceptable face of capitalism'.[18] The public witnessed the unusual spectacle of company directors, normally anonymous and remote figures, engaging in an undignified public slanging match. And the interest with which the public followed the story was increased by the fact that some of the contestants were well known in their public and political roles, particularly Sandys and du Cann.

The issues that stirred widespread political reaction were that highly respectable directors were able to avoid tax; that large sums of money were being paid to them, apparently for very little work; and that some of them lived in expensive, rent-free houses. To most people, the fact that Lonrho was a multinational operating in Africa was not of particular interest. It was the events set in their British context that caught the headlines. A Labour Research Department pamphlet issued in July 1973 used Lonrho as one example of inequality in Britain, with stress given to the high pay of directors, tax havens, Hedsor Wharf, and the compensation payments.[19]

There seems to have been little surprise over the activities that the affair revealed: the British public had become somewhat cynical about the practices of top management. Indignation was excited rather by the sheer size of the sums of money involved. The course of the 31 May proceedings did little to still resentment. When Dennis Healey, Labour's Shadow Chancellor, spoke of the affair during a party political broadcast on television shortly afterwards, he must have summed up the feelings of many people:

Lonrho is an unpleasant and unacceptable face all right . . . But the shareholders do not think so. So far as they are concerned, Helen of Troy could not hold a candle to it. Last Thursday three thousand of them crowded into the Central Hall at Westminster, and almost fainting with greed, they voted by over six to one for all the things Mr Heath had condemned – golden fortunes poured out to part-time consultants, the tax avoidance, Mr 'Tiny' Rowland's £350,000 company mansion . . .[20]

The Lonrho affair could not have come at a less opportune time for the government. The Conservatives, elected in 1970 on a programme of restoring to public life a framework in which market forces were to be allowed free play, had in a space of three and a half years made themselves exceedingly unpopular with the labour movement. It was their intention to bring within a more rigorous system of control trade unions, which in their view had for too long enjoyed the freedom to strike without the responsibilities that should accompany this right. Their policies were seen as an attempt to circumscribe labour movement activities on the American pattern, and made trade union hostility inevitable. The Conservative Industrial Relations Bill had been almost unanimously rejected by the labour movement but had become law despite strenuous resistance inside and outside parliament. Most trade unions refused to recognize or cooperate with the new law.

This tense political situation was made worse by an intensifying internal and international economic crisis, whose chief feature was inflation. Trade unions which attempted to win higher wages to compensate for rising prices were accused by the government and the City both of causing inflation and of greed at the expense of economically weaker members of the community. Up to the end of 1972 the government suffered major defeats at the hands of the Labour movement. The miners' strike of 1972 finally convinced it of the need for a statutory incomes policy. That this was going to make relations between trade unions and government still worse was clear from the start. The trade union movement had never supported such measures.

The Conservative incomes policy began at the end of 1972 with a total freeze on wages. The rise in some prices had been temporarily halted through voluntary restriction by members of the Confederation of British Industry. At the beginning of 1973 this was replaced by the second phase of the policy, which allowed for wage increases on the formula of £1 plus four per cent, with no rises above £250 a year, although long-term agreements were to be allowed to go ahead. There were price controls, but industries whose costs rose because of higher imported raw material prices were to be exempted. The cost of imports, seasonal foods and rents was not controlled and this led to complaints that the brunt of the measures to control inflation fell on wage rather than price restriction, while profits were soaring. The government replied with a much-publicized control over dividends as well as by setting a profits ceiling and by pointing out that those at the top of the salary scale were just as much subject to wage restriction.

The Lonrho affair showed that large sums were indeed being paid to those at the top of the management hierarchy, while trade unionists were being accused of greed for attempting to keep pace with the rise in the cost of living. To add insult to injury, while workers were taxed under the PAYE scheme, company directors were seen to be legally avoiding full taxation on extremely high remuneration.[21] It was an inauspicious background to the 'Phase Three' discussions taking place at that time, which proposed to relax but not remove wage restrictions.[22]

Some unions and the Labour Party did receive resolutions from their branches condemning aspects of the affair. On the day following Heath's famous statement on the Lonrho affair, Vic Feather, the General Secretary of the Trades Union Congress, said that it was a pity that British workers had never thought of trying to get their 'Phase Two' increases paid in the Cayman Islands; 'but if we all started using tax havens, the Government would find some way of stopping it. Because then it would look like tax evasion, which is illegal, instead of tax avoidance, which is of course strictly legal.'[23] Subsequently, the General Council of the TUC issued a statement which observed that although the Lonrho case was not unique, 'as some principals in the case have already testified', it was made public by an unusual combination of events. 'The suspicion must remain that such situations are by no means unheard of elsewhere.' Tax havens were an aspect of the non-accountability of multinationals over which the TUC was becoming increasingly concerned. The General Council 'consider that there are matters of wider public interest at stake in this case'. They demanded a public inquiry into the case, 'coupled with an examination of the degree to which such practices occur elsewhere'. Such an inquiry should be a preliminary to changes in company and tax law.[24]

One of the few official reactions from an individual trade union came in the journal of the Technical, Administrative and Supervisory Section of the Amalgamated Union of Engineering Workers, which said in its editorial:

The court case revealed a number of practices which it was assumed would be quite unacceptable to the shareholders. They met with the full knowledge of the '*unpleasant and unacceptable*'. They proceeded to confirm 'Tiny' Rowland in office and in effect the system of handouts, fat salaries payable in the Cayman Islands and free houses.[25]

It pointed out that the sums mentioned in the case were not unusual. Leading trade unionists used Lonrho as an illustration of inequality in Britain. Ken Gill, General Secretary of the Technical Administrative and Supervisory Section, for example, said about Conservative economic policy, during the 1973 TUC Congress:

You have to remember who the other side of this bargaining is and what the other side of this bargain will be. It is offered by a gang who have brazened their way through a jungle of electoral promises, call-girl scandals[26] and the even more sordid Lonrho affair. While our rulers indulge themselves in bed, pot and boardrooms, Ted's plan for us is one of self-discipline and restraint.[27]

Trade union officers were not particularly surprised by the revelations. They pointed out several times that they met management representatives across the bargaining table frequently, and were well aware of what went on in the boardroom.[28] Their reaction cannot be separated from the wider context; trade unionists tended to see Lonrho in the light of their hostile relations with the Conservative government. While it cannot be said that Lonrho materially altered trade union attitudes towards 'Phase Three' – the policy towards which was clear and had already been laid down – it added ammunition. The TUC reaction was also a part of a concern about the activities of multinationals.

Far more political capital was made out of the affair by the Labour Party. Their attacks in parliament showed how closely it was linked with the economic situation and Conservative policy and with the indignation aroused by tax avoidance. Heath made his statement at a time when the incomes policy was coming under concerted attack from Labour MPs. But it was in answer to a question from the Liberal, Jo Grimond, who stated that 'the goings-on at Lonrho ... will be fatal to the counter-inflation policy', and that 'greed does not now seem to be the monopoly of the trade unions', that the Prime Minister condemned Lonrho.[29] At the height of the scandal Edward Short, Deputy Leader of the Labour Opposition, declared: 'The Lonrho disclosures simply heighten the sense of frustration, deprivation, misery and hardship caused by the government's policy ... The Secretary of State for Trade and Industry is the defender of all the sleazy aspects of capitalism in this country.'[30]

The Labour attack was not confined to parliament. Harold Wilson, leader of the Labour Party, speaking at a public rally in Blackpool which included many miners, pointed to the inequality that the case had highlighted: 'What has now emerged into the light is a graphic illustration of the system of society Mr Heath and his government exist to sustain.' He went on to ask: 'What sort of form does a pitman have to fill up to have his wages paid to him in some sunny tax haven?'[31] The Labour Party pointed out that nothing about the affair was 'illegal or particularly unusual. It is part of the philosophy of the City whereby rewards come to those who deal in financial assets which produce nothing for the community. Even Mr Heath has been moved to call the Lonrho Affair an "unpleasant and unacceptable face of capitalism".'[32]

The Labour attack concentrated on two major aspects of the affair: the contrast with the austerity demanded by the government's wages policy, and the tax avoidance practised by some members of the board. The new information about Lonrho's Rhodesian interests caused much less stir. In the House of Commons at the time, a rare reference to it came from Healey, who asked Heath: 'What action do you propose against those involved in the Lonrho affair who have been reported to have evaded sanctions through mining companies for which Lonrho is responsible? This is one of the more unpleasant and unacceptable faces of capitalism'.[33] The Lonrho scandal would have been a political gift to the Labour Party at any time but they were particularly lucky that it occurred just then. It fitted in with a comprehensive criticism of Conservative policy then being formulated in a period of acute political conflict. This had been created by government policies over a wide range of issues: free school milk, the Housing Finance Act, the Common Market, trade union and wage policy, student unions and grants. These had all added to the criticism that the government was drawn from and interested solely in the welfare of big business. Such an analysis seemed to fit perfectly with the revelations from Lonrho.

For some members of the Labour Party, as well as groups outside parliament, the implications of the Lonrho affair revealed what was wrong with the capitalist system itself. This was well illustrated in a Labour Party motion: 'That this House recognizes that the activities of the firm of Lonrho are not so much the unpleasant and unacceptable face of capitalism, as the inevitable logic of capitalism.'[34] As a correspondent of the *Guardian* commented: 'The principal signatories included a number of MPs not normally identified with the left of the party . . .'.[35] The motion compared Sandys' payments with the wages of hospital ancillary workers and demanded legislation to tighten up the laws relating to tax havens. There can be no doubt that the Lonrho affair showed up the City in a most unattractive light. Hence the press statements that reflected the Establishment view of Lonrho as an exception: 'Lonrho is not typical of British industry as a whole'.[36] But the point was not lost on the British left. In the Labour Party considerable rank-and-file hostility existed towards the City and the abuses which its self-regulating mechanisms seemed unable to control. While conceding the importance of its financial institutions to the balance of payments, Transport House[37] pointed out that 'The City has another side to it. Practices such as asset-stripping are now infamous . . . This sort of thing does no service to the community as a whole . . .'.[38] Lonrho was a powerful argument for reform.

The Conservative Party was quick to realize the implications of the scandal. This sensitivity probably lay behind Heath's swift denunciation of the practices of the Lonrho board. His statement was pre-emptive and designed to head off the criticism that Lonrho reflected any essential part of the system his government was determined to preserve. Other leading Conservatives also expressed their condemnation of these 'excesses'. The Conservative view was that while people should be duly rewarded for business ability, it was not obvious that this had been the case at Lonrho.[39] To some, however, to indict these aspects of capitalism was to condemn the whole system, as the left was doing. The *Spectator* said that 'Businessmen, after all, are in it for the money and the power', concluding that 'it is aggressive entrepreneurs like Mr Rowland that this country needs'.[40]

When Grimond suggested that Heath should ask the CBI to condemn the Lonrho affair, the Prime Minister replied that the CBI was a responsible body which would make its own statement. But the CBI refused to make any comment on the grounds that Lonrho was not a member.

The Conservative attempt to pre-empt criticism did not work; 'the unacceptable face of capitalism' rebounded on Heath and his party and was used to condemn all that he was trying to defend. Single events in the business world do not generally have a discernible impact on political developments, but Lonrho was possibly an exception. The General Election of February 1974 came soon enough afterwards for the revelations still to be fresh in the minds of the electorate. The Labour Party election campaign associated the Conservative government with big business and its scandals. It is possible that Lonrho helped the Conservatives to lose a crucial election. Even in the October 1974 election, reverberations of the affair were felt; Wilson quoted Heath's notorious phrase in his election speeches.

The Lonrho affair also gave impetus to longstanding discussions about company law reform. By the late sixties the major parties were agreed on the need for changes. This consensus about what had been a low-priority non-political issue began to disintegrate in the early seventies, as policy differences emerged, partly as a result of Lonrho and other City scandals – although the major political parties stressed that they had been aware of the abuses and that their plans for reform considerably pre-dated Lonrho.[41] Lonrho happened at a time when reforms were known to be imminent, and there was widespread discussion of the issues. The Conservative government published a White Paper on the subject which appeared in July 1973. The Labour Party was also working on proposals for reform. Concern was not confined to specific business abuses; it seemed that companies would have to impose upon themselves a code of behaviour, or have it imposed on them. A CBI report on the responsibilities of public companies had urged the need for 'an ethical dimension in corporate activity'.[42] It was in an atmosphere of heightened awareness of the issues involved that the Lonrho affair had its impact.

The boardroom crisis gave rise to press and City speculation that it would itself lead to specific changes. For example, *The Times* headlined one of its editorials, 'Lonrho May Change the Companies Act',[43] while elsewhere it was said that 'many changes are expected in the next Companies Bill, and it is a fair bet that some of them will be a direct result of recent happenings at Lonrho'.[44]

Among the most important specific reforms, the need for which was highlighted by Lonrho, was that of fuller disclosure by directors. Even before the publication of their White Paper, the Conservative government conceded this point. In answer to a question suggesting that similar practices might be found in other companies, James Prior, a member of the Conservative Cabinet, said: 'In their current review of company law the Department of Trade and Industry are considering *inter alia* the extent to which further disclosures will be required from companies.'[45] Although the need for this had become more obvious, it did not constitute a policy innovation; the 1970 Conservative Election Manifesto had promised that a Conservative government would 'sharpen the disclosure requirements in the accounts of public companies . . .'. The Labour Party Green Paper of June 1974 stressed the necessity for this, adding that the amount of directors' emoluments paid overseas should be disclosed.

The Lonrho affair also gave added edge to discussions about how to reform management so as to make it more responsive to the public interest and representative of employees as well as shareholders. The Liberal Party pointed out, 'The Lonrho affair quite clearly shows that the direction of companies is often capable of more democratic control.'[46] The press urged a greater emphasis on non-executive directors – who were supposed to represent the more general public interest – and Smallpeice in this position had done his best.

But the boardroom crisis seems to have done little to bring about any specific changes in the proposed legislation. The

Conservative White Paper, while it stressed the need for greater disclosures and for a code of conduct, was far more concerned with such matters as insider trading and non-voting shares, and so was their Bill published in December 1973. The only provision which dealt with the practices illustrated by Lonrho was that the relationships between directors and their interests in other companies were to be controlled more strictly. While the *Economist* said that the White Paper had been redrafted to take account of 'Lonrho and other unedifying situations that had cropped up',[47] this had been denied by Conservatives.[48] The Department of Trade also discounted suggestions that Lonrho affected company law reform proposals.[49]

The effect of the Lonrho affair was probably greatest in influencing Labour Party policies, in particular by strengthening the hand of those who wanted to see strong measures of reform formulated with some speed.[50] Lonrho had turned the issue of reform from one which excited little public interest into a political issue.

Tax avoidance had been seen as the most outrageous aspect of the affair and had led to expressions of concern on all sides. It was a clear example of the way in which companies were not fulfilling their responsibilities to the community and it was expected that the boardroom row would lead to a tightening-up of legislation. The standard reply to questions on the matter in parliament, that this was a matter for the routine of the Inland Revenue, only served to highlight inadequacies in the law. It was announced that further action was being considered.[51] When the Labour Party proposed in 1974 to tighten up the tax laws relating to resident foreign businessmen, Joel Barnett, Chief Secretary to the Treasury in the new Labour government, said that the need for action stemmed from the Lonrho affair. At the time, there had been criticism of the use of tax havens, but Britain itself was 'something of a tax haven'.[52]

The scandal may have had an impact on other aspects of Labour policy. The Labour Party had for some time been demanding a compulsory register of MPs' business interests. The fact that in an affair as controversial as Lonrho two of its leading figures were prominent Conservative MPs undoubtedly added substance and pressure to this demand. And while Lonrho did not change Labour Party policy on nationalization, it may well have promoted the efforts of those members who wished to see the policy pursued with somewhat more determination. Even at the time, Lonrho was seen as providing a good argument for radical proposals. Mr Benn, referring to the dangers exposed by the Lonrho affair, said: 'That is one reason why the Labour Party must allow the public to control or own key industries and financial centres on a far greater scale than in the past. A case for this is becoming stronger every year as economic and industrial power gets more and more concentrated and less and less accountable.'[53]

The public row certainly did Lonrho itself no good; share prices fell and potential investors were scared off. Finally, it brought about the DTI investigation. It also did not improve Lonrho's long-term prospects. While it firmly established Rowland's business acumen, it did not generate sympathy for him either in business or in trade union circles. Nor could it have done much good to Lonrho's reputation in Africa.

In British politics, the boardroom row was significant in coming just at the time when the role of private enterprise in the community and the differential rewards of investment and work were the subjects of so much discussion. This, by and large, is why the affair was treated as such an important event by the press and politicians. If the practices which so outraged public opinion were not unlawful, they did have the effect of focusing attention on the underlying issues.

Edward du Cann spoke for the City when he said, 'I deeply and bitterly regret that anyone should have thought it necessary to drag all these matters into public daylight.'[54]

Eight

An Embarrassment of Riches

The publicity surrounding Lonrho's affairs in the spring and summer of 1973 included editorial and other press claims that Lonrho was avoiding economic sanctions against Ian Smith's white Rhodesia. One of the best documented reports appeared as a feature article in the *Observer* at the beginning of June. Entitled 'How Lonrho Bust Rhodesia Sanctions', it produced evidence showing how one of Lonrho's local subsidiaries was managing, contrary to United Nations sanctions, to get exports of Rhodesian copper out of the country, with the help of a disused mine in the backwoods of Mozambique.[1] Another case prompting speculation was that of the Nyaschere copper mine in Rhodesia itself, and the £3 million loan advanced for its development over a five-year period. The Lonrho subsidiary putting up the money had not been named in the latest Annual Report. There was press comment that if it had been a London-based company, or indeed any company in the Lonrho group incorporated outside Rhodesia, then Lonrho would have been responsible for pumping development finance into a country which was in open rebellion against the Crown and which member states of the United Nations had been called upon to boycott. The legal and political implications of this might have been substantial for a company which prided itself on what it claimed as its identity with black Africa. However, Lonrho's own answer was that the money had been advanced by a Rhodesian subsidiary, Lonrho Investment Company. But the case was confused by another distinct issue on which most of the attention focused: the personal involvement of Rowland, Ball and Ogilvy as shareholders in Nyaschere Copper (Pvt) Ltd.[2] This diverted attention from suspicions that United Nations sanctions against Rhodesia had been breached.[3] These suspicions were not one of the issues preoccupying the attention of the court and failed to disturb shareholders. A member of the audience who raised the question of Rhodesia at the stormy Extraordinary General

Meeting on 31 May received scant attention and less enlightenment. Despite Lonrho's long and well-established connections with Rhodesia, its interests in that country today are one of the least known and least discussed aspects of the group's operations.

The position of all British companies with branches and subsidiaries inside Rhodesia became an ambiguous one after Ian Smith's Unilateral Declaration of Independence in 1965. While it is clear that international trading and investment sanctions against Rhodesia were avoided on an extensive scale after UDI, the inadequacies of the relevant legislation were such that only a handful of prosecutions were successfully brought under British law. By using routes through South Africa and Mozambique, companies were able to give considerable support to the Smith government in its efforts to surmount international disapproval, with little risk to themselves. British companies which could show that their Rhodesian interests had since UDI been managed by independent local boards of directors beyond the reach of control from London, could not be held legally accountable for the latter's actions. By continuing to operate in Rhodesia, Lonrho's subsidiaries were by 1974 highly lucrative; but their retention and expansion after UDI were an open challenge to the strong views of black Africa.

Rhodesia's breakaway from Britain came at a time when Lonrho was making important advances in a number of independent African countries north of the Zambezi; and as it became increasingly obvious that the Smith government was set on a path of convergence with the apartheid policies of South Africa, the company's assets inside Rhodesia became something of a diplomatic liability. Lonrho's Rhodesian origins were, indeed, to be one of the chief ingredients in the row which shook the Organization of African Unity at the beginning of 1974.[4] The London board of Lonrho deplored Ian Smith's action, and Rowland himself expressed his personal distaste for UDI on a number of occasions. In May 1973 he stated in court that after 1965 he had decided against increasing his personal interests in Rhodesia, on the grounds of his opposition to UDI.[5] It is possible that the feeling was mutual. The return of a Rhodesian Front government in the December 1962 elections in Rhodesia had removed from power several of Rowland's allies in the United Federal Party, and the changeover may have been a factor in the company's concern

147

from 1963 onwards to move into fresh territory. The Rhodesian Front was committed to the perpetuation of white settler rule and to the achievement of independence from Britain, and as Malawi and Zambia were granted the right to secede from the Central African Federation, the whites single-mindedly set about realizing their ambitions. In April 1964 the Prime Minister of the Rhodesian Front government, Winston Field, was displaced by his more intransigent deputy, then Treasury Minister, Ian Douglas Smith. UDI was now simply a matter of timing, and it was on the morning of 11 November 1965 that the document was finally signed by the members of the Rhodesian cabinet.

The Labour government in London, for whom the despatch of troops to Salisbury to quash the rebellion was never a serious possibility, now embarked upon a series of ultimately ineffectual measures designed 'to restore a situation in Rhodesia in which there can be untrammelled loyalty and allegiance to the Crown'.[6] The first set of measures against the Smith regime was announced by Harold Wilson on the afternoon of 11 November. The export of British arms and aid was to cease; Rhodesia was to be removed from the Sterling Area and from access to the London capital market; there were to be no further imports to Britain of her tobacco; and her Commonwealth Preferences, including those on sugar, were to be removed. An Enabling Bill, to be brought before parliament on 15 November, was drafted to allow further sanctions to be introduced as necessary. On 1 December, embargoes were placed on imports to Britain of asbestos, copper and copper products, iron and steel ores, antimony, lithium and chrome, maize, meat and other foodstuffs. These items, Wilson assured the House, would together account for more than ninety-five per cent of Rhodesia's exports to Britain and efforts were now being made to persuade other countries to impose similar measures. On 3 December the assets of the Reserve Bank of Rhodesia in London were confiscated by the British authorities. The Rhodesians, who were already taking steps to locate alternative markets for their exports and had abolished the preferential tariffs which British exporters to their country had enjoyed, retaliated by blocking the remittance of profits, rents, interests and dividends, and the repatriation of capital, to residents of Britain. From the point of view of companies such as Lonrho, obstacles were rapidly being placed in the path of normal business and trading relations by British and Rhodesian authorities alike.

The United Nations, meanwhile, was taking its own steps to combat the Smith regime. The first resolutions on UDI were passed by the Security Council on 12 November and 20 November, calling for sanctions on a more ambitious scale than any that Britain had so far applied and including a ban on all oil and petrol supplies. It was this last that put Lonrho in a diplomatic quandary, perhaps more awkward than the company had ever had to face before, and one which probably put paid for the time being to any more ambitious schemes that may have existed for expanding its operations inside Mozambique. Although only just over a quarter of Rhodesia's energy requirements were at this time met from oil, the bulk of imported crude oil supplies was pumped across Mozambique from the port of Beira through Lonrho's pipeline. Since January 1965, when its commercial operations began, over 146 million gallons of crude oil had been delivered though the pipeline to the new Feruka refinery near Umtali, bringing in a gross revenue of over £2 million and realizing Rowland's ten-year-old ambition to construct this vital link with the coast. The whole achievement was now to be put in jeopardy.

In mid-December, Harold Wilson returned to London from addressing the United Nations in New York and informed the House of Commons that oil sanctions were now to be imposed against Rhodesia. British subjects or companies would henceforth be prosecuted for supplying or carrying oil to the regime. What was debatable was how far the other countries would go in enforcing similar provisions upon their own personnel and, even more to the point, how in the absence of a military blockade or some other show of force, privateers and others eager to exploit the situation would be prevented from doing so. Despite such obvious loopholes, pumping did stop at the Beira end of the pipeline as tankers ceased to off-load at the port, and a rough-and-ready method of rationing diesel oil and petrol was introduced by the Rhodesian authorities. Lonrho, which had attracted considerable criticism in Salisbury at the time that the crucial pipeline agreements were being négotiated, for selling out to the Portuguese,[7] soon found itself in a difficult position. Although Lonrho possessed a sixty-two per cent holding in the Companhia do Pipeline Moçambique-Rhodesia, owners of the pipeline and of the various concessions attached to it, the Portuguese were in a majority of five to four on the board. While Rowland, Ball, Ogilvy and Caldecott, the four British directors, were bound under British law to observe the sanctions now being imposed on Rhodesia by the government in London, they had agreed at the end of 1962 that if the pipeline ceased to operate for reasons that were not satisfactory to the Portuguese, it should be handed over to the latter's ownership and control. On 9 March, after the Portuguese chairman of the Companhia do Pipeline had used his casting vote against the four Lonrho directors and in favour of the resumption of pumping operations, Lonrho announced that the pipeline would perforce have to remain open.

The Lonrho directors, caught between Portuguese pressure to honour their concessionary obligations and the potential threat of prosecution by the British authorities for one of the first cases of sanctions-breaking, had apparently decided that the second was the lesser of two evils. Events were to prove them right. Perhaps partly due to pressure from Lonrho, which pointed out to the Foreign Office that if pumping were resumed, it would be without the permission of the British directors of the Companhia, the British government now despatched the aircraft carrier 'Ark Royal', and the frigates 'Rhyl' and 'Lowestoft', to intercept any tankers with cargoes destined for Rhodesia that attempted to dock at Beira. Lord Walston, Parliamentary Under-Secretary at the Foreign Office, was sent hot-foot to Lisbon to try to talk reason to the Portuguese and a request was forwarded to the United Nations to adopt an appropriate mandatory resolution. On 9 April the Security Council authorized Britain to use such force as was required to make the ban effective, and from then on, though it did nothing to improve Anglo-Portuguese relations, the pipeline remained closed. Nevertheless the company was now faced with substantial unpaid bills under the construction agreement with John Hume, the South African company which had undertaken the building of the pipeline, and the South African Industrial Development Corporation, which had financed it. Over the period April to September 1966, the British government was persuaded to dispense a total of £324,000 in compensation for loss of revenue to the Companhia do Pipeline, to pay for repair and maintenance work. From October, however, no further subsidy was forthcoming. To add insult to injury, the Rhodesians quickly found ways and means, as with other vital supplies, to get round the inconvenience of an inoperative pipeline. The South Africans were the first to leap to the rescue by sending supplies of petrol and oil northwards by road across the Beit Bridge. Then, by the autumn of 1966, the bulk of Rhodesia's requirements was being railed across Mozambique from the state-owned Portuguese refinery at Lourenço Marques: a return to the method of transportation that Rowland's first big venture into the oil world had been designed to replace.

The decision to cut the Beira–Umtali oil pipeline was, of course, one of the measures by which the British government had promised to bring the Rhodesian regime to its knees 'in weeks rather than months'. It was still closed, and Ian Smith still in control of Rhodesia, more than a decade later. From 1966 Lonrho itself bore the cost of maintaining the pipeline, a sum of around £300,000 a year. According to a letter that Rowland wrote to the *Daily Telegraph* in 1970, the company had tried to persuade the British government to take the pipeline over but without success.[8] It was clearly an expensive liability, unlike the group's interests inside Rhodesia itself, which continued to operate successfully despite the sanctions barrier.

Apart from a number of South African firms such as Anglo-American, the Messina group, and Rand Mines, Lonrho and Rio Tinto-Zinc were the two most important mining houses in post-UDI Rhodesia. In some contrast to Lonrho, RTZ omitted any mention of its Rhodesian subsidiaries from its Annual Reports in the 1970s, on the grounds that their profits and losses were not included in the group accounts and that accurate information was, in any case, not available. Its gold, nickel and emerald mines in Rhodesia, however, continued to flourish, while Lonrho subsidiaries in Rhodesia also did well. After UDI, Lonrho's main management and service arm in Salisbury became the Lonrho Investment Company. In 1965 this had a number of subsidiaries including, for example, Unit Trust Fund Managers, the first unit trust in Rhodesia open to public subscription and set up in 1961 by former Lonrho director Sir Peter Bednall. The North Charterland Exploration Company (1937) Ltd had interests in 1965 in real-estate development in the Salisbury suburbs, as well as owning several thousand acres of land in Zambia and a substantial holding in an amethyst-mining enterprise there. Willoughby's Consolidated Company Ltd owned two ranches in the Umvuma area south of Salisbury and a further two near Bulawayo. Consolidated Motors and Norton Motors, which had been taken over from Rowland when he joined Lonrho's board, dealt in motor spares and distributed several well-known vehicle makes. Among Lonrho's most important assets in Rhodesia, however, were its gold and later its copper mines. Since 1963 the bulk of these had been held by the company's South African subsidiary, Coronation Syndicate.

From the mid-sixties, a veil of secrecy hung over these embarrassing assets. Direct references to Rhodesia in the Lonrho Annual Reports became few and far between, and most of these – significantly, in view of its conspicuous losses – concerned the pipeline. The 1973 Annual Report, for example, remarked that 'the Group ranches over 100,000 head of cattle on over 1.5 million acres', and that 'a substantial increase in profit from the copper mines was recorded', without indicating that both these operations were located mainly in Rhodesia. Such omissions were remarked on by South African commentators, as well as by the Rhodesian press.

At various times rumours circulated that Lonrho was considering pulling up sticks in Rhodesia. Such a decision would indeed have been in keeping with the company's declared feeling of distaste for the Smith regime. Over the winter of 1971–2, for example, as Peat Marwick Mitchell was preparing its report on the company's liquidity problems, a number of Rhodesian assets were disposed of, including a transport company, a chain of breweries and Consolidated Motors, the motor spares company. A complete withdrawal from Rhodesia would not have been without precedent; the American mining company Roan Selection Trust, for example, decided at the end of 1967 that the political and economic prospects were too uncertain, and sold off a package of its Rhodesian interests to the South African company, Messina (Transvaal). In March 1972 Rowland, asked whether Lonrho might withdraw from white southern Africa completely to concentrate on the independent states, replied, 'That is one of the things we are considering.'[9] Two years later, at the company's Annual General Meeting in the London Hilton Hotel, one of the board assured a questioner that Lonrho's policy was now one of concentrating investment north of the Zambezi.[10] Sir Basil Smallpeice gave a similar undertaking at a press conference during the boardroom row, when he suggested that Lonrho was unlikely to expand its Rhodesian operations, although it did intend to hold on to them for the time being.[11]

Meanwhile, Lonrho had not merely stayed put, but its Rhodesian subsidiaries in several cases had undergone considerable – and in certain crucial instances, dramatic – expansion during the years following UDI. A number of new companies were acquired in Rhodesia after 1965. The Rhodesian Star Mining Company, for example, was registered in 1966 and subsequently taken over by the Lonrho Investment Company; the Rhodesian Wattle Company was one of the assets taken over in the group's package deal with Slater Walker in the summer of 1969; Zambezi Coachworks Ltd, also acquired in 1969, was the largest body-builders for buses and commercial vehicles in Rhodesia. David Whitehead and Sons (Rhodesia), the largest textile spinners and weavers in the country, was taken over when Lonrho acquired the British parent firm in 1968. Nippon Motor Sales Rhodesia Ltd, a subsidiary of the Norton Motor Company, was registered more than a year after UDI, with a board which included Rowland himself and his father-in-law, Lionel Taylor.[12] Lonrho's capacity for expansion in Rhodesia was not dulled by the exposures of the boardroom row or Rowland's bid to secure Lonrho's appointment as oil consultants to the Organization of African Unity.[13] Between 1973 and 1974, the number of Lonrho's subsidiaries in Rhodesia increased by a quarter, from thirty-two to forty.[14] It was in mining, however, that the company saw its most profitable and successful development. From 1965 on, it diversified from being one of Rhodesia's main gold producers into copper, and transiently scheelite and gemstones.

The growth of the mining sector, particularly in copper, was one of the most notable features of the post-UDI Rhodesian economy, and in contributing to it Lonrho followed a trend in common with several other major mining houses. From 1967 there was a distinct upturn in the number of Exclusive Prospecting Orders awarded by the Rhodesian government to companies hot on the trail of new mineral strikes. And Lonrho's Rhodesian subsidiaries put in for a whole range of permissions to prospect for copper and gold, beryllium, tungsten, coal, mineral oils and natural gases. In 1971 the Lonrho group companies ranked fourth in the list of prospectors, with Orders covering 2,377 hectares.[15] The search for new sites went along with schemes to open up old mines that had for one reason or another fallen into disuse. In 1969, for example, Lonrho's subsidiary, Homestake Gold Mines (Pvt) Ltd, acquired the interests in the Shamva gold mine, abandoned by Roan Selection Trust in 1967–8. The mine had been closed in 1930 when it was producing only a very low grade of ore, but it remained one of the largest disused mines in the country and Lonrho believed that rich pockets of gold might still exist. It was not long before the adjacent Cymric mine, where production was envisaged at between 15,000 and 20,000 oz. of gold a year, was opened up by Lonrho. Early in 1974, it was reported that Lonrho had taken up an option from the Rhodesian Mining Promotion Corporation on a disused gold and copper mine, Falcon Athens, a hundred miles south of Salisbury at Umvuma.[16] There were optimistic plans to bring the mine back to life and a programme to explore the old workings was soon undertaken.

It was the two copper mines of Nyaschere (Shamrocke) and Inyati that were without question Lonrho's most successful mining ventures inside Rhodesia after UDI. The group acquired its major copper interests only after Rowland joined the board, yet the development of Inyati and Nyaschere put Lonrho in a position to challenge such established giants of Rhodesian copper mining as MDT Mangula Ltd, a part of the South African-based Messina group. Inyati, a mine owned by Coronation Syndicate, was brought into large scale production in 1966–7. It was one of the most important post-UDI mining ventures in Rhodesia and by 1973 was contributing over half of the total operating profits earned by Coronation. Nyaschere, a mine in which Lonrho in London had a fifty per cent interest, was said in the same year to be earning profits of the order of £600,000.[17]

The mining sector is, of course, an industry geared to the export and sale of its products on world markets. At UDI, Rhodesia's minerals were among the first targets of international sanctions. It was iron and steel, copper and chrome, that were later the subjects of some of the most dramatic cases of sanctions-breaking. Except for those against oil and petrol, the first sanctions imposed by the British government and the United Nations were 'voluntary' ones, depending for their success on the peaceful persuasion of trading partners, whether companies or countries. Having rejected the use of force as a means of bringing the Smith regime to heel, the Wilson government embarked upon a series of seemingly endless, and in retrospect futile, talks with the Rhodesian cabinet, while the United Nations debated the issues and African governments shuffled their feet with impatience. On 8 December 1966, after the Six Principles for a Settlement put to Smith during talks with Wilson on HMS 'Tiger' had been rejected by the Rhodesian Front, George Brown, then Foreign Secretary, went to the United Nations to propose that 'selective mandatory sanctions' now be imposed on exports of copper, asbestos, chrome, iron, sugar, tobacco, meat and leather.[18] A year later, certain members of the United Nations were calling for a military blockade of sanctions-breaking ports such as Beira and Lourenço Marques in Mozambique, and the use of United Nations troops for enforcement purposes. In June 1968, by Resolution 253 (1968) of the Security Council, blanket mandatory sanctions were imposed.

It was an important decision. Yet as events and the Sanctions Committee, convened by the United Nations as a watchdog, were to show, the fatal flaw was the deliberate omission from the sanctions provisions of any machinery to ensure that, above all other UN members, South Africa and Portugal toed the line. Between 1966, the first year of UDI, and 1972 Rhodesia exported merchandise valued at a total of 1,557 million Rhodesian dollars.[19] According to estimates made by the United Nations Sanctions Committee, 1,107 million dollars' worth of this reached world markets via South Africa and Mozambique. In 1972 a comparison of the figures for exports from the Southern African Customs Union, as submitted by the South African authorities, with those from twenty-three importing countries who reported back to the Sanctions Committee, showed a discrepancy of 317 million US dollars. This was interpreted by the United Nations as largely attributable to consignments of Rhodesian goods, exported illegally via South Africa. For Mozambique, the discrepancy for the same year was 90 million US dollars.[20] Close links between Rhodesia, South Africa and Portugal existed long before UDI, of course, and Ian Smith's UDI was in many respects an expression of white Rhodesia's urge to align herself more closely with the apartheid policies of the Republic of South Africa. It was in 1959 that Dr Verwoerd, then South Africa's Prime Minister, first put forward the idea of a 'Southern African Common Market' and in 1965, six months before UDI, Ian Smith was publicly showing enthusiasm for a tripartite military alliance. From the mid-1960s onwards, the Rhodesian Front took pains to close the gap which still persisted between Rhodesia's own laws and constitution and those of the 'pure' apartheid state.

The reaction of South Africa and Portugal to the imposition of United Nations and British sanctions was predictably hostile to the mainstream of world opinion. Sanctions were bitterly attacked by Dr Verwoerd in his 1966 New Year broadcast, and he let it be clearly understood that South Africa's normal financial and trading relations with Rhodesia were not merely to be continued but would be stepped up in active support of the rebel regime.[21] In June 1966 Dr Diederichs, the South African Minister for Economic Affairs, in a clash with an American motor company, indicated that the South African government was not prepared to tolerate foreign companies with subsidiaries in South Africa which imagined that they could continue to observe international sanctions while on South African ground.[22] The traditional flow of trade and investment between Rhodesia and the rest of white-ruled southern Africa in fact made it impossible for other countries to impose sanctions without a confrontation of some kind with South Africa and Portugal. Firms with subsidiaries in South Africa, which in turn had subsidiaries in Rhodesia, were perhaps better placed than any others to beat the sanctions barrier. Once Rhodesia's goods had been carried across the border into the Republic in the course of 'normal' trading relations, there was little difficulty in re-exporting them with new certificates of origin to markets anywhere in the world. Overseas capital injected into South African companies could with comparative ease be forwarded on for development projects inside Rhodesia, while exchange controls applied by the Rhodesian authorities to contain the outward flow of funds were modified where the destination was South Africa.

Lonrho's Coronation Syndicate, owning several gold and copper mines in Rhodesia, took on crucial significance at the end of the 1960s in consequence of its South African registration, although it is probable that the original motive for administering the Rhodesian mining subsidiaries in this way was rather different. In 1963, after Rowland had joined the Lonrho board, Lonrho operated a total of five principal gold mines: Coronation Syndicate, at that time only an associate of Lonrho, owned the Arcturus and Muriel mines; Mazoe Consolidated Mines, an almost wholly-owned subsidiary of Lonrho, operated the amalgamated Connaught and Bucks mines; Mashaba Gold Mines had Empress; and Kanyemba Gold Mines, the Kanyemba Mine. In the summer of that year, it had been decided that all these should now be brought under Coronation's control and in November Lonrho had accepted Coronation's offer of 185,059 fully paid-up shares in return. The result was that all five gold mines became wholly-owned subsidiaries – or virtually so – of Coronation Syndicate, while Lonrho acquired approximately 62 per cent of the issued capital of Coronation, enough to convert it to a subsidiary and to give Lonrho working control. A further reorganization occurred in 1964, when Lonrho interposed two holding companies between itself and Coronation. Lonrho's total holding of 3,734,111 shares in Coronation Syndicate was sold to Tweefontein United Collieries, a subsidiary of the wholly-owned Lonrho subsidiary Henderson's Transvaal Estates. The deal had put £1,120,000 into Lonrho's pocket at a time when ready cash was in short supply. Through Henderson's, Lonrho now held 59 per cent of the shares in Tweefontein, which in turn held the 62 per cent in Coronation. While this meant that Lonrho Ltd of London's stake in the profits of Coronation's Rhodesian mines had been reduced to 36 per cent, it had retained working control over their operations through the two intermediary companies.[23] In 1965, shortly before UDI, a holding company for the five mines, Corsyn Consolidated Mines, had been set up as a wholly-owned Rhodesian subsidiary of Coronation Syndicate. One of the reasons for all these transactions at the time may have been the economies that would accrue from operating all the mining properties through a unified management structure, but it was from the end of 1965 onwards that they began to bear their most politically significant fruit. These transsactions meant in effect that a number of Lonrho's Rhodesian mines were controlled from South Africa, by Coronation Syndicate. This link with the outside world became important with the imposition of United Nations sanctions against Rhodesia.

The impression created by the London board of Lonrho after UDI was that all profits earned in Rhodesia were frozen inside the country as a result of currency controls imposed by the Smith regime. Probably the most precise estimate to come from a director of Lonrho of exactly how important these profits were was that volunteered by Gerald Percy who, next to Rowland himself, was better qualified than any other member of the London board to express an opinion. He had longstanding connections with Rhodesia and was a personal friend of Garfield Todd, the former Rhodesian Prime Minister who in due course was put under house arrest by the Smith regime. At the time of the boardroom crisis, Percy still owned a house in Rhodesia and was a regular visitor there.[24] Shortly before his defeat at the May 1973 EGM, he said that about half of Lonrho's non-remittable profits, which in the 1972 financial year amounted to forty-five per cent of the group's total profits after tax and minority interests, came from

Rhodesia.[25] In May 1973 Sir Basil Smallpeice assured journalists that 'profits being made by the company in Rhodesia were being ploughed back into operations there'.[26]

Nevertheless it is perfectly clear that in certain years after UDI permission was obtained from the Rhodesian exchange control authorities for remittances out of the country to South Africa, through Coronation Syndicate. In 1973 Coronation resumed the payment of a dividend to its shareholders after a three-year break, and in the same year the Rhodesian authorities allowed a total of $320,000 (Rhodesian) in respect of dividends declared in 1968 and 1969, but subsequently blocked, to be sent out of the country. By the time that Coronation's Annual General Meeting took place in January 1974, a total of $1,350,000 (Rhodesian), less fifteen per cent non-resident shareholders' tax, had been allowed out in respect of the 1973 profits.[27]

From 1969 Coronation had been committed to a massive programme of capital expenditure that left little scope for hand-outs to its shareholders in South Africa. The main purpose was to bring Inyati into full production and in 1971 Coronation's chairman, Richard Lee, had to explain to shareholders at the Annual General Meeting that 'the capital developments over the last few years have put considerable strain on the company's resources and we have depended upon financial assistance from associated companies to achieve the favourable results'.[28] By the end of the financial year 1972, Coronation had run up a bank overdraft of 2.8 million rand (about £1.7 million) and its total indebtedness to banks and fellow subsidiary companies was around 3.3 million rand (about £2 million).[29] By the end of 1973, however, the company had substantially paid off its debts and was being described as 'flush with cash'.[30] It was noted in the Chairman's Review for the year that the profits from mining that had been realized were more than double the forecast that had been made at the beginning of 1973 (an increase on the forecast of over 3 million rand), largely due to increases in gold and copper prices.[31] In the past, the company's debts had caused funds to be blocked inside Rhodesia but now that it was well into the black shareholders could relax. In the first half of 1974, as metal prices soared, a dividend of fourteen cents was followed by one of thirty cents, plus a special twelve-cent bonus in respect of 1972–3 profits, confounding the most optimistic forecasts. The *Rand Daily Mail* enthused:

Not even Lonrho's chief executive, Mr Tiny Rowland, can denigrate the performance of the Southern Africa companies, and Lonrho's profits will receive an appropriate boost from this corner of the continent.[32]

By the middle of 1974, it was being forecast that Coronation would reach the end of the year with a pre-tax profit of around ten million rand (£6 million).[33] This would almost double the 1973 figures and multiply those for 1972 nearly six times. Over the financial year ending 30 September 1972 (the period to which Percy was probably referring when, in May of 1973, he estimated the value of Lonrho's Rhodesian profits), Coronation Syndicate had made a profit of 1.7 million rand after directors' fees, prospecting and other costs.[34]

In the event, Coronation Syndicate reached the end of the 1974 financial year with profits which were fifty-nine per cent up on those for 1973.[35] Falling world copper prices over the summer and autumn of 1974 had removed some of the earlier elation, although Coronation as a group which also had interests in gold was better placed than some to withstand market fluctuations. With a permanently resident Rhodesian labour force, it was also unlikely to suffer from the shortages of migrant African labour which in 1974 and 1975 were besetting many gold mines in South Africa.[36]

Through Tweefontein United Collieries and Henderson's, the intervening holding companies in South Africa, Coronation's profits, once they had been allowed out of Rhodesia, could legally be remitted to the United Kingdom. Lonrho's share in Coronation's earnings, however, through Henderson's and Tweefontein (fifty-nine per cent owned by Henderson's), amounted to only just over a third of the total after minority interests, an arrangement which doubtless encouraged Lonrho to make an offer subsequently for the outstanding share capital.

The Inyati mine, and the nearby shaft of Mkooi, in the Eastern Highlands area eighty miles east of Salisbury, were taken over in the early sixties by Coronation Syndicate after the two original promoters – a businessman, Michael Haddon, and a farmer, Charles Bunn – found themselves without the necessary cash to continue exploration work. By the autumn of 1966, it was being whispered in Salisbury that Lonrho was on to something very valuable indeed and the accounts of Coronation Syndicate, whose capital expenditure regularly exceeded profits, indicated that a programme of expansion and development of no mean proportions was getting under way. Coronation's Annual Report for the year ending 30 September 1967 announced that to finance the whole venture, the company's authorized capital was to be nearly tripled and its borrowing powers substantially increased. It was rumoured that a six-figure sum was being injected into Inyati alone, quite apart from the development work in progress at Coronation's other mines. The gamble certainly paid off; from the end of September 1967 to March 1968 the average copper content in the ore being sampled nearly doubled, and the milling rate was expected to rise to ten thousand tons a month. By the end of the financial year 1970, the mine was milling over 20,000 tons a month and had made a working profit for the year of 1,530,066 rand, or nearly twice that of the three main gold mines of Arcturus, Mazoe and Muriel put together. However, after the Annual General Meeting of Coronation Syndicate in Johannesburg in 1968, no further bulletin was issued on Inyati's progress by the Coronation board, and in the Report for the year 1968 its results were amalgamated with those from three other mines that had recently been opened – Sabi Vlei and Kakonde, and the Ball scheelite mine. It was not until more than three years later that the full details of Inyati's fortunes emerged.

At the end of 1968, as the expansion programme at Inyati mine was getting under way, Lonrho made a bid for the outstanding share capital of the three main South African subsidiaries of Henderson's Transvaal Estates – Witbank Consolidated Coal Mines, Tweefontein United Collieries and Coronation Syndicate. It soon became clear that the takeover was not going to be achieved without a struggle. The details of Lonrho's offer were released for approval on 16 July 1969; three Coronation Syndicate shares, total value 105 cents (South African), were to be relinquished for one Lonrho share, valued at 145 cents (South African), to be held on the Johannesburg register. Despite assurances, however, that 'all statements of fact and opinion relating to Lonrho and Corsyn . . . have been authorized by the directors of Lonrho and Corsyn respectively', and that 'each of their respective boards accept individually and collectively responsibility therefor and consider that no material fact has been omitted from this statement',[37] the text of the offer made no mention either of Inyati or of the newly-opened gold mine at Shamva in Rhodesia.

This omission was felt by some minority shareholders, particularly those who had knowledge of conditions in Rhodesia, to be a serious one. Lonrho later stated that it was bound, under the special Rhodesian security regulations, not to reveal details of mines in Rhodesia. Such regulations were certainly in force, although the rigour with which they were to be interpreted was a matter of some debate. Inyati in particular had enormous potential, and this fact cast some doubt on the generosity of Lonrho's offer to Coronation's shareholders.

In the event, Lonrho decided not to pursue its offer for Coronation, Witbank and Tweefontein, and it was quietly withdrawn. The interesting aspect of the bid was that it involved valuable assets inside Rhodesia, a country cut off from the outside world by United Nations sanctions. If the bid had been pursued, Inyati and perhaps other ventures inside Rhodesia would have received publicity outside and it is possible that the reaction of independent African states to such an eventuality was one of the considerations.

Two years later, in July 1971, investigations into Coronation, which were believed to concern among other things the Inyati mine, were opened by the Commercial Branch of the South African Police. According to press statements issued by Lonrho's London board, a group of people who had bought a large number of shares in Coronation, perhaps in anticipation of a lucrative rise in their value after a Rhodesian settlement, had persuaded the South African police that there was a case for investigation. The board suggested that the whole affair stemmed from the spite of a few disgruntled share-dealers who had lost a lot of money.[38] In Johannesburg, it was learned that the stockbroking firm of J. Edgar Barclay had been sequestrated; the trustee who had been appointed to take over its affairs attributed its insolvency to the use of borrowed funds to buy 770,000 rands' worth of Tweefontein and Coronation shares, which had subsequently dropped in value rather than risen as had been hoped.[39]

On 24 September 1971, Frederick Butcher, a director of Lonrho and of a number of its subsidiaries, including Henderson's Transvaal Estates, was arrested in Johannesburg, shortly after flying in from London on a business trip. He was charged with fraud and granted bail of 5,000 rand. In the weeks that followed, three more directors of Lonrho subsidiaries, Clifford Bentley, Richard Lee and Kenneth Scheepers, were arrested on fraud charges. On 11 October, the South African police, accompanied by the Rhodesian CID, visited the Salisbury headquarters of the Lonrho Investment Company, interviewed two directors, and removed a number of company documents. According to the court records of the Johannesburg Regional Court, charges of fraud were brought against Lee, Bentley, Scheepers and Butcher in their personal capacities; against Coronation Syndicate, represented by Lee; against Tweefontein United Collieries, again represented by Lee; and against Lonrho Ltd, represented by Frederick Butcher. The charges alleged that Lonrho and the two subsidiary companies, through its directors or servants, committed fraud while trying to buy up the outstanding share capital in Coronation and Tweefontein in 1969. According to a report in the British press, the charges alleged

that the accused pretended to the merchant bankers handling the take-over offer, to its attorneys and to minority shareholders that all material facts about the financial position of Corsyn and Tweefontein had been made public.

The charge sheet says that the accused omitted to disclose that Corsyn had made a major copper strike, about which the directors of Lonrho, Corsyn and Tweefontein had information, but about which the general public knew nothing.[40]

Three years later, all the charges were in fact withdrawn.[41]

It was reported at the time that the series of arrests took place after a complaint had been lodged with the police. Following the withdrawal of Lonrho's offer for Coronation, Witbank and Tweefontein, private investigations into Lonrho's affairs had been pursued by a Mr J. P. Esterhuysen, an authorized dealer in the Johannesburg stockbroking firm of J. Donaldson. Together with Phil Ward, a mining expert, and Edgar Barclay, a stockbroker (of J. Edgar Barclay Ltd), he had bought heavily into Coronation, Witbank and Tweefontein at the time of Lonrho's offer, in an effort to raise the price. The three men were said to be aware of the potential of the Inyati mine and to have considered that the true value of Coronation's assets had not been taken into account in the terms of Lonrho's offer. After Lonrho's withdrawal of the offer, the collapse of the share price led to the bankruptcy of Barclay's company.[42]

On 12 January 1973, during a two-minute court hearing which brought to a close a whole series of adjournments and postponements, the fraud charges against the Lonrho executives and the companies they represented were dropped by the South African authorities. Investigations did continue into other allegations against the Lonrho group, but in September 1974 these too were withdrawn. According to an announcement issued by the London board and published by a number of national dailies, the decision not to prosecute the company, taken by the Attorney-General of the Transvaal,

confirms that there was no justification for the damaging allegations or charges against Lonrho and its officers. The material cost, damage and the loss of reputation needlessly sustained by Lonrho, its officers and shareholders in the course of a three-year wait for this vindication has been considerable.[43]

The withdrawal of the charges clearly removed a pressure point from the company. The London board seem to have been active on behalf of their colleagues in South Africa. The *Sunday Times* of Johannesburg subsequently claimed that Rowland and Ball themselves had paid a personal visit to Dr Hendrik Luttig, South African Ambassador in London at the time, at the South African Embassy in London:

Mr Rowland complained about harassment of Lonrho and pointed out to Dr Luttig that Lonrho had a lot of influence with the Black states of Africa and had always been a friend to South Africa. He said that should Lonrho continue to be harassed, the South African Government would lose the goodwill of Lonrho and the Black states would take a stronger line against South Africa.[44]

In addition, Duncan Sandys appears to have made personal efforts on behalf of Lonrho in his capacity as consultant to Lonrho South Africa, a post to which he had been appointed in the summer of 1971 at a fee of £10,000 a year.[45] Sandys was known to be a friend of both Dr Hendrik Luttig and Dr Hilgard Muller, the South African Minister of Foreign Affairs. The *Sunday Times* of Johannesburg later reported that Sandys had 'had chats with both men about the Lonrho indictments . . .'.[46]

Over the period of police investigations, the prospect of further arrests was sufficiently unnerving to convince a number of Lonrho executives, in particular Rowland, that it would be unwise to travel to South Africa until the fuss had died down.[47] The irony of the situation was not entirely lost on the South Africans, and the *Financial Mail*, in festive mood, suggested that a suitable New

Year 1972 gift for Mr Rowland might well be a complimentary air ticket to Johannesburg.[48]

Besides Inyati, certainly the most valuable of Lonrho's copper assets, there were two other mines in the Lonrho group which at various times attracted press speculation and comment – Nyaschere, in Rhodesia; and Edmundian, in the Vila Manica region of Mozambique, just across the Rhodesian border from Umtali.

The Nyaschere mine, or Shamrocke as it is sometimes called, had a confusing history of different ownerships.[49] As late as September 1973 a High Court action about the ownership was started in London against Rowland and subsequently Lonrho as well by a South African called Graham Beck.[50]

After 1966, when Lonrho agreed to purchase a half share in the mine,[51] this fifty per cent passed first into the hands of Corsyn Consolidated, Coronation's holding company in Rhodesia. In August 1969, however, it was transferred to the Lonrho Investment Company in Salisbury, again on the grounds that Coronation did not have the money to develop it. In February 1970 it passed to the Johannesburg company, HCC Investments, and Rowland also arranged for his shares to be held through HCC.

The Nyaschere copper mine had been developed with the help of a £3 million-odd loan, put up, according to Lonrho's Annual Report for 1972, by 'the group'. It was not immediately clear to which company or companies within the Lonrho fold this referred. A legal representative for Rowland hastened to point out that 'the money advanced to Nyaschere came from funds frozen in Rhodesia and not from Lonrho in London ... "the group" in the Lonrho annual report did not refer to the parent company but to its Rhodesian subsidiary, Lonrho Investment'.[52] But this did not explain why it was necessary to set up, in Johannesburg, the subsidiary HCC Investments to hold the Nyaschere shares. The question was posed: if no capital was flowing into Rhodesia, and no profits flowing out, what was the purpose of the various transactions involving Borma A.G. and Yeoman Investments; and the removal of the ownership of the Nyaschere mine out of Rhodesia, via South Africa, Switzerland and the Bahamas to, ultimately, London, to Lonrho Ltd, Rowland, and the Ball and Ogilvy family trusts?

As far as the loan for developing Nyaschere is concerned, the money seems to have been provided locally. In other instances of expansion by Lonrho subsidiaries inside Rhodesia much of the capital required seems to have been raised locally. Early in 1971, for example, 4,500 of the ordinary shares in David Whitehead and Sons (Rhodesia), ultimately owned by Lonrho, were put onto the market in Rhodesia. The effect was to turn David Whitehead from a private into a public company over which Lonrho retained executive control, but it raised useful cash at a time when the programme to bring Inyati and Nyaschere into full production was at its peak. The sale of Lonrho Rhodesia's 50.01 per cent holding in Heinrich's Chibuku Breweries (1968) Ltd to Rhodesian Breweries at the end of 1971 raised $2 million (Rhodesian), to be paid in cash; while the disposal of Consolidated Motors in 1972 brought in a considerable sum. From the vantage point of London, these sales could have seemed to be the first stage of Lonrho's withdrawal from Rhodesia; but to those on the spot, they were straightforward money-raising deals to ease the illiquidity of Coronation Syndicate, then in the course of running up its 2.8 million rand bank overdraft.[53] In 1967 a number of Lonrho's smaller Rhodesian subsidiaries, including Mashaba Gold Mines which had operated the then defunct Empress mine,[54] and the Lonrho Exploration Company, a prospecting venture, were liquidated through the Salisbury High Court.[55] Once creditors had been paid off, equipment, stores and so on could have been sold for use elsewhere. Nyaschere was one mine to which such supplies, available inside Rhodesia, were transferred in this way. The company whose assets were utilized was Kanyemba Gold Mines Ltd.

In December 1969, one of the directors of Nyaschere Copper (Pvt) appeared in the Sinoia Magistrate's Court in Rhodesia, charged with driving a vehicle that was too heavily laden. He pleaded guilty and was duly fined. What the intrepid executive was doing, it appeared, was transporting equipment from the worked-out Kanyemba mine – whose disgruntled shareholders had long since given up hope of a worthwhile return on their investment – to Nyaschere. In November 1970, a reporter from the Johannesburg *Financial Mail* confirmed after a visit to the site that both men and materials from Kanyemba were being used at Nyaschere.[56]

Such transactions did not always improve Rowland's image with the Rhodesian authorities, despite the contribution that Lonrho's ventures into copper production were undoubtedly making to the mining sector of the Rhodesian economy. Another attempt to raise funds locally occurred early in 1969, when, as part of its share deal with Slater Walker in London,[57] Lonrho had acquired the Rhodesian Wattle Company Ltd. Rhodesian Wattle was based in Umtali, where it employed around 2,500 Africans and between 80 and 100 Europeans. It owned substantial estates and was engaged in a variety of farming operations, in addition to growing wattle and producing wattle extract. In May 1969, Rowland visited Rhodesia on a 'whistle-stop' visit, and circled over the estates in his private plane.[58] It was then announced that a drastic trimming operation was to take place; all the sidelines that had grown up alongside the wattle interests were to be wound up; 5,000 head of cattle and the company's houses in Umtali were to be sold; and the headquarters shifted to Salisbury. The assets disposed of in this way would have raised an estimated £1½ million there and then, and possibly a further £2 million in the longer term from the sale of land.[59] On the other hand, it would have made well over half of Rhodesian Wattle's white staff redundant, a situation that neither they nor the Rhodesian government – who since UDI had taken considerable pains to encourage European immigration through the prospect of skilled and well-paid jobs – was prepared to countenance. The white employees' representatives pressed their case to the Minister of Commerce and Industry, Mr Mussett; and ten days later the government gazetted an order under the Emergency Regulations (Control of Manpower) preventing the dismissal of any employee without the express authority of the Minister of Labour. Rowland's attempt to trim the company's operations was effectively blocked; and from now on, Rhodesian Wattle, along with oil supplies and the motor trade, was a 'controlled industry' under Rhodesian law.[60] 'With this and the closing of his Beira-to-Umtali oil pipeline, few can blame Rowland from [sic] feeling pretty fed up with Rhodesia', commented the *Financial Mail*. 'He should be allowed to go ahead with his plans . . .'.[61] Despite such setbacks, both Inyati and Nyaschere were brought into successful production and there is no evidence that capital for the ventures was required in addition to that available on the Rhodesian market.

Another cause for concern voiced in the British press was that Coronation Syndicate, Lonrho's South African subsidiary, was exporting copper from its Rhodesian mines after UDI contrary to United Nations sanctions. After 1965 there was certainly extremely limited scope for selling the output of two large copper mines inside Rhodesia itself, yet all these ventures showed handsome profits. The mine that was named in connection with these suspicions by the British press was the Edmundian in Mozambique.[62]

The Edmundian mine was an old shaft that had produced copper on and off since 1903 and had in the past been worked by Portuguese interests. It had reportedly not been active for a number of years when it came into Coronation's possession. In July 1968, Corsyn Consolidated Mines Ltd acquired an option to purchase the Edmundian mine for 70,000 rand from Hochmetals, a Johannesburg-based metal-dealing firm whose parent firm was a Brazilian mining company. Further payments of either 80,000 rand or royalties of up to 130,000 rand were due if the mine proved to be workable. In September 1969 Corsyn transferred its rights in Edmundian to Eastern minerals, another wholly-owned Rhodesian subsidiary of Coronation Syndicate.[63] In January 1970, however, the option was ceded to the Henderson group of wholly-owned Lonrho subsidiaries on the grounds that Coronation, which had been carrying out a programme of heavy capital expenditure, did not have the ready money to develop the mine.

At Coronation's Annual Meeting on 11 March 1970, the chairman, Richard Lee, said that 'prior to cession of the option no exploratory drilling was undertaken on the property', and that while 'about 130m of underground driving had been done . . . no economic orebody had been found'.[64] As there had been no engineer's report available on the mine at the time that Coronation had acquired the option either, clearly rather little was known about its potential. Fifteen months later, however, in April/May 1971, it was duly reported in the South African press that the Edmundian mine had been opened up by Lonrho and, according to official sources in Lourenço Marques, was milling at the rate of 2,000 tons of ore a month, to be raised to 10,000 by the end of that year.[65] It was estimated that by then, the mine could be bringing in a gross revenue of 1.5 million rand, and the speed with which the whole operation had been conducted, from the initial exploratory surveys through to production itself, left observers bemused. 'Lonrho shareholders . . . will be pleased that this entrepreneurial risk has been so handsomely rewarded,' commented the *Financial Mail*. 'Indeed, the mine seems to have come to production so rapidly that there has not, as yet, been an opportunity to give shareholders any information about it . . .'.[66]

On 13 August 1969, just before Coronation acquired its option to purchase Edmundian from Hochmetals, the British government sent a Note to the United Nations Sanctions Committee, expressing fears about the real purpose to which the Edmundian copper mine was shortly going to be put. The mine had been purchased, according to the text of the Note, by an unnamed 'Johannesburg Company', although it had not been worked for a number of years and had been written off as a 'completely uneconomic proposition' by an expert who had carried out an investigation in 1968. According to information that had been made available to the Foreign Office, however, plans were now in hand to reopen the mine and bring it into production that very month, August 1969. The Sanctions Committee was warned that:

The purpose of this activity is understood to be to provide a cover for Rhodesian copper exports. Copper may be shipped by rail to Beira and Lourenço Marques where it may be redocumented as originating from the Edmundian Mine: the actual production from the Edmundian Mine may amount to only a small proportion of the volume of copper exported and declared as originating from that mine.

According to the same information production has not yet begun at the Edmundian Mine, but a shipment of Rhodesian copper has already been falsely documented and described as originating from that mine.[67]

The shipment to which the Note referred consisted of bags of copper concentrates, each marked with three distinctive purple stripes, that had been loaded at Beira on 18 April 1969 onto a Dutch ship, 'Tjipondik'. Its cargo was destined for Japan, and the shipper was Hochmetals, a company that had in fact been repeatedly named in Notes to the Sanctions Committee for its dealings in Rhodesian metal products.[68]

The British government had warned the Sanctions Committee of their suspicions about the origin of the 'Tjipondik's' cargo in an earlier Note dated 12 May 1969. They had also pointed out that according to the figures published in the official monthly bulletin of statistics of the Province of Mozambique, no copper or copper concentrates were at that time being produced in the territory.[69] The Sanctions Committee circulated UN member states, while the 'Tjipondik' steamed serenely on towards Japan, calling at ports along the East African coast, Singapore and Hong Kong. On 26 May it entered Kobe harbour and was investigated by the

Japanese authorities. The cargo consisted of around 500 tons of copper concentrates, together with a Certificate of Origin issued by the Chamber of Commerce in Beira, stating that they were of Mozambican origin. In view of the fears that had been aroused, the Japanese withheld customs clearance but then informed the Sanctions Committee in October that they judged the cargo to be genuine. (A second shipment of copper, however, packed in exactly the same type of purple-striped bags and loaded at Beira on 4 June on the 'Eizan Maru', was sent back to Beira by the Japanese authorities after docking at Yokohama on 7 July.)

It was in July 1968, of course, that Coronation's subsidiary, Corsyn, acquired the option over Edmundian from Hochmetals of Johannesburg. According to what Lee, the chairman of Coronation, later said, no exploratory drilling had been undertaken and no economic orebody had been found when the option was ceded to Henderson's in January 1970. The South African and Rhodesian press in due course reported the fact in 1971 when the mine was brought into production under Lonrho's management. In the light of these later reports the Edmundian mine could not have been producing substantial amounts of copper at any time in 1969. Where, then, had the cargoes of the 'Tjipondik' and the 'Eizan Maru' come from?

In 1973 the former Company Secretary of Hochmetals, who it now emerged had been the British Foreign Office's original informant on the Edmundian affair, gave an interview to Charles Raw of the *Observer* in London. He had resigned from Hochmetals, he said, because of his misgivings about the sanctions-busting operations which he was called upon to help organize. Hochmetals, he told the newspaper, had been Lonrho's agents in South Africa for the export of copper from the Inyati mine for some time. To begin with, there was little difficulty in transmitting it for sale on world markets under 'South African' Certificates of Origin. In 1968, however, Hochmetals began to look around for alternative outlets as buyers in various parts of the world became more discriminating, and the United Nations made efforts to tighten up the sanctions net. It was then that the company hit upon the idea of using the Edmundian mine as a 'front' for Lonrho's copper, shipping it from Beira or Lourenço Marques accompanied by false Mozambican documents.[70] The old shaft could be opened up and made to produce enough copper to pass muster at any investigation that might be conducted. Consignments of copper from inside Rhodesia would meanwhile use Edmundian as a staging-post *en route* for shipment from Mozambique.

On the basis of this evidence, Lonrho's subsidiaries in South Africa and Rhodesia were involved in a calculated operation to leap the United Nations sanctions barrier. However, no evidence of a direct connection between the Lonrho group and Hochmetals was put before the UN Sanctions Committee.* The only further information on the 'Tjipondik's' cargo to be made available to the United Nations' Sanctions Committee was of a decidedly negative kind. In a reply to the Secretary-General of the United Nations dated 15 July 1970, the Japanese government informed the Committee that they had undertaken an on-the-spot investigation of the Edmundian mine between late July and early August 1967 – when it was still in Hochmetals' possession. The Japanese authorities had 'collected information on the production, shipment and export of copper products from the competent Mozambique authorities, as well as from persons associated with the said mine'. Who these were was not specified. However, 'as a result of the investigation, it became clear that the mine had not been abandoned but that it had been producing copper though on a small scale, and had accumulated a stock of copper products'.[71] Richard Lee, however, stated at Coronation's Annual General Meeting a few months later, in March 1970, that 'no economic orebody had been found' at that time. The Japanese government gave permission for the 'Tjipondik's' cargo, which had been impounded at Kobe since 26 May of that year, to be imported, and 'did not seek to obtain the producer's certificate concerning the copper concentrates in question'.[72]

It was at this point that the Edmundian affair would seem to have been dropped by the authorities concerned. Lonrho was never named in any Note to the Sanctions Committee.

It is quite clear from the figures available to the United Nations that, in general, sanctions against Rhodesia were bypassed on an extensive scale from the mid-1960s on. Companies involved in sanctions-breaking activities obviously took pains to cover their tracks; and as far as the great majority of British firms with

* Considerable detail of the negotiations involving Edmundian was published in July 1976 in the Report of the Inspectors of the Department of Trade.

branches in Rhodesia was concerned, such evidence as existed was almost entirely circumstantial.

The Lonrho group had other interests in Rhodesia producing exportable commodities; in 1973, for example, Lonrho owned 400,000 hectares of ranching land in Rhodesia, supporting 60,000 cattle.[73] There were other ranches in Swaziland, although these were less extensive. Meat and meat products were traditionally among Rhodesia's most important exports. In July 1974 a Rhodesian subsidiary of Lonrho, the Norton Motor Company (Pvt) Ltd, was named in the British press in connection with the import of Datsun-Nissan car kits for assembly inside Rhodesia. The information had come into the hand of the *Sunday Times* in documents originally supplied by Mr Kenneth McIntosh, the Scottish banker imprisoned earlier that year by the Smith regime for leaking information about the arrangements made to finance the expansion of the Rhodesian Iron and Steel Corporation with European and American capital. According to the McIntosh papers and to Datsun-Nissan's shipping agent in Japan, the Norton Motor Company was in 1974 in receipt of Datsun kits imported through Mozambique by an agent called Gerber. Gerber's parent company, Gerber-Goldschmidt of Switzerland, had a branch in Rhodesia, which was in turn a shareholder in Norton.[74] (The Norton Motor Company was one of those acquired by Lonrho from Rowland. In 1973, it was listed in Braby's Commercial Directory of South, East and Central Africa as the sole agents in Rhodesia for Mercedes-Benz, and as agents for Toyota.)

Naturally, the London board denied the charges of sanctions-breaking which were from time to time brought against Lonrho, and in June 1973 the company protested very strongly over allegations made by Denis Healey, then Labour's Shadow Chancellor, in a press release.[75] Nearly a year later, Rowland, questioned on the issue of sanctions, assured *Africa* that, to his knowledge, no Lonrho subsidiary was engaged in sanctions-busting.[76]

There are several reasons why the extent to which Rhodesia continued to trade with the outside world after UDI was out of all proportion to the number of prosecutions actually brought against those who were assisting the Smith regime to do so. No effective international machinery was created for enforcing sanctions legislation; and the arrangements for apprehending suspected cases of breaking and avoidance, involving a number of separate watchdog committees as well as the authorities of the various countries concerned, were slow and cumbersome. At the request of the Sanctions Committee, the UN Secretary-General would circulate relevant information to member governments, but it was their sole responsibility to take action against their own nationals. The cargo of the 'Tjipondik', for example, was not impounded until it had reached Japan, the country for which it was destined, although it had already been investigated by the authorities of both the Netherlands and Hong Kong. After UDI, there continued to be considerable scope – notably by making use of strategic South African connections – for British and other foreign firms with Rhodesian subsidiaries to continue to operate there without breaking the letter of the law; and even greater scope for activities which, while certainly not in the spirit of United Nations resolutions on the subject, left very little evidence behind them. The right of British companies to retain their assets in Rhodesia, and even to expand their operations there, was never in question under the law, so long as parent boards could produce evidence that they no longer had control over their Rhodesian subsidiaries and that the latter were not receiving any funds directly from Britain. On 15 June 1970, the British representative to the United Nations Sanctions Committee, speaking at its thirty-fourth meeting, said that

It was meaningless to talk of removing fixed capital assets from Southern Rhodesia. Moreover, it had long been accepted that associate companies should not be subordinate to their parent companies and should act independently in accordance with the laws of the country in which they conducted their business.[77]

The implication that Rhodesia, a state in rebellion against the Crown and whose government had never been recognized by any other country, possessed laws which other nationals were bound to obey, was a surprising one.

At the time of the boardroom dispute in 1973, the Conservative government was asked in both Houses of Parliament to spell out what action it proposed to take against Lonrho in view of the allegations of sanctions-breaking that had been made about the company. The answers were designed to reassure questioners by directing them to the investigation then being carried out by the Department of Trade and Industry. Lady Tweedsmuir, Minister of State for Foreign Affairs in the House of Lords, replied to Lord

Caradon on 20 June that 'specific allegations about breaches of control were being investigated. As far as Lonrho was concerned, she said she did not think it right to comment "before an investigation had been conducted".'[78] It was feared that sanctions were rather low down on the list of priorities as far as the Department of Trade and Industry was concerned. Their investigations at the time helped Lonrho to shift the spotlight of publicity away from its dealings with the Smith regime. In May 1974 Rowland, challenged on the sanctions issue, suggested that 'as the Department of Trade and Industry in Britain is still investigating, perhaps the matter could be regarded as *sub judice*'.[79] The DTI inquiry, however, did not preclude comment or discussion on the company's operations in Rhodesia.

Official encouragement of mining ventures and generous subsidies for white farmers, on top of the ample support forthcoming from South Africa and Portugal, enabled the Rhodesian economy to expand in the years following UDI. Up to 1972, it achieved an average real growth rate of 5.9 per cent a year; in 1972, it topped 8.4 per cent; and in 1973, despite a severe drought, it still managed to reach 6.5 per cent.[80] The expansion of the mining sector was particularly spectacular. Lonrho's Rhodesian subsidiaries unquestionably contributed to the growth of the Rhodesian economy. Apart from Coronation's Rhodesian subsidiaries, David Whitehead (Rhodesia), for example, flourished in the absence of foreign competition following UDI. The clamp-down on imports meant an upsurge in demand for locally-produced cloth; and by the end of 1973 the chairman, Sir Peter Bednall, could report: 'The group is now operating at maximum activity. Further growth now depends on additional plant, and it is the intention of the board to expand as soon as foreign currency is made available for this purpose.'[81] Zambezi Coachworks Ltd, one of Lonrho's most important acquisitions in Rhodesia since UDI, also had a part to play. In 1973 the local Rhodesian manager pointed out that 'the output of this one company represents an important saving in foreign exchange ... It also plays an important part in assisting both commerce and industry.' In general, he felt that Lonrho in Rhodesia was doing more for the country than people realized; 'we have developed considerably in Rhodesia since we became autonomous after UDI,' he remarked.[82]

By continuing to operate inside Rhodesia after 1965, Lonrho's subsidiaries were more than just a morale-booster for the beleaguered whites. Their development was in line with the post-UDI trends of import substitution and expansion of the mining and agricultural sectors, and they earned profits which could be ploughed back to finance further development schemes. The acquisition of new subsidiaries for Lonrho's Rhodesian portfolio was only one indication that there was no shortage of cash in Salisbury. Without such support from British and other foreign firms, the Smith government would have been hard put to it to survive at all. Lonrho was, after all, a company whose roots in Rhodesia went back long before its meteoric rise in black Africa, and its subsidiaries employed several respected members of the Rhodesian business establishment. Major-General Sir Peter Bednall, for example, the chairman of David Whitehead (Rhodesia), was also in 1974 the Branch President of the London-based Institute of Directors. The London Council included Angus Ogilvy, and its South African Branch President was Harry Oppenheimer of Anglo-American. Mr B. Hewitt, the Managing Director of Rhodesian Wattle, taken over by Lonrho from Slater Walker in 1969, was at the time a director of the Reserve Bank of Rhodesia. In 1966 Hewitt had been appointed to the committee of the local branch of the Anglo-Rhodesian Society, a London-based organization, which actively supported the Smith regime and opposed the imposition of international sanctions.[83] Duncan Sandys, appointed as Lonrho's chairman in 1972, had been another prominent advocate within the British political establishment of the case against sanctions. Lonrho, whose Rhodesian connections were undoubtedly an embarrassment in its dealings with independent African states, had a strong vested interest in a settlement between the British government and the Smith regime. After UDI, the Beira–Umtali pipeline had developed into something of a white elephant, while the profits from Lonrho's Rhodesian operations, leaving Coronation Syndicate aside, were for the time being effectively beyond the reach of its shareholders in London.

Lonrho's Rhodesian interests, notwithstanding, were highly lucrative. The profits they actually contributed to the group were an aspect of its financial performance that provoked considerable speculation, and estimates varied widely. In 1974, for example, the right-wing Rhodesian monthly, *Property and Finance*, using the evidence available on the spot to observers in Rhodesia and South Africa, arrived at a figure of close on seventy-five per cent for Rhodesia's contribution to the group's net attributable profits (i.e. after tax but before minority interests). This was in some contrast to Gerald Percy's estimate the year before, of around twenty-two per cent of the group profit after both tax and minority interests.[84]

Discrepancies on this scale can perhaps be explained in part by Coronation Syndicate's ambiguous position as a company incorporated in South Africa but earning its money in Rhodesia. *Property and Finance* included Coronation in its calculations of Lonrho's Rhodesian profits; but in situations where minimizing the Rhodesian interests carried a diplomatic pay-off, it could well have been expedient to exclude this particular company. Lonrho, moreover, had its own definition of 'Southern Africa', and one which was at variance with much established usage. From 1970, when the group first began to give regional breakdowns of its earnings, 'Rhodesia' was included in the Annual Reports under 'East and Central Africa', while 'Southern Africa' was defined as 'Botswana, South Africa, Swaziland and Lesotho'. This did not merely leave a very large question mark over the final destination of Coronation Syndicate's profits in the regional breakdown, but it ignored the political and economic realities of the white-dominated southern tip of the continent.

The treatment of the Rhodesian assets after UDI was an unconventional one in another respect as well; in contrast to those of Rio Tinto-Zinc, Lonrho's Rhodesian profits were consolidated in the group accounts with those from other parts of Africa and Europe. In 1974 the Lonrho Investment Company and the other subsidiaries in Rhodesia did not publish separate Annual Reports and referred an inquiry to Lonrho in London.[85] In 1973 Lonrho's chief accountant, Roger Moss, explained the practice of consolidation in an interview on the grounds of his belief that 'the exclusion of Rhodesian assets from the group balance sheet would present shareholders with a very misleading picture'.[86] His remarks suggested, at the very least, that the assets involved were substantial.

In September 1968 a private survey of Lonrho undertaken by a commercial firm calculated that the effect of a Rhodesian settlement would be to add half a million pounds to Lonrho's profits (after minority interests but before tax), as a result of the freeing of Rhodesian earnings. Overall, the survey 'strongly recommended' the purchase of Lonrho shares.[87] For the financial year ending on 30 September 1968 Lonrho's pre-tax profit was £7.2 million, and its net profit after both tax and minority interests was £2.6 million. Between 1968 and 1973, of course, Lonrho opened up two major copper mines in Rhodesia, took over Rhodesian Wattle and Zambezi Coachworks, and expanded David Whitehead's textile production plant. In November 1971, when the prospects for a settlement in the wake of the Pearce Commission's visit to Rhodesia seemed bright in the City, the *Sunday Times* calculated that 'No less than twenty-eight per cent . . . of the group's £16 million pre-tax profits come from its Rhodesian interests, and though these have continued – with the exception of the famous Beira–Umtali pipeline – to make money over the past five years all income has remained blocked in Rhodesia.'[88] By the 1972 financial year, Rhodesia was still said to be contributing around a quarter of the pre-tax profits; but between September 1972 and September 1973, Coronation Syndicate more than tripled its earnings, and in 1974 was well on the way to doubling them again. All the evidence suggests that from UDI up to 1973, the expansion of Lonrho's operations in Rhodesia kept well in pace with the growth of the Lonrho group as a whole; and in 1974, when the spin-off from the boom in commodity prices was added to the completion of the Inyati development programme, it may well have outstripped it on a considerable scale. Yet it was during the winter of 1973–74, as the profits flowing into South Africa from the Inyati mine approached flood-like proportions, that Rowland found himself able to assure the Organization of African Unity of the unimportance of Lonrho's southern African interests. In May, 1974, Rowland, interviewed by *Africa*, said:

I can assure [you] that I am not aware that any Lonrho subsidiary is engaged in sanctions-busting. I would be very, very disturbed if the contrary were the case. However, I should like to point out that our Rhodesia company, Lonrho Investment Company, is obliged to comply with the general policy of the illegal Rhodesia regime and we have no control whatever over its activities. The same goes for other Rhodesian companies in which Lonrho has interests.[89]

According to Lonrho's 1970 and 1973 Annual Reports, where the same wording appeared, the group's Rhodesian operations had since UDI 'been under the control of local boards following the resignation of all senior Lonrho executives'. As far as British law in 1974 was concerned, the directors of British-based companies with Rhodesian subsidiaries could not be considered responsible for illicit dealings with the regime so long as evidence could be brought forward that these resulted exclusively from decisions taken by completely autonomous local boards. This, the London board maintained, was precisely Lonrho's situation.

Despite UDI, there were never any major obstacles in the path of close liaison between London and Johannesburg, the head-quarters of Coronation Syndicate. Sydney Newman, for example, the managing director of Lonrho South Africa and in 1974 the chairman of Coronation Syndicate, was in close touch with Cheapside House and was present at the Annual General Meeting held in March 1974 in the London Hilton Hotel. Two other directors of Coronation in 1973–74, Richard Lee and Denis O'Donovan, were in fact British subjects and the company was represented in London on transfer work by a committee which included Frederick Butcher. From South Africa, it was easy enough to reach Salisbury, carrying a British passport or other-wise.

Rowland himself certainly visited Rhodesia after UDI, and it was after his 1969 visit that the decision was made to run down a sizeable proportion of the assets of the Rhodesian Wattle Company. He remained on the board of Nyaschere Copper until the summer of 1969, nearly four years after UDI, and his father-in-law, Lionel Taylor, in addition to staying on at Gatooma as Rowland's farm manager, served on the boards of both Nyaschere Copper and Eastern Minerals, the Rhodesian subsidiary of Coronation. Rhodesia was by no means cut off from the outside world after UDI; in Lonrho's case, as in that of other British companies, it would have been highly surprising if contacts be-tween London and Salisbury had broken down entirely. At all events, the profits of Coronation Syndicate set the seal on the status of Rhodesia as a vital and continuing area of the group's operations.

Nine

The Sudanese Springboard

In the early months of 1971 Rowland made the first decisive moves to establish Lonrho in Sudan, Africa's largest country in size if not in population. Sudan was a bridge between black Africa and the Arab world, combining an Arab culture in its northern provinces with black African traditions in the south, where in 1971 a bitter secessionist war was still raging. It seems likely that Rowland first met his closest Sudanese ally, Khalil Osman, in West Africa.[1] At any rate, their personal friendship soon became a close one, and this was to become an important political factor.

General Numeiry's government had come to power in 1969 through a broadly-based left-wing *coup*, supported by the Communist Party of Sudan. He had at first included several communists within the cabinet and adopted left-wing policies, including the nationalization of many foreign-owned businesses and indigenous firms. But although Osman was the richest and most successful Sudanese entrepreneur, his interests escaped nationalization. Gradually the Numeiry administration tried to rid itself of its left-wing allies. In February 1971 Numeiry issued a stern warning to the communists, whom he accused of attempting to sabotage the planned Federation of Arab Republics between Egypt, Libya and Sudan. The accusation was not unjustified, but it was not only the communists who were opposed to the federal plans, as later became clear. To the military leaders in Egypt and Libya, Khartoum's remaining left-wing bias was unacceptable. For this and other reasons, the Sudanese government was trying to rebuild its bridges with the West, attempting in particular to resume economic links with Britain.

British aid had been halted the previous year because of the nationalization of British banks and other interests. But after the arrival of a Lonrho mission in Khartoum in June, talks about a £10 million British credit for Sudan, to be underwritten by the Export Credit Guarantee Department, were started. The talks took place in London between a Sudanese delegation which had arrived on 10 July and British government officials. Lonrho helped the Sudanese to negotiate the credit.[2] There were curious aspects to the ECGD deal. A credit of £10 million seemed large by comparison with Britain's exports to the country, which were running at about £12 million a year. It was also out of keeping with British policy, particularly under a Conservative government, to be so helpful to a country which had nationalized British assets and not yet offered acceptable compensation terms.

On 19 July 1971 Sudan's left-wing officers, the Free Officers Movement, which had grown increasingly concerned at Numeiry's moves to the right, staged a coup which put them into power and Numeiry into prison. Three days later this coup was reversed by Egypt and Libya. In the confusion of that week the main event, for international and particularly British opinion, was the forced landing in Libya of a BOAC plane, carrying two of the revolutionary Sudanese leaders on a scheduled flight back to Khartoum. The officers were arrested by the Libyans and executed, together with many other left-wingers, on Numeiry's orders a few days later.

To understand what happened and the implications of the events, it is necessary to examine the movements of some of the principal persons involved on a day-to-day basis.

10 July. The Sudanese negotiating team arrived in London, led by the Sudanese Defence Minister, General Hassan Abbas. Also in the party were the Treasury Minister, Mohammed Halim, and the Industries Minister, Ahmad Suleiman – a former communist who had remained loyal to Numeiry. Present also were two senior ministers, the Tank Corps Commander, Brigadier Awad Khalif, and the Quartermaster General, Brigadier Siddick Hamad. Osman assisted at the negotiations.

18 July. The Sudanese team, with the exception of Halim and Osman, left for Belgrade.

19 July. Halim spent the night of 19 July at the Sudanese embassy in London. He was to have left for Kuwait the following day, but on hearing of the left-wing coup he changed his destination for Cairo. In Sudan, Major Hashim al-Atta took power in a bloodless overthrow of the Numeiry regime. But the leader of the Free Officers Movement, Lieut-Colonel Babiker el-Nur, and another left-wing leader, Major Faruk Osman Hamdallah, were in London. Their stay, they said, was 'coincidental'; el-Nur was in Britain for medical treatment. El-Nur was nominated Sudan's new president, and both prepared to return to Khartoum surrounded by publicity about all their moves.

20 July. A Lonrho jet (the Mystère) flew to Yugoslavia to pick up the Defence Minister, Abbas, and his party and rush them back to the Middle East. They arrived in secrecy at Cairo that night, where they met Halim.[3]

21 July. The Sudanese party, headed by Abbas, arrived in Tripoli, accompanied by the Egyptian War Minister. Abbas broadcast over Libyan radio, ordering an armed force loyal to Numeiry to advance on Khartoum. According to a subsequent statement by Colonel Gadaffi, the Libyan leader, the meeting of Sudanese, Egyptian and Libyan leaders that day 'made their plan with maps' and resolved 'to support the Sudanese people against those who rose against them'.[4] The first plan was to enter Sudan within seven days, but this was abandoned when it was realized that el-Nur and Hamdallah were in transit to Khartoum.

22 July. The BOAC plane carrying the two Sudanese revolutionaries had a special dispensation from the revolutionary government to land at Khartoum, which was otherwise closed. During the early hours it arrived in Libyan air space and was ordered by the Libyans to land at Benina. The pilot, Captain Bowyer, had already been in touch with BOAC headquarters in London because his course had been queried by several air traffic controllers; he ignored the order to land and turned back towards Rome. As he approached Maltese air space, he was given clearance by the Maltese. A few miles from safety he received another Libyan message: 'For the sake of the safety of all souls on board, land at Benina, or your aircraft will be bombed.' There were reports on subsequent days that Malta refused landing permission at the last minute, but this has been vigorously denied by the Maltese. Captain Bowyer landed at Benina, and the two Sudanese leaders agreed to leave the plane for the sake of the other passengers who would otherwise have been endangered.

The arrest of the two leaders, according to a member of the Libyan government, caused Libya and Egypt to 'cancel the plan to intervene within one week and substitute it with a plan calling for intervention within twenty-four hours'.[5] As a result of Abbas' broadcast, the Egyptian military academy inside Sudan seized Khartoum airport, and Egyptian troops were flown in large air carriers to Khartoum and to the Egyptian air base fifteen miles north of the capital.

By 24 July, Numeiry was back in the saddle, executing his enemies and praising the role of Defence Minister Abbas. By rushing Abbas back to the Middle East in time to organize the counter-coup and to consult with the Libyans about forcing down the BOAC plane, Lonrho played a small but crucial part in changing the course of political events. President Sadat of Egypt admitted that he had intervened to bring down the revolutionary government: 'Our teeth are sharp – as was proved in the case of the Sudan.'[6]

In London, Joseph Godber, Minister of State at the Foreign Office, said that his government took 'a most serious view' of the action taken by the Libyans in forcing down the plane.[7] A week later, after the execution of the two leaders, Britain's representative at the United Nations sent a letter to the Secretary-General, U Thant, which said that the incident had 'grave international implications'.[8] The Libyans remained unperturbed and there was wide press speculation that Western, and probably British, intelligence services had assisted in the kidnapping of the Sudanese officers. *The Times*, for instance, said that 'the speed of the operation and the forcing down of the BOAC plane have suggested to many that Western intelligence agencies were involved. This is possible'.[9]

Despite the appeal by Sir Alec Douglas Home, Britain's Foreign Secretary, to Numeiry to save the lives of el-Nur and Hamdallah, and the fact that this went unheeded, relations between Britain and Sudan improved. As far as Lonrho was concerned, the next few weeks saw a number of significant developments, indicating its standing with both the British and Sudanese authorities. Rowland, Osman and Sandys were later said to be the only people in the months following the coup who could see Numeiry without appointment.[10] Osman went on television in Khartoum within days of Numeiry's counter-coup to congratulate all concerned for triumphing over the red menace. By coincidence, perhaps, on 26 July Britain's Overseas Development Administration issued a press release announcing the appointment of Colonel W. H. L. Gordon as 'adviser on private investment' in developing countries to the Foreign Office, of which the Overseas Development Administration was a part. He had just resigned as Managing Director of Lonrho (Exports) Ltd. At the beginning of August there were rumours that Lonrho was to become buying agent for the Sudanese government for all official purchases in Britain. A Lonrho spokesman said that he was 'not prepared to make any comment at all' about any kind of deal.[11] But an agency report on 1 September announced that Lonrho (Exports) had been appointed by Sudan 'as sole agents for state purchases of capital and semi-capital goods in the United Kingdom'. Lonrho (Exports) also agreed to act as purchasing agents for the Sudanese government in other countries, when required to do so.[12] The agreement for the ECGD £10 million credit, which Lonrho had helped to negotiate, was signed in Sudan on 28 August. The Sudanese Industries Minister, Ahmed Suleiman, who had been part of the negotiating team which visited London in July, announced that the British government had granted Sudan one hundred scholarships worth nearly £100,000.

Some people suggested that Britain's new readiness to help Khartoum involved more than an improvement in economic relations. A correspondent in the *Guardian* found that there were 'political overtones to the £10 million investment guarantee . . . and the interest which the British finance company, Lonrho, is showing in the Sudanese project'.[13] The first major purchase that Lonrho made for Sudan involved Massey-Ferguson tractors worth £2 million. As Massey-Ferguson had been associated with Sudanese agricultural development since 1946, it was not quite clear what specific service Lonrho was rendering. In the past, the buying of British goods had been done through the Sudanese embassy, whose purchasing department performed this service at a cost which was said not to exceed 0.2 per cent of the value; Lonrho's charge was fixed at 2 per cent of the total, plus bank interest charges for the financial services involved in the transactions.[14] To some extent Lonrho's sole purchasing rights annoyed Sudanese officials who had been accustomed to break their routine with visits overseas to carry out such deals.

Lonrho did not remain a passive buying agent. By the end of 1972 it had announced a scheme for the joint production of sugar with the Sudanese government and a deal with Osman's company, Gulf International, for a textile factory. This, it was reported, 'is the type of investment venture that is most likely to bring success at a time when Sudan is disenchanted with the Soviet bloc and is trying to build bridges to the West'.[15] There was praise for Numeiry's new policy of favouring private investment which was often linked with Rowland's company: 'For Britain, Lonrho has been leading the search for fresh investment opportunities as the

Khartoum revolutionary regime modifies the nationalization drive in 1969 and 1970.'[16] A new law – the Development and Promotion of Industrial Investment Act, 1972 – exempted companies whose production was based on local raw materials from profits tax for the first five years of operation and reduced their obligations for further periods. Such concerns also enjoyed other privileges, including freedom from customs duty on imported machinery and raw materials, lower electricity charges and favourable leasehold terms for land. Repatriation of profits was to be free, as was withdrawal of capital. 'The proposed Lonrho deals seem the type of venture most likely to succeed in Sudan, and President Numeiry has commended the company's attitude.'[17]

In March 1973 agreement was reached between London and Khartoum on the question of compensation for the assets of British companies nationalized in 1970. It was a fitting end to Numeiry's state visit to Britain that month, and the agreement included military co-operation. During the visit, he spent a day at Hedsor Wharf; Rowland boasted:

> When President Numeiry of the Sudan was in London on a State visit, he dined with the Queen at Buckingham Palace, with Mr Heath at 10 Downing Street. He also came and spent the day with me – the President, his entire Cabinet of sixteen, and a variety of ambassadors.[18]

British advisers were already at the staff college in Khartoum. Now it was openly stated that Sudan would be purchasing military equipment, though it is not certain whether such requirements were considered to be capital or semi-capital goods of the kind mentioned in Lonrho's buying agency contract. Discussions on the supply of British military equipment had been going on for over a year, linked with a possible further loan. Once compensation was agreed, British aid was resumed. *The Times* reported a programme 'worth £15.7 million for the next four years. A number of suggestions for military co-operation were also examined.'[19]

Sudan's economy had not yet improved to any marked extent, despite the new welcome given to foreign investment. The International Monetary Fund had vainly urged Khartoum to cut expenditure, but Osman scoffed at the economists' concern over inflation: 'Put $21,000 million into Egypt and the price of land will double. But put that amount into Sudan and we have the land – we will absorb it like a sponge.'[20] The Economy Minister, Ibrahim Mansour – also a director of Osman's enterprises – agreed that there was no solution to Sudan's development problems except more development. He was leading a campaign to revitalize private business and to open the door to foreign investment.

Cotton was responsible for 60 per cent of the country's foreign exchange earnings. But debt-servicing consumed about 12 per cent of export earnings, and the proportion was thought by some to be as high as 17 per cent. Although the Sudanese foreign debt was high and rising rapidly, Lonrho's confidence was not shaken, and one of the company's officials made the commendable observation that 'there is no point in waiting for a country to become rich. If you give it help in development, the country will be able to repay its debts.'[21] Lonrho estimated that Sudan would have no debt-servicing problem once revenue started to flow in from agricultural development schemes. Sudan, according to the company, should be able to absorb an inflow of around $500 million in investment. *African Development* commented that 'in its unofficial "merchant bank" role, Lonrho has been gingering up British aid to Sudan, and awaking [sic] the British Government to the possibilities of trade. As a start the Export Credit Guarantee Bank has extended £10 million of cover to British exporters, which in turn has acted as a pump primer, with the American Export-Import Bank coming in to cover the new fleet of Boeing 737s, and the Japanese and French equivalents also under pressure by their businessmen to extend guarantees.'[22]

Lonrho advised the Khartoum government to lessen its dependence on cotton and put new irrigated acreages under sugar cane. When the sugar scheme was first mooted, the cost was estimated at £40 million and the project was publicized as the largest development in the country after Gezira cotton. Lonrho was to manage, arrange finance for, and have a forty-nine per cent stake (in partnership with the government) in the undertaking. The company anticipated no problems with finance because the scheme would be self-financing, with the export of sugar repaying the foreign debt. Arab interests were reported to have expressed willingness to put up some of the money. Britain's Overseas Development Administration had agreed to underwrite Lonrho's feasibility study. An ODA press release said that this 'support is being given under its new scheme for encouraging pre-investment studies by British firms in developing countries'.[23] Lonrho then applied to the British government for financial assistance for the sugar scheme itself, without success. According to an ODA official, the cost of the scheme had grown so great that Lonrho experienced difficulty in finding backers for it. *Initial* production was given as 'approximately 300,000 metric tons per annum'.[24] In fact, expected total consumption in Sudan for 1976–7 – the target date for Lonrho's first sugar-crushing season – was 380,000 tons, and the two existing factories were expected to produce half of domestic needs. Lonrho was not the first or only foreign expert in the field.

For a time nothing new was heard of the Lonrho venture, and there seem to have been difficulties about finding a suitable site. By the end of 1973 the site was reported to be Kenana, and initial production was now put at only 125,000 tons and Lonrho's final target at 300,000 tons; when this was reached Lonrho and other sugar producers should have achieved a surplus of 200,000 tons for export, reported *African Development*. 'Three quarters of this figure has been provisionally allocated as Lonrho's quota.'[25] Lonrho was to get Arab finance in return for assured future sugar supplies.

The general impression created was that Lonrho was an enormous boon to Sudan, not only in creating a new industry where none had existed, but also in reducing the import bill and creating export earnings which would be used to pay Sudan's debts. When Booker McConnell announced in January 1974 that its subsidiary, Fletcher and Stewart, had been awarded a £15.4 million Sudanese government contract for the design and construction of a sugar factory for the north-west Sennar scheme, it became clear that Lonrho's would not be the first factory off the ground.[26] Moreover, Booker McConnell managed to arrange finance through the British EGGD guaranteed credit of £10 million, with the remainder made available by the Kuwait Fund for Arab Development – financial provisions which had until then been connected almost exclusively with the name of Lonrho in Sudan.

Finally, at the end of December 1974, Lonrho's scheme was announced as a joint venture linking European, Japanese and Arab capital with that of the Sudanese government. The cost was given as £77 million, of which £11 million was to be equity and the rest loans. Most of the loan funds were to come from Arab sources. Lonrho was to have a twenty per cent interest, plus the management contract, and the company was said to have spent £1.25 million on preparatory studies since 1971. However, the scheme was behind schedule – production was not expected before November 1977 – and while the sugar estate was said to be capable of expanding to one million tons a year, capacity was set at 350,000 tons of white sugar a year in the immediate future. The scheme was said to be the largest in the world, but the *Investors Chronicle*, commenting that the project would not affect Lonrho's profit and loss account for several years, found it 'surprising' that 'no firm marketing arrangements have been made'.[27] In February 1975 it was reported that Fletcher and Stewart had agreed to a Sudanese government request to advance the date for the start of production from August 1976 to December 1975. This request was probably linked with serious student protests in December 1974, after the Numeiry government had raised sugar prices.

Lonrho's textile scheme might have filled a real need. Despite its vast cotton crop, Sudan imported textiles worth just under twenty per cent of the country's total import bill. The group's partnership with Gulf International was first proposed in 1972 and was for the production of thirty million yards a year of grey cloth, part of which was to have been exported for finishing in Britain, where the textile industry was suffering from the competition of developing countries and man-made textiles. As with so many other Lonrho schemes said to be in the pipeline, nothing more was heard of this.

In 1973 Rowland spoke of even greater things to come: 'We have suggested that Marconi puts up a telecommunications satellite for Sudan ... We have an option to link the Egyptian and Sudanese railway systems ... We would like to link Sudan's railways with the East African systems ...'.[28] There was also talk of a Port Sudan–Khartoum pipeline contract. Most, if not all, of these projects were mentioned in connection with 'Kuwaiti money' – presumably a reference to Osman and his powerful Kuwaiti backers. Osman's purchase of Lonrho shares was announced with a flourish at the Annual General Meeting in 1974.[29] At that time, Kuwaiti interests were variously reported as holding between 3.5 per cent and nearly 10 per cent of the share capital.

Discussing Sudan's development plan soon after the counter-coup, the British financial press had looked for salvation to Osman: 'A fairly substantial amount of private Kuwaiti investment and perhaps money from other sources may come through Mr Khalil Osman, the only Sudanese industrial magnate of any size.'[30] Not that Kuwait had been put off helping Sudan during its socialist phase; the Kuwaiti Arab Development Fund gave nearly 15.5

million Kuwaiti dinars[31] to Sudan between 1961–2 and 1971–2 – more than to any other country. In 1972 Sudan continued to head the list of the Fund's beneficiaries. Arab aid as a whole that year, for Sudan's capital development, amounted to £13 million, out of a £21 million total of foreign aid to Sudan.

The loose ends of what were Lonrho's original development plans – waiting, as it were, to be tied to somebody's purse strings – were a feature of the group's approach elsewhere, too, but their lack of rapid progress on the ground in Sudan was unlikely to have worried Rowland unduly. He had achieved a major objective in fashioning Khartoum into a springboard for his larger visions. These were embodied in his prediction: 'In the future I see a partnership between Western technology, Arab oil money and African resources',[32] a sentence echoed by Sudan's Foreign Minister, Dr Mansour Khalid: 'We envisage as our ultimate aim a partnership between Europe, with her technology and skills, the Arabs, with their oil wealth, and Africa, with her great untapped natural resources . . .'.[33] A few months later Sudan's Minister for Industry and Mining, Moussa Awad Ballal, said, 'My vision is that of European technology being combined with Arab oil money to develop the Sudan.'[34]

Mansour Khalid played a vital role in 1974, when Lonrho wanted to translate Rowland's vision into reality through obtaining the vantage point of oil consultants to the Organization of African Unity.[35] President Numeiry reshuffled his cabinet in January 1975. Mansour Khalid was demoted to become Minister of Education; Numeiry explained ,'I do not want a Foreign Minister at the present time'.[36] According to press reports, the changes followed accusations that the Economy Minister, Ibrahim Mansour, had granted 'seven local businessmen a licence to operate a new import and export company in which the Minister had a personal interest'.[37] Ibrahim Mansour, a member of the board of Gulf International, was dismissed from the government altogether.

In 1973 Rowland, claiming that he had recognized the 'unbeatable combination' of European skills, Arab oil and African potential 'years ago', elaborated on the idea: 'Africa's problem has always been one of finance. I think it quite natural that Africa should look to the Arab countries for their development funds. The Arab countries have the money, and they are already putting it into Africa.' Lonrho was to act as an 'honest broker' between the various parties. Gazing into his crystal ball, Rowland continued: 'In the near future, I see the establishment of a Grand Arab Dinar, not based on the US dollar – which is based on gold – but on oil, which will be by far the most valuable commodity in the future.' The Arab countries, looking for somewhere to invest their money, would be 'pouring billions of new dinars' into the development of Africa.[38]

Some of that spare Arab oil money came to Lonrho at the end of 1974, when Sheikh Nasser Sabah al Ahmed, the son-in-law of the ruler of Kuwait, purchased eight million Lonrho shares on behalf of himself and other Kuwaiti interests. Lonrho told its shareholders that this transaction was additional to 'the 2.9 million shares already held by Sheikh Nasser and his associates'.[39] Sheikh Nasser's family had sponsored Khalil Osman in his early business ventures, and they controlled Gulf International, the Kuwaiti-based firm of which Osman was the managing director. When the share deal between Lonrho and the Kuwaiti princes was announced, Alan Ball said: 'They have been looking at what we have done in Africa and regard us perhaps as a reasonably pro- gressive company. We are involved in some of the things that they like, such as gold and sugar.'[40] At the Extraordinary General Meeting called in December to ratify the transaction, Sandys de- clared in his introductory remarks that Lonrho had established a relationship of mutual confidence with a number of African governments. He went on to say:

In the last year or two, Kuwait, like other Arab countries, has shown an active desire in taking an active part in furthering the economic progress of developing countries in Africa. Sheikh Nasser, who is a keen believer in this policy, rightly recognized that Lonrho, with its widespread contacts and experience, is uniquely placed to provide the organization and qualified personnel to carry out development projects of this kind.[41]

Khalil Osman, who (as at the Annual General Meeting in May of that year) had been invited by the board to address the audience, remarked: 'Thank God you have endorsed the policies that Mr Rowland takes.'[42] Two months later Lonrho announced that it was proposing to issue a further block of equity to Kuwaiti in- terests whose identity was not at first revealed.[43] The sale was to be of 8.8 million new shares, giving the Kuwaitis a total of about 22 per cent of the issued capital. Rowland's share, as a result of this and other dilutions, fell to around 16 per cent. The

Daily Telegraph, reporting this announcement, commented that the money that Lonrho had received from the earlier December transaction 'has already been earmarked for a £2.68 million deal under which Lonrho is buying 29.51 per cent of London Australian and General Exploration from Jessel Securities and for an as-yet-unquantified deal under which Lonrho is buying Balfour Williamson from Lloyds Bank International'.[44] London Australian's interests included a gold mine and other property in South Africa,[45] while Balfour Williamson had assets in Australia, New Zealand, the United States, Brazil, Mexico, Japan and Switzerland. These ventures contrasted with those envisaged by both Sandys and Sheikh Nasser at the Extraordinary General Meeting in December, when they had said that the petrodollars would be used 'to assist developing African countries'.[46]

It may well be that Rowland's introduction into leading Egyptian and Libyan circles was effected by a grateful Numeiry after the defeat of the left-wing coup. In any case, the close co-operation in those critical days between Osman, the pro-Numeiry generals and Egyptian and Libyan ministers established important contacts for Rowland in Tripoli and Cairo. The reports about Lonrho's Libyan petrochemical venture early in 1972[47] originated in Cairo: first reports quoted 'Cairo sources',[48] which were then confirmed by Lonrho spokesmen in London. The Egyptian role in this was interesting, since suggestions that Libya needed Lonrho's oil expertise would scarcely have emanated from Tripoli. 'The project was seen by Libya as its entry into the international scene as a new force in petrochemicals, said the reports from Cairo. They added that this would strengthen Libya's hand in bargaining with international oil companies.'[49] Since Libya's bargaining in 1970 had set the pace for all the other oil price increases which followed in subsequent years, the Libyans hardly needed the assistance of a company like Lonrho which, despite its far-flung interests, had no conceivable hope of affecting international oil giants like Shell or the American companies. (Libya's brilliant technique of negotiating with companies one by one, starting with those least able to afford government-imposed cutbacks in production, broke the united front of the companies. It was a novel bargaining method in the oil industry, with a genuine Libyan flavour.) Lonrho had little to offer the Libyans by way of investment capital, but it may have appeared to have potential as a go-between with British government circles. In April 1973 Rowland said that the British government had asked him to negotiate a compromise with Gadaffi during the previous November, to save British Petroleum's Libyan interests from nationalization; he claimed that a deal was in sight, 'but the Foreign Office just did nothing about it for a fortnight'.[50] In view of Lonrho's part in the 1971 negotiations between the Foreign Office and the Sudanese government, Lonrho may have been closer to diplomatic circles in Whitehall than was generally known.

The Gadaffi government was piling up oil revenues faster than it could spend them. The same was true of many other oil-rich Arab states: in fact, Rowland's declared intention was to get money from the Arabs for his African development plans. Nor was he the sole Western businessman with interesting ideas about the creation of an Arab currency or other suggestions about the utilization of spare oil funds. His main attraction may have been his claim to have influence in black Africa, which at that time was becoming important in the battle for world opinion over the Middle East. In the months leading up to the 1973 Arab–Israeli war, almost all African countries broke off relations with Israel: this followed determined diplomatic campaigning, spearheaded by Libya and supported by Egypt, conducted through the Organization of African Unity. For countries like Kuwait and Saudi Arabia, it had been obvious for some time that the African continent could either protect or threaten their western flank, not only in the context of the Middle East struggle but also as far as revolutionary influences were concerned. Arab investment in Africa always had the twin purposes of creating international allies and strengthening politically 'safe' governments.

Sudan's support of Lonrho's North African plans remained effective for only a short time because relations between Khartoum on the one hand and Egypt and Libya on the other soon started to deteriorate. At the beginning of 1972 the Numeiry government ended its longstanding war against the southern Sudanese secessionists; and one of the conditions of the peace agreement was that Sudan would not become a member of the Federation of Arab Republics without the consent of the largely non-Moslem southerners. Egypt and Libya had already formed their federation, with Syria replacing Sudan, although Khartoum's eventual adherence to the pact was still hoped for. Moreover, Numeiry's relations with Washington improved at a time when the

United States was still regarded as an enemy of the Arabs in their quarrel with Israel. This rapprochement was partly necessary if Khartoum was to find adequate funds for the reconstruction of the war-torn areas in the south. But the breaking-point probably came in May 1972, after a visit by Gadaffi to Khartoum during which the Libyan leader preached the need for Arab unity. Gadaffi also said that he had given Sudan one last opportunity 'which expires on 25 May' to join the Federation, and he let it be understood that Libya's financial aid to Khartoum depended on Sudan's decision.[51] Later that year Numeiry closed down two important Egyptian business concerns and criticized Gadaffi and Sadat for setting up the Federation 'without caring about our internal conditions'.[52] Cairo and Tripoli accused Numeiry of ingratitude, particularly in the matter of the July 1971 counter-coup.

But when this estrangement between the former allies set in, Rowland had already made his North African contacts. In October 1971 Lonrho registered a new subsidiary, Lonrho North Africa Ltd. The memorandum of association entitled it to trade or invest in almost every field, but its main purpose was to serve as a holding company. Among its directors were Ball, Rowland and Olympio. One of Rowland's former associates commented later that this company had been set up in a 'fit of enthusiasm' to be used 'if and when any North African interests were developed'. The only Annual Report filed in the first three years of its existence noted that the company had not traded, so that no profit and loss account had been prepared.

Rowland's next major North African initiative in company-building came two years later, when Lonrho Arab International was set up – again with Ball and Rowland among the directors. According to press reports, this company was formed to 'concentrate on the Sudan and Arab Peninsula, and Lonrho North Africa to look after Egyptian and Libyan interests'.[53] Apart from these two wholly-owned subsidiaries, Lonrho set up a joint company with the Arab International Bank having 'broadly similar aims' with this institution.[54] The latter had been formed in September 1972 by the Egyptian International Bank and the Arab Libyan Foreign Bank to promote trade and investment in Egypt, Libya and other Arab states. Lonrho was to have a thirty per cent share in the new scheme, alongside those financial interests, but it is quite possible that this particular venture fell victim to the estrangement which had by then also divided Libya and Egypt.

At any rate, the next news from Lonrho's North African front was that it 'is taking a firm stake in the Middle East and is now in equal partnership through a subsidiary of the newly formed Arab International Bank under the presidency of the renowned Egyptian financier, Dr Kaissouni'.[55] Commander Anderson, described as an Arabist from London, had gone out as the company's representative and was actively looking for joint investment ventures with Arab governments. In the middle of 1974 discussions were reported to be under way about a joint Egyptian–Zambian copper processing scheme in which Zambian copper would be shipped to the Alexandria Free Zone where the factory would be situated. Lonrho, according to British and East African gossip, was to be involved in this. Later that year, when Lonrho's nine months' profits were announced, Rowland was reported to be looking on Egypt – not one of the oil-rich Arab states – as 'the biggest potential growth area in the Middle East'. A new company, Lonrho Egypt, was being established with 'Arab interests as major shareholders'.[56]

For the time being, however, the buying-agency agreement in Sudan remained the company's only profitable investment in the Arab world. And even this notable success may have been less well founded than had seemed at first. When Khalid was asked at the beginning of 1972 during a visit to Britain whether his government was satisfied with the recent exclusive purchasing agreement established with Lonrho (Exports), he said that the agreement had been signed on a three months' trial basis only: 'We will then see whether they can deliver the goods and whether they can do the job more economically than an alternative arrangement, like setting up our own purchasing office here in Britain.'[57] Although the agreement was continued, Khalid's uncertainty may have been caused by the recent publicity about the arrest of the company's directors in South Africa, which drew attention to Lonrho's embarrassing links. As a former Sudan ambassador to the United Nations, the Foreign Minister should have known that Lonrho had grown up in Rhodesia and was operating in white-ruled African countries. His attention was drawn to this fact during the same 1972 visit to Britain. The occasion was a press luncheon, when he was asked to explain his government's relationship with Lonrho in the light of OAU attitudes to apartheid. Khalid replied that he was 'not aware' of the company's operations in South Africa or Rhodesia.[58]

Lonrho's involvement in Khartoum pre-dated the Sudanese up-heavals by a few weeks, for at a press conference in the Sudanese capital on 9 June, given by the Under-Secretary for Planning and Information, a journalist asked whether the agreement with Lon-rho which was being negotiated was in line with Sudan's professed policy of non-cooperation with interests which upheld the white racist governments of southern Africa. The Under-Secretary replied that his Ministry was aware only of Lonrho's interests in Swaziland and Kenya and knew nothing of its south-ern African connections.

Having received this answer, the journalist in question decided to enlighten the Sudanese government and handed the Under-Secretary a dossier setting out Lonrho's southern African ramifi-cations. Perhaps as a result of this, Sudanese diplomatic circles made inquiries from opponents of the South African regime, re-questing the fullest possible details on this question. The informa-tion was gathered in London at the end of 1971 and a report was handed to a senior Sudanese official with a copy to the organizers of the African liberation movements' summit which met in Tripoli a few months later. A year later, a further request for information on Lonrho's southern African links was made by senior Sudanese figures, this time through the United States, and a detailed dossier was prepared and forwarded in February 1973, with a copy to the OAU. Apart from the usual press information which revealed in considerable detail Lonrho's far-flung interests, the Sudanese government had been kept directly briefed, making its ignorance on the question surprising. This fact is of considerable importance in view of the role which Sudan played during 1973 and 1974 in the events which led to the appointment of Lonrho as economic advisers on oil matters to the OAU.

Ten

The Commanding Heights*

In the middle of the boardroom row in May 1973, Rowland was asked what would happen if he were sacked from the board. 'What I would like to do,' he replied, 'is to act as an unpaid economic adviser to the Organization of African Unity, if I was acceptable. I would volunteer my services. Africa has been good to me and I would like to do something in exchange. In the whole of this crisis Africa has been loyal to me in contrast to what has happened here in London.'[1] Whether he said this on impulse, or whether he had already planned to establish links with the OAU, his opportunity came soon afterwards as a result of the 1973 Middle East war and the world oil crisis. The African countries had expressed concern about the effect which this might have on their economies and Rowland employed this widespread anxiety to facilitate Lonrho's appointment as consultants on oil matters to the OAU. The appointment caused a political storm, with results which seriously damaged the organization.

The OAU was just ten years old and although it had scarcely fulfilled the expectations of its founders, it was Africa's most important policy-making body. Any disarray in its secretariat was bound to affect the co-ordination of Africa's basic unity on such questions as apartheid in South Africa or Rhodesia's UDI, not to speak of other important issues. At the time of the Middle East war, the organization was preoccupied with the issues arising from this conflict, particularly the price of oil and Africa's petrol supplies. The vast majority of African countries supported the Arab cause, and after the war was over the Arabs promised their support for black Africa by extending their oil embargo to Rhodesia, South Africa and Portugal.[2]

The decision to impose sanctions on southern Africa was taken by the Arab summit meeting in Algiers at the end of November

* For a time-table of the events with which this chapter is concerned, the reader is referred to Appendix 2.

1973. It was in response to a resolution passed at an emergency meeting on the Middle East held by the OAU Council of Ministers at Addis Ababa a week earlier, calling on Arab countries to impose an oil embargo on South Africa, Portugal and Rhodesia 'until these countries conform with the resolutions of the General Assembly and the Security Council of the United Nations'.[3] The Arab summit also decided to set up an Arab Agricultural and Industrial Development Bank for Africa, with an initial capital of $125 million. The implementation of this plan was to be discussed between the Secretary-General of the Arab League and the Secretary-General of the OAU. The OAU meeting had discussed the effects of the world energy crisis on OAU member states. To protect their economies and co-ordinate action, the Ministerial Council appointed a seven-nation committee to study the implications and methods of a new oil strategy. The role of this Committee of Seven in practical terms was to serve as a liaison between the OAU and the Arab League. It consisted of Botswana, Cameroun, Ghana, Mali, Tanzania, Sudan and Zaire.

The only one of these seven in which Lonrho had no known interests was Mali. Tanzania had nationalized the Lonrho newspapers, sisal estates and other interests but some compensation questions may have remained unsettled. Lonrho's interests in Botswana were minor[4] but there had been a rapprochement with Zaire, and Ashanti Goldfields still remained the company's largest single profit-earner. Lonrho was influential in Sudan; and in Cameroun, the home country of OAU Secretary-General Nzo Ekangaki, the company had recently established trade links.[5]

None of these seven countries was an oil producer and they represented a cross-section of those hardest hit by the price rises. It was feared that the embargo imposed on Israel's friends might lead to oil shortages in Africa as well, not because the Arab producers were restricting supplies to that part of the world but because the international oil companies were not expected to consider African markets as their priority customers at a time of shortages in Europe. The Middle East tensions and the cutbacks in oil output by Arab producers also led to a tough price policy by the Organization of Petroleum Exporting Countries. Prices for crude oil had more than doubled by the end of the year and were to double again early in 1974. Dr Mansour Khalid, then Sudanese Foreign Minister and one of Lonrho's close African friends,[6] who was elected chairman of the Committee of Seven, calculated that the African states' payments for oil could increase from $400 million to $1,000 million a year.[7]

The key to what happened between Lonrho and the OAU is to be found in the first meeting of the Committee of Seven, held at Addis Ababa on 29 December 1973. The morning session was attended by some African diplomats and other observers, including the Secretary-General of the United Nations Economic Commission for Africa, which, like the OAU, had its headquarters in Addis Ababa. Robert Gardiner made a brief statement in which he expressed his appreciation to the committee for inviting the ECA to attend, and promised ECA co-operation with the committee in carrying out any studies or other tasks. One of Gardiner's officials was to represent the ECA throughout the committee's deliberations. The Secretary-General of the OAU, Ekangaki, then gave his assessment of the problems posed by the oil situation, stressing the need for 'immediate adequate arrangements for the flow of fuel to member states and ensuring continuous flow in the future'.[8] This at least was the public version which was noncommittal and did not disclose the grand scheme which Ekangaki put to the committee: the possibility of establishing an African oil company to co-ordinate the supply of member states, and the formation of a tanker fleet.

This was an old Rowland dream; he had already spoken about wishing to help the oil states to go into the transport of oil: 'I have always thought that they would own their own tankers, and we would be glad to use our expertise to help them get into this field, in partnership or some other agreement.'[9] In August 1973 a new subsidiary, Lonrho Energy Resources Ltd, had been incorporated in Britain. According to *African Development*, this company was planned 'as the link between Arab oil producers and Africa's coastal refineries'.[10] Its memorandum and articles of association gave as the first objective for which the company was established 'to carry on the business of purchasing, selling, blending, refining, transporting, storing and dealing in lubricating oils and greases, petroleum and other mineral and vegetable oils, industrial alcohols and other hydrocarbon products of all kinds' – in other words, the operations involved in running an oil tanker fleet, refineries and petrochemical industries. Presenting his proposals for a long-term solution to the Committee of Seven meeting on 29 December, Ekangaki listed the threats posed to African countries if they continued to be supplied by Western oil monopolies.

'We need to arrange for Africa to have its own oil company that would gradually take over from the multitude of Western oil companies now supplying individual African states. The company would also make appropriate necessary arrangements to ensure refining possibility for each OAU member state. Even from the point of view of prices and conditions of payment, it would be quite feasible for a single African company to strike specially favourable terms from the Arab producing countries, within the framework of a general policy of Arab-African co-operation.' And he concluded:

The Ministerial Committee may therefore wish to charge the General Secretariat to make a study of the possible formation in the near future of an OAU oil company that would be an intermediary between the African consuming states and the Arab producing states in all spheres of transportation, transformation, storage and commercialization of petroleum and petroleum products between Africa and the Arab world. The most immediate task of the company would be to constitute a tanker fleet to supply African countries within the framework of the negotiations now going on or to be undertaken. Such a company could broaden its spectrum in future to deal not only with fuel but with trade in general between African and Arab states. The formation of this company would constitute the most important concrete development in Arab–African relations.[11]

The seven Foreign Ministers debated this proposal in the committee's closed session that afternoon and decided that such complex questions needed more detailed study, which they requested Ekangaki to carry out, for consideration at some later date. But they agreed that the repercussions of the international oil situation on African countries should be treated as an urgent matter. 'Each country should make its own arrangements for the movement of its own oil supplies, after general global arrangements have been agreed between the OAU and the Arab oil producing countries for the supply of oil to the OAU member states.'[12] But, most significant for Lonrho, the committee apparently requested Ekangaki to 'give all necessary assistance to the member states in the detailed arrangements for securing adequate supply of oil, and to this end authorized him to appoint a consultant or consultants who could provide the necessary technical advice and expertise on the said arrangements'.[13]

In fact, Ekangaki himself had insisted, first, that he should negotiate oil contracts for each member state with Arab suppliers through the OAU Secretariat, and then that he could not do this without outside help: 'The General Secretariat cannot discharge the above assignment without expertise provided by a company that has experience in the business'. He went on:

The committee may therefore wish either to contract the services of a company that is sufficiently introduced both in Africa and in the Arab world and which is in the fuel business. The honour of working in partnership with the OAU and of being introduced by the OAU to thirty-seven of its member states would constitute the consideration for the company's assistance, and thereby not involve the OAU in any financial commitment.[14]

Mansour Khalid afterwards said that the committee had made it clear it wanted consultants who were not actively engaged in the oil business, so as to avoid companies with vested interests in Africa that might be detrimental to the continent. He recalled that the particular idea had been mentioned of appointing consultants from Yugoslavia or other non-aligned countries and that he himself had pressed for Rumanian involvement.[15] The Tanzanians later said that the committee had instructed Ekangaki to choose his experts from non-aligned states. The committee also decided to call for 'a joint meeting of Arab foreign ministers and ministers of petroleum with the OAU Committee of Seven at an early date, preferably before the end of January 1974, to discuss arrangements for alleviating the impact of the oil embargo on African states';[16] in anticipation of this meeting, Ekangaki was to prepare 'in collaboration with the ECA and any consultants he may appoint all studies needed to facilitate subsequent work of the committee'.[17]

The question of expert consultants cropped up in other contexts as well. Ekangaki suggested technical assistance from Arab countries and a fund to finance 'projects executed by African experts as well as by experts from other countries friendly to the African and Arab states, especially where these experts were not obtainable from the African and Arab countries themselves'.[18] The same theme reappeared, to be stated in almost identical words, some five weeks later at the African oil conference in Libya, at which Gardiner played a prominent part.[19] This conference was organized quite independently of any programme with which the Committee of Seven was involved but the recommendations it made were similar to Ekangaki's proposals for an African oil company, a tanker fleet, refineries and outside consultants. In particular, it called on the OAU, in collaboration with the ECA, to make a comparative study of legislation and agreements relating to the oil industry. The information was to be provided urgently by member countries 'for study by a group of experts to be appointed by the OAU'. The conference also recommended periodic meetings of experts to exchange information about the oil industry 'and in particular the experience gained in the provision of advisory services'. A documentation centre was to be established and 'transferred to an African oil organization when it is established'. The OAU and the ECA were to make 'detailed studies and prepare the necessary documents to enable the African countries to begin establishing an African oil organization'. Regarding consultative services and joint projects, the conference recommended that pending new sources of finance becoming operational, 'requests and offers for financial and technical aid should be submitted through the OAU'. The OAU and ECA, in cooperation with various other international institutions, 'shall be called upon to work out a co-ordinated plan for building oil refineries in the African continent'. In the field of the petrochemical industry, 'every member state should appoint experts to participate in the preparation of economic studies and in the drafting of subregional projects'.[20] Dr Gardiner emphasized the need for direct oil exports from producer countries to African consumers, without apparently referring to the discussion of Ekangaki's parallel proposals at the 29 December meeting of the Committee of Seven, at which the OAU had asked the ECA to prepare a list of consultants – African if possible, but also of non-African ones. In this connection the ECA service submitted to Gardiner a list of fifteen research organizations, most of them African. According to one report from Addis Ababa, Gardiner replied that the information had come too late, as an agreement was on the point of being concluded. It could only have been the Lonrho agreement.[21] Ekangaki later recalled that between 29 December and 9 January – the date of the Lonrho agreement – his secretariat 'along with the ECA were making maximum efforts to get a list of consultants from which to choose'.[22]

The 29 December meeting sent a delegation headed by the Tanzanian Foreign Minister and including representatives from Botswana and Sudan, as well as one of the OAU Assistant Secretary-Generals, to Cairo on 30 December. It was to underline the urgency of the oil question in its meeting with the Arab League and arrange a conference between the full Committee of Seven and the representatives of the Arab oil-producing states. This preliminary delegation to Cairo met the Assistant Secretary-General of the Arab League and emphasized the gravity of the oil problem. According to Ekangaki, the Arab League representative replied that his organization had been waiting for detailed quantitative information about the oil requirements of African countries 'since about the middle of December 1973'. Ekangaki went on:

He further indicated that it was because they had not received this information that they themselves had not arranged for a meeting to take place between the Committee of Seven and the representatives of the Arab League. He then went on to say that as soon as the actual figures indicating the African requirements were received by the League, a meeting would be arranged.[23]

The meeting eventually took place in Cairo on 22 January 1974, and the results were disappointing. The general African hope was for a preferential oil price to be set by the Arab producers for their African friends. This was refused. Khalid, chairman of the Committee of Seven, concentrated his argument on the need to establish an African oil transport and distribution system, including the building of adequate terminal facilities, the acquisition of a tanker fleet, and the co-ordination of distribution methods. There was, according to one report, some Arab response on the need for a tanker fleet, because this would reduce the need to use American carriers and the Arabs were still in an anti-American mood.[24] In practical terms, the only success scored by the Committee of Seven on that occasion was an Arab promise of a $200 million loan fund, but the Arab League Secretary-General, Mahmoud Riad, emphasized that this was for economic aid and not a subsidy for oil purchases.

Moreover, Riad's estimate that the Africans were importing only about ten million tons of Arab oil per year appeared to differ from the figures produced by the Committee of Seven on the basis of Ekangaki's calculations.[25] These, he admitted himself, were 'a very rough approximation' of the total requirements of the thirty-six non-oil-producing states whom he had asked to supply details of their oil imports. Only nineteen had responded to his questionnaire and his calculation was based on the statistics supplied by the nineteen, with 'an interpolation' to include the seventeen whose needs were unknown. Ekangaki's calculation had produced a total of 33.3 million metric tons, and, unsure whether such an approximation would in fact cover the thirty-six countries for whom the committee had been set up, he had suggested that 'it would be wise to present the figure of thirty-five million metric tons as the African requirement for 1974'.[26]

The necessity of collecting these figures was Ekangaki's argument for having engaged Lonrho in such a hurry, without consulting anyone except his immediate assistants – or, at least, some of them. At the end of December, while the first delegation was in Cairo conferring with the Arab League, which demanded detailed quantitative information about African oil needs, he telexed the thirty-six affected states, requesting the relevant information. Then, on 5 January, as he afterwards explained, he consulted with his assistants

as to what to do. It was noted that the second meeting of the Committee of Seven was scheduled to take place on 20 January 1974, to be followed by a meeting with the Arabs on 22 January 1974. The General Secretariat therefore had only two weeks to implement the decisions of the first session which included the appointment of a consultant who was to make contact with member states to discuss with fellow technicians and obtain additional necessary data likely to be useful to the Committee in their negotiations with the Arabs. For all these reasons, the Administrative Secretary-General and his assistants decided unanimously:

(a) to appoint Lonrho without prejudice to appointing other consultants in the future;

(b) to introduce the firm to member states to facilitate the discharge of their duties, especially those that had to be undertaken before the two meetings mentioned above;

(c) to continue efforts with the ECA with a view to looking for other consultants.[27]

In fact, Lonrho had already put in a formal letter, dated 21 December, offering the company's services to the OAU in working out a comprehensive oil programme. This letter had followed preliminary contacts soon after the setting-up of the Committee of Seven at the end of November, when a Lonrho delegation arrived in Addis Ababa to suggest that it might act for the OAU as a whole, as well as for individual member states. Ekangaki later explained that 'during the time the General Secretariat and the

ECA were searching for consultants, the application of the firm Lonrho was already lying in the files of the General Secretariat'.[28]

Could this explain why Ekangaki's proposals to the Committee of Seven on 29 December – just a week after Lonrho's first application – contained so many of Rowland's ideas concerning Afro-Arab cooperation and oil? Ekangaki later gave as a principal reason for signing with Lonrho that the company was well established in Africa, and 'the fact that several OAU member states had officially and publicly given support to the present Chief Executive of this firm during a boardroom dispute last year'.[29] This was inaccurate, but Ekangaki may well have believed this to have been the case in view of the widespread press reports to this effect. Moreover, Lonrho had informed the OAU of 'its absolutely pro-African and Arab policy and that its present leadership was now being harassed and persecuted by business interests with a colonial mentality, and that this pro-African stand is known and endorsed by several African heads of state and Government'.[30]

Nevertheless, Ekangaki took the precaution of writing to Rowland to inquire 'if Lonrho Ltd is involved in business in South Africa, Zimbabwe [Rhodesia], Angola and Mozambique, and to what extent, as you are no doubt aware of the attitude of the OAU to discourage any economic activities in these territories which assist to sustain and perpetuate the unjust political regime there'.[31] The letter was dated 8 January and addressed to the Chief Executive of Lonrho in London. Rowland's reply, addressed to Ekangaki in Addis Ababa, was also dated 8 January. His reply did not deal with the extent of the company's involvement, about which Ekangaki had inquired; it merely said that some of Lonrho's subsidiaries and associated companies had had interests 'since the 1890s' in southern Africa. His views on the 'temporary' regimes in southern Africa coincided entirely with those of Ekangaki, and he was in no way deterred by the baseless and deliberately misleading newspaper coverage which had been intended to discredit him in African and Arab eyes. He took the opportunity of forewarning Ekangaki that the intensity of these attacks against Lonrho might increase. This also would not deter him, although the effect that this might have on the uninformed might, he admitted, embarrass Ekangaki. He hoped that the OAU would continue unmoved by attacks from sources so hostile to what he called 'our common objectives'.[32]

Ekangaki must clearly have been impressed with this reply. He had already been told by the company that its southern African business interests were

historical and that they only administered them now by proxy, as they were themselves banned from entering the areas because of their pro-African policy. That at one time, they thought of giving them up and selling out their equities but were advised by friendly African heads of state and government whom they consulted that they should not, as this would only increase the financial empires of the enemies of Africa in that region.[33]

The claim that Lonrho or its directors were barred from South Africa probably referred to the earlier reference by Rowland to the possibility of arrest in South Africa and neighbouring countries.[34] Rowland later repeated the point he had made to Ekangaki on Lonrho's 'historical' South African interests.[35]

Ekangaki later said that, despite Rowland's reassurances, he weighed up what he called the 'disadvantages and the inconveniences of using Lonrho against the advantages'. On the debit side was the fear that 'the declared pro-African policies of the new Lonrho administration were not widely known and that the image of Lonrho as an imperialist pro-South African firm might continue to pervade'. But he hoped that through direct contact between Lonrho and the African states, 'the real situation will be known gradually'. He was also aware that 'Lonrho's methods in its dealings with certain states are considered by some people as unorthodox, but felt that this is a matter for each state to judge independently'.[36]

But none of this became public until much later, and even then Ekangaki's apologia and detailed explanations remained buried in OAU documents which were not released to the general public. The secrecy in which the Lonrho agreement was signed heightened suspicions when the appointment became general knowledge in February 1974. The best investigative coverage of the OAU–Lonrho affair appeared in *Jeune Afrique* between 23 February and 30 March. *African Development*, which had in the past reported very assiduously what Lonrho was up to and which had taken a strong pro-Rowland line during the boardroom dispute, remained almost completely silent on the company's OAU adventure. *Jeune Afrique* had heard rumours of the deal before it became public and had mounted an investigation. Neither Lonrho headquarters in London nor Ekangaki's office at the OAU would comment or answer the most direct questions. There was comment on the rapidity with which everything had been signed and sealed in view of the fact that the Committee of Seven was due to meet on 20 January.

Ekangaki wasted no time in ordering Lonrho to go ahead with its consultancy work. In an undated letter to Rowland, he instructed the company to undertake immediately 'a preliminary survey of fuel requirements of the thirty-six member states and seek to submit a report to me by 21 January 1974'. Lonrho was also instructed to 'hold yourselves available to attend negotiations between the Organization of African Unity representing the thirty-six member states and the oil-producing states of the Arab League in Cairo from 22 January onward'. The company was to undertake a fuller survey of the fuel requirements of each member state, although Ekangaki did say that this was to be done 'upon agreement of the member state concerned and in conjunction with the government of that member state'. The Committee of Seven had decided at its first meeting to defer consideration on such complex matters as an African oil company and a tanker fleet. Nevertheless, Ekangaki asked Lonrho 'to prepare proposals for the establishment of a tanker fleet to supply African countries within the framework of negotiations now going on or to be undertaken'; and to 'study and prepare recommendations for the formation of an OAU oil company that would be an intermediary between African consuming states and the Arab producing states in all spheres of transportation, transformation, storage and commercialization of oil and petroleum products between Africa and the Arab world.'[37]

These services were to be rendered under the terms of the agreement. This appointed Lonrho as a consultant to the OAU to assist in the implementation of certain general objectives, including the achievement of self-sufficiency of member states in their energy requirements, whether by the development of natural resources or the signing of long-term contracts with oil-producing states. Mention was also made of refining and the transportation of oil, as well as its transformation 'into such products as lubricants, fertilizers and petrochemicals' and the development of internal distribution systems. Specifically, Lonrho 'is hereby required by OAU to establish direct contact with member states affected by the oil embargo', so as to assist them. While Lonrho was barred from acting in any way as the agent of the OAU except with the organization's written authority, it was stated that

where any project falling within the objectives is approved by OAU and/or one or more of its member states, Lonrho shall be entitled, without prejudice to fair competition on a commercial basis, to be appointed to act as contractors, to act as managers, to act as buyers and/or as confirmers in respect of requisitions for services, capital equipment, consumable stores and other goods and services and/or to secure where necessary long and short term finance facilities for capital projects and shall be entitled to take such participation as may be offered to Lonrho in such projects by member states.[38]

In other words, Lonrho was not only entitled to help as a consultant in planning but to become contractors in the construction phase, and even managers, bankers and part-owners of the schemes they helped to draw up: a remarkable latitude for a company whose expertise in the oil and petrochemical fields had never been established and whose financial resources would certainly not have stretched to undertaking multi-million-dollar projects. What later particularly annoyed Africans was that Lonrho was to have opened an office in Addis Ababa and that the OAU promised to issue Rowland and other officials with the diplomatic 'OAU Laissez Passer', which had until then been the prerogative of OAU officials. Nevertheless, Ekangaki may have had some premonition about African reactions to the deal, for the agreement contained a clause stating that 'nothing in this agreement shall be construed as placing any obligation on a member state to engage the services of Lonrho against the will of such a member state'. Member states could not, of course, have been forced to cooperate with Lonrho, even if this clause had been omitted.

Ekangaki said later that immediately upon signing the agreement he had written to the heads of state of the thirty-six countries concerned, 'introducing the firm Lonrho and forwarding to each of them a copy of the agreement. Since the Administrative Secretary-General knew that Lonrho may not be acceptable as a consultant to some countries,' he had also sent a telegram to each member state, requesting direct information about their oil needs to be forwarded to himself.[39] Nevertheless, without awaiting their reactions and despite his admitted doubts about their attitude to the company, he forwarded to Lonrho the oil statistics of those countries which had already responded to his original request for information. This only emerged during the second meeting of the

Committee of Seven on 20 January in Addis Ababa, when Ekangaki's progress report disclosed that the information received from the nineteen countries out of thirty-six, in response to his inquiry, 'has been passed on to the Cairo office of the OAU consultant, that is, Messrs Lonrho Limited of London'.[40] Further on he wrote that the appointment had been made by him 'in accordance with the authority granted to him by the committee last month', and that he had chosen Lonrho 'after considering other possible consultants'. The secretariat and Lonrho had formulated a questionnaire requesting more information; this would 'facilitate awareness both of the OAU secretariat and of the consultant' of the countries' long-term needs and their arrangements to meet them. Ekangaki added that, as promised by Gardiner, the ECA was 'working very closely with the secretariat in pursuing this matter'.[41]

The Committee of Seven reacted strongly. Accounts vary about the precise nature of the discussion which ensued, but even Ekangaki conceded that 'considering the observations that were made during the debate on the agreement, the Administrative Secretary-General has so far refrained from assigning any new tasks to Lonrho at the general secretariat level'.[42] However, despite the Committee's 'reservations' about the appointment, Ekangaki claimed that 'the consensus as summed up by the Chairman was that the Administrative Secretary-General had acted within the mandate given him and done so in good faith'.[43] The chairman was Mansour Khalid of Sudan, according to whom the committee 'didn't want to pass a judgement'. Ekangaki 'was technically mandated to make a contract but should have appointed a consultant in the framework of what we had said – he should have taken the hint about vested interests and non-aligned countries'. The reaction of some members had been, 'Why appoint this company which hasn't been involved in the oil business?' Khalid himself thought that 'politically it was not right', but he could see how Ekangaki had come to believe that it might have been: 'In spite of everything else, Lonrho has been accepted in many African countries, and there was no reason to think it would cause such a row.' He claimed that nobody had dwelt on Lonrho's southern African links. Even Tanzania had made little reference to these, and Ghana had been talking of the problems it had with Ashanti Goldfields. He felt that the angry reaction had been prompted by the fact that the agreement in itself was in some ways unacceptable, particularly in conferring diplomatic privileges on the company. It had been concluded in a clumsy way: 'Ekangaki never tried to read between the lines or see the political implications'. But what seemed to annoy Khalid most was the reference in the agreement to access to heads of state, which, he said, 'made it look not like the work of technical consultants – it might perhaps touch on the sovereignty of nations'. There might also have been an element of jealousy among the seven Foreign Ministers, he thought: 'No Foreign Minister would like a company to have access to heads of state, bypassing the Foreign Office. It was an impropriety which makes one suspicious about it all.'[44]

Despite Khalid's later doubts, he still thought that the company had been aiming at what would have been 'beneficial to Africa and in tune with what Tiny Rowland has always advocated. Bypassing the multinational corporations with their own tanker fleet, making bilateral deals, us having our own industrialization, our own fertilizer plants. They would have been able to achieve what they were always hoping to.'[45] The ambivalence of his feelings towards Lonrho might be explained by the fact that he spoke several weeks after the event, when the scandal had become an embarrassment to all concerned. But his views differed from those of many other African leaders who had been involved.

The story broke when General Amin of Uganda got to hear of it and despatched one of his famous telegrams to Ekangaki, with copies to General Yakubu Gowon, the Nigerian leader and 1973–4 chairman of the OAU, and Riad, Secretary-General of the Arab League. This read:

I have been informed that last month you signed an agreement with a representative of Lonrho company, in effect giving that company the sole agency of dealing in oil products between the Arab and African countries. If that is so, it is most regrettable and unfortunate.

In the first place, your action does not appear to be backed by the OAU mandate of any kind, in spite of the fact that there is a standing Committee of Seven countries specifically charged with the subject of oil supply from the Arab countries to the African countries.

In the second place, Lonrho is obviously widely known throughout Africa as being one of the leading imperialist and Zionist companies, with roots in southern Africa where it specializes in supplying racist minority regimes with military weapons, propaganda machinery and petroleum products among other things, for fighting OAU member states, as well as for suppressing patriotic and nationalist movements in those parts of the continent still under imperialist and colonialist slavery.

He demanded that the Lonrho agreement be cancelled, and that Ekangaki furnish an explanation for having signed it, failing which he would insist that this 'unauthorized action and improper behaviour should be the subject of very serious debate at the next summit'.[46]

· Amin's characteristic of overstating the case made it easier to refute: there was no evidence that Lonrho had any Zionist tendencies or was a supplier of weapons to southern Africa. Ekangaki replied that he had been authorized to appoint consultants and he stressed that he had not appointed the company as sole agents. Moreover, the facts available to him about Lonrho's position in Africa, as well as its policy in southern Africa and towards Israel, were 'at complete variance' with those stated by Amin. He would place the full facts before the Ugandan leader at the earliest opportunity before the next summit, 'in view of any action Your Excellency may then contemplate'.[47] But once Amin had spoken out publicly, the political storm was bound to break. Ekangaki's failure to foresee the consequences of his actions was to have grave consequences for the OAU.

The OAU had withstood numerous serious crises and despite regular predictions that it was about to disintegrate it was still in existence. The main bond between its members was their opposition to apartheid and the white minority regimes of southern Africa: if there was none on anything else, there was full accord on questions such as racialism, foreign exploitation and the evils of neocolonialism. While members differed widely in their approach to these problems, a formula to express a broad common position was generally found, and the resolutions passed by the annual summit meetings allowed the secretariat to adopt a more radical approach in representing African views internationally than some heads of state who had voted for the resolutions may have intended. At least this is what had happened in the first eight years of the OAU's existence, when its Secretary-General had been Diallo Telli, a radical politician from Guinea, who had built up the secretariat within the framework of the charter on which the OAU was founded in 1963. He had four Assistant Secretary-Generals, appointed by the only decision-making body recognized by the organization: the assembly of heads of state which met annually to lay down policy. The most able diplomat among the four was the Algerian Mohammed Sahnoun, in charge of the political department.

By 1972 Telli had come to be disliked in a considerable number of African countries, particularly those with conservative governments which complained that he was exceeding his authority in various ways. The charter of the OAU had carefully limited his room for independent action, to the extent of inserting – as an afterthought – the word 'Administrative' to designate his functions. The Administrative Secretary-General, by definition, could not supersede the political wishes of member countries. And the same was true even of the Council of Ministers: the assembly of Foreign Ministers which met biannually and thrashed out the political differences between member states, formulating compromises which had to be confirmed by summit resolutions. At the eighth annual summit meeting, which took place at Rabat in the summer of 1972, Telli's second term of office had come to an end; although he presented himself for re-election, the post went to a rival candidate.

This selection had been the subject of preliminary bargaining between member countries and the candidature of Ekangaki, a Camerounian, represented a compromise. He came from a much less radical country than Telli, but nevertheless one which had always adopted a correct attitude towards southern African questions. President Ahidjo of Cameroun had been a recent chairman of the OAU and had filled that office to the satisfaction of radical as well as conservative member states. Besides, Cameroun had the advantage of combining two territories, one of which had been administered by Britain, the other by France, before independence. Camerounians were therefore supposed to have an understanding of Commonwealth politics as well as of the peculiar relationship between the francophone states and France. Ekangaki, who came from the English-speaking western part of Cameroun, was fluent in French as well as English. Before his election as OAU Secretary-General he had been virtually unknown in Africa, although he had served as a minister in Ahidjo's government and accompanied his president on various international missions. His inexperience of inter-African politics caused some concern, particularly among the more radical member countries; to make his man more acceptable, Ahidjo is said to have agreed with President Boumedienne of Algeria that Sahnoun would work closely with the new Secretary-General to retain the diplomatic drive which Telli and Sahnoun had conducted on behalf of the organization. Nevertheless, a year after his election Ekangaki shuffled his assistants around to different departments. This was done at a moment when both diplomacy and economic expertise were more necessary than ever before: the OAU members were about to negotiate a new relationship with the Common Market, and the first successful meeting between African and European Economic Community representatives in Brussels had just been organized. Boumedienne, annoyed that his compromise with Ahidjo had thus been scuttled, recalled Sahnoun. Sahnoun later resigned, and was appointed soon afterwards as an Assistant Secretary-General of the Arab League in charge of relations with African countries.[48]

Some African quarters explained Ekangaki's political ineptitude in signing up a company like Lonrho as the result of 'lack of administrative experience', but he did not lack competent advice.[49] The attack on the Lonrho agreement was led by Tanzania's Foreign Minister, John Malacela, who claimed that Ekangaki had not been mandated by the first meeting of the Committee of Seven on 29 December to engage consultants. The Committee had merely resolved that a firm be given the contract after the OAU secretariat, in consultation with the ECA, had prepared a list of competent groups or individuals and submitted this to the Committee, to allow it to select an adviser. 'The list of experts,' he said, 'has not yet been submitted to the Committee. So the position of the Committee, in which Tanzania is a member, has not changed. We are still waiting for the list so that we can choose from it.' He explained that any agreement could become valid only after ratification by the Committee or by OAU member states. He denied that there was any controversy on this matter, 'because the issue is very clear. And as far as Tanzania is concerned, the agreement between the OAU secretariat and Lonrho is non-existent.'[50]

The question of whether Ekangaki had been authorized to engage consultants is difficult to settle, since the only documentary evidence consists of Ekangaki's statements, reports and minutes. Apart from Malacela, only the Ghanaian Foreign Minister, Kwame Baah, seems to have made any public statement; the other Committee members maintained a discreet silence and the chairman was publicly noncommittal. According to Baah, Ekangaki was acting within his mandate, although Baah himself strongly disagreed with the choice of Lonrho as consultants; he later explained that his government rejected Lonrho politically in view of what he called its notorious dealings with South African racists.[51] The state-owned Ghanaian *Daily Graphic* carried a leading article entitled 'Ekangaki Must Resign', which described the agreement as 'a criminal sell-out of the continent to our enemies' and 'a smear on the Africans'. The Ghana government reiterated its 'full confidence in his integrity and his ability to steer the affairs of the OAU'. However, it added that it had already made known its opposition to the appointment of Lonrho.[52]

In Kenya, Vice-President Moi announced that 'signing an agreement of this nature would be against the leadership of the OAU'. Kenya 'would not be a party to it'. It would be 'contrary to the UN sanctions against Rhodesia, if we African nations, who have made a big noise against Rhodesia, would now accept Lonrho, a firm deeply rooted in Rhodesia and hence in South Africa, to be an oil agent between us and the Arabs'. Moi's assistant, Martin Shikuku, added that 'the best and noble thing Mr Ekangaki can do is to resign his position'.[53] Nigeria's External Affairs Commissioner, Dr Okoi Arikpo, said that while Nigeria maintained an open mind until all the facts surrounding the consultancy deal had been established, his government would not accept Lonrho as oil consultants. He regretted that despite Lonrho's well-known business interests in South Africa, more than twenty African governments were doing business with the company.[54] A spokesman for the Zambian Ministry of Foreign Affairs said that Zambia was not aware of any special powers delegated to the OAU Secretary-General authorizing him to sign the agreement.

These critical attitudes leave no doubt as to why Lonrho was opposed: the legal question of whether Ekangaki had been authorized to commit the OAU to any particular consultants came second to the political implications of his having appointed a company with strong southern African links. Ekangaki chose to ignore the more serious political attacks on his action and defended himself on other grounds, at least in the first instance. In a statement replying to the Tanzanian attack, he accused Malacela of 'complete and deliberate distortion of the facts'. Some African governments had already confirmed to him in writing their willingness to utilize Lonrho's services; 'contrary to those who may think

I have acted *ultra vires*, I was duly authorized by the Committee of Seven to appoint a consultant or consultants'. Since the matter had become one of public interest, he was going to explain to the Council of Ministers, which was due to meet on 28 February, on what authority he had acted. 'If after that the Council of Ministers is not convinced of the legality of my action and my good faith, I shall resign, because that would be the fitting and honourable course of action for anyone who respects his convictions and his dignity.'[55]

When Amin came out with the news of Lonrho's appointment, three weeks had elapsed since the second meeting of the Committee of Seven at which Ekangaki had formally told it of the agreement. Why, then, had nobody mentioned the matter before in public? In particular, why had Tanzania, which claimed that the consultancy had been unanimously rejected- on 20 January and which was so strongly opposed to it, not protested publicly? In view of the damage which the public debate of the issue subsequently did, it is easy to see why any member state concerned with the survival of the organization should have hoped to get the deal revoked without inviting world attention. Tanzania's President Nyerere was Africa's most incisive critic of the OAU, and had openly analysed its shortcomings on several previous occasions. That Tanzania had not challenged the appointment of Lonrho publicly before was doubtless due to its hopes that the situation might be rectified without an open scandal damaging to the OAU, whose prestige had fallen so low.

But Ekangaki himself found it necessary to come out with a defence of his actions, even before the meeting of the Ministerial Council which was scheduled for 28 February. In a document intended for the ministers, which appeared to have been leaked to the press, he claimed to have conducted 'exhaustive' inquiries into the company's southern African links, and to have been satisfied.[56] Apart from the 'good audience' enjoyed by the company in Africa and the Arab world, it was

totally independent of any of the existing major international oil companies. In its shipping group, Loncom Shipping Company Limited, it is currently already undertaking the shipping of crude oil for some African states. In their application to the OAU the firm state that His Excellency, President Anwar El Sadat, President of the Arab Republic of Egypt, has been kind enough to agree that his ex-Minister of Petroleum, Eng. Aly Wally, who has some thirty years of experience in the oil industry, should be permitted to work for the firm and is presently a full-time executive with the firm dealing with petroleum negotiations.[57]

Aly Wally had also been in charge of the Sumed project, Egypt's planned Suez–Mediterranean pipeline. In May 1972 he was dismissed from his post, following strong public criticism of the political and economic implications of the scheme. Its opponents pointed out that Egyptian sovereignty was being infringed by the manner in which it was being financed: revenues from the pipeline were to have been transferred to the French-led consortium of international bankers with whom Aly Wally had negotiated. After retiring from public life, he set himself up as a consultant, and it was presumably in this capacity that Rowland had come across him and acquired his services for Lonrho – with Sadat's permission.

Khalid later observed that if the basic consideration which had led Ekangaki to choose Lonrho was Aly Wally, was it necessary for him 'to go all the way to London to get this man? Couldn't we have gone to the Egyptian government?'[58] When Ekangaki instructed Lonrho to hold itself available for the 22 January Cairo meeting between the Committee of Seven and the Arab League, he said, 'The presence of Eng. Aly Wally would be particularly beneficial.'[59] Aly Wally did accompany the Committee of Seven to Cairo and was present during the conference. But what, if anything, he achieved remains obscure. Certainly this Egyptian trump card counted for little when the Council of Ministers met at Addis Ababa on 28 February.

The meeting started under inauspicious circumstances: the first stage of the Ethiopian army's revolt had just started, and shooting could be heard in the distance. Most of the ministers who assembled for the occasion were determined to get to the bottom of the Lonrho affair. For instance, the Nigerian External Affairs Commissioner, Arikpo, who was then chairman of the Council of Ministers, said on his departure from Lagos, 'I expect him [Ekangaki] to know what to do if it is proved that he has acted improperly.'[60] Ekangaki's apologia – the document entitled 'The Question of Consultants on the Effects of the Oil Embargo on African States' – was distributed to some delegations, though not to all; the OAU secretariat explained that French translations had not yet been prepared. When the meeting started the Guinean ambassador demanded that the agreement be cancelled and was applauded. At that point Ekangaki felt compelled to announce that he had suspended the operation of the consultancy, but this only stiffened opposition. The Algerian Minister of Commerce, Yaker Ayachi, replied that they were not debating the suspension of the agreement, 'but its annulment pure and simple'.[61] It was clear that Ekangaki was in for a difficult time, but at that moment the Ethiopian Foreign Minister asked for the adjournment of the meeting because of the deteriorating Ethiopian situation, and it was decided to re-convene the session in Kampala at the end of March.

Lonrho played it cool and refused to comment when the storm first broke – possibly because Rowland was in Khartoum at that time and the London Head Office did not know enough about the deal. However, the company was understood to believe that the agreement had been validly negotiated. A week later, Alan Ball claimed that it had been signed in the presence of representatives of a number of OAU member states, and that members of the Committee of Seven had been present. Ekangaki had the authority from the Committee to conclude the deal. Was the Committee present when it was signed? Ball replied, 'I know that all its members were not present. He signed it in the presence of a number of his staff on 9 January, but I do not know who they were.'[62] Ball told journalists that the agreement involved no payments of any kind to Lonrho by the OAU. Moreover, it had been an African initiative: 'The approach was from them – the Ministers of the OAU Committee – to us. We were appointed honorary consultants, and I would stress the word honorary, because it makes it clear that no fees were involved.'[63] Ekangaki's version of how Lonrho came to accept a major consultancy post without prospect of financial remuneration was that as the introduction of the company was 'a potentially major advantage to the firm', he had insisted that they should not ask for monetary reward for their services to the OAU which were to be rendered 'at the general secretariat level in the form of certain studies'.[64] Rowland, when he was asked to explain why a commercial firm had agreed to carry out consultancy work without a fee, said,

We love Africa. We have interests in about twenty OAU Member states, and the second largest Lonrho shareholder is Kuwait, an Arab country and one of the largest oil producers. So when, in a period of emergency, the OAU asked us to do a service we are well qualified to do and have all the necessary resources to do, what is the point in asking for fees? Of course, if the agreement had gone ahead, we would have reaped some benefits indirectly.[65]

But the company did not comment on the political storm in Africa which its entry into OAU affairs had caused. After the interrupted session of the Council of Ministers in Addis Ababa, there cannot have been any doubt that benefits, direct or indirect, would not be reaped.

Ekangaki was in deep trouble, and it was clear that he would be forced to cancel the contract when the session was resumed in Kampala at the end of March. Any further debate could only weaken Lonrho's position in African countries where the company was already established. Although a number of Lonrho's supporters throughout Africa went into action,[66] Lonrho formally asked to be released from the contract. In a letter to Ekangaki dated 11 March, Rowland reviewed all the arguments he had already advanced about his operations in African and Arab countries. He also referred to the boardroom row of 1973, and said that the shareholders had by a large majority sacked all those directors 'who in any way favoured the racist and minority regimes of southern Africa'. Rowland assured Ekangaki that there was no one left in the company who was opposed to the fundamental decision that 'all' Lonrho's business future lay with independent Africa and in the Arab world. It therefore came as a complete surprise to him, Rowland wrote, when the consultancy was greeted with ill-informed criticism by the press. But in view of the unfair image of 'my company' which had thus been created, and in view of the adjournment of the Council of Ministers session, he felt that it would be in the interests of all concerned to terminate the consultancy forthwith. Should the OAU see fit in future to accept Lonrho's services, the company would be most willing to respond.

Hopes that this withdrawal would stifle further debate proved to be unjustified. The fact that Lonrho had found it expedient to cancel the agreement with Ekangaki did not dampen the desire of many African leaders to discover how the deal had been arranged in the first place. Arikpo, for instance, announced on the eve of the reconvened Council of Ministers meeting that 'mere withdrawal by Lonrho is not the end of the whole affair. It is within the competence of individual delegations to inquire into the conduct of the Secretary-General of the Organization.'[67] In fact, the Lonrho affair gave rise to a very heated debate when the

OAU ministers resumed their deliberations in Kampala at the end of March, although little of this was reflected in the press at the time. However, Ghana's state-owned newspaper did report that the agreement 'came in for unanimous condemnation from the delegates'.[68]

This time the discussion was opened by the Zambian delegation. Khalid, the Sudanese Chairman of the Committee of Seven, was absent from the meeting. Malacela said again that the Committee was dissatisfied with Ekangaki's handling of the matter, and there were wide demands for an explanation of Ekangaki's motives. When the Committee of Seven presented its report, the meeting demanded 'more substantial' work[69]; it was felt that the two-and-a-half-page document was nothing but a summary of what had already been reported – 'a catalogue of meetings and travels', one diplomat said. Some delegates tried to insist on a formal declaration, stating that Lonrho's agreement had been annulled because it had been rejected by the OAU ministers in Addis Ababa, and not because the company had backed out. This question was left open and on the next occasion – during the OAU summit meeting in Somalia in June – it was submerged in a much wider debate on the position and functions of the OAU Secretary-General.

The weeks following the Ministerial Council meeting in Kampala were critical ones for Ekangaki. Ahidjo had become extremely embarrassed by his protégé's actions, and at the meeting of the OAU Liberation Committee in Cameroun in May, he reportedly refused to receive him. (At the OAU summit in June, Ahidjo walked out of the conference hall when Ekangaki rose to give his annual report.)

Ekangaki resigned as Secretary-General at the end of May, just two weeks before the OAU summit, although he stayed nominally in office until the end of August. His letter to Gowon, as chairman of the OAU, gave 'personal reasons'. But it was generally assumed that he had resigned over the Lonrho affair. This he denied: 'The assumption that I would have resigned because of the Lonrho affair is completely incorrect. I knew all along that the Committee of Seven with which I was working on the oil situation had absolute confidence in me.' He had resigned

because of an internal situation within the OAU, both at the level of the secretariat and at the level of member states. The proportions which the Lonrho affair assumed were just one manifestation of [the] existing internal situation.

The publicity as well as the 'tendentious interpretations and obnoxious innuendoes' had been aimed 'to discredit me personally'. There was a 'disgruntled group' within the secretariat which had, with outside help, 'decided on a course of open subversion of my person as Secretary-General in order to make me fail in my mission'. He had then discovered to his dismay that 'the machinery of the organization did not give me the power to deal with such an internal situation as far as order and discipline are concerned'. But to fight for more power while still Secretary-General 'would only confirm to my accusers that I am selfishly motivated. It was better that I sacrifice myself [by resigning] if it could serve some good cause for the organization.' He added that he would 'have occasion to give my own side of the inside stuff on the Lonrho affair'.[70]

Ekangaki's allegations of a vendetta against him were no doubt linked to the dissatisfaction within the secretariat at the posting of his four assistants to different departments; he had probably created enemies for himself among the staff over this and other issues. But his initial popularity had been dissipated in other ways too: one instance was his behaviour over his official residence. The OAU had rented a small palace from the Ethiopian royal family for the use of the Secretary-General while an OAU house was being planned, but he moved into a house of his own choice which he vacated in turn – leaving the OAU to pay $782 in lieu of notice. The OAU auditors were highly critical of his use of official funds for non-official purposes; for instance, they remarked that he was 'not entitled' to the $1,500 which the OAU paid for his wife's trip to London for medical treatment. His claims for restaurant bills, laundry services and other items on his hotel bill were criticized because they were personal and 'should have been met by the Secretary-General himself'.[71]

The most immediate effect of Ekangaki's resignation was that the 1974 summit in Mogadishu, the Somali capital, was diverted from more urgent issues into a wrangle over the choice of his successor. The military coup in Portugal on 25 April 1974 had changed the situation in southern Africa so drastically that the OAU should have been fully occupied studying its implications and co-ordinating its policy towards the liberation movements of Angola and Mozambique. Instead, the attention of delegates was taken up with the lobbying of candidates for the post of Secretary-General. There were two main contenders: the Somali Foreign Minister, and the Zambian Foreign Minister, Vernon Mwaanga, until recently the government-appointed editor of Lonrho's newspaper, the *Times of Zambia*, in which capacity he had expressed strong views on such issues as the Lonrho boardroom crisis.[72] Mwaanga was an experienced diplomat: a former Zambian ambassador to Moscow, he had headed his country's delegation to the United Nations until assuming the editorial post. He was popular with the liberation movements. Under different circumstances there is little doubt that he would have been elected to the OAU position, in which a Zambian at that particular time might have brought a touch of realism to the organization. After all, Zambia was the most exposed country in the confrontation with the white-ruled South; both Salisbury and Pretoria had issued frequent threats of military retaliation in response to its support of liberation movements. As a neighbour of both Angola and Mozambique, Zambia would also have been well suited to provide the OAU at that particular stage of Portuguese decolonization with a Secretary-General who was better informed than most other African diplomats about developments in these crucial territories. Nevertheless, Mwaanga did not obtain the necessary number of votes; many delegations may well have been reluctant to support a former employee of Lonrho, which was now regarded with considerable suspicion. The voting remained tied until a compromise candidate broke the deadlock.

Ironically, Ekangaki's successor, Mr W. A. Mboumoua Eteki, was another Camerounian protégé of Ahidjo. He too was relatively unknown outside his own country. After serving as president of the UNESCO assembly in Paris, he became Special Technical Adviser to the Presidency in Cameroun. His lack of experience in inter-African affairs was a handicap to the new Secretary-General in his most urgent task: to pull the organization together again. One of the most obvious signs of the disarray into which the OAU had fallen was its decision at Mogadishu to hold the 1975 summit in Kampala. Since the host of the annual summit conference usually becomes chairman of the organization for the following year, this honour was due to fall on the idiosyncratic Ugandan leader, General Amin. In view of the tensions between Amin and some of Uganda's East African neighbours, particularly Tanzania, this was an uneasy prospect. A functioning OAU secretariat might have prevented the choice of a controversial host country, as it had on past occasions, but the confusion created at OAU headquarters by the Lonrho affair had crippled the organization's administrative and diplomatic functions.

No other company had tried to involve itself so deeply in OAU politics as Lonrho had, and there were Africans who feared that it might be a potential security risk. The argument that was advanced, in particular through *Jeune Afrique*, stressed the magnitude of Lonrho's southern African investments. The oil embargo extended to South Africa by the Arabs at the Algiers conference in November 1973 had met with strong reactions from Pretoria, and *Jeune Afrique* quoted Dr Hilgard Muller, the South African Foreign Minister, as saying that South Africa would 'not accept any neutrality on this question'.[73] The article continued: 'What will Lonrho do if Pretoria exacts confidential information and details of supplies, or even demands the re-routing of the [oil] traffic?'

Ironically, one of Ekangaki's last actions as Secretary-General was to preside at the Mogadishu summit over the presentation of a report prepared by the OAU secretariat, naming Lonrho's Rhodesian interests as among the largest in the country's gold and mineral development and exploration. Those present who had had occasion to study Ekangaki's apologia recalled that one of his justifications had been that Lonrho would help to tighten sanctions. In fact, in his own words,

The Secretary-General requested Lonrho whether they would accept to use their wide machinery in the business world to help the OAU in detecting sanctions-busters in southern Africa, particularly when the petrol embargo should be fully in operation, and Lonrho accepted to do this.[74]

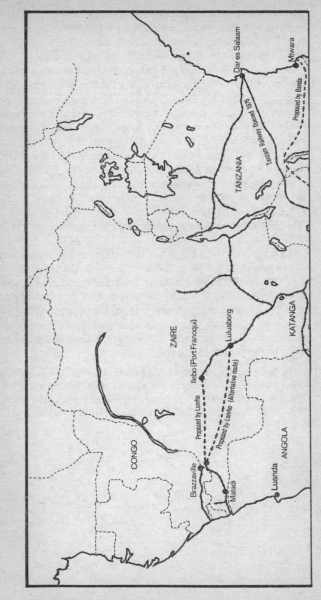

The Southern African Railway Network

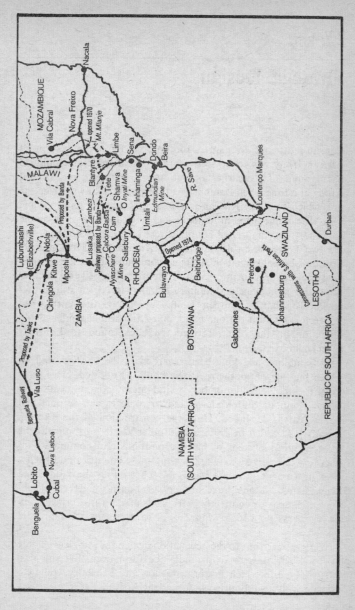

MOZAMBIQUE

Nacala

Nova Freixo

Vila Cabral

Mt. Mlanje
opened 1970

MALAWI

Limbe
Sena
Dondo
Beira

Blantyre

Proposed by Banda

Tete
Shamva
Inhaminga

Zambezi
O Inyati Mine
Edmundian
Mine

R. Save

Railway proposed by Banda
Cabora Bassa
Dam

Lourenço Marques

Lubumbashi
(Elizabethville)

Ndola

Lusaka

Nvaschere
Mine

Umtali

Durban

SWAZILAND

Chingola
Kitwe
Mpooshi

Salisbury

RHODESIA

Opened 1974

Pretoria

Connections with S. African Ports

LESOTHO

ZAMBIA

Bulawayo

Beitbridge

Johannesburg

Proposed by Tanks

Benguela Railway

Via Luso

BOTSWANA

Gaborones

REPUBLIC OF SOUTH AFRICA

Lobito
Nova Lisboa

Benguela
Cubal

NAMIBIA
(SOUTH WEST AFRICA)

221

Eleven

Strategic Designs

Lonrho's attempt to gain a foothold in the Organization of African Unity has to be seen against the strategic and political background of its earlier operations in southern and central Africa at a time when Zambia was trying to break away from the grip which southern African interests retained over its economy. The African liberation movements had started their assault on the white fortress comprising South Africa, Namibia, Rhodesia, and the two Portuguese-ruled territories, Angola and Mozambique. Lonrho's entanglement in strategic communications and associated projects drew it into some of the most explosive issues preoccupying politicians and military planners in Africa and further afield. The battle between white supremacy and entrenched Western capital on the one hand, and African independence and liberation on the other, formed the background to Lonrho's spectacular expansion.

Mozambique had long been regarded as the battleground on which the fate of southern Africa would be decided, largely because it commanded a number of vital lines of communication on which Rhodesia and Malawi, and to some extent Zambia and South Africa, depended. Until the construction of the Tanzam railway – regarded in Pretoria and other Western capitals as the most ominous portent of black aspirations and communist influence – the railway network serving these countries had been a vital instrument in white hands for controlling the landlocked black states. At one stage or another Lonrho had become involved, directly or indirectly, with each of the three crucial railway systems on which white hopes to pre-empt Tanzam were pinned.

Western reactions to the new nationalist and ideological climate in black Africa were to promote the formation of a southern African bloc in which Pretoria, Lisbon and Salisbury would co-operate with neighbouring independent African states, exporting their skill and capital in return for a certain degree of accommodation by the black leaders in accepting the existing power structure in the sub-continent. The crucial country was Zambia, partly because of its strategic copper wealth and partly because it was geographically in the forefront of the pan-African bloc. Since the break-up of the Central African Federation, it had been precariously balanced between economic necessity which tied it to the south, and a sense of political destiny which made it part of the black continent. Attempts by Pretoria to include Zambia in a southern African bloc were persistent. In 1968, for instance, South Africa's Prime Minister remarked that his government had 'the best possible relationships with Botswana, Lesotho, Swaziland, Rhodesia and Malawi', while the Portuguese and the South Africans 'understand one another'. He went on: 'The time will come when Zambia and South Africa will understand each other . . . not only because of good relationships and everything that will flow from these relationships, but because of the need for southern Africa to be kept free of communist infiltration.'[1]

President Kaunda of Zambia resisted such approaches for a long time, though he had to move cautiously to avoid an outright attack. In the years before independence, he and Dr Banda had led the campaign for the right to secede from the Federation, while Welensky, supported by Britain and South Africa, was trying desperately to keep it together. The Federation had been conceived as a bastion of Western stability in which 'partnership' between the races would prevent the emergence of militant African movements determined to achieve command over their peoples' destinies. But partnership, as Sir Godfrey Huggins, the Rhodesian Prime Minister, so aptly described it, was that of the rider and his horse – with the white man firmly in the saddle.

In practical terms, the Federation was intended to give the white settlers, most of whom lived in Rhodesia, the benefit of Zambia's copper wealth. When the African nationalists lobbied London in their bid to escape from white domination, it was suggested in Salisbury that the Federation should be allowed to break up, but with the copper belt, which had been developed by 'white skill and capital', and possibly Katanga[2] included in a Rhodesian state. While the Federation lasted, taxes from the copper industry were diverted to the south. Between 1954 and 1960 the net drain from Zambia to the rest of the Federation was estimated at £56 million, and the total tax loss to Zambia during the entire Federal decade at nearly £100 million. In 1953, when the Federation was formed, Zambia had a national debt of £22 million; when it was dissolved ten years later, the debt stood at £97 million. This flow of capital to the south attracted business and industry to Salisbury, the capital of the Federation as well as of Rhodesia, and the centre of white settlement. Federal government policy deliberately encouraged development projects based in Rhodesia, and the economic imbalance which was thereby created stood in bleak contrast to liberal assertions of partnership and progress.

Lonrho, of course, had been established in Rhodesia since the early years of the century, and in the fifties it was well connected in federal circles. Lonrho House, a stately office block built in the centre of Salisbury in 1959, was a fitting symbol of Lonrho's faith in the political and economic future of Welensky's Federation.

Federalist hopes were, however, confounded not only by black nationalism but also by white fear. The realization that Welensky was only paying lip-service to 'partnership' did not reconcile Rhodesia's whites to his superficial liberalism. When the Federation broke up and Malawi and Zambia achieved independence, white Rhodesia was determined to rid itself of the last vestiges of restraint by Britain over Salisbury's African legislation, which had encouraged Welensky's liberal hopes. On 11 November 1965 Ian Smith made the Unilateral Declaration of Independence, and the line of southern Africa's racial divide was drawn at the Zambezi. The issues at stake had been crystallized.

Zambia, which bordered three hostile countries – Rhodesia, Mozambique and Angola – was the outpost of black African independence and was now wide open to attack. The fact that Zambia's main export route ran south from Lusaka gave Pretoria, Salisbury and Lisbon a potential stranglehold over Kaunda's government. Zambia's support of policies with which southern Africa's white rulers disagreed made it subject to political and economic blackmail. Difficulties were immediately created for Zambia after UDI when Rhodesia banned the movement of railway tankers and oil across the border, in breach of the agreement concluded between the two countries in December 1963, under which the assets of the Central African Federation had been divided at its dissolution. The railway system had been jointly owned, and Salisbury and Lusaka had agreed to run the line as a unitary system. Zambia was supposed to have equal ownership and control, as well as responsibility for half the liabilities, despite the fact that most of the assets, including the headquarters and workshops, were sited in Rhodesia.

Kaunda had been conscious since before independence that Zambia's reliance on hostile neighbours for its lines of communication was a weakness which had to be overcome. In 1963 Lonrho carried out a survey to connect Zambia with the Indian Ocean, through the Tanzanian port of Dar-es-Salaam – the eventual route of the famous Tanzam railway. Earlier studies, dating from before the Federation, had concluded that such a link could not be economically viable.[3] It has been suggested that the retention of exclusive prospecting licences by the big mining houses had created an obstacle to its construction. According to one observer, overseas finance in a rail link with East Africa might have been found 'if the Zambian government had been able to grant mining concessions to consortiums involved in the construction and financing of the railroad'.[4] Lonrho would certainly have been interested in such a proposition; its survey was followed by offers to finance the railway on condition that the company was awarded a monopoly to carry copper over the route.[5]

Although the scheme fell through, Lonrho remained interested. In February 1965 the company's newly-acquired Zambian newspaper, the *Northern News*, reported that the rail scheme merely awaited Kaunda's favourable decision and an editorial comment mentioned that China was 'ready to finance the work on the Tanzania side'.[6] This seemed a remarkable prophecy, for President Nyerere's visit to Peking, during which the Chinese indicated their willingness to back the project, occurred only at the end of that month. Two years later, after Peking's support for the scheme had been settled, Lonrho was once again mentioned in connection with the project. The West had by this time woken up to the fact that the Chinese were in earnest, and that Tanzania and Zambia had decided to accept Peking's assistance. A whole spate of last-minute bids to bring the railway under Western control followed.[7] Since neither Tanzania nor Zambia was prepared to go back on its agreement with the Chinese, alternative schemes were proposed with the object of pre-empting the Tanzam plans or diminishing the importance of the railway once it was constructed.

Following UDI, Lonrho was already handling Zambia's copper and tobacco exports by road through the Smith and Youngson transport company[8] to the Salima railhead in Malawi, and then by Malawi Railways through Mozambique to the coast. When

225

Chinese support for the Tanzam scheme was confirmed, new proposals were made for the transport of Zambia's copper via Malawi, particularly through the new Nacala railway link from Salima to the coast. Zambia did have a limited outlet through the Benguela railway, which connected the copper belt with the Atlantic Ocean on the other side of the continent, via Zaire and Angola. Proposals were now made to shorten and improve this line. At the same time, Lonrho was planning a new link in Zaire between Port Francqui and the Atlantic, which would have joined up with part of the Benguela line.

The importance for independent Africa, and Zambia in particular, of the new outlet through Tanzania was obvious: it would rid Zambia of the threat of economic blackmail by the white-dominated south and open the way to a completely new political and economic reorientation. This 'wind of change' might have swept further afield, for example into Botswana, a hostage to South Africa, except for one small border point with Zambia, which had long been the road to freedom for political refugees from the white south.[9]

But it was Zambia that mattered; the prospect of Chinese influence, added to the deliverance of Zambia from her dependence on white-controlled lines of communication, manifestly worried the white regimes of southern Africa. Feelings in Pretoria on this matter were reflected in a book on 'terrorism' by a member of the South African police force.[10] The author, pointing out that Tanzam was to use the 3ft 6in. gauge which, despite its awkward narrowness, was prevalent in southern Africa, suggested that the railway had 'revolutionary' potential as a vehicle for Chinese ambitions. But the prospect of Chinese soldiers disembarking in Johannesburg, which this seemed to suggest, was not the chief concern of South Africa's foreign policy experts. As the author put it,

The simple fact is that Zambia is landlocked and that the only roads and railways able to support the necessary heavy supply [transports] are those from its 'white-controlled neighbours' . . . Complete disengagement would be, of course, a major step towards removing what I shall term a buffer of economic composition: once this has gone, we shall all be one step nearer to hell.

The most significant factor in lessening Zambia's economic dependence, the writer pointed out, was the Tanzam railway, but 'not so much because of the economic aspect as because of the ideological influence'.[11]

On 28 May 1969, at the annual conference of the Tanganyika African National Union – Tanzania's ruling party – Nyerere said in Kaunda's presence that the Tanzam railway had 'a lot of enemies. A profusion of railway projects is being canvassed in southern Africa at the present time, and all of them have one goal – to prevent our railway being built. I do not believe that these plots to sabotage our plan will succeed.'[12] *African Development* reported that the statement

gave no comfort at all to Lonrho, which has been making a great song and dance about its plans to build a railway through the Congo [Zaire]. In theory that railway would offer an alternative route to Tanzam and take business away from it. Nyerere also clearly sees some connection between big United States interest in the Congo's current structure and this new challenge to the Chinese-sponsored Tanzam line.[13]

In view of the feelings aroused by the Tanzam railway plan in Western circles, Tanzanian fears about Western sabotage of the project were not exaggerated. In February 1970, for instance, a well-known British Conservative MP, John Biggs-Davison, referring to the Chinese in Tanzania, said that the 'Tanzam Railway survey has brought them [the Chinese] into the heart of the continent. Well-armed, well-indoctrinated terrorists trained in Tanzania, are staged through Zambia and are infiltrated into Rhodesia and further south . . .'.[14]

The answer to the Tanzam railway for many Western strategists was the existing Benguela railway. Owned by the Bahamas-based British company, Tanganyika Concessions Ltd (known as Tanks), it reached as far into the Zambian copper belt as the Tanzam rail scheme was to go. The importance of the Benguela railway was underlined early in 1970 when a working group within Britain's Conservative Party produced a report on defence outside NATO which referred to the Benguela railway as

the most obvious sign of the economic interdependence of Angola, the Congo and Zambia. Portugal's relations with the Congo are improving . . . Despite the competition which the Chinese building of the Tanzam rail-link will bring, the Benguela railway will still serve the shortest and most economic sea route from Lobito for the shipping of Central African copper to Europe and will therefore continue to act as an important lever for the establishment of more normal and neighbourly relations with the Congo and Zambia.[15]

The Benguela railway was already used by Zambia to export a substantial part of its copper; Lord Colyton, the chairman of Tanks, was anxious to get more of this traffic. It was also carrying the bulk of Zaire's copper to its terminal at Lobito, a port on the Atlantic. Following informal contacts with Kaunda during the Commonwealth Prime Ministers' Conference in London in January 1969, Colyton made two secret visits to Lusaka. The second time he was accompanied by Dr Alexandre Pinto Basto, president of the Benguela railway company, and an influential member of the Portuguese political and business establishment. The purpose of these visits was to propose to the Zambians that Tanks would carry out, at its own expense, a £100,000 survey for constructing a direct link between Zambia and Angola that would connect with the existing Benguela line and bypass the lengthy detour through Zaire. Zambia refused.[16]

Soon after the first approaches by Colyton to the Zambians, Lonrho was rumoured to be making a takeover bid for Tanks and hence the Benguela line as well: a revival of a suggestion made in Salisbury six years previously, when the pros and cons of alternative coastal outlets for Malawi were being considered.[17] At that time, too, Lonrho was said to have had half an eye on the Benguela line.[18] Tanks would certainly have been a prize for Lonrho, eliminating an important competitor, for apart from the Benguela railway it had valuable assets in Zambia and a seventeen per cent stake in Union Minière, the Zairean copper giant. Furthermore, in 1969 Tanks had just announced that it was spending £10 million on improving the Benguela line to provide a faster and more efficient link between the Zambian copper belt and the Atlantic Coast – the Cubal variant.

The Benguela railway itself was threatened by Lonrho's Zaire scheme[19] – one of the major challenges to the Chinese Tanzam plans. This coincided with rumours of Lonrho's bid for Tanks, demonstrating perhaps Rowland's determination to manage one or both of central Africa's copper export routes to the Atlantic. The plan was to build a railway through Zaire, linking the copper mines of Katanga with the port of Banana, and cutting out the tedious river shipments involved in the existing route through Port Franqui and Matadi.[20] During the second half of 1968 a consortium headed by Lonrho had launched into a feasibility study of the 800-mile route. Construction of the line – according to Lonrho – was due to start in 1971. Its completion would have posed a direct challenge to Benguela, which was carrying most of Zaire's copper. Until things began to go seriously wrong for Lonrho in Zaire during the following year, the company's hope to manage both Zaire's and Zambia's export routes to the Atlantic seemed a dangerous one for both Tanks and Tanzam.

The most serious potential threat to the Tanzam railway, and to a militant African nationalism in its challenge to white rule in the south, centred on Malawi whose crucial location, poised on the edge of the southern African bloc, along with Banda's pro-South African stance, were seen by the *Daily Telegraph* in London as

major obstacles in the path of pan-African forces bent on the destruction of white rule in South Africa. In the growing racial confrontation Malawi could not be more strategically placed. Its northern tip points towards the Tanzania–Zambia railway now being built by the Chinese, while its southern border is within a hundred miles of the Cabora Bassa dam.[21]

Malawi had been strengthened by South African capital even before independence, with the clear intention of rendering the country 'safe'. And Lonrho had played a part in this. As a writer in *Sechaba*, the journal of South Africa's African National Congress, put it in 1971:

Dr Banda has encouraged foreign investments in Malawi by capitalist interests – most notable of these being the powerful Lonrho (London–Rhodesia) Group who have long been active in Malawi ... A senior member of Lonrho is employed by Dr Banda's cabinet in an advisory capacity, providing a splendid example of neo-colonialism in Africa today.[22]

The 'senior member' of Lonrho was not named.

The company certainly had powerful friends in the Banda administration. Sir Peter Youens, a senior colonial official, became Secretary to Banda and the Malawi cabinet after independence. When he retired in 1967, he became a Lonrho director. Gerald Percy, Lonrho's managing director in Malawi, was appointed to the board of the Malawi Development Corporation. During that period the Banda government encouraged both South African and Portuguese private investment.

Malawi's strategic position was particularly important to Mozambique, where the Portuguese were under growing pressure from one of the most successful liberation movements in Africa,

Frelimo (the Front for the Liberation of Mozambique). After the British, the Portuguese were probably the largest resident European community in Malawi and in March 1962, in an address to the Portuguese Association in Blantyre, Banda had assured them that he saw no reason why Malawi and Mozambique could not live amicably side by side. He said that he stood for a 'live and let live' approach; while he might not agree with every aspect of Portuguese colonial policy, he had no intention of interfering with the Portuguese so long as they did not interfere with Malawi.[23]

As a landlocked country, Malawi was in a similar position to Zambia in many ways, and at independence also faced problems of transporting bulk exports and imports either through the existing southern route or by constructing a railway running north through Tanzania. At independence in 1964, Malawi's only railway ran to the Mozambican port of Beira, so connecting it firmly with the white south. The line as a whole was at this time divided among four separate companies. Malawi Railways Ltd and its wholly-owned subsidiary, the Central Africa Railway Company Ltd, owned the line from Salima on the southern shore of Lake Malawi through to the border and for twenty-four miles into Mozambique, as far as the bridge across the Zambezi. The Trans-Zambezia Railway Company, a British-registered group, owned the next 179 miles from Sena on the south bank of the river to Dondo, where the track joined up with the main line from Salisbury to Beira. The last eighteen miles from Dondo to Beira were the preserve of the Caminhos de Ferro de Moçambique, the state railways. Trans-Zambezia and Malawi Railways were closely interconnected; for thirty years, up to the time of Lonrho's take-over, they had shared local management staff, London office staff and accommodation, and there were other arrangements for pooling the supply of rolling stock, and for dividing up the revenue received from through traffic from Malawi. There was also considerable overlap between the boards. Both the Federal government and Malawi Railways had the right to appoint directors to Trans-Zambezia; when Lonrho took over the line in Malawi, Alan Ball joined Trans-Zambezia's board. Taking over the latter completely would certainly have given Lonrho a valuable foothold inside Mozambique and an entry into a number of related enterprises covering a whole range of interests.

Before independence, Banda seemed to fear that his vital lifeline to the sea might be cut off by the Portuguese for political reasons and while he tried to get on better terms with his white neighbours he also explored the possibility of creating new outlets through Zambia and Tanzania. Shortly before independence he despatched simultaneous missions to the Portuguese and to Nyerere, while another mission went to Kaunda. The general idea was to build a railway from the copper belt in Zambia to the northern shores of Lake Malawi and onwards to the Tanzanian port of Mtwara – a line running roughly parallel to and south of today's Tanzam.

Lonrho seems to have been involved in these plans: in February 1963 it was linked in the Rhodesian press with the prospect of a Zambia–Malawi–Tanzania railway connection. As the company having executive control over Malawi Railways, it would have had an obvious interest in staking a claim to any alternative route.

But plans for a Malawi outlet independent of Mozambique were dropped as Banda grew increasingly certain that he would enjoy Portuguese friendship and support. In April 1962 Dr Pereira Bastos, Portugal's consul in Salisbury, had confirmed that 'the harbours and railways of Mozambique . . . are all at Dr Banda's disposal'.[24] Bastos also said that Banda was to visit Portugal, which he did in June of that year, to meet the Portuguese Foreign Minister, Dr Franco Nogueira. Banda had already told the Portuguese Association in Blantyre: 'I don't mind telling you that I am interested in your ports . . . I also want you to build that railway.'[25] What he was referring to here was a new rail link with the coast on which he pinned much hope for Malawi's future economic development. At the time, the line belonging to Malawi Railways was not only the sole coastal outlet in existence, but at its terminal, the congested port of Beira, loading and unloading were becoming subject to increasingly lengthy and frustrating delays. Work on the new outlet finally began in 1966 with a loan from the South African Industrial Development Corporation which Lonrho had first introduced into Malawi. It linked the railway town of Novo Freixo in Mozambique with Mpimbe in Malawi to connect the Malawi rail system with the port of Nacala. Malawi's position within the white-controlled southern African bloc had now been firmly determined.

The decision to build the Nacala link coincided with the take-over from Lonrho by Malawi of the controlling block of shares in Malawi Railways. As Banda put it, 'When I decided that the government should acquire the controlling block of shares . . . I also decided that this country should use a port other than

Beira.'[26] At the end of 1966 the twenty-four miles of line from the Malawi border to the Zambezi and the bridge across the river itself were still in the hands of the Malawi Railways' subsidiary, the Central Africa Railway Company. In March 1967, six months after Lonrho had been removed from control of the two companies, three transportation agreements were signed in Lisbon between Malawi and the Portuguese government. One formalized the understanding between the two countries concerning the construction of the Nacala link and guaranteed Malawi's right of access to both Beira and Nacala. The other two dealt with the ownership of the existing line to Beira. Under the agreements the Malawi government sold its holding in the Trans-Zambezia Railway Company to the Portuguese government and handed over the entire share capital of the Central Africa Railway Company, including the rights to the Zambezi Bridge and the line connecting it with the Malawi border, for a total of £3.35 million. But in 1971, and again in 1973, it was claimed in the British press that Rowland himself, against the advice of Banda's British civil servants, had been involved in negotiating the sale of the bridge to the Portuguese – a strategically crucial asset in the light of later plans to develop the Cabora Bassa hydro-electric scheme.[27] The claim, if no more than that, indicates the reputation that Lonrho had acquired as a powerful influence in Malawi.

The plans for a rail link between Zambia and Malawi, this time to give the Zambians an outlet through Nacala, were revived in 1970 when actual construction of the Tanzam was about to begin: 'President Banda envisages the railway as an outlet for Zambia ... Zambia and Tanzania recently signed a contract for construction of the railway from Lusaka to Dar-es-Salaam by Communist Chinese.'[28] Banda had also proposed to link the Nacala railway with Rhodesia and as this was well known in Lusaka the Zambian link-up with Malawi's Nacala outlet stood little chance. An extension westwards from Cabora Bassa to Shamva in Rhodesia, as proposed by Banda, was widely seen in black Africa as a telling expression of his readiness to support a campaign of beating sanctions.[29]

Such a link with the coast through Malawi was becoming of increasing interest to the Rhodesians. It would have provided an alternative export outlet to the Umtali railhead and overcrowded Beira, running through two countries at that time amicably disposed towards the Smith regime. It would also have been of singular interest to mining companies, since the Headlands area east of Salisbury, centred around Shamva and Umtali, was at that time the scene of an intensive programme of mineral prospecting, spurred on by government subsidies, and a number of important finds, including the renowned Inyati copper mine. Lonrho and its subsidiaries were in 1969 in possession of a number of Exclusive Prospecting Orders covering concessions in the Headlands area, and in the first months of that year had taken over Roan Selection Trust's disused gold mine at Shamva itself.[30]

Banda's numerous railway schemes were at least partly an expression of the need felt in the white south to consolidate its position by extending its sphere of influence – through sponsored transport links and other means – as far north in black Africa as possible. The visit of the Governor-General of Mozambique, Rebello de Souza, to Malawi in November 1969 marked an important point in these strategic designs. At a press conference in the presence of his guest, Banda announced his intention to visit Mozambique when the Nacala rail link was opened. Referring to the idea of the rail extension to Shamva, 'the President reiterated his belief that the establishment of an international transport system among countries of southern Africa would enhance and accelerate the economic development of the area'. Malawi radio reported him as saying that 'this area included Mozambique, Rhodesia, Malawi, Zambia and even the Congo, which are economically and geographically one area'.[31]

Banda's old acquaintance, Dr Nogueira, mapped out a similar design soon afterwards in London, during a discussion of the Cape Route. Calling for the recognition of southern Africa 'as a separate entity', he said that this area was the only part of Africa still secure for the West. Hence

the Republic of South Africa, Rhodesia, the Portuguese provinces, Madagascar, Malawi, Swaziland, Zambia, Lesotho, Botswana should cooperate with each other and with the West and should be the nucleus of some kind of organization which could contribute, by promoting such cooperation, to the stability of the area, preserving it from communist influence and eventual domination.[32]

What was at stake was, of course, not the security of Western oil tankers along the Cape Route, but the control of the entire subcontinent with its strategic resources. This was spelled out during the same discussion by Biggs-Davison. In sounding an alarm about Chinese influence and guerrilla infiltration, he pointed out that South Africa was

the heartland of an unwritten alliance and expanding economic zone. It gives increasing technical and financial assistance to Black Africa. Our own economy and that of Western Europe rests in large measure on southern African minerals.

In the autumn of 1969, Lonrho and Portuguese interests, represented by the Champalimaud group, along with the Malawi Development Corporation, established Alcoma for the exploitation of the Mlanje bauxite deposits. With the exception of extensive deposits of bauxite (from which alumina, the raw material of aluminium, is produced) in the Mount Mlanje area in the southwest of the country near its border with Mozambique, Malawi had few mineral resources. It was envisaged that the formation of Alcoma could transform the Malawian economy by earning, perhaps, as much as £12 million a year in exports. Through their partnership in Alcoma, Lonrho had, however, become involved in a project whose strategic significance far outweighed its economic implications.

It had always been clear that the inaccessibility of the Mlanje deposits – 65 million tons of them, situated 9,000 feet up on the steep volcanic outcrop of Mount Mlanje at a considerable distance from any road or rail connections – would be a difficult problem for any mining company to overcome. Efforts to interest developers had been started some years before Lonrho's concession was announced. Feelers had been put out to the Japanese in 1965 during discussions on the financing of the Nacala railway – part of the money for which came from Japanese sources. Then in November 1967 a team of economists commissioned by the South African government to survey Malawi's development potential, headed by Dr Rautenbach, Chairman of the South African Resources and Planning Council and an adviser to Prime Minister Vorster, considered the project. This suggested that the Mlanje deposits could employ power from the vast Cabora Bassa hydroelectric scheme, planned for a stretch of the Zambezi River in the Tete region of north-west Mozambique, and pointed out that the bauxite could be used by the South African aluminium industry.

The Cabora Bassa dam on which construction work began in 1970 was a scheme designed on an enormous scale to consolidate white power in southern Africa. It would not only provide hydro-electric power in sufficient quantity for South Africa, Rhodesia and Mozambique, but would open the way for a programme of massive white settlement and mineral exploitation in the fertile Zambezi valley in Mozambique, putting the Portuguese government firmly in control of the remote and vulnerable Tete province. Tete shared a border with Zambia which was one of the countries supporting Frelimo, and Frelimo had made the proposed dam a specific target of attack. The successful exploitation of the Mlanje deposits was crucially dependent on both the Cabora Bassa electricity and Malawi's access to the port of Nacala. It would also require coal from Mozambique and fuel oil from Durban or Lourenço Marques. The *Financial Times*, listing these requirements, commented that the Cabora Bassa scheme was

vital if the aluminium smelter [which was to be part of Alcoma] is to be made profitable. Other recent developments which have encouraged the Mount Mlanje project to go ahead are the construction of the Richards Bay aluminium plant in South Africa ... and the completion of the Malawi rail link with Port Nacala.[33]

Mlanje meant business for Cabora Bassa, while access to an African source of bauxite for the aluminium smelter being planned at the Richards Bay port as a possible alternative to an Alcoma smelter would reduce South Africa's dependence upon supplies from Canada and Australia.[34] By the autumn of 1970 Lonrho, through Alcoma, had completed a road to the foot of Mount Mlanje and was engaged in constructing a cable-way up the mountainside, and an airstrip at the top. The consortium, filled with optimism despite earlier judgements from both Anglo-American and British Aluminium that the project would prove uneconomic, felt that mining could begin five or six years after the completion of a two-year feasibility study. In the summer of 1972, after drilling and sampling had been completed, a report was submitted to the Malawi government.

The Champalimaud group, Lonrho's partners in Alcoma, was represented in Mozambique by a man who had become one of Banda's closest friends, Engineer Jorge Jardim. They had met at a crucial stage in Malawi's political evolution. Jardim, who played a decisive part in shifting Banda's opinion of the Portuguese from suspicion to friendship and cooperation, had introduced himself to the Malawi leader in the autumn of 1961, shortly before Lonrho entered Malawi. He was one of the richest and most influential men in Mozambique, owning a major newspaper in Beira, and well placed as a senior executive of the giant Champalimaud group to keep an eye on events in both Lisbon and its African colony. Antonio Champalimaud, one of Portugal's leading financiers and a major investor in Mozambique, had been responsible for the establishment of Portugal's first steel works, and by 1960 was head of a vast industrial empire which included steel mills and foundries, cement and fertilizer plants, banks and insurance companies.[35]

Like Champalimaud, Jardim was close to Salazar, Portugal's dictator for more than forty years, and as a young man had been an Under-Secretary for Trade and Industry in Lisbon. From the late fifties Jardim was involved in opening up Mozambique's business potential. In the sixties he was a frequent visitor to Blantyre and his daughters were said to have spent their holidays in Banda's household to learn English. Jardim thus succeeded in striking up a friendship with Malawi's Head of State and in 1964, following an economic agreement with the Portuguese authorities, he became Malawi's honorary consul in Beira.

Jardim's political interests in Malawi were combined with a number of industrial and commercial projects in association with the Malawi government, and in the case of Alcoma, at least, with Lonrho as well. He had already become chairman of the Oil Company of Malawi, Oilcom, founded in 1968, in which the Portuguese firm Sonarep had a majority shareholding. Sonarep operated the refinery at Lourenço Marques which since UDI had become Rhodesia's main oil supplier; one of the refinery's major shareholders was the French oil company, Total, with whom Lonrho had earlier been associated in Malawi through a joint scheme to distribute oil and oil products throughout the country.[36] In 1969 Jardim also became chairman of a joint enterprise with the Malawi government, the Commercial Bank of Malawi.[37]

Lonrho's instant success in Malawi may have been connected with the pro-Portuguese climate created by Jardim from the end of 1961 onwards. The company was, by all accounts, already well connected in the Portuguese business world which Banda had started to court. The negotiations for the construction of Lonrho's Rhodesian oil pipeline from Beira to Umtali, concluded in the final months of 1962, are said to have taken Rowland to Lisbon, as well as to Lourenço Marques and Beira, for a whole series of meetings with the Portuguese authorities and with representatives of the Companhia da Moçambique, Lonrho's partners in the pipeline venture[38] and the second largest investors in Mozambique. The Companhia da Moçambique had been incorporated by Royal Charter in the nineteenth century and granted sovereign rights over all the territory between the Rhodesian border and the coast between the rivers Save and Zambezi. It subsequently established the town and port of Beira, where Jardim became the leading businessman, and in 1962 it retained a degree of control over the Trans-Zambezia line running through its territory. The Companhia's subsidiaries and associates included the Companhia Carbonifera de Moçambique, the railway's main coal suppliers. Another link was with the Sena Sugar Estates Ltd, a British-registered company with local boards in both Lisbon and Mozambique. It was the largest producer of cane sugar in Mozambique and from 1969, when a spur was opened to connect the main railway line to its cane plantations, one of Trans-Zambezia's most influential customers. Although Sena was not directly linked with Lonrho's sugar interests, there were some indirect connections. The chairman of Sena Sugar was Lt.-Col. John D. Hornung, who was until November 1962 on the boards of both Malawi Railways and Trans-Zambezia. Another Sena director, Vivian L. Oury, continued on Trans-Zambezia's board after Lonrho's takeover of Malawi Railways, and in 1973 was both its chairman and managing director. In 1962 Lonrho was clearly keen to extend its interests in Mozambique, and it was very soon after the railway deal that Rowland was reported in Salisbury to have gained a concession from the Portuguese for the handling of Rhodesia's maize exports.[39]

Banda's attitude towards UDI in Rhodesia was equivocal, perhaps because Malawi's tobacco exports benefited from the sanctions imposed on the Rhodesian crop. However, he did make it clear that he could not go along with sanctions in so far as these might harm Malawi. In November 1969 he expressed his hope for a settlement between Wilson and Smith which, he argued, 'would be of advantage and benefit not only to Britain and Rhodesia . . . but to all countries in southern Africa'. He went on, 'Malawi has kept contact with Rhodesia and will continue to maintain this contact.'[40] The desire for an early settlement was of course shared by all companies with interests in Rhodesia, as well as by Lisbon,

Pretoria and the West as a whole. When Sandys went on a tour of southern Africa in 1971 – shortly before he joined Lonrho as a consultant – he embodied many of these hopes. In South Africa he was a guest of the government. He then visited Malawi, where he saw Banda, and continued to Mozambique. He was reported to have commented that

the Cabora Bassa dam project will rank among the greatest engineering achievements of the world . . . When completed [it] will offer neighbouring countries a new and vitally needed source of industrial power. Mr Sandys added he feels Mozambique is a happy country whose peoples of all races are working constructively in harmony and friendship.[41]

From Mozambique he flew on to Salisbury, where he had a private meeting with Smith. His interest in reopening negotiations between Britain and the Smith regime was clear. In Malawi he probably found that Banda's attitude towards Rhodesia had softened considerably, for the previous year, during a private visit to Blantyre as a guest in Banda's household, Welensky and Banda had buried the hatchet. On his return to Salisbury in September 1970, Welensky spoke of his impressions of Malawi and particularly of Banda's foreign policy. 'My feeling was that he would welcome a settlement of the Anglo-Rhodesian issue because he feels that the difficulties which exist in this field just add to the general problems of Central Africa.'[42]

Welensky and others in Salisbury, Pretoria, Lisbon and London were concerned at the increasingly successful Frelimo campaign and were looking to Malawi to play a 'positive' role in stemming the tide. The fact that the southern half of Malawi jutted into Mozambique, partly dividing that territory's northern provinces from the more industrialized southern ones, gave rise to an ingenious plan designed to cushion the white-ruled countries from the growing Frelimo threat. The idea was based on that of the ancient and shadowy 'Maravi kingdom' of central Africa; Banda believed that Malawi had some historical claim to areas in Mozambique as well as in Zambia and Tanzania. At first it appeared that he might use this pre-colonial history to help the people of Mozambique to free themselves from Portuguese oppression. Before independence, for example, he had said, 'When Nyasaland is free, I will not rest until the greater part of Mozambique is joined to it. We are all the same people.'[43] By 1963, however, he had been given to believe that northern Mozambique might be ceded one day to Malawi; whether this suggestion emanated from government circles in Lisbon, whom Jardim represented in his first contacts with Banda, or whether it was linked with a possible white settlers' UDI in Mozambique, is uncertain. In November 1969, at the time of the visit to Malawi by Mozambique's Governor-General, who was accompanied by Jardim, the idea gained fresh currency. A contemporary report in *Le Monde* about the white settler 'independence' movement in Mozambique, led by Jardim, linked him with the plan to merge the northern part of the territory with Malawi. Jardim was described in the French newspaper as 'a fervent supporter of Dr Salazar' and as 'an intimate friend of Dr Banda, the President of Malawi; of Mr Smith and Mr Clifford Dupont, the *eminence grise* of the Rhodesian Prime Minister'. The Champalimaud group which he represented had shown

a marked preference for the area north of the Zambezi River, where it has built an important cement factory and is getting ready to create new industries. Most industrialists, on the other hand, prefer the area south of the Zambezi because of the climate of insecurity created in the north by Frelimo guerrillas. Those industrialists who have learned about Mr Jorge Jardim's independence plans know that, if they are realized, the northern part of the territory which comprises the provinces of Niassa, Cabo Delgado and Mozambique, will be handed over to Malawi to form a buffer between Tanzania and 'white Mozambique', and to give Malawi direct access to the sea.[44]

Lonrho, like Champalimaud, had not been deterred from investing in territory subject to Frelimo attack. It had acquired the Edmundian copper mine and in 1972 it was reported to have gained concessions to prospect for copper, gold and other minerals in the Manica region across the border from Shamva, where it had acquired its gold mine in 1969.[45] Lonrho also had timber interests in Mozambique. In April 1965 Ball had told shareholders that a company had been formed with Portuguese associates to develop extensive timber concessions in the territory for the eventual export of hardwoods to South Africa. A company – Moçambique Florestal SARL – was set up; like the Beira–Umtali pipeline company, it was an associate of the Companhia da Moçambique of Beira. In their Annual Report for 1974 Mozambique was listed as one of the countries in which Lonrho maintained representation.

The scheme for dividing Mozambique surfaced again in 1974 as the Portuguese – after the changes in Lisbon – were moving towards a transfer of power in Mozambique to Frelimo leaders. There was talk in Pretoria of a secret agreement, supposedly reached between Zambia, Malawi and Swaziland, to carve up Mozambique in the event of a breakdown of law and order after the Portuguese had withdrawn.[46] This was hotly denied by Zambia, and later also by Swaziland, but Malawi, which had broken off diplomatic relations with the new government in Lisbon, remained silent. The breach had come after accusations had been made from Lisbon that Jardim – by now clearly identified as a leading figure in white plots to seize control in Mozambique – was using Malawi as a base where he was reported to have been in contact with ex-Congo mercenaries.[47]

In the days following the fall of the Caetano regime in April 1974, Jardim had taken refuge in the Malawi embassy in Lisbon to evade the new authorities. He made his escape to Spain and from there travelled to France, Rhodesia, South Africa, Swaziland and Malawi. His manoeuvres worried Lisbon. A Portuguese government request for his expulsion from Malawi was refused by Banda, even though a warrant was by this time out for Jardim's arrest.

Jardim's plans for Mozambique had envisaged 'a government comparable to that of Dr Banda in Malawi . . .'.[48] Malawi, Jardim's model, had been one of Lonrho's most successful areas of investment. A parallel system in Mozambique would have been welcomed by eager Western investors. In the summer of 1974, about six weeks before the formal transfer of power to Frelimo, du Cann was reported as saying that he was 'eagerly watching the throes of the Portuguese colonies in Africa. In a black-ruled Mozambique in particular, he sees great opportunities for Lonrho . . .'.[49]

Conclusion

The Smiling Face of Development?

Like other multinational companies, Lonrho's prime purpose is to make profits. As the company's accountant himself said, 'When it comes down to it, there is only one thing that matters, and that's the cash we can expect to receive in London'.[1] But in certain other respects Lonrho is uncharacteristic. It is rare enough, in an era when the proprietorship of big business has increasingly grown divorced from its management, for a company the size of Lonrho to be managed by an individual, Rowland, whose personal shareholding is second only to that of the Kuwaiti royal family. What is rarer still is that it should be a multinational. At the beginning of February 1975, Rowland personally held about seventeen per cent of Lonrho's issued share capital. And rare, too, for one of its size, the company has few institutional investors, so that until the advent of the Kuwaitis Rowland could pursue his aims virtually untrammelled by powerful voting blocs. From the late sixties onwards, there were those in the City who thought that Lonrho was outgrowing its management structure and becoming too big and complex to operate at full efficiency under the control of one man, particularly as its interests were so diverse. But the real complaint was that Lonrho's phenomenal period of success in Africa seemed to be ending. And those who pointed this out came close to identifying perhaps Lonrho's most important divergence from other multinationals: its overwhelming involvement in operations on the African continent, and so its vital connection with political events there.

Most if not all multinationals operating in Africa do become involved in politics at some level. In order to carry on business, they have to interact with governments which increasingly exercise close supervision over their own economies, and to enter into negotiations for the best deal that they can get. The importance of such political manoeuvring to Lonrho has been particularly great because it has challenged the position of companies far more securely established in black Africa, and with financial power very much greater than its own. Thus in seeking to displace them, as in Zaire and Sierra Leone, Lonrho has disregarded some commercial practices.

In order to expand rapidly the company had chosen to operate in overtly political ways by utilizing the local political situation. Rowland himself pointed to his influential contacts in 1973: 'When I'm abroad, I am entertained, and do business with Rulers, Presidents and Prime Ministers, who entertain me and look after me.'[2] His most fruitful contacts have probably been among the new generation of well-connected African capitalists who have been brought up as members of a Westernized business élite.

Rowland has said, 'We believe in Independent Africa. We will do anything we can to help Independent African countries to achieve their full economic potential.'[3] This emphasis on the role that Lonrho can play in development is interesting, both in the light of the controversy that multinationals have caused and of the longstanding debate about the effects of foreign investment in developing countries. Apologists for their activities claim that multinationals potentially have a considerable part to play in the promotion of development. They can import fresh capital investment into the economy, embarking on schemes which employ valuable technology and expertise beyond the reach of indigenous entrepreneurs. They can bring to bear their network of marketing organizations, and can help to reduce the high levels of unemployment present in so many parts of Africa, not only by the jobs that they provide directly, but also by indirect stimulation of the economy.

Against this, however, must be balanced the negative aspects of foreign investment for development. Some profits are usually repatriated instead of being reinvested in the areas where they are earned. Moreover, foreign companies may try to raise capital locally, instead of bringing in the extra investment that is so desperately needed. It has even been argued that, in the long run, developing countries should not encourage foreign investment.[4] For, as the governments of developing countries increasingly have to intervene directly in key sectors of the economy, they come up against well-established foreign companies, whose policies clash with their aims. And this sometimes arouses the hostility not just of the foreign company but also of its host government, which may then affect the attitude of international aid and credit agencies, if not encourage more direct forms of intervention.

These problems have been tackled in different ways. Some countries, like Tanzania, have proceeded to outright nationalization; others, such as Zambia, have tried to control foreign capital by pursuing joint participation policies. Rowland has said: 'We like to approach a country and give them ideas and suggest a feasibility study and a partnership deal so they can get in right from the start . . .'.[5] The implication that Lonrho has been somehow exceptional in promoting joint ventures with governments has been accepted by many, including some leading African officials. The company has certainly been eager for such schemes in the Arab world.[6] It is nevertheless true that all companies, whatever their attitudes, have in certain countries been obliged to accept some form of government participation or pull out. Some indeed, like Consolidated African Selection Trust in Ghana, have reconciled themselves to the changing conditions more quickly than Lonrho.[7] Companies have continued to do well out of what has been called 'exploitation by participation'.[8]

Certainly Lonrho's operations in Africa have earned it large profits, although it is very reticent about the proportion of these attributable to southern African ventures.[9] Remittability has been an important issue for Lonrho since the late sixties and the pressures on it in this respect have been particularly acute, partly because it had substantial interests in areas where the repatriation of profits to parent United Kingdom companies was restricted. It was also a legacy of the 1971 liquidity crisis and the Peats recommendations.[10] During the 1973 boardroom battle, Rowland assured shareholders that every effort had been made to maximize the proportion of profits remittable to the United Kingdom.[11] If this was so, Lonrho was committed to a policy which might reasonably be considered disadvantageous to the interests of developing countries.

Rowland's statements in 1973 were in some contrast with his claim of the following year that 'I have always insisted that the profits made in Africa should be used to develop the continent, and that is the policy I will continue to pursue as long as I am chief executive of Lonrho.'[12] Again, during the 1973 crisis, Rowland claimed that he had implemented the Peats recommendations that the negative cash flow from the United Kingdom be halted and that projects be financed from other sources. There were, he said, only two instances in which this had not been done since 1971: Western Platinum, and the extension of the Sugar Corporation of Malawi, where no local capital was available. In Kenya, complaints were being made at this very time that Lonrho was financing its expansion by borrowing local capital, instead of bringing investment funds into the country.[13]

Lonrho has, indeed, started new schemes in some African countries, so fulfilling what is sometimes assumed to be the crucial role of multinationals in development. It promoted the growth of the Malawian sugar industry, partly by attracting South African loan guarantees, and has initiated schemes in Sudan and Ivory Coast which will help these countries to substitute local production for imports. In Sudan and Ivory Coast it was not providing the great bulk of the finance as such, although its involvement possibly helped the governments concerned to find other sources. The company put money into industries such as brewing and construction.

Helping in the task of development, however, is not simply a matter of haphazard investment. One interesting example of this, in a scheme in which Lonrho was involved, was the Ivory Coast sugar project. This made some contribution to solving local economic problems. When fully operational, the scheme was envisaged as providing four thousand jobs in an area where local people had traditionally been obliged to migrate south as daily labourers upon wealthier and more fertile farms. But in some ways, the sugar scheme was unnecessary and a burden on the economies of other African sugar producers. Ivory Coast had prevously been supplied with sugar under an agreement concluded among the members of the Afro-Malagasy Common Organization (OCAM). This was an association of most of the ex-French and Belgian colonies, which Mauritius had also joined.[14] Its member states devised economic cooperation schemes, and in particular one concerning sugar. Under this, the sugar producers in OCAM – Congo-Brazzaville, the Malagasy Republic, and Mauritius when it joined – were to supply the other members. Lonrho's sugar in Ivory Coast would have been as expensive as OCAM's.[15]

But a large part of Lonrho's expansion in the sixties was through the acquisition of existing productive businesses like John Holt rather than through fresh investment and this scarcely brought significant new funds to developing countries. The company did invest in Africa by stepping up the activities of some subsidiaries: production at Ashanti, for instance, was increased on the lines of an expansion programme already under way when Lonrho took over the mine. The activities of David Whitehead, the cotton textile firm in Malawi, were also considerably expanded, in partnership with the Commonwealth Development Corporation. This was a response to a situation of increasing demand which held opportunities for growth: Lonrho's Rhodesian cotton interests were also being extended. Similarly, some of the expansion at Ashanti took place when gold prices were rising sensationally.

According to the Annual Report for 1974, the group and associated companies had 90,000 employees, of whom 3,000 worked in the United Kingdom. The remaining 87,000 were scattered among the company's operations in Africa and Sri Lanka, with a substantial proportion being employed in southern Africa. The provision of these jobs does contribute to development. Rowland said in 1973 that he saw no contradiction between his wish to advance African economic development and his desire to make profits.[16] Elsewhere, he has said: 'We love Africa'.[17]

Yet, while Lonrho stresses its sympathy with the aspirations of black Africa, it also has substantial, profitable and expanding interests in the white supremacist states of South Africa and Rhodesia. When Rowland was asked whether he saw a conflict between the company's interests in South Africa and those in black Africa, he replied:

There could be a conflict of interest. But, you see, the South African interests are historical; they were inherited, and with our emphasis on Independent Africa, we are left with three alternatives: sell up, maintain them or expand them. We decided not to expand; our preference was to sell, but we were advised not to sell by several African leaders who thought that to do so would be increasing the strength of the enemies of Independent Africa.[18]

Lonrho's public relations officer maintains that the southern African interests are a subject of constant debate within the company. It must also be borne in mind that Lonrho contends the London board has no control over the activities of the local Rhodesian management, who finance development from funds frozen in the country. It is interesting, however, that during the boardroom row, the eight dissident directors appeared to think that the London board did have control over Rhodesian activity, for they said they would not expand in that country if they succeeded in ousting Rowland, because of the problems involved in remitting profits from there.[19]

In fact, profitable businesses like Western Platinum and Inyati are ventures which originated and were developed in the late sixties and early seventies. The embarrassment, and even harm, they can cause Lonrho was seen in the OAU affair. Nevertheless, Rowland mentioned Western Platinum several times during the boardroom crisis when he was defending the group's profitability and prospects for remitting profits.[20]

The gap between the two fields of activity is bridged largely by Rowland himself, and his ability to get on with African leaders and other influential figures. When Rowland argued in May 1973 that his presence was essential for Lonrho's continued prosperity, his case was a strong one. He had built up Lonrho from a small company, whose activities were in the main confined to Rhodesia, into a multinational which operated in a number of black as well as white African countries; Lonrho's most ambitious schemes clearly derived from his enthusiasm and energy. It was Rowland above all who managed to perform the skilled balancing act between Lonrho's conflicting interests, so that both areas of activity have so far been safe and profitable. In the sense that his dismissal would have changed the company's policy and the way it operated through a network of influential figures, his presence as chief executive was indeed essential.

This bridging activity could only be a temporary expedient, however. Did Rowland think otherwise? Or did he have in mind some other, more long-term, solution to the contradiction between Lonrho's two spheres of activity? A kind of strategy does emerge from what he has said of the future of his own company and of Africa. When he declares his faith in independent Africa and his wish to see it free of colonial and white domination, there is no reason to think that he is not perfectly sincere. He has said: 'I am convinced that South Africa will be governed by Africans in ten to fifteen years from now, and in five years from now Rhodesia will be Zimbabwe.'[21] In the long run, the wish to see a solution of some kind to the racial confrontation in southern Africa is a logical one for all companies in Africa, particularly those like Lonrho which are active on both sides of the black–white divide. As the economic and political conflict intensifies, the position of such companies becomes more precarious and the climate of uncertainty increasingly damaging to their interests. There is always the lurking fear that an anti-imperialist struggle may easily turn into an anti-capitalist one.

In 1974 the possibility of such a progression seemed to have been advanced by events in Mozambique. On 20 September 1974, a transitional government was installed in which Frelimo representatives were predominant and Frelimo's president, Samora Machel, declared:

> The power belongs to the people. It has been won by the people, and must be exercised and defended by the people. Before the popular victory, the power belonged to colonialism; and was an expression of the domination exercised by [commercial] companies over our country. Who was ruling? The rulers were those who served the interests of a handful of big exploiters . . . We shall rebuild our country in our own way . . .[22]

Western business would do much to discourage both the implementation of such a programme, and the emergence of similar situations elsewhere in white-ruled Africa. The politicization that accompanies guerrilla warfare and industrial strife is a major threat to the long-term growth of profits, and the more far-sighted companies have appreciated the need for some compromise.

Lonrho is thus at the centre of a process in which Western capital is attempting to restructure its attitude towards Africa and its nationalist aspirations. In accepting the independent Africa that emerged with the 'wind of change', and in cooperation with its governments, companies in Africa have gone some way towards this. Lonrho's role, through its contacts with the African élite, has been to promote a climate of opinion in independent Africa favourable to the continuing presence of foreign companies.

Rowland hopes that the future of Africa will be one in which his kind of 'creative capitalism' will have elbow-room. He recognizes that this requires a new set of compromises from companies like Lonrho in the form of partnership agreements and concessions to the desire of developing countries for economic and political independence. The effect of Lonrho's style of operations has been to prepare the ground for the acceptance by black Africa of a solution to racial confrontation in southern Africa which would still leave room for Western investment. Its operations in countries such as Malawi have already opened the door for the entry of South African capital, skills and ideas. Its involvement in the strategic southern bloc was bound to steer the company into this role of go-between if it was to retain the goodwill of both black and white, a necessary condition for its expansion.

Lonrho's ambitions now stretch beyond the borders of black Africa. Rowland has said that 'the future lies with international companies, with consortia set up by different nations getting together and tackling today's needs all over the world'.[23] He has expressed his approval for the policy of Arab countries in obtaining control of their oil industries and has visualized an investment of the proceeds in the economic development of Africa:

> I am totally in sympathy with this type of revolutionary capitalism. If you have that, you won't get nationalization. It's much better that they should use their money this way than on buying Russian arms, and there is no greater opportunity than in independent Africa. Clearly the future of a company like Lonrho depends on being able to take part in this development.[24]

The real challenge to Lonrho's future lies in the possibility of an African and Arab challenge to capitalism itself and to its major agencies in the multinational companies. The devotion of these to the priorities of private profit have come under increasing attack even by conservative Arab regimes, which have sought to dispossess the oil multinationals of their traditional role in dominating supply and marketing. How much more, then, must the role of the multinational be questioned in African states where popular discontent at economic inequalities and pressures for more rapid economic development promote radical regimes, with a commitment to some form of socialism. In an era when there is mounting hostility, within the very homelands of capitalism, to the role of the multinational as an exercise of power without accountability, the role of the multinational is unlikely to escape searching criticism in Africa. And the criticism must be the more searching to the degree that the multinationals are inevitably associated with Western economic dominance. Ultimately, however, the question must and will be asked whether the sort of system represented by the multinationals is necessarily the most just and productive for Africa. The issue is not whether Lonrho is the unacceptable face of capitalism, but whether capitalism is going to have an acceptable face in Africa at all.

Postscript[1]

Rowland's ambition to use Arab oil money for the development of black Africa, and the company's expressed intention not to expand in white-ruled southern Africa, were little in evidence in 1975. On the whole, Lonrho's developments in black Africa were routine, and followed the pattern of the previous period.

During the year a project was started in Kenya to establish a commercial vehicle assembly plant in which Lonrho's subsidiary, Kenya Motor Holdings Ltd, played a part, together with the government, the Industrial Development Bank Ltd, Inchcape Mackenzie, and Associated Vehicles Assembly. At the same time Lonrho became subject to parliamentary discussions in Nairobi; in March a Kenyan MP, Mr Wichira, was reported by Kenyan state radio to have substantiated claims that the Nairobi Chibuku Company – distributors of Chibuku beer – was owned by Lonrho, and that both Udi Gecaga and his uncle, Nyoike Njoroge, were involved in the company.[2] Although Lonrho have no equity in the Company there was Kenyan comment on the involvement of some of its top personnel in Chibuku's complex system of holding companies.[3] Gecaga and other members of the Kenyatta family also bought heavily into Inchcape in Kenya.[4]

The Kenyan press came under general parliamentary criticism for its reporting of events surrounding the murder of J. M. Kariuki at the beginning of March.[5] The report of the commission of inquiry set up to investigate the murder had criticized the police for 'a massive cover-up operation'[6] and while other newspapers published the report in full, the Lonrho-owned *Standard* – formerly the *East African Standard* – omitted vital sections implicating top police personnel.[7] The *Standard*'s reportage of the matter took place under a new editor-in-chief, Henry Gathigira, who had just replaced Michael Peirson. Peirson had lost his post following criticism by the paper of the government radio station, a matter for which it was attacked in Parliament by the

Assistant Minister for Information and Broadcasting, Elisha Godana.[8] A few weeks earlier Ugandan reports on Kariuki's death recalled that 'the *Standard*, a Lonrho subsidiary, was criticized strongly over the mother company's connections in South Africa'.[9] Lonrho, as the largest commercial group in Kenya's private sector, was particularly vulnerable to government displeasure.

Kenya was not the only African country in which Lonrho newspapers came under pressure that year. In Zambia the two Lonrho papers, the *Times of Zambia* and the *Sunday Times* (of Zambia) were nationalized at the end of June, together with Lonrho's chain of cinemas. Printpak, a printing company in which Lonrho retained forty per cent, was also earmarked for eventual complete nationalization. No mention of compensation was made; nevertheless, Rowland said he was 'delighted' by this development[10] – surprisingly, perhaps, since the threat of Zambian nationalization had been his major argument during the 1973 boardroom row. In September it was stressed in Lusaka that Lonrho was not to retain its two editorial representatives on the newspapers.[11] In November William Saidi, the deputy editor-in-chief of the *Times of Zambia*, who had been brought in by Lonrho in consultation with the government, was dismissed by Kaunda because his philosophy was inconsistent with 'the philosophy and spirit of the paper' as the ruling party's new mouthpiece.[12] The nationalization followed the dismissal in May of several public figures, and the suspension of Amok Phiri, Zambian High Commissioner in London during the critical months of 1973, who had become a cabinet minister, for failing 'to honestly submit details of their private property' in accordance with the Zambian leadership code.[13] At the same time Vernon Mwaanga – the former *Times of Zambia* editor[14] – who had become Foreign Minister, was moved to the Central Committee of the party, from which post he resigned on 1 January 1976.

From Zaire came reports that Lonrho, in cooperation with the Belgian company Segtraco and a consortium of banks, had signed an agreement with the government in Kinshasa to survey an important railway branch line on the Ilebe–Kinshasa route. The work was expected to take six years.[15] The previous year Lonrho's Cominière was said to have been in the running for the construction of the main Ilbe–Kinshasa line, though this was still very much in the air because of cost and other considerations. Lonrho was said to have been 'interested in the project since its inception and considers [it] is now back in the running'.[16]

In Ghana the 1974–5 gold output was the lowest on record; it had been a deliberate policy of Ashanti to reduce the average grade of ore mined.[17] Miners' wages, which had been subject to regulation by the Chamber of Mines, had gone up by ninety-eight per cent since the government had taken a majority share in the mine. In July it was announced that a new shaft had been completed at Ashanti which was expected to prolong the life of the mine by fifteen years,[18] although net profits were down on the previous year. At the Lonrho Annual General Meeting in March Sandys was asked whether any progress had yet been made in the Ashanti gold mine compensation negotiations with the Ghana government. He replied that the matter had not yet been fully resolved: 'Discussions are still going on in a friendly and constructive atmosphere. While negotiations are proceeding I don't think it would be useful to give any details about what is being discussed.'[19]

In Nigeria, which had become an important sphere of operations for Lonrho through a variety of enterprises, Rowland paid a visit to the country's leader, General Gowon, and was entertained at the official residence at Dodon Barracks. It was rumoured that Lonrho was proposing a scheme to clear the critical congestion in Lagos harbour, where several hundred ships, mainly with cargoes of cement, were queueing up. Even if this rumour was true it is unlikely that anything could have come of such a venture as Gowon's government was overthrown in a bloodless coup a few weeks later.

Lonrho's Arab connections, rather than its black African performance, received most of the attention in the British press during 1975. This was not surprising in view of the importance which Arab oil money assumed for an increasingly depressed British economy. By the end of the year, after a long and complex series of share deals, Arab interests owned around twenty-six per cent of Lonrho's equity, with an option to purchase another four per cent.[20] The main Middle Eastern countries involved were Kuwait and the United Arab Emirates.

Considerable press publicity was given at the end of December to the transfer of a twelve per cent stake in the equity between United Fisheries of Kuwait and Gulf Fisheries, part of the Gulf International group. United Fisheries, in which the Kuwaiti government had the majority holding and Sheikh Nasser (son-in-law of the ruler of Kuwait) a further thirty-five per cent, had been revealed a few months earlier as the unidentified purchaser at the beginning of the year of 8.8 million new shares.[21] Gulf International, which was described as the largest private industrial concern in the Middle East, was wholly controlled by members of the Kuwaiti royal family, notably Sheikh Nasser and his brother. As a result of the December 1975 transaction, Khalil Osman, the Sudanese managing director of Gulf Fisheries, replaced Suleiman Khalid Al-Sahli, a representative of United Fisheries, as a Lonrho director. Al-Sahli had joined the London board in January 1975. Rowland said he was 'delighted' at the deal (which in itself did not change the overall size of the Arab holding in the company): 'I think it's only the beginning. I think they will be taking an increasing interest in Lonrho.'[22]

The greatly increased Arab stake in Lonrho since the end of 1974 prompted rumours that the company was considering changing its domicile, possibly to Belgium or the Middle East.[23] It was said that the Arabs would have welcomed the company. The suggestion reappeared towards the end of the year, when it was reported that Lonrho had instructed its solicitors to investigate the possibility. But it was pointed out that Bank of England permission would not necessarily be easy to obtain.[24] Rowland seemed to be considering another possibility: turning Lonrho into a private company by acting in conjunction with the Arabs to buy out the small shareholders, most of whom were in Britain. Confirming that he would very much like to make Lonrho a private company, he remarked 'I do not like the City overmuch, there are too many hypocrites around.'[25] Furthermore, he added, 'if we do not take over the company and carry on as we are we may or may not move the domicile'.[26] Commenting on these remarks and the latest Arab deals, *The Times* said:

> Shareholders should ask for a clear statement on the purpose and intent of the Arab holding. They also need to know more about the board's philosophy: why, for example, a change of domicile is being so seriously considered, and what benefits it might bring.[27]

One reason for the continuing antipathy between Rowland and the City, it was suggested, was the City's unease about the impending findings of the Department of Trade whose report on their investigations into Lonrho had yet to be published. Rumours about the publication date of the report had punctuated the year. In March at the AGM Sandys told a questioner that he did not know when it would be published. In April Clinton Davis, Parliamentary Under-Secretary of State for Companies, Aviation and Shipping, said that the investigation was in its closing stages. Publication of the report would be 'as soon as is practicable'.[28] Six months later it was reported that the inquiry was 'in its concluding stages'.[29]

As a result of the dealings over the previous year, the impression had gained ground by the end of 1975 that the Arab interest represented an important shift of emphasis towards projects in the Middle East, but City comment indicated some reservations: although a lot of money had changed hands as a result of the Arab connection, Lonrho had been 'notably coy' about revealing what actual business it had picked up in the Middle East; recent expansion had, in fact, been conspicuously in the United Kingdom and South Africa.[30] A deal greeted as evidence of Lonrho's capacity to play some part in development projects in the Middle East was the acquisition of twenty per cent of the ordinary share capital of Richard Costain Ltd, the British construction group. The shares involved had been purchased in December 1974 by Mohammed Al-Fayed and associates from Slater Walker Securities, and were bought by Lonrho in March 1975. Costain's chairman, John Sowden, later stressed that Lonrho had given a written undertaking not to raise its holding in Costain by more than a small amount, and to retain its stake as a long-term holding.[31] Al-Fayed was described as a shipowner and banker who lived in Dubai; as a result of the Costain transaction he joined Lonrho's board as executive director 'with special responsibilities for shipping and construction'.[32] He also became Lonrho's representative on Costain's board. Costain had important interests in Africa and the Middle East, particularly the Gulf states. At the time of the deal it was building a dry dock complex in Dubai.

According to press reports Lonrho's acquisition of the twenty per cent stake in Costain had been arranged by Mahdi Al-Tajir, the United Arab Emirates' ambassador to London and Western Europe.[33] Tajir had business connections with the Dubai dry dock scheme; he also advocated the concept of an Arab dinar based on oil rather than gold – an idea which was close to the heart of Rowland.[34] Al-Fayed was said to be acting on Al-Tajir's behalf in the Costain negotiations with Lonrho. Al-Tajir was also reported to have a twenty-five per cent stake in the El Sara Fund, a Swiss company which was half owned by a company half owned by Lonrho. The remaining El Sara equity was owned by another Middle Eastern businessman, Kamal Adham, a former adviser to the Saudi Arabian King Faisal; Adham also had top-level diplomatic links with Egypt. Sara had reportedly secured an exclusive concession from the Egyptian government to handle heavy goods transport between the Suez Canal and the rest of the country, and had been granted a licence for an air taxi firm; its longer-term plans were said to include the building and financing of an entire new city outside Cairo – echoing, perhaps, Lonrho's corniche scheme.[35] When President Sadat of Egypt visited Britain in November 1975 he met a group of British industrialists, including Duncan Sandys.

Costain's African interests, particularly in Nigeria, must have been an attraction to Lonrho; at Costain's AGM in June Sowden said that Costain (West Africa) in Nigeria was the main contracting subsidiary and 'we are doing extremely well there'.[36]

The year 1975 saw further announcements about the finalization of Lonrho's sugar involvement in Sudan. At the AGM Sandys announced 'the recent conclusion of the agreement setting up the Kenana sugar project'. There had been nearly four years of preparatory work in Sudan which had included 'extremely difficult financial negotiations'.[37] Nevertheless, further negotiations seem to have been required, for it was not until January 1976 that *African Development* reported, 'at last the financial package for Sudan's Kenana sugar project is finally tied up'. During the year it emerged that Lonrho's share in the company was only twelve per cent (instead of the twenty per cent earlier reported); Gulf Fisheries – Lonrho's partners in other ventures – held five per cent. The Sudanese government retained majority control. The Arab Investment Company – owned by twelve Middle Eastern governments – held seventeen per cent in the Kenana Sugar Company; it also agreed to lend the sugar project $15.75 million. Lonrho, the managers, appointed as their managing director Réné Leclezio, the sugar expert whose family had long been associated with Lonrho's southern African sugar interests.[38]

Lonrho's relations with the Arabs were not entirely trouble free. The first danger signal came in March, when Volkswagen and the associated company Audi-NSU were threatened by the Arab Boycott Office in Cairo with economic sanctions unless they withdrew a licence to an Israeli firm, Savkel, to produce Wankel rotary engines. According to the *Financial Times*, they were given a three-months' final warning.[39] Lonrho, which together with Audi-NSU controlled licensing rights for the manufacture of Wankel rotary engines, remarked at the time that the 'Israeli company presumably does still have a stake. But we are not involved.' Volkswagen also disclaimed responsibility for granting the licence to Savkel.[40] In September, however, a further six-months' warning was issued by the ABO, this time specifically naming Lonrho as well as Volkswagen. If the companies allowed rotary engines to be built in Israel they would be blacklisted, the ABO said. Lonrho indicated that it would probably withdraw the licence, and Ball, pointing out that the Volkswagen–Savkel licensing agreement had been concluded in 1969 before Lonrho had become involved with Wankel GmbH. (in 1971),[41] said that no engine plant had been set up in Israel. 'We shall talk to the Arabs,' he said. 'Someone at the bureau has got the wrong end of the stick.'[42] Lonrho was clearly trying to extricate itself from an embarrassing situation. A few weeks later it was reported that Savkel was in the process of building a $12 million plant with a capacity to manufacture in five years' time 100,000 Wankel engines. Production was expected to start in 1976 for export to North America, Europe and South Africa.[43]

Almost immediately after the warning Lonrho announced that it had bought Volkswagen (GB), the sole British distributor of Volkswagen, Audi and NSU vehicles from Thomas Tilling for £8.68 million in shares and cash. Ball justified the deal by explaining that it would bring in valuable United Kingdom earnings; it certainly was a move away from the group's emphasis on black African projects. Lonrho's holdings in Britain were further increased in the autumn of 1975 by the acquisition of an 18.8 per cent holding in the Yorkshire-based firm of Charles Roberts, manufacturers of road tankers and industrial plant. In October the Roberts board recommended acceptance of £1.76 million cash offer from Lonrho for the outstanding equity. Charles Roberts was part of the troubled business empire of Oliver Jessel, and its acquisition followed on from the purchase of Jessel's London Australian and General Exploration (LAGS).

In January 1975 Lonrho bought its 29.5 per cent stake in LAGS, making it the largest shareholder.[44] Despite its name the vast majority of LAGS' subsidiaries were incorporated in South

Africa, and there had been talk of a possible change of its domicile from Britain to the Republic. Nearly a third of its shareholders were South Africans. Apart from its mining interests in South Africa its operations there included property development, computer services, record and videotape manufacture. In 1973 Oliver Jessel had pointed out that eighty-five to ninety per cent of LAGS' profits were derived from South Africa.[45] Over the year to 30 June 1974 LAGS' central and southern African interests brought in seventy-nine per cent of total turnover and all of the profit, whereas the British end of the business made a £210,000 loss. Lonrho's purchase into LAGS was also the beginning of Lonrho's growth in Britain.[46] LAGS also had minor interests in Rhodesia and a number of black African countries, including Mozambique.

LAGS had an overwhelming bias towards southern Africa, but Lonrho was predictably reticent about having increased its stake in apartheid. In his introduction to the 1975 AGM Sandys described LAGS as a company

engaged in the manufacture of cold rolled steel and plant for steel works in Britain. It has subsidiary and associated companies in Africa which are involved in the mining of gold, coal, anthracite and asbestos, as well as in the general trade and motor car distribution. In this way the operations of LAGS will, as you see, dovetail well with our own.[47]

He made no mention of South Africa. In May du Cann joined the board of LAGS as its chairman, replacing Oliver Jessel. It was a surprising move because du Cann had resigned as chairman of Keyser Ullmann less than two months before on the grounds of his heavy public duties and other commitments. He had been widely tipped for appointment to a prominent position in the Conservative Party under Margaret Thatcher's leadership. Robert Dunlop also joined LAGS, bringing the Lonrho contingent on the board to seven. In July Lonrho started negotiations for the outstanding equity of LAGS, and the offer – consisting of one Lonrho share for every three in LAGS – was declared unconditional in September. Some shareholders apparently thought that Lonrho's offer did not reflect the true value of LAGS' assets, notably in South African mining.[48] LAGS held a seventy-five per cent stake in Duiker Exploration Ltd, which in turn had interests in a gold prospect in the Orange Free State, Erfdeel/Dankbaarheid. This prospect, being investigated by Anglo

American, had produced very encouraging results.[49] Duiker also had a holding in Unisel Gold Mining Company Ltd. Lonrho's bid for LAGS was finalized in December.

In March 1975 Lonrho followed up its acquisition of Balfour Williamson, the Lloyds Bank subsidiary with interests in the Far East, Australia and Brazil,[50] by purchasing a 16.6 per cent stake in San Paulo (Brazilian) Railway. San Paulo's assets in South America had been expropriated many years previously by the Brazilian authorities, but it had only a few weeks earlier received £4 million in compensation from the Brazilian government. Soon after the deal with Lonrho, San Paulo's name was changed to SPR Investments ('SPRINTS') and three Lonrho directors – Rowland, Ball and Butcher – joined the board, Ball becoming the chairman. There was speculation that Lonrho was intending to invest SPRINTS' £4 million in South Africa, and that the plan was to use the company alongside LAGS as a vehicle for further South African ventures.[51] There were growing commercial and political links between Brazil and South Africa at that time, and Sandys confirmed, in answer to a question at the March 1975 AGM of Lonrho, that the company was ready to consider further South American possibilities. However, he said, 'In the immediate future we have got our eye more on expanding in South East Asia and perhaps Australia'.[52] Sandys was referring to the new Balfour Williamson interest, and after the meeting Rowland elaborated: 'I would like Balfour Williamson to be the first British company in Hanoi and Peking', and he said that he was planning to fly to Hanoi 'any day now'.[53] The war in Vietnam was in its closing stages; perhaps Rowland felt that there would be scope for Lonrho's brand of 'revolutionary capitalism'.

Despite such far-flung plans, Lonrho did not neglect its proven profit-earners in southern Africa which had, of course, been expanded through the acquisition of LAGS. Dr Piet Koornhof, the South African Minister of Mines, told Parliament in Cape Town in June 1975 that Lonrho was to be the first company to put to commercial use at their Brakpan refinery new processes for refining platinum group metals, developed by South Africa's National Institute for Metallurgy. Lonrho, he said, was 'actively interested' in building a full-scale extension to the Brakpan plant to produce platinum group metals of higher purity than had been possible in the past.[54] However, there was little comment in London about this or other aspects of Western Platinum's operations. Under the heading 'Platinum' in the Annual Report for 1974, Rowland told shareholders that 'wage increases took place during the year and other substantial rises will be effected this year. In line with company policy, a considerable amount is being spent on additional amenities for mine employees.' No details were given.

Sugar continued to be a major profit-earner. Swaziland Sugar Milling's operations in Swaziland, South Africa and Mauritius broke all records as a result of the boom in world sugar prices. Earnings went up fivefold in the year to March 1975, and though subsequent months brought a decline the board remained optimistic that 'highly satisfactory' results would again be obtained.[55] However, in July forty per cent of Swazi Sugar's subsidiary in Swaziland itself, Ubombo Ranches, was taken over by the Swazi government. The agreement was signed by HM King Sobhuza and Rowland in a ceremony on the king's birthday: 'Today we are founding a new partnership,' commented Sandys who was also present, having recently visited South Africa and Malawi, where he inspected Lonrho's interests.[56]

The slump in world metal prices brought to an end the 1974 profit boom of Coronation Syndicate in Rhodesia; working profits for the year ending September 1975 all but halved, and forecasts for 1976 by the chairman – now Sydney Newman – envisaged some further decline.[57] In Britain, however, a more optimistic view prevailed: 'Coronation Syndicate, Lonrho's Rhodesian copper and gold producer, is a share which will appeal to those who want a speculation on the copper and gold prices and a satisfactory Rhodesian settlement'.[58] Lonrho's southern African interests were clearly bound up with the success of *détente*.

Mineral exploration, particularly for gold, by Lonrho's Rhodesian subsidiaries continued. In April the Rhodesian Minister of Mines announced that the Athens mine at Umvuma, which had been taken over by the Lonrho subsidiary, Homestake mines, a year earlier,[59] should feature 'prominently' as a gold and copper producer in the near future.[60] Homestake mines, who were working the Athens and the neighbouring Falcon mines, reported that 'encouraging' bodies of gold-bearing ore had been discovered. A pilot plan on the site was treating 3,000 tonnes of ore a month, producing a concentrate containing silver and copper as well as gold.[61] Coronation Syndicate was reported to be considering the takeover of the Tatcoll Mining Company Ltd which held the option for the dormant Ayrshire gold mine north-east of Salisbury.[62]

Lonrho's orthodox Rhodesian subsidiaries obviously continued to operate along well-established lines within the economic and political framework of the white minority regime. At the beginning of October a Lonrho employee, Petrus Snyders, was shot dead in an incident in the eastern border area of Rhodesia about eighteen miles south of Umtali. Snyders, a manager on a border estate of the Rhodesian Wattle Company, was patrolling the border with Mozambique in a company vehicle when, according to official Rhodesian reports, he was killed by FRELIMO troops just inside the Rhodesian border. This and similar incidents led to a protest by the Mozambique government against what was seen as aggression on the part of the Rhodesian regime.

Meanwhile it was reported in the British press that an economist connected with Lonrho, Mr Tim Curtin, had travelled to Rhodesia early in 1976 to act as adviser to the African National Council[63] in its constitutional talks with Ian Smith. Lonrho had already shown an interest in establishing rapport with African nationalist groups in Rhodesia. In May it was reported that a new company financed by Lonrho had been formed to start a newspaper for African readers. The proposed editor-in-chief was to be Herbert Munangatire, who was reported at the time to be a Lonrho employee, and the chairman of the company concerned was to be Mr Amon Jirira, a member of the ANC executive.[64] A fortnight later a Rhodesian press report stated: 'it is authoritatively known that Lonrho interests in London, South Africa and Zambia have been investigating the possibility [of starting a newspaper] for about six months now. ... It is learned that Lonrho's chief executive, Mr Tiny Rowlands [sic], supports the project and will give the go-ahead once he feels the political climate is ripe.' Munangatire was reported to have made several visits to Rhodesia to sound out the opinions of the ANC and African journalists, and to have gone to see the Lonrho press in Zambia.[65] Nothing came of the newspaper plan at that point: according to the South African press, 'certain ANC officials objected to involvement with Lonrho whose future operations, it was thought, might conflict with the aims of a Black government'.[66]

The newspaper scheme was very much in keeping with the kind of approach Lonrho had developed over the years in black African countries: to gain influence with important political groups as a step towards securing the company's interests and future operations. Lonrho had a lot to lose in Rhodesia and its approach here fitted in well with the whole concept of southern African *détente* as an 'understanding' between black and white interest groups in the hope of avoiding the overthrow of the economic *status quo* in the region.

Report of the Inspectors of the Department of Trade

On 6 July 1976, while this book was in page proof, the long-awaited Department of Trade report on Lonrho was published.[1] The bulk of the report dealt with the company's activities in Rhodesia and South Africa, particularly the transactions relating to the Nyaschere and Inyati copper mines; it also dealt with Wankel, and with the financial relationships between Rowland and others in the company. The report was highly critical of many aspects of the company's operations, presenting the evidence it had collected in considerable detail. The British press headlined Ogilvy's resignation from his remaining directorships as a result of the report's criticisms of him personally, but gave less attention to the implications of the inspectors' findings for the company's operations in Africa.

Dealing with Inyati the inspectors gave their opinion that 'Mr Rowland, Mr Ball and Mr Butcher were more closely involved in matters relating to the financing and in consequence the development of the Inyati mine than was consistent with the terms of UK sanctions legislation . . .'.[2] The most far-reaching aspects of the report were the implications that the inspectors' findings had for Lonrho's position in Africa. In particular, the evidence that the report presented of the constant and close liaison that members of the London board, notably Rowland, maintained with the company's Rhodesian and South African interests was in contrast with the assurances that Rowland had so often given to black Africa.

Rowland maintained that he was unaware of negotiations concerning the acquisition of the Edmundian mine, telling the inspectors that the London board had not even been consulted about its purchase: 'I do not know what happened because I was never present at any of the conversations or meetings.'[3] Nevertheless, the report quotes a letter from Lonrho's Salisbury office to London headquarters dated 19 July 1968 headed 'Edmundian Investments (Pty) Ltd' which refers to a visit Rowland and Ball paid to Rhodesia 'regarding the acquisition of the above named company' and enclosing a copy of the agreement 'covering this purchase made through Hochmetals Africa (Pty) Ltd as nominees'.[4]

Lonrho's sensitivity on these matters was indicated by Rowland's initial reaction to the publication of the report. He accused a number of British companies of avoiding sanctions. The allegations were contained in a letter written at the beginning of April to the Inspector of Companies at the Department of Trade, which he now released to the press, and in a company statement which rejected the report's criticism concerning sanctions-breaking 'because it is superficial and disregards the realities of the Rhodesian situation as accepted by the UK government'. Lonrho also answered in detail some of the inspectors' findings, and stressed that its position was 'far less open to criticism than that of many British companies who have continued through South Africa or elsewhere to supply oil, vehicles and banking and insurance services'.[5]

In view of the inspectors' criticisms concerning sanctions, it was ironical that at the time of the report's publication Rowland was being subjected to criticism in the Rhodesian parliament on the grounds that he supported the leaders of militant African liberation movements.[6] In reality, Rowland has long been concerned that Rhodesia's constitutional dilemma should be solved in such a way as to leave a place for companies such as Lonrho. The inspectors' report acknowledged Rowland's talents in building up Lonrho and gave a revealing insight into his conviction that the pursuit of African independence could be made to work to Lonrho's advantage. It quoted from Sir Basil Smallpeice's punctilious notes of his conversations with Rowland. After a meeting in June 1972 Sir Basil recorded a long statement by Rowland

of all his personal interests in helping free Africa, whether black or Arab, to develop, and how he had only this morning been to see the political adviser at the American Embassy in London, when he said it had been agreed that a special message would be sent to President Nixon outlining his ideas for the solution of the problem of Africa. He went on to add that he thought that as a result of securing a political solution to the problem of Africa, Lonrho could develop into a company earning profits of £50 to £100 million a year! . . . He said that he had two basic interests. One was personal and predominated over the other. The first was his interest in the political evolution of Africa and the generation of better relations between emergent Africa on the one hand and Europe and America on the other. The second was Lonrho. If there was a clash between the two, he would choose the first and willingly give up any participation in Lonrho.[7]

In reality, if the inspectors' report revealed nothing else, it showed the indivisibility of these two facets of the Rowland philosophy which has moulded Lonrho.

Appendix 1

Coronation Syndicate and the Rhodesian Mining Profits

From 1969, the profit figures show that Coronation Syndicate, a South African registered company, developed into an increasingly valuable asset for the Lonrho group. Coronation, of course, operates some of Lonrho's most valuable assets in Rhodesia – its gold and copper mines of Arcturus, Muriel, Mazoe and Inyati.

In its Annual Reports, Lonrho defines 'Southern Africa' as comprising South Africa, Botswana, Swaziland and (when the group possessed interests there) Lesotho. Rhodesia is included under 'East and Central Africa'. Since 1970, the Annual Reports have included territorial breakdowns of Group Turnover and Profit. The Accounts do not, however, indicate under which region Coronation Syndicate, as a company which is incorporated in South Africa but earns the vast bulk of its profits in Rhodesia, is included.

	Year ending 30 September:					
	1969	1970	1971	1972	1973	1974
	(£ *million*)					
Lonrho Ltd: total profit before taxation[1]	14.44	14.61	15.09	19.30	29.37	46.48
Coronation Syndicate Ltd: Group profit before taxation[2]	0.45	0.79	e0.67	1.04	3.34	6.19
Coronation Syndicate Ltd: Group profit before taxation as a *percentage* of Lonrho's pre-tax total (%)	3.12	5.41	e4.44	5.39	11.37	13.32
Lonrho Ltd: total profit before taxation from Southern Africa[3]	NA	1.46	0.91	1.01	2.03	7.44

(*e* = estimate; *NA* = not available)

1. Including both group companies and associates, and before tax and minority interests. (After taking account of minority interests, shareholders of Lonrho Ltd have a 39 per cent beneficial interest in the net profits of Coronation Syndicate. Lonrho's subsidiary, Tweefontein United Collieries Ltd, holds 66 per cent of the equity of Coronation Syndicate.) *Source:* Lonrho Ltd, Annual Report and Accounts for 1974.

2. Coronation's profits before payment of Rhodesian tax have been calculated using the approximate exchange rate of 1 rand (South African) equals £0.60. This underestimates them slightly in British currency. *Sources:* Coronation Syndicate Ltd, Annual Reports and Accounts for 1970, 1973 and 1974; *Rand Daily Mail*, 29 February 1972 (from which the 1971 profit figure has been estimated).

3. Up to 1973, Lonrho's Annual Reports included an Analysis of Group Turnover and Profit, broken down by activity and by territory, which *excluded* profits from associated companies. In the 1974 Annual Report, however, associate companies were *included* in the activity and territorial breakdown. This made no difference to the turnover and profit figures given for 'Southern Africa' for the year 1973, however. *Source:* Lonrho Ltd, Annual Reports and Accounts.

Coronation's gold and copper mines represent only a part of Lonrho's operations in Rhodesia as a whole, although, as assets owned by a company which is South African based, they occupy a particularly significant position.

In 1974, Lonrho possessed the following subsidiary and associated companies in Rhodesia:

A.O.P. of Rhodesia (Pvt) Ltd (*oil pipeline*)
*Autorama (Pvt) Ltd
*Ballarat Mines (Pvt) Ltd
*Brake-Rite (Pvt) Ltd
*Brake Services (Pvt) Ltd
*Capital Holdings (Pvt) Ltd
Corsyn Consolidated Mines Ltd (*holding company for Coronation's mines in Rhodesia*)
    Alton Mining Co. (Pvt) Ltd
    Eastern Minerals (Pvt) Ltd
    Kakonde Mines (Pvt) Ltd
Crittall-Hope (Rhodesia) Ltd
*Eastern District Engineers (Pvt) Ltd
Greystone Development Co. (Pvt) Ltd (*property development*)
*Koben Investments (Pvt) Ltd
Lonrho Investment Co. Ltd
    Chemcap Properties (Pvt) Ltd
    W. Dahmer & Co. (Pvt) Ltd
      Ace Engineering (Pvt) Ltd
      Italian Coachbuilders (Pvt) Ltd
    Homestake Mines (Pvt) Ltd (*gold-mining*)
    Lonrho Finance Co. Ltd
    Mobile Motors (Pvt) Ltd
    Nippon Motor Sales Rhodesia Ltd
    Norton Motor Co. Ltd
    Rhodesian Gemstone Mines (Pvt) Ltd
    Rhodesian Star Mining Co. (Pvt) Ltd
    Unit Trust Fund Managers (Pvt) Ltd
The North Charterland Exploration Co. (1937) Ltd
Reliance Metal Windows (Rhodesia) (Pvt) Ltd

Rhodesian Spinners Ltd (*textile production*)
   David Whitehead & Sons (Rhodesia) Ltd
      Strongweave Textile Mills (Pvt) Ltd
   Textile Investments Ltd
Rhodesian Wattle Co. Ltd (*wattle and farming*)
   Rhodesian Wattle Co. Provident Trust (Pvt) Ltd
*Simms Electrical and Diesel (Bulawayo) (Pvt) Ltd
*Simms Electrical and Diesel Services (Pvt) Ltd
*Simms Electrical and Diesel (Umtali) (Pvt) Ltd
 Zambezi Coachworks Ltd
    J. H. Plane (Central Africa) Ltd

*Acquired since 1972–3 financial year.
 Source: *Who Owns Whom*, 1973–4 edition.

There is every reason to believe that the profits from these Rhodesian-based companies, which according to statements made by Lonrho's London board have been frozen inside Rhodesia since UDI, have been substantial. The Lonrho Investment Co. Ltd and its subsidiaries do not publish separate accounts, but over the first six months of 1974 David Whitehead (Rhodesia), for example, made pre-tax profits of over £1 million (*Property and Finance*, June 1974). Like David Whitehead, Zambezi Coachworks is a leader in its own field. The capacity of Lonrho (Rhodesia) for continued expansion in the 1970s indicates that there has been no shortage of cash in Salisbury.

Appendix 2

Time-table of Events Surrounding Lonrho's Organization of
African Unity Consultancy Deal

1973

May	Rowland speaks of his desire to act as unpaid economic adviser to the OAU.
8 August	Lonrho Energy Resources Ltd is incorporated in London.
21 November	Emergency session of OAU Ministerial Council calls on Arabs to extend oil sanctions to southern Africa; it also appoints Committee of Seven to deal with oil issues.
28 November	Arab summit meeting in Algiers agrees to extend oil sanctions; it also sets up a bank for African development with an initial capital of $125 million.
21 December	After preliminary contacts, Lonrho submits formal application for appointment as OAU oil consultants.
29 December	First meeting of Committee of Seven: OAU Secretary-General Ekangaki advises on the need for oil consultants and proposes OAU oil company, tanker fleet, etc. Sudan's Foreign Minister is appointed chairman of the Committee, which authorizes Ekangaki to appoint or search for likely consultants.
30 December	Committee of Seven sends preliminary team to Cairo to fix a meeting between the Arab League and the Committee.
31 December	Ekangaki begins quest for information about the oil requirements of the OAU's thirty-six non-oil-producing members.

1974

5 January	Ekangaki decides to appoint Lonrho.
8 January	Exchange of letters between Ekangaki and Rowland about Lonrho's southern African activities.
9 January	Lonrho agreement is signed; soon afterwards Ekangaki instructs Lonrho to study the oil needs of the thirty-six countries, as well as the formation of an African oil company, etc.

20 January	Second meeting of Committee of Seven which is informed of Lonrho's appointment; there are protests at Ekangaki's deal.
22 January	Committee of Seven, accompanied by Ekangaki and Lonrho's Egyptian oil consultant, meet Arab League.
13 February	First news of Lonrho appointment made public by the Ugandan leader, General Amin, who criticizes Ekangaki.
19 February	Ekangaki says he will explain himself to OAU Ministerial Council Meeting at end of month; he threatens to resign if Council finds that he has acted *ultra vires*.
28 February	OAU Ministerial Council Meeting in Addis Ababa hears demands for cancellation of Lonrho appointment, but the session is cut short by Ethiopian upheavals.
11 March	Rowland writes to Ekangaki, asking that Lonrho be released from its contract.
31 March	OAU Ministerial Council resumes its interrupted session in Kampala; Ekangaki is severely criticized.
24 May	Ekangaki resigns for 'personal reasons'.
16 July	OAU summit elects new Secretary-General.

Appendix 3

Copy of the agreement between the Organization of African Unity and Lonrho, as presented by OAU Secretary-General Nzo Ekangaki in OAU document OEM/Cttee.1/5 (II) – Report on the First Session of the Committee of Seven on the Effects of the Oil Embargo on the OAU Member States, held in Addis Ababa, 29 December 1973 – Annex II.

AGREEMENT

BETWEEN:

The ORGANIZATION OF AFRICAN UNITY (hereinafter described as 'OAU') having its corporate address in Addis Ababa, Ethiopia and acting through its Administrative Secretary-General of the first part

AND

LONRHO LIMITED (hereinafter described as 'LONRHO') a company registered in England and having its registered address at Cheapside House, 138 Cheapside, London, EC2 of the second part.

WHEREAS the Administrative Secretary-General of the OAU who is duly authorized to enter into this Agreement on behalf of OAU has defined certain objectives (hereinafter described as 'the Objectives') for ensuring the future self-sufficiency in energy requirements and economic independence of the Member States of OAU, namely that:

(A) In respect of its energy requirements, it is in the interest of each Member State that it should be self-sufficient, whether by the development of its natural resources or the signing of long-term contracts with the oil producing countries in order to ensure continuity and security of supply;

(B) It is in the interest of each Member State for the refining of its crude oil supplies to be under its own control, while recognizing that for economic reasons a measure of interdependence may be desirable amongst Member States;

(C) In order to further assure the security of supply the transportation of oil should be under the control of African States, while recognizing the benefits accruing from the pooling of such operations into larger more economic units;

(D) The transformation of oil into such products as lubricants, fertilizers and petrochemicals should similarly be under the control of African States but that by reason of the benefits accruing from the operation of plants of greater size than the needs of any one State, this should not preclude the processing and production of these products by Member States acting in consortium together;

(E) It is in the interest of each Member State to work out and develop an efficient internal distribution system to ensure the continuity of supply to all regions within the state and to exercise control over such system;

(F) It is essential for all parties concerned to bear in mind the permanent concern of the OAU for more intensified inter-African economic co-operation in all fields.

WHEREAS OAU has requested LONRHO to assist in the bringing to fruition and in the implementation of the Objectives.

NOW IT IS HEREBY AGREED AS FOLLOWS:

(1) LONRHO is hereby appointed as Consultant to OAU and to provide services to OAU as hereinafter mentioned for the purpose of carrying out the policy of OAU in accordance with the Objectives and otherwise as may be mutually agreed between the parties hereto.

(2) More specifically LONRHO is hereby required by OAU to establish direct contacts with Member States affected by the oil embargo and to advise, assist and undertake all other such duties in respect of these Member States on behalf of the General Secretariat of the OAU as LONRHO may determine with the Government of each Member State concerned.

(3) The Member States referred to in the foregoing paragraph are countries that are not importers [sic]* of oil and specifically comprising the following Member States of OAU:

BOTSWANA	IVORY COAST	SENEGAL
BURUNDI	KENYA	SIERRA LEONE
CAMEROON	LESOTHO	SOMALIA
CENTRAL AFRICAN REPUBLIC	LIBERIA	SUDAN
CHAD	MADAGASCAR	SWAZILAND
DAHOMEY	MALAWI	TANZANIA
ETHIOPIA	MALI	TOGO
EQUATORIAL GUINEA	MAURITANIA	TUNISIA
GAMBIA	MAURITIUS	UGANDA
GHANA	MOROCCO	UPPER VOLTA
GUINEA	NIGER	ZAIRE
GUINEA BISSAU	RWANDA	ZAMBIA

* This appears to be a mistake since the Member States now listed are specifically those which import oil, and would be affected by an oil embargo. [Authors' note.]

(4) This Agreement shall continue in force for a minimum period of three years and shall thereafter continue until terminated by either party on the expiration of twelve months notice given in writing.

(5) LONRHO shall not at any time commit, or act in any way as agent of the OAU except with the written authority of OAU.

(6) Notwithstanding the foregoing provisions, where any project falling within the Objectives is approved by OAU and or one or more of its Member States, LONRHO shall be entitled, without prejudice to fair competition on a commercial basis to be appointed to act as contractors, to act as managers, to act as buyers and or as confirmers in respect of requisitions for services, capital equipment, consumable stores and other goods and services and or to secure where necessary long and short term finance facilities for capital projects and shall be entitled to take such participation as may be offered to LONRHO in such project by Member States.

(7) LONRHO shall open a permanent office in Addis Ababa to maintain contacts with OAU and its Member States. OAU will use its good offices to secure for sinor [sic] expatriate staff employed by LONRHO for this purpose privileges and immunities normally accorded to OAU consultants and other consultants of International Organizations.

(8) In pursuit of the Objectives LONRHO shall ensure that its Office in Cairo maintains contacts with Arab States, with their office in Addis Ababa and with the OAU.

(9) The OAU shall issue the Diplomatic 'OAU Laissez Passer' to the Chief Executive of LONRHO as well as to such other staff of LONRHO engaged in making contacts with the Member States, for whom the granting of such facility, in the opinion of the Administrative Secretary-General of the OAU, shall be deemed necessary in the interest of the objectives.

(10) LONRHO shall not assign any of its obligations or benefits arising under this Agreement PROVIDED THAT it shall be at liberty to assign any such obligations or benefits to any subsidiary or company controlled or managed by it for the better performance thereof within the LONRHO Group.

(11) Any disagreement between the parties as to the interpretation or operation of this Agreement shall be referred to a mutually acceptable arbitrator in Addis Ababa who shall apply the general principles of International Law and whose decisions shall be final and binding on both parties. Failing selection of an arbitrator acceptable to both parties the arbitrator shall be appointed by the Chief Justice of the Imperial Government of Ethiopia.

(12) The Administrative Secretary-General of the OAU undertakes to introduce LONRHO formally to the Heads of State and Government of the Member States referred to in paragraph 3 above and to communicate copies of this Agreement to the Government of the Member States.

(13) Nothing in this Agreement shall be construed as placing any obligation on a Member State of OAU to engage the services of LONRHO against the will of such a Member State.

(14) Any notice to be served under this Agreement shall be sent by hand or registered post to the address of the party shown in the preamble to this Agreement or otherwise at its corporate or registered office for the time being.

(15) This AGREEMENT shall come into effect immediately after the date of signature.

SIGNED this ninth day of January in the year one thousand nine hundred and seventy-four.

For and on Behalf of
ORGANIZATION OF
AFRICAN UNITY   ADMINISTRATIVE SECRETARY-GENERAL

For and on Behalf of
LONRHO LIMITED   CHIEF EXECUTIVE

Appendix 4

The Smith Regime and International Sanctions

At its 1428th meeting on 29 May 1968, the United Nations Security Council adopted resolution 253 (1968) concerning the situation in Rhodesia, calling upon Member States to take action against the illegal Smith regime and 'to render moral and material assistance to the people of Southern Rhodesia in their struggle to achieve their freedom and independence' (paragraph 13). The resolution called for the imposition of blanket mandatory sanctions against Rhodesia and set up the United Nations Sanctions Committee, as a committee of the Security Council, to monitor their operation in practice.

The main paragraphs of the resolution relating to sanctions, paragraphs 3 and 4, read as follows:

The Security Council

3. *Decides* that, in furtherance of the objective of ending the rebellion, all States Members of the United Nations shall prevent:

(a) The import into their territories of all commodities and products originating in Southern Rhodesia and exported therefrom after the date of this resolution (whether or not the commodities or products are for consumption or processing in their territories, whether or not they are imported in bond and whether or not any special legal status with respect to the import of goods is enjoyed by the port or other place where they are imported or stored);

(b) Any activities by their nationals or in their territories which would promote or are calculated to promote the export of any commodities or products from Southern Rhodesia; and any dealings by their nationals or in their territories in any commodities or products originating in Southern Rhodesia and exported therefrom after the date of this resolution, including in particular any transfer of funds to Southern Rhodesia for the purposes of such activities or dealings;

(c) The shipment in vessels or aircraft of their registration or under charter of their nationals, or the carriage (whether or not in bond) by land transport facilities across their territories of any commodities or products originating in Southern Rhodesia and exported therefrom after the date of this resolution;

(d) The sale or supply by their nationals or from their territories of any commodities or products (whether or not originating in their territories, but not including supplies intended strictly for medical purposes, educational equipment and material for use in schools and other educational institutions, publications, news material and, in special humanitarian circumstances, food-stuffs) to any person or body in Southern Rhodesia or to any other person or body for the purposes of any business carried on in or operated from Southern Rhodesia, and any activities by their nationals or in their territories which promote or are calculated to promote such sale or supply;

(e) The shipment in vessels or aircraft of their registration, or under charter to their nationals, or the carriage (whether or not in bond) by land transport facilities across their territories of any such commodities or products which are consigned to any person or body in Southern Rhodesia, or to any other person or body for the purposes of any business carried on in or operated from Southern Rhodesia;

4. *Decides* that all States Members of the United Nations shall not make available to the illegal regime in Southern Rhodesia or to any commercial, industrial or public utility undertaking, including tourist enterprises, in Southern Rhodesia any funds for investment or any other financial or economic resources and shall prevent their nationals and any persons within their territories from making available to the regime or to any such undertaking any such funds or resources and from remitting any other funds to persons or bodies within Southern Rhodesia except payments exclusively for pensions or for strictly medical, humanitarian or educational purposes or for the provision of news material and in special humanitarian circumstances, food-stuffs;

(United Nations Security Council: Report by the Secretary-General in pursuance of Resolution 253 (1968) adopted by the Security Council at its 1428th meeting on 29 May 1968 concerning the situation in Southern Rhodesia. s/8786 28 August 1968.)

By a letter dated 31 May 1968, the Secretary-General of the United Nations transmitted the text of resolution 253 (1968) to the Government of the United Kingdom of Great Britain and Northern Ireland. Relevant legislation was duly laid before the British Parliament on 2 July 1968, to come into operation on the following day, 3 July. The Southern Rhodesia (United Nations Sanctions) (No. 2) Order 1968 laid down that:

2 (1) Except under the authority of a licence granted by the Minister, all goods that have been exported from Southern Rhodesia after the commencement of the Southern Rhodesia (United Nations Sanctions) Order 1968 are prohibited to be imported into the United Kingdom.

3 (1) Except under the authority of a licence granted by the Minister, no person shall export any goods from Southern Rhodesia.

   (2) Except under such authority as aforesaid, no person shall –
     (a) make or carry out any contract for the exportation of any goods from Southern Rhodesia after the commencement of this Order; or
     (b) make or carry out any contract for the sale of any goods which he intends or has reason to believe that another person intends to export from Southern Rhodesia after the commencement of this Order, or
     (c) do any act calculated to promote the exportation of any goods from Southern Rhodesia.

4 (1) Except under the authority of a licence granted by the Minister, all goods are prohibited to be exported to Southern Rhodesia.

6 (1) Except under the authority of a licence granted by the Minister, no person shall import any goods into Southern Rhodesia.

(Statutory Instruments: 1968 No. 1020 *Southern Rhodesia*. The Southern Rhodesia (United Nations Sanctions) (no. 2) Order 1968; paras. 2 (1), 3 (1) and (2), 4 (1) and 6 (1). HMSO 1970 (reprint).

Notes

Introduction

1   *African Development*, London, June 1973, p. 9.
2   *Guardian*, 1 June 1973.
3   *African Development*, op. cit.
4   Lonrho Ltd, Annual Report for 1973.
5   The Annual Report for 1974 did mention that 'with associates in Lonrho North Africa, operating from our office in Cairo, a joint venture has been set-up [sic] with the Ministry of Electricity to develop a modern power despatch system based on up-to-date computerized real time technique for the whole of the Egyptian power network'. No further details were given.
6   *Star*, Johannesburg, weekly airmail edition, 1 March 1975; *Guardian*, 1 March 1975.
7   *Financial Times*, 4 March 1975. The Savkel agreement has now been terminated. See also Postscript.
8   Lonrho Ltd, Annual Report for 1974.

Chapter 1. The Colossus of Cheapside House

1   *Sunday Telegraph*, 13 May 1973.
2   ibid.
3   ibid.
4   ibid.
5   *Observer*, 17 October 1971.
6   J. G. Lockhart and C. M. Woodhouse, *Rhodes* (Hodder & Stoughton, 1963), p. 19.
7   *Daily Mail*, 17 May 1973.
8   The company changed its name formally to 'Lonrho' in 1963; it was, however, known as 'Lonrho' even before then, and will be referred to by the shorter and better-known name throughout the book.
9   *Daily Mail*, 17 May 1973.
10 According to many accounts his father was a German national, although evidence on this point is lacking.
11 The official document registering his change of name, in which this description occurs, number J 18/410 11509, dated 12 October 1939, was signed in the presence of E. Bryden Besant, solicitor; Cyril Theodore Carton, shipping agent, testified he had known Rowland for many years.
12 *Property and Finance*, Salisbury, Rhodesia, April 1967.
13 *Sunday Times*, 28 November 1971.

14   *Financial Mail*, Johannesburg, 28 April 1972, vol. XLIV, no. 4, p. 291.

15   *Sunday Times*, 28 November 1971.

16   *Investors Chronicle and SEG*, 18 May 1973, p. 777.

17   *Observer*, 17 October 1971.

18   *Sunday Times*, 28 November 1971.

19   *Property and Finance*, March 1960; also a reference in a survey of Lonrho, dated September 1968, by Pidgeon, Stebbing, Gow and Parsons.

20   The interests handed over by Shepton Estates to Lonrho comprised the following:

     96 per cent (i.e. 29,689 Ordinary £1 Shares) of the issued capital of the Norton Development Company Ltd, distributors of Mercedes-Benz;

     90 per cent (i.e. 72,000 Ordinary £1 Shares) of the issued capital of Consolidated Holdings (Pvt) Ltd, dealers in motor spares;

     36.33 per cent (i.e. 550,000 Ordinary five shilling Shares) of the issued capital of Kanyemba Gold Mines Ltd, a public company which operated the Kanyemba and Hepworth gold mines near Gatooma;

     100 per cent (i.e. 10,000 Ordinary £1 Shares) of the issued capital of Mashaba Gold Mines (Pvt) Ltd, operating the Empress gold mine in Fort Victoria district;

     51 per cent (i.e. 51 Ordinary £1 Shares) of the issued capital of Associated Overseas Pipelines (AOP) of Rhodesia (Pvt) Ltd, a company set up by Rowland to promote a scheme for an oil pipeline from Rhodesia to the Mozambique coast.

21   *Property and Finance*, October 1961.

22   For the sake of simplicity, 'Zambia' and 'Malawi' will be referred to as such throughout the book; likewise, 'Rhodesia', known until the dissolution of the Federation as 'Southern Rhodesia'.

23   See above, p. 12.

24   Memorandum and Articles of Association of Lonrho Ltd, p. 1 (reprinted April 1965).

25   At the end of 1960, the proven ore reserves had been calculated as standing at 211,300 tons. At the end of September 1961 they were down to 68,890 tons of a lower grade (*Property and Finance*, February 1962).

26   *Property and Finance*, February 1962.

27   The Empress gold mine shared much the same fate. In August 1961, it was stated to contain 160,000 tons – three years' supply – of ore reserves and to be earning £3,000 a month, but development results declined and at the end of 1963 normal mining operations were suspended (*Property and Finance*, January 1964). In 1967 Mashaba Gold Mines (Pvt) Ltd, the company that owned the Empress mine, was liquidated.

28   *Property and Finance*, June 1962.

29   See below p. 29ff.

30   *Property and Finance*, November 1962.

31   ibid., February 1963.

32   ibid., June, November, December 1962.

33   ibid., February 1962.

34   The compensation required amounted to a minimum of £1.5 million a year.

35 *Property and Finance*, August 1962.
36 Lonrho's Annual Report for 1962 lists the four agreements signed concerning the pipeline as:
    – Between Lonrho and the Federal government, under which Lonrho undertook to 'construct, maintain and operate' a crude oil pipeline;
    – Between Lonrho and the Rhodesian government, whereby Lonrho were granted a concession to construct and operate the pipeline from the Mozambique border to Feruka;
    – Between the Province of Mozambique and the Companhia do Pipeline Moçambique-Rhodesia S A R L – an 'indirect subsidiary' of Lonrho, set up to construct and operate the pipeline inside Mozambique;
    – Between Lonrho and the consortium of seven oil companies who were building the Feruka refinery, establishing the terms under which Lonrho would supply the refinery with crude oil.
37 After weeks of waiting for the Federal authorities to release the details of the agreements, the Articles of Association of the Companhia do Pipeline were published by the Salisbury magazine, *Property and Finance*, who provided their own translation from the Portuguese in February 1963.
38 See Chapter 8, p. 150.
39 *Property and Finance*, February 1963.
40 ibid., August, November, December 1962.
41 *The Rhodesian Farmer*, Farm Journal of the Federation, 4 January 1963, vol. XXXIII, no. 36.
42 ibid.
43 *Property and Finance*, August 1964.
44 In 1964 Lonrho attracted angry criticism from a number of tea transportation companies in Malawi for a plan which, by undercutting the conventional rates for the carriage of the tea crop to the railhead, would virtually force all competitors out of business. (*Times*, Blantyre, Malawi, 10 November 1964). See also Chapter 2, p. 33.
45 In October 1962, Lonrho made an offer – in due course successful – for the entire share capital of Halls Holdings Ltd, an unquoted company operating a motor business in Malawi's capital, Blantyre, and holding the franchise for a number of well-known makes of motor-car. It seemed a reasonable choice although there had been little if any profit for some time and the company was clearly facing business difficulties of some magnitude, but with Angus Ogilvy on the Halls board there was a direct link with Ogilvy's patron, Harley Drayton, and the security of his financial empire. And, of course, it gave Rowland a foothold in new terrain. His much more important takeover of Malawi Railways (see below) followed very shortly after.
46 *Property and Finance*, December 1963 – text of speech taken from the *Malawi News*, Limbe, Malawi.
47 *Times*, Blantyre, Malawi, 12 November 1963.
48 *Property and Finance*, December 1963.
49 ibid.
50 At that time known as 'Nyasaland Railways' – the name was changed at Malawi's independence.

51 See map, pp. 220–21.

52 *Nyasaland Times* (renamed *Times* after Malawi's independence), 20 November 1962.

53 ibid.

54 *Financial Mail*, Johannesburg, 26 April 1963, overseas air edition, pp. 728–9.

55 *Property and Finance*, December 1962.

56 For example, *Sunday Times*, 28 November 1971; *Financial Times*, 2 May 1973.

57 *Times*, Blantyre, Malawi, 26 August 1966.

58 ibid.

59 *Daily Mail*, 29 May 1973.

60 Lonrho also acquired a controlling interest at this time in the Central Africa Transport Company (CATCO). CATCO had been started in 1921 by Colonel John Sanders, a retired army officer whose pioneering efforts to establish a system of road transport in what was then a remote and underdeveloped country were the inspiration for Edgar Wallace's novel, set on the west coast of Africa, *Sanders of the River*. In 1934, Jomo Kenyatta, later President of Kenya, acted the part of a minor chief in Korda's famous film of the book, the fee being one guinea a day. The film portrayed the British colonial approach at its frankest and later aroused controversy among Africans, who thought it degrading. See *Kenyatta* by Jeremy Murray-Brown (Allen & Unwin, 1972), p. 187.

61 *Times*, Blantyre, Malawi, 5 November 1963.

62 ibid., Blantyre, Malawi, 8 November 1963.

63 See Chapters 4 and 11.

Chapter 2. Black African Allies

1   *African Development*, London, December 1971, p. 13.

2   *Nyasaland Times*, Blantyre, Malawi, 25 October 1963.

3   Richard Hall, *The High Price of Principles* (Hodder & Stoughton, 1969, p. 212; Penguin Books, 1973): 'Lonrho wanted a guarantee that it would be given all the copper traffic to the coast – more than 600,000 tons a year – at rates to be agreed. The copper companies were alarmed when they caught a whisper of this . . .'.

4   Mark Bostock and Charles Harvey (eds.), *Economic Independence and Zambian Copper* (Praeger, New York, 1972), pp. 108–9.

5   Dr Anton Rupert, who was a leading South African exponent of the 'outward-going' policy towards black African states and owned Rothmans. He founded the Economic Development Bank for Equatorial and Southern Africa (EDESA) to promote 'dialogue' between black and white Africa. Its main purpose was to combat left-wing militant tendencies near South Africa's borders, and to exploit development opportunities in black Africa. It was registered in Luxembourg, with headquarters in Zurich.

6   See pp. 123–4.

7   *Zambia News*, 14 February 1965, reported in *Property and Finance*, Salisbury, Rhodesia, March 1965.

8 *Property and Finance*, June 1965.
9 *African Development*, April 1969, p. 5.
10 See p. 250.
11 See p. 33.
12 *Property and Finance*, February 1965.
13 See pp. 40–41.
14 *The Times*, 20 March 1970.
15 *Morning Star*, 4 June 1973. See also p. 126.
16 Mr J. M. Kariuki, Parliamentary Debates, Nairobi, col. 1162, 8 May 1973.
17 *The Times*, 11 December 1974, and *Financial Times*, 11 December 1974. He threatened to ban the Lonrho-owned daily.
18 See p. 38.
19 *African Development*, November 1969, p. 11.
20 ibid.
21 Parliamentary Debates, Nairobi, col. 1215, 8 May 1973.
22 ibid., col. 1466, 17 May 1973.
23 Interview with James Fox, *Sunday Times*, 1974.
24 Kariuki was found murdered in March 1975, and his death caused a serious political crisis in Kenya because of his widespread popularity. This popularity was connected with his outspoken criticism of the increasingly close relationship between government and big business.
25 *Property and Finance*, April 1964.
26 Memorandum and Articles of Association, Special Resolution, 14 April 1965, Clause 12A.
27 *African Development*, February 1973, p. 39. This comment referred to Chibuku, explaining Lonrho's reluctance to allow the Ghana government a majority of their nominees on the board.
28 Anthony Martin, *Minding Their Own Business* (Hutchinson, 1972, p. 199; Penguin Books, 1975).
29 See pp. 28–9.
30 Martin, op. cit., p. 198.
31 In a letter to shareholders dated 25 November 1974 Lonrho stated: 'The Company has guaranteed up to Zambian Kwacha 2,000,000 (£1.33 million) in respect of the overdraft of Contract Haulage Limited, now owned by a Zambian parastatal corporation.'
32 Martin, op. cit., p. 111.
33 Zambia and Malawi, having been partners in the Central African Federation, were particularly used to South African and Rhodesian firms.
34 *African Development*, April 1969, p. 8.
35 See pp. 228–9.
36 *West Africa*, London, 28 February 1970, pp. 225–6.
37 *African Development*, October 1969, p. 15.
38 ibid.
39 *Financial Times*, 23 July 1970.
40 ibid.
41 The story of Lonrho's Zairean entanglements and the Cominière dispute are reported in some detail in *African Development*, April 1969, October 1969, November 1970 and December 1970.

42   *West Africa*, 12 December 1970, p. 1439.

43   *Sunday Telegraph*, 8 December 1974.

44   *African Development*, March 1974, p. 7.

45   *West Africa*, 8 February 1969, p. 150.

46   ibid., 22 March 1969, p. 333.

47   ibid., 2 August 1969, p. 897.

48   *Financial Times*, 2 May 1973, and *West Africa*, 2 August 1969, p. 897.

49   See pp. 52–3. The Gulf Fishing Company was reported in 1971 to have gone into partnership with the Rivers State government to form a £4 million company, Rivers Gulf Fisheries, with ambitious plans which included processing and exporting. Little more was heard of this. See *West Africa*, 14 March 1970, p. 297. A joint company, the Star Match Co., is said to have been formed between the Rivers State government and Gulf Fisheries.

50   John Holt and Company (Liverpool) Ltd., Report and Accounts 1968/69.

51   *Daily Telegraph*, 17 May 1973.

52   *West Africa*, 21 May 1973, p. 674. The picture also appeared in *African Development*, June 1973, with Mtine cut out of the picture, and the mistaken caption describing the photograph as 'Roland "Tiny" Rowland and his African friend, Tom Mitine [*sic*]'. A correction appeared in the August issue of the magazine.

53   *West Africa*, 21 May 1973, p. 674.

54   *West Africa*, 4 June 1973, p. 751. A member of *West Africa*'s editorial staff told the authors that the correction was inserted at Lonrho's request.

55   *Daily Times*, Lagos, 16 March 1974.

56   ibid., Lagos, 28 February 1974. See p. 207.

57   *Financial Times*, 14 March 1974.

58   *West Africa*, 26 February 1971, p. 225.

59   ibid.

60   *Daily Times*, Lagos, 10 December 1974.

61   See pp. 196–7.

62   *West Africa*, 15 October 1973, p. 1463.

63   West Cameroun, the English-speaking part of the country, was then administered by Britain as part of the Nigerian federation.

64   *Africa*, January 1974, p. 41; *West Africa*, 15 October 1973, p. 1463.

65   See p. 46.

66   *Financial Times*, 24 April 1973.

67   ibid.

68   Authors' transcript of 1974 Annual General Meeting.

Chapter 3. Gold and Diamonds

1   *West Africa*, London, 30 April 1971, p. 474.

2   ibid., 16 November 1968, p. 1350.

3   ibid., 29 March 1969, p. 366.

4   For every three 4s. ordinary shares of the mining company, Lonrho offered 22s. 6d. of a new 7½ per cent convertible unsecured loan stock (1984/89) and one new ordinary 5s. Lonrho share. *West Africa* (2

November 1968, p. 1293) said that the convertible Lonrho stock would be fully convertible into ordinary shares 'on the basis of a conversion price expected to be 40s.'.

5   *West Africa*, 16 November 1968, p. 1350.
6   ibid.
7   *African Development*, London, February 1969, p. 6.
8   *West Africa*, 28 December 1968, p. 1551.
9   *Financial Times*, 22 January 1970.
10 *West Africa*, 31 January 1970, p. 147.
11 ibid., 26 October 1968, p. 1247.
12 ibid., 28 March 1970, p. 344.
13 *SWB/ME/2945/B/5 Accra radio, 6 December 1968.
14 *West Africa*, 8 March 1969, p. 282.
15 SWB/ME/3016/B/1, Accra radio, 3 March 1969.
16 *West Africa*, 5 November 1971, p. 1292.
17 SWB/ME/3018/B/3, Accra radio, 5 March 1969.
18 *West Africa*, 29 March 1969, p. 366.
19 ibid.
20 *West Africa*, 15 March 1969, p. 291.
21 ibid.
22 *Standard Bank Annual Economic Review of Ghana*, 1971, p. 9.
23 *West Africa*, 29 August 1970, p. 1010.
24 Lonrho, Annual Report for 1969, p. 5.
25 *West Africa*, 30 July 1971, p. 871.
26 ibid., 21 February 1970, p. 210.
27 ibid., 20 September 1969, p. 1126.
28 ibid., 27 November 1972, p. 1598.
29 ibid., 4 June 1971, p. 625.
30 ibid., 21 July 1972, p. 948. This additional option was later valued at £3.7 million.
31 ibid., 18 August 1972, p. 1102.
32 ibid., 25 December 1972, p. 1735.
33 *Standard Bank Review*, September 1972, p. 10.
34 *West Africa*, 25 December 1972, p. 1735.
35 *African Development*, March 1973, p. 80.
36 ibid.
37 *West Africa*, 30 April 1971, p. 483.
38 For Lonrho as a whole, profit after taxation and minority interests, and excluding extraordinary items, was as follows (the Ashanti component is given in brackets):

    1969 £5.01 million (£1.53 million)
    1970 £5.64 million (£1.16 million)
    1971 £4.24 million (£1.20 million)
    1972 £6.46 million (£2.96 million) *This was also due to the revaluation of the Ghanaian currency*
    1973 £11.19 million (£2.23 million)

    Rowland admitted in the Annual Report for 1973 to a net profit in 1973 of £5.1 million for Ashanti Goldfields, 'in which the company is

* S W B: *Summary of World Broadcasts; published by the BBC Monitoring Service.*

interested to the extent of 45 per cent'. An indication of how difficult Lonrho's accounts are to unravel can be found in the other figure, given by Rowland, that of £12.9 million being 'the gross profit before mineral duty and royalties'. One had to look elsewhere to find the pre-tax profit of Ashanti Goldfields – about £9 million – to understand that the mine's taxes amounted to about £3.8 million in mineral duties and royalties, and to secure a basis for comparison with previous years (*Standard Bank Review*, July 1974, p. 13).

39   *Daily Telegraph*, 27 November 1970. By the end of 1975 ore reserves had increased from 3.2 million to 6.5 million. The expansion of production had arisen because the company had been mining at a lower grade, according to Lonrho.

40   *New Statesman*, 8 June 1973, p. 842.

41   ibid.

42   *Sunday Times*, 13 May 1974.

43   See p. 76.

44   See p. 42.

45   In the event, the projected takeover negotiations with Delco did not take place, and the company remained in British hands.

46   Sorenson became a director of Diminco, the joint SLST/government company, set up later.

47   *Daily Mail*, Freetown, 9 June 1970.

48   *West Africa*, 21 March 1970, p. 311.

49   *Financial Times*, 16 June 1970 and 7 July 1970. *African Development*, July 1970, p. 2.

50   *Daily Mail*, Freetown, 13 June 1970.

51   *The Times*, 16 June 1970.

52   *Financial Times*, 16 June 1970.

53   *Daily Mail*, Freetown, 18 June 1970.

54   ibid., 3 July 1970.

55   *African Development*, July 1970, p. 2.

56   ibid., August 1970, p. 2.

57   There was widespread speculation at the time that Sardanis had been brought in to introduce some sort of order into Lonrho's African interests, which were suffering from nearly a decade of rapid and somewhat uncoordinated growth (*Financial Times*, 9 July 1971). With Rowland, Sardanis was to be joint managing director of a new subsidiary, the African Industrial and Finance Development Corporation Ltd (AIFCO). This was to oversee Lonrho's entire operations in independent Africa, including Comincor, on whose board Sardanis was to have been (Lonrho Ltd, Annual Report for 1970). It is probable that the neutral choice of name stemmed from the group's growing self-consciousness about its Rhodesian connections. Sardanis's period of employment with AIFCO lasted for less than three months; in July 1971, before he had even attended a board meeting, he departed from Cheapside House, 'because I found myself in basic disagreement with Lonrho's objectives and its style of management'. He criticized as inconsistent with development criteria the practice of raising capital within the local economy. He accused Lonrho of inefficient management, and

policies that were based on no coherent long-term strategy. Lonrho volunteered that Sardanis had left because he was homesick. (*Financial Times*, ibid.)

58 *Daily Mail*, Freetown, 3 October 1970.
59 In November 1974 Forna and fourteen others were condemned to death after being found guilty of treason and of attempting to overthrow the government. They were accused of trying to kill a number of leading officials, including the Minister of Finance, Kamara Taylor, who had negotiated the SLST agreement in 1970. The events were reported in *West Africa* (9 September 1974, p. 1113, and 25 November 1974, p. 1443). Forna was executed in 1975.
60 *West Africa*, 12 November 1970, p. 1439.
61 ibid.

Chapter 4. The White 'Homelands'

1 *Financial Mail*, Johannesburg, 23 May 1969, vol. XXXII, no. 8, p. 689.
2 ibid.
3 One rand was then worth just over £0.6.
4 *Today's News*, 9 November 1972. Issued by the Department of Information, South African Embassy, London.
5 Paper by S. C. Newman, extract from *Transactions*, Section A of the Institution of Mining and Metallurgy, London, 1973, vol. 82. The manuscript was first received on 12 December 1972 and published in April 1973.
6 *Today's News*, 12 December 1972.
7 *Financial Times*, 21 October 1972.
8 *Financial Mail*, Johannesburg, 23 May 1969, vol. XXXII, no. 8, p. 689.
9 *West Africa*, 25 April 1970, p. 468.
10 *Daily Telegraph*, 4 July 1970.
11 *Financial Times*, 4 April 1972.
12 Peat, Marwick, Mitchell and Co., Report to Shareholders.
13 *Financial Times*, 28 August 1970.
14 Lonrho Ltd, Annual Report for 1969.
15 *Daily Telegraph*, 15 July 1971.
16 ibid., 27 November 1970.
17 However, earlier in 1975 free market platinum prices again took a downturn after having reached £127 per oz. in 1974. The official prices were reduced to between £51.50 and £53.50. Free market prices were a few pounds higher.
18 *Daily Telegraph*, 27 November 1970.
19 *Today's News*, 19 July 1973.
20 ibid., 3 January 1973.
21 Newman, op. cit. For instance, up to 1975 the Impala platinum mine was not obliged to pay the agreed 13 per cent of its fixed profits to the Bafokeng tribe on whose land it was situated, because of a tax loss as a result of high capital expenditure. In 1974, however, a new agreement was reached under which the Bafokeng were to receive 10 per cent of the mine's dividends instead (*The Times*, 13 November 1974).

22   *Report from South Africa*, July–August 1971, p. 15. Issued by the Department of Information, South African Embassy, London.

23   ibid.

24   *Star*, Johannesburg, 20 November 1968. Quoted in United Nations Unit on Apartheid, *Bantustans in South Africa*, Notes and Documents no. 26/70, December 1970.

25   Expenditure Committee of the House of Commons (Trade and Industry Sub-Committee), *Wages and Conditions of African Workers Employed by British Firms in South Africa* (HMSO, 1973), vol. IV, p. 619. In 1974 Western Platinum, like many other South African mines, suffered from a shortage of migrant labour which affected performance. (*Star*, Johannesburg, weekly edition, 25 January 1975.) All mines in South Africa recruit through a central labour organization which undertakes the negotiations and is used by all mining companies.

26   *Bantustans in South Africa*, op. cit.

27   *Africa*, London, May 1974, p. 13.

28   Expenditure Committee, op. cit., p. 618. Western Platinum is a subsidiary of Lonrho South Africa Ltd, which in turn is a subsidiary of Lonrho Ltd of London. The 51 per cent mentioned earlier in this chapter refers to Lonrho South Africa's holding in Western Platinum.

29   *Star*, Johannesburg, 22 January 1974.

30   *Rand Daily Mail*, Johannesburg, 4 March 1974.

31   See p. 55.

32   *Daily Mail* interview, reported in *West Africa*, 17 March 1972, p. 326.

33   *Africa*, May 1974, p. 13.

34   See p. 162.

35   *Daily Telegraph*, 25 May 1973, reporting the Thames Television programme, 'This Week'.

36   According to at least one report, Sandys had been employed as a consultant in Lonrho South Africa since the summer of that year at a fee of £10,000 a year (*Sunday Times*, 27 May 1973).

37   Jack Halpern, *South Africa's Hostages* (Penguin Books, 1965).

38   *Financial Times*, 5 April, 8 April 1972.

39   *The Times*, 5 April 1972.

40   *Financial Times*, 8 April 1972.

41   Expenditure Committee, op. cit. Five volumes.

42   P. N. Pillay, *A Poverty Datum Line Study Among Africans in Durban*, Department of Economics, University of Natal, Occasional Paper no. 3, June 1973. This is the definition cited by the Expenditure Committee, op. cit. Fifth Report, p. 39.

43   Expenditure Committee, op. cit. Fifth Report, p. 40.

44   ibid., p. 66.

45   Transcript by the authors.

46   The Annual General Meeting took place on the same day. The document was duplicated.

47   South African Chamber of Mines, 'General Conditions of Recruitment and Service of African Employees on South African Mines', 25 March 1974.

48   Expenditure Committee, vol. IV, p. 631.

49   *Financial Times*, 2 October 1974.
50   *Africa*, May 1974, p. 12.
51   *Guardian*, 29 March 1974.
52   ibid., 28 March 1974.
53   Britannia and Highland were estates owned by Anglo-Ceylon and General Estates, an old London-registered colonial company that Lonrho had taken over in 1967 when its interests consisted mainly of sugar cane plantations in Mauritius and tea estates in Sri Lanka. It was subsequently developed by Lonrho as a holding company for a whole range of other operations.
54   *Times of Swaziland*, 12 September 1969.
55   ibid. Development Survey in a Special First Anniversary of Independence issue, 4 October 1969.
56   See p. 231.
57   V. S. Naipaul, 'Mauritius – the Overcrowded Barracoon', *Sunday Times* magazine, 16 July 1972. In 1974 Lonrho remained well established in Mauritius, and featured in a special survey on the island in the November issue of *African Development*. Its subsidiaries in Mauritius were listed in the 1973-4 edition of *Who Owns Whom* as Exotic Exports Ltd, held through Anglo-Ceylon; Lonrho Mauritius Ltd; Merville Ltd; Mon Trésor et Mon Désert Ltd; Roglon Ltd.
58   *Rand Daily Mail*, Johannesburg, 4 March 1974.
59   ibid., 21 January 1974.
60   *West Africa*, 11 February 1974, p. 154. Report based on *Newsweek*.
61   Transcript of Annual General Meeting made by authors.
62   Interview with authors.
63   *Rand Daily Mail*, Johannesburg, 21 January 1974.
64   By buying only a proportion of Jessel's total holding of 33.58 per cent in LAGS, Lonrho just avoided the necessity, under the Takeover Code, of making an outright bid for the company. Lonrho's purchase was ironical, in view of Oliver Jessel's own bid for Rowland's personal holding in Lonrho at the time of the boardroom row in 1973. Jessel had then been reported as saying that his own operations in South Africa, earning £8 million a year, could certainly help Lonrho in that area. (*Sunday Telegraph*, 22 April 1973.)
65   *Financial Times*, 27 January 1975.
66   *Daily Telegraph*, 23 January 1975.
67   *Financial Times*, 23 January 1975, 27 January 1975.

Chapter 5. City Trouble

1   *Mining Journal*, 27 June 1969, p. 575.
2   See pp. 51–2
3   *Investors Chronicle and SEG*, 21 February 1969.
4   See p. 54.
5   Annual Report for 1969.
6   *Financial Mail*, Lusaka, January 1965.
7   See *African Development* for monthly share index.
8   *Financial Times*, 19 August 1969; *Investors Chronicle*, 22 August 1969.

9   See pp. 43 and 81.

10   *Investors Chronicle and SEG*, 25 July 1969, p. 408.

11   ibid., 16 July 1971, p. 329.

12   ibid.

13   This section of the Act says: 'If, in the opinion of the directors of a company having, at the end of its financial year, subsidiaries, the number of them is such that compliance with subsection (1) of this section would result in particulars of excessive length being given, compliance with that subsection shall not be requisite except in the case of the subsidiaries carrying on the businesses the results of the carrying on of which, in the opinion of the directors, principally affected the amount of the profit or loss of the company and its subsidiaries, or the amount of the assets of the company and its subsidiaries.'

14   *African Development*, April 1971, p. 53.

15   *Financial Mail*, Johannesburg, 27 November 1970, vol. XXXVIII, no. 9, p. 885.

16   *Investors Chronicle and SEG*, 16 July 1971, p. 329.

17   See p. 44.

18   See p. 72.

19   *African Development*, February 1972, p. 63.

20   Letter from Peat, Marwick, Mitchell and Co. to shareholders and owners of convertible loan stock, 22 March 1972.

21   See p. 148.

22   *Daily Telegraph* and *Guardian*, 8 October 1971; *The Times*, 9 October 1971; *Sunday Times*, 10 October 1971.

23   *Sunday Times*, 10 October 1971.

24   *Financial Times*, 3 January 1972 and *Daily Telegraph*, 5 January 1972.

25   *The Times*, 3 March 1972.

26   *Sunday Telegraph*, 5 March 1972, quotes this statement.

27   Peat, Marwick, Mitchell and Co., 'Report to the Shareholders and the Holders of the Convertible Loan Stocks of Lonrho Limited', 1 March 1972.

28   This was later the subject of dispute. See pp. 115–16.

29   Because the diamond scheme had collapsed (see p. 94). Lonrho retains a presence in Mauritian agriculture and tourism, through Lonrho Mauritius Ltd.

30   See p. 82.

31   *The Times*, 5 April 1972.

32   Peat, Marwick, Mitchell and Co., op. cit.

33   See pp. 12, 14, 108.

34   *Sunday Times*, 5 March 1972.

35   *The Times*, 9 May 1973.

36   Peat, Marwick, Mitchell and Co., op. cit.

37   On the publication of Lonrho's interim results for the 1974 financial year, the *Financial Times* commented: 'Fully diluted earnings are reported at 20p a share with no mention of their remittable content. Lonrho apparently feels that its improved liquidity now makes such disclosure unnecessary' (*Financial Times*, 11 December 1974). However, the remittability content was disclosed in the annual accounts.

38   *Accountancy Age*, 25 May 1973.
39   ibid.
40   Letter from Smallpeice, Percy, *et al.* to Shareholders, 17 May 1973.
41   *Financial Times*, 21 December 1972.
42   See p. 188.
43   *Financial Times*, 12 December 1974.
44   See p. 92.
45   *Sunday Telegraph*, 9 February 1975, 26 January 1975.
46   *Financial Times*, 8 February 1975; *Daily Telegraph*, 8 February 1975.
47   *Sunday Telegraph*, 26 January 1975, 9 February 1975.

Chapter 6. The Public Daylight

1   *Daily Telegraph*, 15 May 1973.
2   *Daily Mail*, 15 May 1973.
3   *The Times*, 9 May 1973.
4   *Evening Standard*, 15 May 1973.
5   *Sunday Telegraph*, 20 May 1973.
6   *The Times*, 10 May 1973.
7   ibid.
8   *Guardian*, 15 May 1973.
9   *Sun*, 15 May 1973.
10   *Evening Standard*, 15 May 1973.
11   ibid.
12   *Daily Telegraph*, 15 May 1973.
13   *Guardian*, 10 May 1973.
14   *The Times*, 9 May 1973, 10 May 1973; *Sunday Telegraph*, 13 May 1973.
15   *Sunday Telegraph*, 20 May 1973.
16   Shortly after the boardroom crisis, Butcher retired as Finance Director
      and Basil West left the Automobile Association to take over his post.
17   Franklin was appointed to the Lonrho board, as alternate for du Cann,
      during the 1973 crisis.
18   *Guardian*, 22 May 1973; *Sunday Telegraph*, 20 May 1973.
19   Sandys may have been an especially valuable asset for Lonrho in
      Brussels and South Africa. See Chapter 2, p. 44 and Chapter 8, p. 163.
20   *Sunday Times*, 13 May 1973.
21   *Daily Telegraph*, 10 May 1973.
22   *Sunday Telegraph*, 13 May 1973.
23   *Daily Telegraph*, 25 May 1973.
24   ibid., 30 April 1973.
25   ibid., 18 May 1973.
26   *Financial Times*, 11 May 1973.
27   *Daily Telegraph*, 18 May 1973.
28   *Evening Standard*, 15 May 1973.
29   *Daily Telegraph*, 18 May 1973.
30   *Evening Standard*, 15 May 1973.
31   *Daily Telegraph*, 25 May 1973.
32   *Evening Standard*, 15 May 1973.
33   *Guardian*, 1 June 1973.

34   *Daily Mail*, 26 May 1973.
35   *Financial Times*, 19 May 1973.
36   *Daily Mail*, 18 May 1973.
37   *Financial Times*, 3 May 1973.
38   *Guardian*, 22 May 1973.
39   See Chapter 3, p. 66.
40   *Guardian*, 10 May 1973.
41   See Chapter 2, p. 44.
42   *Daily Telegraph*, 9 May 1973.
43   ibid.
44   *Financial Times*, 10 May 1973.
45   *African Development*, June 1973, p. 9.
46   This did in fact happen.
47   *Guardian*, 15 May 1973.
48   *Sunday Times*, 13 May 1973.
49   *Financial Times*, 10 May 1973.
50   See Chapter 8, p. 164.
51   *Observer*, 20 May 1973.
52   *Property and Finance*, July 1973.
53   The name 'Borma' was said to have been made up from the initial
     letters of 'Ball, Ogilvy, Rowland Mining Associates'.
54   Rowland explained that he had let Ball and Ogilvy into Yeoman because
     he wanted to give them the benefits he felt would accrue from a large
     equity stake in Lonrho. But the Ball and Ogilvy trusts would only
     benefit from Rowland's Lonrho shares when he had been fully repaid,
     out of the dividends otherwise accruing to Ball and Ogilvy, for all the
     money he had put up to buy the shares. Large amounts were still
     outstanding. See, for instance, *Observer*, 20 May 1973.
55   *Daily Telegraph*, 9 May 1973.
56   ibid., 10 May 1973.
57   *Sunday Times*, 13 May 1973.
58   *Financial Times*, 10 May 1973.
59   ibid.
60   *Observer*, 27 May 1973.
61   *Daily Telegraph*, 12 May 1973. According to Lonrho's Annual Report
     for 1974, published in February 1975, 'The share capital of Nyaschere
     Copper (Private) Limited ("Nyaschere") continues to be held as to
     50 per cent by a subsidiary of a company controlled as to 70 per cent
     by Mr R. W. Rowland, as to 20 per cent by family trustees of Mr A. H.
     Ball, a Director, and as to 10 per cent by trustees of a family trust of the
     Hon. A. J. B. Ogilvy, a former Director, and as to the other 50 per cent
     by a subsidiary in the Lonrho Group. The Group acquired its 50 per
     cent interest in Nyaschere in 1968 for approximately £20,000 from a
     third party unconnected with the Group. Mr R. W. Rowland has held
     an interest since the incorporation of Nyaschere in 1958. It was re-
     ported in last year's accounts that Mr R. W. Rowland had contracted
     to dispose of his interest for a deferred consideration but it has proved
     impossible to carry out this contract because of the trustee share-
     holdings above mentioned. Consideration will be given in the ensuing

year to achieving an alternative solution. As at 30 September 1974 the amount of the loans advanced by the Group to Nyaschere totalled £1.30m (1973 – £3.49m).'

62   *Guardian*, 21 April 1973.
63   *Daily Telegraph*, 2 May 1973.
64   *The Times*, 15 May 1973.
65   *Guardian*, 15 May 1973.
66   See p. 102.
67   *Guardian*, 25 May 1973.
68   *The Times*, 10 May 1973.
69   *Guardian*, 15 May 1973.
70   Dated 16 May 1973.
71   Dated 19 May 1973.
72   News release, 21 May 1973, 'Programme for the new Lonrho'.
73   *Financial Times*, 21 May 1973.
74   *The Times*, 22 May 1973. Also *Guardian*, 22 May 1973.
75   *Daily Telegraph*, 25 May 1973.
76   *Financial Times*, 1 June 1973.
77   Dated 22 May 1973.
78   *Guardian*, 23 May 1973.
79   In the 1973 financial year the ratios were somewhat improved, but well over a third of total profit still remained unremittable.
80   *Guardian*, 22 May 1973.
81   ibid., 18 May 1973.
82   ibid.
83   *Daily Mail*, 26 May 1973. At that time there was very little to remit from Ivory Coast.
84   *Daily Mail*, 22 May 1973.
85   See Chapter 7, p. 136.
86   *Zambia Daily Mail*, 2 May 1973.
87   *Evening Standard*, 19 April 1973.
88   During his bid for the OAU consultancy deal (see Chapter 10), Rowland made a similar point. *African Development*, June 1973, p. 9.
89   *Daily Telegraph*, 12 May 1973.
90   *Daily Graphic*, Accra, 11 May 1973.
91   *Evening Standard*, 15 May 1973.
92   *The Times*, 9 May 1973.
93   *Financial Times*, 12 May 1973.
94   *Daily Telegraph*, 9 May 1973.
95   ibid., 11 May 1973.
96   *Guardian*, 8 May 1973.
97   *Times of Zambia*, 11 May 1973.
98   *Daily Express*, 16 May 1973; *Daily Telegraph*, 16 May 1973.
99   *The Times*, 17 May 1973. Also a conversation between Phiri and author, during which Phiri explained that his whole attitude towards Lonrho had been formed by Mitchley's statement.
100 *Daily Express*, 16 May 1973.
101 *Daily Telegraph*, 16 May 1973.
102 *Daily Mirror*, 31 May 1973.

103 ibid.
104 See Chapter 2, pp. 40–41.
105 See Chapter 2, pp. 37–8.
106 Parliamentary Debates, Nairobi, cols. 1464–1465, 17 May 1973.
107 See Chapter 2, p. 38.
108 *African Development*, July 1973, p. 5.
109 *Daily Graphic*, Accra, 7 May 1973.
110 ibid.
111 *Daily Telegraph*, 1 June 1973.
112 *African Development*, June 1973, p. 9.
113 *Daily Mail*, 26 May 1973.
114 *Financial Times*, 1 June 1973.
115 The Drayton Corporation was one of the few large institutional investors.
116 Segrue: Statement to Fellow Shareholders, 25 April 1973.
117 ibid.; also *Financial Times*, 24 April 1973.
118 *Daily Telegraph*, 30 April 1973.
119 Segrue, ibid.
120 *Daily Telegraph*, 30 April 1973.
121 ibid., 2 May 1973.
122 ibid., 28 April 1973.
123 *Evening Standard*, 23 May 1973.
124 *Daily Telegraph*, 25 May 1973.
125 Interview with Martyn Marriott, 10 July 1974.
126 Marriott: Letter to Shareholders, 31 May 1973.
127 *Evening Standard*, 22 May 1973.
128 Interview with Martyn Marriott, 13 July 1974.
129 Marriott: Letter to Shareholders, ibid.
130 *Guardian*, 1 June 1973.
131 *Daily Telegraph*, 1 June 1973.
132 *Financial Times*, 1 June 1973.
133 ibid.

Chapter 7. The Unacceptable Face

1   *Sunday Telegraph*, 29 April 1973.
2   Parliamentary Debates, House of Commons, col. 368, 17 May 1973.
3   Companies Act, 1948, Sections 168, 169.
4   *Investors Chronicle and SEG*, 18 May 1973, p. 775.
5   *The Times*, 19 May 1973.
6   *Guardian*, 25 May 1973.
7   Parliamentary Debates, House of Commons, col. 265, 22 May 1973; cols. 22–24, 18 June 1973.
8   Garret resigned soon afterwards, when it emerged that the firm of accountants to which he belonged had audited the accounts of Lonrho's subsidiary, Ashanti Goldfields. His place was taken by Sir William Slimmings.
9   Department of Trade and Industry, Press Notice, 23 May 1973.
10 Parliamentary Debates, House of Commons, col. 23, 18 June 1973.

11   ibid., col. 24, 18 June 1973.
12   ibid., col. 650, 24 May 1973.
13   ibid., col. 23, 18 June 1973. Meacher asked a series of questions, e.g.
     cols. 18–19, 10 December 1973.
14   ibid., col. 23, 18 June 1973.
15   *Daily Telegraph*, 19 May 1973.
16   Letter to shareholders, 19 May 1973.
17   Interview with an official of the Department of Trade, 6 August 1974.
18   Parliamentary Debates, House of Commons, col. 1243, 15 May 1973.
19   Labour Research Department publication, 'The Two Nations. Inequality
     in Britain Today', July 1973, pp. 11, 15, 16, 20.
20   *The Times*, 6 June 1973.
21   PAYE stands for 'pay as you earn', the system whereby taxes are
     automatically deducted from wages.
22   The various stages of the Conservative government's strategy against
     inflation were categorized as 'Phase One', 'Phase Two' and 'Phase
     Three'.
23   *Guardian*, 17 May 1973.
24   Report of the 105th Trades Union Congress, p. 306.
25   *TASS Journal*, July 1973, p. 3.
26   A reference to the Lambton–Jellicoe affair.
27   Report of the 105th Trades Union Congress, p. 513.
28   This passage is based on conversations with trade union officers.
29   Parliamentary Debates, House of Commons, col. 1243, 15 May 1973.
30   ibid., col. 265, 22 May 1973.
31   *Daily Telegraph*, 19 May 1973.
32   Labour Party Research Department, *Financial Institutions and the
     City*, Speakers' Notes no. 7A, September 1973, p. 23.
33   Parliamentary Debates, House of Commons, col. 659, 24 May 1973.
34   Order Paper no. 116, 16 May 1973, p. 6294, motion 340.
35   *Guardian*, 16 May 1973.
36   *The Times*, 16 May 1973.
37   The headquarters of the Labour Party.
38   Labour Party Research Department, op. cit., p. 22.
39   For example, Heath, reported in *Financial Times*, 24 May 1973. Also
     interview with official, Conservative Party Research Department,
     2 August 1974.
40   *Spectator*, 19 May 1973.
41   Interviews with official, Labour Party Research Department, 18 July
     1974, and official, Conservative Party Research Department, 2 August
     1974; telephone conversation with official, Liberal Party Research
     Department, August 1974.
42   *Financial Times*, 1 June 1973.
43   *The Times*, 1 June 1973.
44   *Daily Telegraph*, 1 June 1973.
45   Parliamentary Debates, House of Commons, col. 240, 11 June 1973.
46   Evidence and Memorandum on EEC Proposals on Supervisory Boards
     and Worker Participation. Submitted by the Liberal Party's Industrial
     Affairs Advisory Panel. Undated, but issued in May 1973.

47   *Economist*, 28 July 1973, p. 67.
48   Interview with Conservative Party Research Department official, 2 August 1974.
49   Interview with an official of the Department of Trade, 6 August 1974.
50   Interview with Labour Party Research Department official, 8 July 1974.
51   Parliamentary Debates, House of Commons, col. 325, 16 May 1973.
52   ibid., col. 1868, 13 March 1974. Considerable modifications were later made to these proposals.
53   *Observer*, 20 May 1973.
54   *Guardian*, 1 June 1973.

Chapter 8. An Embarrassment of Riches

1   *Observer*, 10 June 1973.
2   *Financial Times*, *The Times* and *Daily Telegraph*, all of 11 May 1973; *Observer* and *Sunday Times* of 13 May 1973. See also Chapter 6.
3   See Chapter 6.
4   See Chapter 10.
5   *Financial Times*, 10 June 1973.
6   Harold Wilson, speaking in the House of Commons on 11 November 1965; Parliamentary Debates (Hansard), Fifth Series, vol. 720, Session 1965–66, p. 359.
7   See Chapter 1, pp. 22–3.
8   *Daily Telegraph*, 27 November 1970.
9   *Daily Mail*, 2 March 1972.
10   Transcript by authors, 25 March 1974.
11   *Guardian*, 18 May 1973.
12   *Property and Finance*, Salisbury, Rhodesia, January 1967.
13   See Chapter 10.
14   *Who Owns Whom*, op. cit., 1972–73 and 1973–74.
15   Anglo-American, in the lead, had rights over 6,955 hectares, and Rio-Tinto (Rhodesia), 1,144 hectares. (*Financial Mail*, Johannesburg, 30 April 1971, vol. XL, no. 5, Supplement on Rhodesia, p. 27.)
16   *Financial Mail*, 26 April 1974, vol. LIII, no. 4, and *Financial Times*, 31 May 1974.
17   *Property and Finance*, February 1974.
18   The Six Principles on which any solution to the Rhodesian situation were to be based were laid down by the British Government in a White Paper published in December 1966:

(1) The principle and intention of unimpeded progress to majority rule, already enshrined in the 1961 Constitution, would have to be maintained and guaranteed.

(2) There would also have to be guarantees against retrogressive amendment of the Constitution.

(3) There would have to be immediate improvement in the political status of the African population.

(4) There would have to be progress towards ending racial discrimination.

(5) The British Government would need to be satisfied that any basis proposed for independence was acceptable to the people of Rhodesia as a whole.

(6) It would be necessary to ensure that, regardless of race, there was no oppression of majority by minority or of minority by majority.

(*Rhodesia – Proposals for a Settlement 1966*, Cmnd 3159, December 1966.)

19 At the beginning of 1975, the Rhodesian dollar was valued at about 77p, rather higher than the South African rand at 63p. (*Financial Times*, 7 January 1975.)

20 The Africa Bureau, *Time for Change*, mimeographed paper, 5 July 1974, and *Sixth Report: Official Records of the United Nations Security Council*, S/11178/Add.2, Annex VI.

21 *Rhodesia: Why Minority Rule Survives* (International Defence and Aid, 1969), p. 24.

22 John Sprack, *Rhodesia – South Africa's Sixth Province* (International Defence and Aid, 1974), p. 46.

23 *Property and Finance*, October 1964, and Lonrho's Annual Report for 1964.

24 *Financial Times*, 17 May 1973 and *Guardian*, 25 May 1973.

25 *Guardian*, 22 May 1973.

26 ibid., 18 May 1973.

27 Coronation Syndicate Ltd, Annual Report for 1973, Chairman's Review.

28 Coronation Syndicate Ltd, Annual Report for 1970, Chairman's Review.

29 Coronation Syndicate Ltd, Annual Report for 1973, Chairman's Review and Consolidated Balance Sheet.

30 *Rand Daily Mail*, 4 January 1974.

31 Coronation Syndicate Ltd, Annual Report for 1973, Chairman's Review.

32 *Rand Daily Mail*, 23 April 1974; and see Appendix 1.

33 *African Development*, June 1974, p. 30, and *Property and Finance*, May 1974.

34 Coronation Syndicate Ltd, Annual Report for 1973.

35 *African Development*, January 1975, p. 85.

36 *The Times*, 28 December 1974.

37 Extracts from the explanatory statement issued with the Coronation offer document, and reproduced in the *Financial Mail*, Johannesburg, 22 October 1971, vol. XLII, no. 4, p. 334.

38 *Sunday Times*, 3 October 1971; *Guardian* and *Financial Times*, 27 September 1971; *Property and Finance*, August 1971.

39 ibid.

40 *Guardian*, 30 May 1972. Around the time of the arrests in connection with the fraud charges, at the end of September 1971, two other directors, Sydney Newman, managing director of Lonrho South Africa, and Mortimer Raath, Lonrho South Africa's finance director, were also arrested by the South African police and charged with offences under the Companies Act concerning unauthorized loans to directors. The

charges against the two, which had nothing to do with Coronation's mines or with Lonrho's takeover bid for Coronation and Tweefontein, were in fact withdrawn in November 1971. Two years later, an appeal from Newman for damages against the State brought him an award of 10,700 rand.

41   See below, p. 163.
42   *Sunday Times*, 3 October 1971; *Property and Finance*, August 1971 and June 1974.
43   *Financial Times*, 12 September 1974, and other British daily papers.
44   *Sunday Times*, Johannesburg, 3 June 1973.
45   *Sunday Times*, 27 May 1973.
46   *Sunday Times*, Johannesburg, 3 June 1973.
47   *Daily Telegraph*, 25 May 1973, reporting an interview with Rowland on Thames TV 'This Week' on 24 May 1973.
48   *Financial Mail*, Johannesburg, 24 December 1971, vol. XLII, no. 13, p. 1095.
49   See Chapter 6.
50   *Guardian* and *Financial Times*, 4 December 1974.
51   See Chapter 6, pp. 116–17.
52   *Daily Telegraph*, 10 May 1973.
53   *Property and Finance*, April 1972.
54   See Chapter 1, p. 18.
55   *Property and Finance*, October 1967.
56   ibid., July 1973; and *Financial Mail*, 27 November 1970, vol. XXXVIII, no. 9, p. 885.
57   See Chapter 5, p. 95.
58   *Financial Mail*, 6 June 1969, vol. XXXII, no. 10, p. 865; and *Property and Finance*, June 1969.
59   *Financial Mail*, ibid.
60   ibid.
61   ibid.
62   For example, *Guardian*, 21 May 1973 and *Observer*, 10 June 1973.
63   *Sunday Times*, Johannesburg, 20 May 1973; *Observer*, 10 June 1973.
64   *Financial Mail*, 14 May 1971, vol. XL, no. 7, p. 558.
65   ibid.
66   ibid.
67   *Third Report: Official Records of the United Nations Security Council*, Twenty-fifth year Special Supplement no. 3, S/9844/Rev.1, Annex VII, p. 157.
68   In May 1974, Hochmetals were implicated in a case involving the illegal importation into Britain of Rhodesian chrome ore. A director of a British metal import agency, Exsud Ltd, admitted that the firm had obtained its supplies from Hochmetals of Johannesburg. Exsud Ltd were fined £6,000 with £150 costs, at Hull Magistrates Court. (*Financial Times*, 3 May 1974.)
69   *Third Report: Official Records of the United Nations Security Council*, op.cit.
70   *Observer*, 10 June 1973.
71   *Fourth Report: Official Records of the Security Council*, S/10229/Add.1, Annex 1, pp. 48–9.

72   ibid.
73   *Business and Financial Review*, Salisbury, Rhodesia, 17 May 1973.
74   *Sunday Times*, 14 July 1974.
75   *Yorkshire Post*, 7 June 1973.
76   *Africa*, May 1974, p. 13.
77   *Third Report: Official Records of the Security Council*, S/9844/Rev.1, Part X, Appendix III, p. 42.
78   *Financial Times*, 21 June 1973.
79   *Africa*, May 1974, p. 13.
80   *African Development*, July 1972, p. 8; July 1974, p. 30.
81   *Property and Finance*, January 1974.
82   *Rhodesia Herald*, Salisbury, 28 June 1973.
83   *Property and Finance*, March 1966.
84   ibid., April 1974.
85   Information from the company secretary of the Lonrho Investment Co., Salisbury, Rhodesia, in a letter to authors dated 1 August 1974.
86   *Accountancy Age*, 25 May 1973.
87   Survey of Lonrho dated September 1968 by Pidgeon, Stebbing, Gow and Parsons.
88   *Sunday Times*, 28 November 1971.
89   *Africa*, May 1974 p. 13.

Chapter 9. The Sudanese Springboard

1   See pp. 52–3.
2   *Daily Telegraph*, 7 August 1971; *African Development*, March 1972, p. 74.
3   The fact of this flight in the Lonrho plane was confirmed by Siddik Hamad in 1974 to James Fox, *Sunday Times*.
4   *Financial Times*, 27 August 1971.
5   *Morning Star*, 28 July 1971.
6   ibid., 24 July 1971.
7   *Financial Times*, 23 July 1971.
8   *The Times*, 30 July 1971.
9   ibid., 6 August 1971.
10   *Africa Confidential*, vol. 16, no. 3, 7 February 1975.
11   *Guardian*, 7 August 1971.
12   *Financial Times*, 3 September 1971.
13   *Guardian*, 30 September 1971.
14   The Massey-Ferguson order remained the largest handled by Lonrho during the first year of its agency; goods bought on Sudan's behalf during the period were reported to have amounted to a total value of £3.5 million.
15   *Financial Times*, 8 December 1972.
16   ibid.
17   *The Times*, 27 March 1973.
18   *Daily Mail*, 22 May 1973.
19   *The Times*, 31 March 1973.
20   *Financial Times*, 28 March 1973.
21   *African Development*, December 1972, p. 14.

22 ibid.
23 O D A Press Release, 10 October 1972.
24 1972 Annual Report.
25 *African Development*, January 1974.
26 *Investors Chronicle*, 3 January 1975, p. 37; *African Development*, January 1975, p.S41; *The Times*, 24 December 1974.
27 *African Development*, January 1974, p. S11.
28 ibid., June 1973, p. 9.
29 See p. 53.
30 *Financial Times*, 23 November 1971.
31 One Kuwaiti dinar equals £1.40.
32 *African Development*, June 1973, p. 7.
33 *Africa*, February 1974, p. 21.
34 ibid., September 1974, p. 61.
35 See Chapter 10.
36 *Guardian*, 27 January 1975. See also *Daily Telegraph*, 27 January 1975 and *Le Monde*, 28 January 1975.
37 *Guardian*, 27 January 1975.
38 *African Development*, June 1973, pp. 7–9.
39 Letter to shareholders dated 25 November 1974.
40 *Daily Telegraph*, 20 November 1974.
41 Authors' transcript of proceedings at the Extraordinary General Meeting, 11 December 1974.
42 ibid.
43 *Financial Times*, 15 February 1975.
44 *Daily Telegraph*, 15 February 1975.
45 See pp. 92–3.
46 Authors' transcript of proceedings at Extraordinary General Meeting, 11 December 1974.
47 See p. 99.
48 *The Times*, 5 January 1972.
49 ibid.
50 *Birmingham Post*, 25 April 1973.
51 *Le Monde*, 2 October 1972.
52 *Guardian*, 26 October 1972.
53 *Daily Telegraph*, 30 November 1973.
54 ibid.
55 *African Development*, December 1973, p. 5. Lonrho's share in this venture is not quite clear. *African Development*, February 1974, p. 13, reported that Rowland 'has taken a twenty per cent share in the newly formed Egyptian International Bank . . .'.
56 *Daily Telegraph*, 28 September 1974.
57 *African Development*, June 1972, p. 83.
58 Reply to a question asked by one of the authors.

Chapter 10. The Commanding Heights

1 *African Development*, June 1973, p. 9.
2 The embargo had originally been imposed on the United States and other Western countries considered friendly to Israel.

3   *Le Monde*, 23 November 1973.

4   In the 1973–74 edition of *Who Owns Whom* a new subsidiary, Pipelines Botswana (Pty) Ltd, made its first appearance.

5   See p. 52.

6   See pp. 187, 192.

7   SWB/ME/4500/ii, Sudanese News Agency, broadcast 14 January 1974.

8   Organization of African Unity Press Release no. 494, 30 December 1973.

9   *African Development*, June 1973, p. 8.

10 ibid., December 1973, p. 5.

11 'The Question of Consultants on the Effects of the Oil Embargo on African States. Presented to the 22nd Ordinary Session of the Council of Ministers, 27 February – 3 March 1974, by the Administrative Secretary-General', Organization of African Unity, Addis Ababa, p. 4.

12 'Report on the First Session of the Committee of Seven on the Effects of the Oil Embargo on the OAU Member States', no. OEM/c'ttee/ 1/5(II), Annex 1, p. 3, Organization of African Unity, Addis Ababa.

13 ibid., p. 3.

14 'The Question of Consultants', op. cit., p. 2.

15 Interview with James Fox, a *Sunday Times* journalist, London, 1974.

16 OAU Press Release no. 494, 30 December 1973.

17 'Report on the First Session', op. cit., p. 4.

18 ibid., p. 5. The Committee also discussed the question of the Arab Agricultural and Industrial Development Bank for Africa, set up by the Arab summit meeting in Algiers the previous month. A number of delegates criticized the commercial nature of the project, and the profit motive said to be the basis of its formulation of policy.

19 The conference was organized jointly by the ECA and the OAU.

20 SWB/ME/4527/B/1, 12 February 1974. Decisions of the African Oil Conference, as broadcast by Tripoli.

21 *Jeune Afrique*, Paris, no. 688, 16 March 1974, p. 33. Translation by authors.

22 'The Question of Consultants', op. cit., p. 6.

23 'Administrative Secretary-General's Progress Report to the Second Session of the Committee of Seven', no. OEM/c'ttee/1/5(II), Addis Ababa, 19 January 1974, p. 2.

24 *Le Monde*, 24 January 1974.

25 The *Financial Times* of 14 February 1974 says: 'OAU statistics show that during 1973 the OAU nations imported over $350 million worth of petroleum products. The figure was based on an average crude oil price of $3.50 a barrel.'

26 'Progress Report to the Second Session', op. cit. Annex IV. Ekangaki's calculation went as follows: the 19 countries which had replied showed total requirements of 16,665,330 metric tons of crude oil. 'In order to account for all 36 African countries an interpolation is made in order to include the 17 countries that did not report their requirements. Hence, estimated total requirements for the 36 African countries in crude oil equivalent equals

$$\frac{16{,}665{,}330 \times 36}{19} \text{ metric tons}$$

This is roughly equal to twice the requirement of the 19 countries which responded to the Secretariat's inquiry. Thus, the approximate total requirement for the 36 African countries affected by the oil embargo could be put at 33,330,666 metric tons.'

27 'The Question of Consultants', op. cit., p. 7.
28 ibid., p. 6.
29 ibid, p. 8.
30 ibid.
31 ibid., Annex I(i).
32 Letter reproduced as Annex I(ii) of 'Report of the First Session', op. cit.
33 'The Question of Consultants', op. cit., p. 8.
34 See pp. 81–2.
35 *Africa*, May 1974, p. 13.
36 'The Question of Consultants', op. cit., p. 10.
37 Letter reproduced in Annex III to 'Report on the First Session', op. cit.
38 The full text of the agreement, which appears as Annex II of the 'Report on the First Session', op. cit., is reproduced as Appendix 3.
39 'The Question of Consultants', op. cit., p. 11.
40 'Progress Report to the Second Session', op. cit., p. 2.
41 ibid., p. 3.
42 'The Question of Consultants', op. cit., p. 12.
43 ibid., p. 11.
44 Interview with James Fox of the *Sunday Times*, London, 1974.
45 ibid.
46 SWB/ME/4527/B/3, Kampala broadcast, 13 February 1974.
47 SWB/ME/4529/B/6, Kampala broadcast, 16 February 1974.
48 According to some observers, Sahnoun was in very bad health, and ready to leave the OAU in any case.
49 *New Nigerian*, Kaduna, 22 April 1974.
50 *Daily Nation*, Nairobi, 19 February 1974.
51 *Daily Times*, Lagos, 28 February 1974.
52 *Daily Graphic*, Accra, 20 February 1974; also SWB ME/4532/B/1, Accra, 19 February 1974.
53 *Daily Graphic*, Accra, 18 February 1974.
54 Lonrho's business interests in Nigeria were, of course, widespread – see p. 45.
55 OAU Press Release no. 501, Addis Ababa, 19 February 1974.
56 *West Africa*, 4 March 1974, p. 227.
57 ibid.
58 Interview with James Fox of the *Sunday Times*, London, 1974.
59 Undated letter to Lonrho, Annex III, 'Report on the First Session', op. cit.
60 *Daily Times*, Lagos, 28 February 1974.
61 *Jeune Afrique*, Paris, no. 688, 16 March 1974, p. 33.
62 *Daily Times*, Lagos, 21 February 1974; *West Africa*, 25 February 1974, p. 215.
63 *Guardian*, 20 February 1974.
64 'The Question of Consultants', op. cit., pp. 9–10.

65 *Africa*, May 1974, p. 13.
66 For example, Mr Ogungbade's full-page advertisement in the Nigerian press (see p. 48).
67 *Daily Times*, Lagos, 1 April 1974.
68 *Daily Graphic*, Accra, 5 April 1974.
69 *The Times*, 8 April 1974.
70 *Africa*, August 1974, pp. 10–11.
71 'Report by the Board of External Auditors. Financial Year 1972/73', Organization of African Unity, Addis Ababa.
72 See p. 36.
73 *Jeune Afrique*, Paris, no. 685, 23 February 1974, p. 19.
74 'The Question of Consultants', op. cit., p. 9.

Chapter *11*. Strategic Designs

1   *Star*, Johannesburg, 28 September 1968.
2   The plan behind Tshombe's secessionist ambitions in the early 1960s was to bring about unified control of the copper-rich Congolese province of Katanga and the adjoining Zambian copperbelt.
3   See p. 33.
4   Mark Bostock and Charles Harvey (eds.), *Economic Independence and Zambian Copper. A case study of foreign investment* (Praeger, New York, 1972), p. 109.
5   R. Hall, *The High Price of Principles* (Hodder & Stoughton, 1969, p. 212; Penguin Books, 1973).
6   Quoted in *Property and Finance*, February 1965.
7   See also pp. 33, 35–6.
8   R. Hall, op. cit., p. 219; *African Confidential*, London, 17 November 1967.
9   After initial opposition from South Africa, a road across the border between Zambia and Botswana was under construction, with American aid.
10 Michael Morris, *Terrorism* (Howard Timmins, Cape Town, 1971). The book had a foreword written by the South African Commissioner of Police, General J. P. Gous, who pointed out that the author had won the 'best student of the year award' in police college, and had participated in the guerrilla war. He was also involved in the South African student protests in 1969, on the side of the authorities. According to the publishers, 'to forestall unwarranted suggestions of police prejudice, he resigned from the Police Force at the end of 1969 to write this book, re-enlisting later in 1970'. The author subsequently resurfaced in London, where he was 'seen and photographed watching an anti-apartheid demonstration outside South Africa House' (*Guardian*, 20 March 1973).
11 Morris, op. cit., p. 150.
12 SWB/ME/3088/B/6. Dar-es-Salaam, 28 May 1969.
13 *African Development*, July 1969, p. 5.
14 *The Cape Route*. Report of a seminar held at the Royal United Service Institution on 25 February 1970, p. 6.

15   Conservative Commonwealth and Overseas Council, 'Overseas Issues Facing the Next Conservative Government. Defence Outside NATO', Ref. CCOC 274, February 1970.

16   *African Development*, June 1969, p. 4; *Financial Times*, 22 May 1969.

17   *The Times*, 19 May 1969.

18   *Property and Finance*, March 1963.

19   See pp. 42–3.

20   *African Development*, February 1969, p. 9; *African Development*, April 1969, pp. 10–11. See also Chapter 3.

21   *Daily Telegraph*, 24 March 1970.

22   *Sechaba*, London, March 1971, p. 14.

23   *Times*, Blantyre, Malawi, 3 April 1962 (formerly *Nyasaland Times*).

24   ibid., Blantyre, 6 April 1962. Quoted in Philip Short, *Banda* (Routledge & Kegan Paul, 1974).

25   ibid., 3 April 1962.

26   ibid., 26 August 1966.

27   *Sunday Times*, 28 November 1971; also *Financial Times*, 2 May 1973.

28   *Daily Telegraph*, 22 September 1970.

29   In February 1975, Welensky said during a visit to London that there was again talk of extending the Nacala link into Rhodesia, and that the South Africans had lent Malawi 19 million dollars for this purpose. (Authors' recording of address to Diplomatic and Commonwealth Writers' Association of Britain, 26 February 1975.)

30   1969 was also the year of the unsuccessful takeover bid for Coronation Syndicate which involved both the Inyati and the Shamva mines. It was in July 1968 that Coronation Syndicate purchased its option over the Edmundian mine in Mozambique – conveniently situated close to the Umtali–Beira railway – from Hochmetals of Johannesburg. See Chapter 8.

31   SWB/ME/3232/B/1, Blantyre, 15 November 1969.

32   *The Cape Route*, op. cit., pp. 2–3.

33   *Financial Times*, 2 July 1970.

34   No immediate action was taken, probably because the escalation of the liberation struggle in Mozambique was making planning difficult and capital hard to come by. As an alternative to the Richards Bay smelter there was talk in *African Development* of developing production facilities more fully inside Malawi itself, using indigenous hydro-electric power. This would to some extent have freed Malawi from dependence on Cabora Bassa, which from 1972 was increasingly subject to guerrilla attacks. (*African Development*, May 1972.)

35   General Spinola, who took power in Portugal after the events of April 1974, was at one time an executive with the Champalimaud steelworks.

36   See p. 30.

37   The share capital was divided in the proportion 20 per cent, 20 per cent and 60 per cent between Press Holdings Ltd, a holding company in which Banda himself held 9,998 kwacha out of the total 10,000 kwacha share capital; the Malawi Development Corporation; and the Banco Pinto e Sotto Mayor of Lisbon, a member of the Champalimaud group. This was the Malawi government's first venture into commercial banking.

38 See Chapter 1.
39 See pp. 24–5.
40 SWB/ME/3229/B/2, Blantyre, 12 November 1969.
41 SWB/ME/3660/B/4, Salisbury, 15 April 1971.
42 *Guardian*, 4 September 1970. The reconciliation also provided ex-Federal MP, Peter Staub, an old business associate of Rowland's, with an opportunity to point out in a letter to the *Daily Telegraph* (2 September 1970) that Staub was 'a personal friend of President Banda and Sir Roy'.
43 *Sunday Mail*, Salisbury, 8 May 1960, quoted in Short, *Banda*, op. cit.
44 *Le Monde*, 13 November 1969. Authors' translation.
45 Anglo-American and Johannesburg Consolidated abandoned their joint exploration of a large area in Tete when Frelimo activities threatened their teams.
46 *Star*, Johannesburg, weekly edition, 20 July 1974; *Daily Telegraph*, 27 August, 1974.
47 *Observer*, 4 August 1974; *Sunday Telegraph*, 4 August 1974; *Daily Telegraph*, 5 August 1974.
48 *Le Monde*, 27 May 1972 (authors' translation from French).
49 *Birmingham Post*, 24 July 1974.

Conclusion. The Smiling Face of Development?

1   *Accountancy Age*, 25 May 1973.
2   *Daily Mail*, 22 May 1973.
3   *Africa*, May 1974, p. 12.
4   Mark Bostock and Charles Harvey (eds.), *Economic Independence and Zambian Copper. A case study of foreign investment* (Praeger, New York, 1972), pp. 19–20.
5   *African Development*, June 1973, p. 9.
6   See pp. 187–8.
7   See pp. 67–72. *West Africa*, 15 April 1974, p. 449. *The Times*, 12 January 1974 (Ghana Supplement).
8   *Daily Mail*, Freetown, 29 June 1970.
9   See pp. 81, 96–7.
10 See p. 102.
11 Letter to shareholders, 16 May 1973.
12 *Africa*, May 1974, p. 13. Over the 1974 financial year, Lonrho's remitted and remittable profits (after tax but pre-extraordinary items) rose to 68.53 per cent of the total, compared with 58.36 per cent in the previous year. (*Daily Telegraph*, 28 February 1975.)
13 See pp. 37–8.
14 From 1973 on, OCAM seemed to be disintegrating with the departure from the organization of Chad, Zaire, Cameroun and Madagascar.
15 *African Development*, February 1971 and May 1972; *West Africa*, 2 April 1971, p. 357.
16 *African Development*, June 1973, p. 9.
17 *Africa*, May 1974, p. 13.
18 ibid.

19   *Guardian*, 18 May 1973.
20   For example, letter to shareholders, 16 May 1973.
21   *Africa*, May 1974, p. 13.
22   SWB/ME/4710/B/1 and 2, Lourenço Marques, 20 September 1974.
23   *African Development*, June 1973, p. 9.
24   *Birmingham Post*, 25 April 1973.

Postscript

1   The main part of the text takes developments into early 1975. This postscript summarizes the more important developments during the remainder of the year.
2   SWB/ME/4849/B/2, 8 March 1975.
3   *Weekly Review*, Nairobi, 17 March 1975.
4   *Sunday Times*, 17 August 1975.
5   See pp. 37–8.
6   *Financial Times*, 5 June 1975.
7   ibid., 5 June 1975; *Daily Telegraph*, 6 June 1975.
8   SWB/ME/4915/B/6, 29 May 1975.
9   SWB/ME/4882/B/7, 19 April 1975.
10   *The Times*, 1 July 1975.
11   SWB/ME/5011/B/8, 19 September 1975.
12   *Rhodesia Herald*, Salisbury, 6 November 1975.
13   *Financial Times*, 28 May 1975.
14   See p. 36.
15   *West Africa*, 2 April 1975, p. 463.
16   *African Development*, January 1974, p. 7.
17   *West Africa*, London, 16 June 1975, p. 692.
18   *Financial Times*, 30 July 1975.
19   Authors' transcript.
20   Press estimates of the actual size of the Arab holding varied.
21   See p. 188.
22   *Daily Telegraph*, 31 December 1975.
23   *Africa*, London, February 1975.
24   *Economist*, 25 October 1975; *African Development*, December 1975.
25   *Daily Telegraph*, 31 December 1975.
26   *The Times*, 31 December 1975.
27   ibid.
28   *Daily Telegraph*, 17 April 1975.
29   *Sunday Telegraph*, 19 October 1975.
30   *Investors Chronicle*, 7 November 1975.
31   *Financial Times*, 28 June 1975.
32   Lonrho circular to shareholders, 4 April 1975.
33   *Europa* supplement of *The Times*, 4 March 1975; *Washington Post* quoted in *Investors Chronicle*, 7 November 1975.
34   See pp. 187–8.
35   *Washington Post* quoted in *Investors Chronicle*, 7 November 1975.
36   *Financial Times*, 28 June 1975.
37   Authors' transcript.

38   See p. 90.
39   *Financial Times*, 3 March 1957.
40   ibid., 4 March 1975.
41   See pp. 115–16.
42   *Daily Telegraph*, 3 September 1975.
43   *Financial Times*, 4 November 1975.
44   See pp. 92–3.
45   *The Times*, 25 September 1973.
46   *Financial Mail*, Johannesburg, 3 January 1975.
47   Authors' transcript.
48   *Sunday Telegraph*, 13 July 1975; *Financial Times*, 14 July 1975.
49   *Financial Times*, 11 July 1975.
50   See p. 103.
51   *Sunday Telegraph*, 23 March 1975.
52   Authors' transcript.
53   *Daily Telegraph*, 25 March 1975.
54   *Star*, Johannesburg, 14 June 1975.
55   *Financial Mail*, 12 September 1975.
56   *Times of Swaziland*, 25 July 1975.
57   *Star*, 3 January 1976.
58   *Investors Chronicle*, 9 January 1976.
59   See p. 154.
60   *Financial Times*, 11 April 1975.
61   *Rhodesia Herald*, 4 December 1975.
62   *African Development*, October 1975.
63   *Rhodesia Herald*, 21 August 1975; *Observer*, 4 January 1976. The ANC was formed in 1971 to mobilize African opinion in Rhodesia against the British–Rhodesian settlement proposals. It later became an umbrella organization for the various competing nationalist movements. Between August and December the ANC split, and Mr Curtin advised that part of it which negotiated with Smith.
64   *Rhodesia Herald*, 13 May 1975; *Star*, 10 May 1975.
65   *Rhodesia Financial Gazette*, 23 May 1975.
66   *Star*, 10 May 1975.

Report of the Inspectors of the Department of Trade

1   *Department of Trade. Lonrho Limited. Investigation under Section 165(b) of the Companies Act 1948. Report by Allan Heyman, QC and Sir William Slimmings, CBE, CA (Inspectors Appointed by the Department of Trade).* HMSO, 1976.
2   ibid., 4.135.
3   ibid., 4.131.
4   ibid., 4.123.
5   Company statement, 6 July 1976, p. 9.
6   *Rhodesia Herald*, 28 May 1976, 10 June 1976.
7   *Report of the Inspectors of the Department of Trade.*

Index

More about Penguins and Pelicans

The Puritans in Africa

A STORY OF AFRIKANERDOM
W. A. de Klerk

'*The Puritans in Africa* is a work of much importance and
the most immediate relevance . . . it is, in a real sense, *the*
story of the people told as it has not been told before' –
Laurens van der Post in *The Times Literary Supplement*

Modern South Africa has generated increasing controversy
and attention for its implementation of a revolutionary
political idea – apartheid. This book relates the history of a
small people, the Afrikaners, and their attempt to remake
their particular world according to a rational plan from the
the radical Right. In no other way, the author maintains,
can the Afrikaners be understood.

'At the end of its moving evocation of Afrikaner history, as
unsparing of its shortcomings as it is alive to its virtues,
The Puritans in Africa shows how the ancient Calvinist and
Huguenot conscience of the Afrikaner is troubling him
today as never before, compelling what is best in him to
clamour for correction of the manifest injustices and
imperfections of his society . . . one has only to read William
de Klerk's book to see what irresistible social forces such a
conscience-inspired movement can realize. For this reason
alone, although there are many others, I cannot recommend
this book too strongly, both to Afrikaners and their
enemies' – Laurens van der Post

The Multinationals

Christopher Tugendhat

In recent years vast international companies have developed which dominate the 'commanding heights of the economy' throughout Western Europe and North America. Firms like Alcan, IBM, Ford, Shell and Bayer have annual sales as large as the gross national products of many countries, and their rate of growth is much faster. Inevitably there are tensions between the companies and governments who see control of a vital sector of the economy slipping from their grasp.

Christopher Tugendhat's book, which won a McKinsey Foundation Book Award in 1971, is a detailed examination of the multinationals and the political implications of their position and influence. His theories and principles, supported with examples from the experience of companies and governments, illuminate a major political and economic problem.

'The importance of this book is not in doubt. It will stand the test of years' – Tam Dalyell in the *New Scientist*

'Mr Tugendhat has called attention to a vitally critical problem' – Thomas Balogh in the *New Statesman*